China deconstruct

Over the last ten years China's economy has grown faster than that of any other nation. By the early part of the next century it is widely suggested that it will be the largest in the world. Yet, as it verges on becoming an economic superpower questions are being asked about China's identity.

This challenge to identity has been triggered by the Chinese economic reform and in particular the decentralization of economic power. The uncertainty surrounding succession politics is bringing the crisis to a head. This book examines the process of internal and external bargaining by analysing reforms in China's political economy. This is done through analysis of key regions, and their external connections, as well as how the outside world is interacting with this less tightly-knit China.

Decentralization has caused a number of fault lines to appear in the structure of authority because power has flowed from Beijing and into the provinces. However, the break-up of China would benefit few, either inside or outside the country. If the outside world believes that it can best accommodate China's rising power through mutual interdependence, then the strongest ties will be woven with the different regions of China.

David S.G. Goodman is Director of the Institute for International Studies at the University of Technology, Sydney and is author of *Deng Xiaoping and the Chinese Revolution*.

Gerald Segal is Senior Fellow at the International Institute for Strategic Studies and coordinator of the ESRC Programme on Pacific Asia. He is also the author of more than a dozen books on China.

China deconstructs

Politics, trade and regionalism

Edited by
David S.G. Goodman and Gerald Segal

London and New York

First published 1994
by Routledge
11 New Fetter Lane, London EC4P 4EE

Simultaneously published in the USA and Canada
by Routledge
29 West 35th Street, New York, NY 10001

Typeset in Times by
J&L Composition Ltd, Filey, North Yorkshire
Printed and bound in Great Britain by
TJ Press (Padstow) Ltd, Padstow, Cornwall

British Library Cataloguing in Publication Data
A catalogue record for this book is available from the British Library.

China deconstructs: politics, trade and regionalism / edited by David S.G.
Goodman and Gerald Segal.
    p.   cm.
    1. China—Economic conditions—1976– 2. China—Economic
conditions—Regional disparities. 3. China–Foreign economic
relations. 4. Regionalism—China. 5. China—Economic
policy—1976– I. Goodman, David S.G. II. Segal, Gerald, 1953–
HC427.92.C4638   1994
330.951—dc20   94–21698

ISBN 0–415–11833–6
      0–415–11834–4 (pbk)

Contents

Figures and tables

FIGURES

TABLES

Contributors

Feng Chongyi is Associate Professor of History, Nankai University, Tianjin. He is currently writing a study of the political development of the peasantry in South China. He is the author of *Peasant Consciousness and China* (Chung-hua Book Company, Hong Kong, 1989), *Bertrand Russell and China* (Sanlian Shudian, Beijing, 1994) and *Chinese Culture in the Sino–Japanese War* (Guangzi Shifandazue Chubanshe, 1994).

Peter Ferdinand was educated at Oxford University and LSE. He has studied or done research at Kiev University, Harvard University and the Chinese Academy of Social Sciences, Beijing. From 1989 to 1993 he was Head of the Asia–Pacific Programme at the Royal Institute of International Affairs in London. Since October 1993 he has held the post of Director, Centre for Studies in Democratisation at the University of Warwick and is the author of *Communist Regimes in Comparative Perspective: The Evolution of the Soviet, Chinese and Yugoslav Models* (Wheatsheaf, 1991); *Take-Off for Taiwan?* and *The New Central Asia and its Neighbours* (both RIIA forthcoming). From 1993–4 he was specialist adviser to the House of Commons Foreign Affairs Committee enquiry into UK–China relations up to and after 1997.

John Fitzgerald studied at Sydney University and the Australian National University before undertaking postdoctoral study at the University of Wisconsin – Madison. He currently teaches East Asian politics at La Trobe University. His research on Chinese nationalism has been published in the *Journal of Asian Studies*, *Modern Asian Studies* and *Modern China*. He edited *The Nationalists and Chinese Society* and his book *The Irony of the Chinese Revolution* is shortly to be published by Stanford University Press.

David S. G. Goodman is Director of the Institute for International Studies at the University of Technology, Sydney (UTS). His publications include *Deng Xiaoping and the Chinese Revolution*, Routledge, London, 1994; *China's Quiet Revolution: New Interactions between State and Society* (edited with Beverley Hooper) Longman Cheshire, Melbourne, 1994; and (with Richard Robison) *The New Rich in Asia: Mobile-phones, McDonalds and Middle Class Revolution*, Routledge, London, 1994.

Lijian Hong is a Research Fellow in the Department of Asian Languages and Studies at Monash University. A native of Sichuan, he conducted research at the Sichuan Academy of Social Sciences prior to completing doctoral studies at the Australian National University. His publications in English and Chinese cover several aspects of Chinese politics.

Ingrid d'Hooghe is with the Documentation Center for Contemporary China at the Sinological Institute of Leiden University, specialising in the regional development of Yunnan province. She has published work on the Dutch–Taiwanese Submarine Affair of 1992 and is co-editor of *China Information*.

J. Bruce Jacobs is Professor, Department of Asian Languages and Studies, Monash University in Melbourne, Australia, where he has been Head of Department and Director, Centre of East Asian Studies. A member of the Australia–China Council, he has published widely in English and Chinese on Chinese and Taiwan politics, society, history and economics.

Anjali Kumar (Ph.D., Cambridge, UK) is a senior economist specializing in industry and trade, at the China and Mongolia Department of the World Bank in Washington, DC. She has also worked on several other transitional and developing economies. Her publications include two books on India's exports (Oxford University Press, UK, 1988) and on public enterprise reform (the Macmillan Press, UK, 1993), as well as seminar and discussion papers, and background papers for the Uruguay Round of the GATT negotiations.

Simon Long works as a journalist and broadcaster for the BBC and the *Guardian* in Hong Kong. He is the author of *Taiwan: China's Last Frontier* (Macmillan, 1991) and *Reform's Last Chance: China to 2,000* (Economist Intelligence Unit, 1992).

Gerald Segal is Senior Fellow (Asian Studies) at the International Institute for Strategic Studies and editor of *The Pacific Review*. He is the author of *China Changes Shape* (Adelphi Paper No. 287, March 1994) and *The Fate of Hong Kong* (Simon & Schuster, London, 1993).

Brantly Womack is Director of the East Asia Center and Professor of Government and Foreign Affairs at the University of Virginia. His current research interests include relations between China and Vietnam, problems of political liberalisation in China, and patterns of Chinese diversification. His research on the border trade between China and Vietnam appears in the June 1994 issue of *Asian Survey*.

Michael B. Yahuda is a reader in international relations at the London School of Economics and Political Science. He is a specialist on Chinese foreign relations.

Dali L. Yang is an assistant professor of political science at the University of Chicago. He is the author of *Calamity and Reform in China: State and Society Since the Great Leap Famine* (forthcoming from Stanford University Press) and the co-editor of *Yan Jiaqi and China's Struggle for Democracy*. He is doing research for a book tentatively entitled *The Era of Decentralization in China*.

Guangzhi Zhao is a Ph.D. student in Political Science at Northern Illinois University. He received his MA from the Institute of Foreign Affairs, Beijing, China in 1988. He taught International Relations and Comparative Government at the Institute of Foreign Affairs from 1988–90. Currently, he is doing research on the development and influences of border trade in China and teaching Comparative Politics at Northern Illinois University.

Preface

The need to reconceptualise our understanding of China's politics and economics has become increasingly acute. Simple models, such as totalitarianism, are clearly no longer appropriate (if indeed they ever were) for describing the increasing complexity of the political and economic environment of the People's Republic of China (PRC) in the 1990s. One area where there is an urgent need for reconceptualisation is regionalism. Policy change within the PRC has led to regional economic growth, particularly in coastal China, through decentralisation, localisation, and the policy of the 'open door'. The neighbouring economies of East Asia, faced with limits to their own economic growth and seeking to restructure, have not only traded with and invested in China's new dynamic regions, but have moved enterprises and even whole industries to off-shore processing and production in the PRC. The result is a new pattern of economic regionalism unlike earlier regionalisms experienced in China, and one whose impact on domestic politics and international relations remains relatively undiscussed. The exploration of that impact, and the reconceptualisation of regionalism in a PRC that appears to be going 'fuzzy at the edges' is precisely the object of this book.

This volume results from a joint project between the International Institute for Strategic Studies, London, and the Asia Research Centre for Social, Political and Economic Change, Murdoch University, Western Australia, and undertaken largely during 1993. A first draft was presented in papers delivered at a workshop held at the Woodrow Wilson Center, Washington, DC in October 1993.

A project of this kind must always depend on the cooperation, assistance and goodwill of many people and not just the contributors to this volume. In particular, we would like to express our gratitude to Sheelagh Urbanoviez of the International Institute for Strategic Studies; Dellas Blakeway of the Asia Research Centre; and Mary

Bullock of the Woodrow Wilson Center. We would also like to acknowledge the assistance of all those who have read and commented on various drafts of the text, including all those who have attended the project's various workshops during 1993.

Funds for the project were provided by the Smith Richardson Foundation and the Asia Research Centre. This volume appears under the auspices of the IISS and the ARC and in the Asia Research Centre's series of *Studies on Contemporary Asia*. An earlier version of Gerald Segal's chapter appeared as part of *China Changes Shape*, Adelphi Paper No. 287, Brassey's for the IISS, March 1994.

David S. G. Goodman
University of Technology, Sydney

Gerald Segal
International Institute for Strategic Studies, London

1 The politics of regionalism

Economic development, conflict and negotiation

David S. G. Goodman

At the start of the 1990s the capacity of the People's Republic of China (PRC) to remain united has become a matter of considerable concern and debate. Drawing on a past frequently characterised by division and civil war, writers of popular non-fiction in the PRC have several times hit the best-seller lists to discuss *guo shi* – 'the project of China' – and ask whether the country can stay united or must break up.[1] Elsewhere in the PRC academics, government advisers and different parts of the state administration have similarly written papers and reports on this topic, even though, to be sure, the issue has sometimes been raised in order to make an inherently political point: to slow the pace of reform, for example, or by those who wish to strengthen centralised government.[2] Many of these themes have been echoed in the writings of external commentators, who focus not simply on the pattern of the Chinese past but on the new challenges facing both the PRC and the Chinese Communist Party (CCP) with modernisation, particularly economic growth, and changes in the international world order.[3]

The collapse of communism and national political disintegration in Eastern Europe, as well as popular interpretations of the PRC's current economic development and recent history all suggest future challenges to the unity of the PRC, and not just the leading role of the CCP. The PRC's rapid economic development since 1978 has been based on decentralisation and an explicit regional policy, in which some regions have been positively encouraged to become wealthy before others. The result is a highly differentiated economic geography and pattern of regionalism that has suggested to some a replay of the 'warlord era' of the 1920s, except that power is now based on economic rather than military might.

China is undoubtedly changing shape, not least because the increasing pressures of modernisation ensure organisational complexity and political sophistication. In the PRC, no less than in any other modernising society, the functions and exercise of central government, and its relationships with regional levels of the state system, have already changed dramatically and will continue to do so for some time, regardless of the fate of the CCP. The CCP has substantially reduced its involvement in government. Government has even more substantially reduced its involvement in the direct management of the economy, turning instead to the principles of macro-economic control.

However, the degree of change is even more dramatic when the PRC's post-1978 transformation is viewed from regional perspectives. Change within the PRC has combined with external changes to produce new patterns of economic – and possibly even political interaction – in and around China. Within the PRC domestic regional policy has abandoned the notion of 'equal poverty' prevalent during the Mao-dominated era of China's politics and based on the creation of a number of regions of economic cooperation and self-sufficiency. In its place have come the notions of a national division of labour and the development of local comparative advantage. Coastal and border areas in particular have been encouraged to utilise the comparative advantage of their geo-political locations for economic involvement – trade, technology transfer and investment – with the outside world. It is in that context that five Special Economic Zones (SEZ) have been created and fourteen cities designated as 'open cities'.

The notion that the coastal and border regions might develop external economic links is itself a major policy change: the abandonment of the principle of 'self-reliance' and the adoption of the 'open policy' in economic relations with the rest of the world. Fortuitously these policy changes within the PRC coincided with increasing pressures on the adjacent NIEs – first Hong Kong and Taiwan, followed more recently by Singapore and South Korea – to restructure their economies because of high factor costs. Their needs to find suitable locations for off-shore processing and production were met by the PRC's new economic and export-oriented outlook and cheap labour costs.

The overall results of the changes of economic outlook in the PRC and within East Asia include not only increased border trade, but also the PRC's integration into the economic order of East Asia. However, the pattern of economic integration has not been even. Though each of the East Asian economies has traded with and invested in the various areas of the PRC, there has been a high degree of specialisation. Different parts of the PRC have established particular economic links with specific – sometimes industry- as well as country- or territory-based – parts of East Asia. Most spectacularly, the economy of Guangdong Province is dominated by its relationship with Hong Kong; that of Fujian Province by its relationship with Taiwan, on which it is almost totally dependent for its industrial development. Domestic developments have thus encouraged economic regionalism within the PRC at the same time as international developments have encouraged China's regionalisation within East Asia.

It is possible that under these various regional pressures China may follow the path of political disintegration mapped out in Eastern Europe and the former USSR. However, any assessment of the prospects for political disintegration must examine the structures that maintain or may even increase integration as well as those that encourage disintegration. They must also take care not to confuse the epiphenomena of the political process – in which the regional dimension has been and remains important – with manifestations of more deep-rooted significance.

Regional economic growth certainly has the potential to lead to political disintegration, but it is not a necessary consequence. Nor is that consequence necessarily signalled by developments in the late 1980s and early 1990s. Such arguments are based on three assumptions that are almost self-evidently too simple: an almost exclusive economic determinism; a simple, conflictual model of relations between centre and province; and the equation of China's new economic regions with the traditional provinces, and the kinds of regionalism that have existed before in China's history.

China's history certainly provides many examples of regionalism. These have at times led to political particularism and separatism, as for example most recently during the Warlord Era of 1917–1927. However, it does not automatically follow that all regionalist tendencies in China are directed towards, or indeed will arrive at, political independence. The centralised state in the nineteenth and twentieth centuries may have stressed a unity based on conformity throughout China, but that is not the only tradition.

Moreover, it is far from clear that the conditions which in the past encouraged a high degree of regionalism are those that apply in the 1990s. In any case, at a basic level, the current economic regions are by no means the same as the traditional provinces, not only in geographical terms, but also administratively, politically and economically. There is a new regionalism that results, as already indicated, from two initially separate processes. Policy change within the PRC that led to the introduction of decentralisation, market economics, and the policy of the 'open door' in the 1980s; and pressures for economic restructuring within the more developed economies of East Asia from the mid-1980s on. Together these two tendencies have created poles of economic growth and dynamism in the PRC that may have little in common with earlier Chinese patterns of regionalism.

Similarly, though there may be tensions between the centre and the regions (or indeed the provinces), their relationship is by no means necessarily antagonistic. In the first place, whatever else has happened in the PRC since the start of the reform era in 1978, it remains a communist party state. The role of the CCP has changed with reform, but it still controls the appointment of senior local leaders, and still exercises that control assiduously, especially at provincial level. With the exception of the major non-Han areas, there are no organisations outside the party-state system that might claim to articulate the wishes of a province or region. Economic development might bring entrepreneurs in a region into conflict with the centre, but that conflict is then mediated by local leaders whose careers depend on their superiors within the CCP, even though they will need to meet a degree of local demand if they are to ensure compliance with central direction and policy.

The position of regional political leadership, as well as the traditions of the CCP which have always encouraged a degree of local flexibility in national policy implementation, have combined to ensure that regionalism has been a constant feature of the PRC's political process and not necessarily a symptom of political disintegration. It is usual to find policies under experimentation regionally before national adoption, and central and local leaders frequently combine to lobby on behalf of specific policy initiatives. The relationship between centre and region is then perhaps more usefully interpreted in terms of negotiation rather than in terms of any necessary conflict leading to political disintegration.

THE POTENTIAL FOR LOCALISM

Three key initiatives of the era of economic reform that started with the Third Plenum of the Eleventh Central Committee of the Chinese Communist Party in December 1978 are typically held to have encouraged local political autonomy and to contain the seeds for potential political disintegration. One is the decentralisation of economic management, which has taken a number of forms. Within the state sector there has been decentralisation of economic management and decision-making, with lower levels now having taken over functions and responsibilities previously the preserve of superior levels. In addition, governments and the state sector have divested themselves of large areas of previous activity, as for example in the retail trade, which used to be the preserve of local government and is now dominated by private enterprise.

Allied to decentralisation is the development of a more market-oriented and market-determined economy. Where previously there was a notion in China that it was a command economy, economic reform has been moving towards an economy regulated by market forces. At times movement has been both erratic and alarming, as in 1988. However, by the early 1990s few prices were still fixed by the state, and resource allocation decisions were increasingly left to the market. The movement towards an economy where government direction is exercised through macro-economic levers rather than direct intervention has been maintained. One consequence has been the development of highly localised markets for both supply and distribution.

Decentralisation and the introduction of market forces together suggest in general terms that the centres of economic power are moving away from the centre to the localities and away from the CCP and the government. Less obviously related are the consequences of the 'Open Door Policy'. The CCP's determination since the late 1970s to utilise its economic and geographic comparative advantages in the international economic system it once shunned may also have assisted in the development of a new economic regionalism. Foreign trade and capital provide those localities that are placed to take advantage of the situation with alternative sources to assist their economic development – sources which have not been channelled through and are therefore not controlled by the central planning process. Guangdong Province is an obvious example: in 1991 the province only obtained 3 per cent of its capital development from Beijing. The remainder comes from either foreign investment or economic activity generated by Guangdong's production for the international market. Fujian Province is another, with some 70 per cent of its industrial output created through investment from Taiwan alone.

Though South China is in the vanguard of such developments, other economic regions are developing relationships with the international economy, and often specific parts of the East Asian market. Economic integration between Guangdong and Hong Kong is such that the movement of goods and people across the border has become relatively unrestricted and locals already acknowledge the emergence of a new synthesis rather than the dominance of one or the other. Fujian's industrial dependence on Taiwan has been noted in the preceding paragraph. In addition, Japanese, Taiwanese and, since 1992, Hong Kong investment and activities in Jiangsu and Zhejiang have been steadily increasing; Shandong and Northeast China have ties with South Korea and the Russian Far East; Xinjiang is becoming economically integrated with the Turkic republics of the former USSR; and Yunnan's economic relationships with Burma and Thailand are considerable, though not always politically sound.

THE APPEARANCE OF LOCALISM

The evidence of national economic management in the early 1990s does at first sight suggest that central government is less able than it once was to exercise control over the provinces and provincial level authorities. One area where new relationships seem manifest is in the determination of the state budget. Another has been in the apparent emergence of a surprisingly high degree of mercantilism exercised by provincial authorities. Both appear to support an argument that economic and by extension political power has passed, or is passing, from the centre to the provinces.

The state of the national budget is clearly a matter of some concern. Since the 1980s, and particularly since 1988 when revenue-sharing between centre and provincial level units based on taxation was introduced, central government has faced increasing budgetary deficits.[4] Necessarily the revenue-sharing system has disproportionately benefited those provinces which have grown fastest during the 1980s – Guangdong, Fujian, Zhejiang and Jiangsu. Central government has stated several times that it would prefer to see the system replaced by one based on profit-sharing, and to reduce the level of its budgetary deficit. Neither has proved politically possible, even though central government had the support of several provincial level units – notably Shanghai and Liaoning – who were resentful of what they considered to be the preferential treatment afforded the fast-growing provinces of the reform era. Particularly at the end of 1990 and beginning of 1991, as part of the discussions which resulted in the Eighth Five-year Plan, Beijing attempted, unsuccessfully, to renegotiate its financial arrangements with a number of the wealthier provinces.

More remarkable is the emergence in and since the late 1980s of phenomena criticised within the PRC as 'duke economies'. Essentially this is a shorthand for mercantilism and economic protectionism, implemented by provinces operating as individual actors. For a communist party state, even one moving towards a market economy, some of the instances of protectionism seem, at least at first sight, somewhat bizarre.

It has become common for provinces to restrict imports from other provinces, to levy high, if informal, taxes on goods whose production is seen as important to the domestic provincial economy, and to create non-tariff barriers. Xinjiang, for example, effectively banned the import of forty-eight commodities on the grounds that they would harm its domestic economy. Jilin refused to market beer produced in the neighbouring provinces of Heilongjiang and Liaoning. In some provinces, local authorities established, and provided finance for, a variety of schemes which promoted the sales of local products. Enterprises from other provinces often have difficulties in finding office space, accommodation, or land for their activities.[5] Competition between provinces can be fierce, and there are numerous tales of 'commodity wars' between provinces over, amongst other items, rice, wool, soy beans, tobacco, coal and steel.[6]

THE LESSONS OF CHINA'S HISTORY

Interpretations of recent developments in China as portents of political disintegration usually misunderstand not only the regionalist nature of post-1949 politics but also the traditions of the state historically. During the Mao-dominated era of China's politics there was a widespread emphasis not only on the unitary nature of the traditional state, but also on its conformism. Such emphases were not without their political purposes. However, the tradition of conformity was both a simplification and over-stated, and should consequently not be taken as the necessary starting-point for any argument that might want to regard all local variation in national policy as an act of opposition to Beijing. Such traditions were created during the late Ming period (1368–1644) and later developed by the Qing (1644–1912) because of the pressures and the various crises of legitimacy facing the imperial system. Before that time, unity based on diversity was a more common tradition.

In any case, the attempt to treat history as though it were an independent variable is clearly fraught with difficulties. History cannot create a propensity towards localism or regionalism within the PRC, though consciousness of specific traditions may play a political role. The economically and politically significant regions of the 1990s may not be the traditional provinces. The traditional province as an historical–cultural identity may not be identical with the post-1949 provincial leadership. There is no reason to suppose an identity of interest among China's provinces, and every reason – given size and geographic diversity – to believe otherwise. Each province is unlikely to have the same traditions of autarky, and it may well be the case that such autonomy does not find its expression at the provincial level. Moreover, there is no necessary reason to believe that the conditions which created any traditions of autonomy remain relevant.

The cultural determination of regionalism in the PRC is clearly an important political factor in relations between the centre and provinces, but may not necessarily result in political disintegration or provincial separatism. It is of course the case that there are parts of the PRC where the desire for local autonomy entails pressure for political separatism. In particular, there are strong local movements for political self-determination in the non-Han areas of Tibet, Xinjiang (Turkestan) and Inner Mongolia: they have separate histories and traditions of independence which may lead to movements to break away from the PRC regardless of the costs. However, elsewhere in the PRC autonomy must be interpreted more subtly.

The dominant 'state idea' throughout Han China remains, as it has always been, that of China as a whole. Provincial autonomy, when it has occurred, been practised, or been encouraged has always been regarded as either a temporary phenomenon or a relative autonomy. Many provincial-level units do indeed have a long history. Their boundaries are not the creation of a modernizing state but result from the circulation of people, goods and ideas over several centuries.[7] At times, such as the collapse of the Empire and the birth of the Warlord Era, provincial independence has been declared.

However, such declarations are regarded as a temporary expedient, with their legitimation grounded not in the province but in the state-idea of China as a whole. For example, in 1921 Sichuan Province proclaimed its Declaration of Independence. Independence was conditional rather than absolute pending 'the establishment of a legal unified government of the Republic of China'.[8] Sichuan's case was further legitimated by traditional political philosophy which even provided for such political behaviour through the concept of *pian an* (partial peace). This was first enunciated with respect to Liu Bei's establishment of Shu during the Three Kingdoms' Period. As a purely transient expedient, when there is imperial disorder, order can be restored in only part of the Empire on condition that it is then extended to the country as a whole, and that restoration is itself a duty incumbent on the partial ruler.

THE LESSONS OF SOVIET HISTORY

The application of the Soviet Union's recent experience of imploding communism as a predictor of the PRC's potential for political disintegration is perhaps even more methodologically suspect than the extrapolation of China's own history. Certainly before 1989 both the PRC and the USSR were communist party states of imperial dimensions. Equally, it was the case that they shared, for the most part, political institutions. The structures of the party state were established with direct Soviet assistance in the PRC during the early 1950s. Nonetheless, there are also significant differences between the experience of communism in China and the Soviet Union that suggest its transformation in the former has at least the chance of a radically different outcome.

In the first place, the PRC's ethnic composition and ethno-administrative politics are very different to those of the former USSR. Ethnically the PRC is considerably more homogenous than the USSR: some 93 per cent of the population of the PRC is regarded, and would regard themselves, as Han Chinese, compared to just over half of the former USSR who are Russian. The non-Han Chinese – the so-called national minorities – are concentrated in the border areas of North, Northwest and Southwest China, and as already indicated, are only really politically significant in Tibet, Xinjiang and Inner Mongolia, where there are, or have been, significant movements for independence. Elsewhere, the national minority peoples are not only dispersed but also largely indistinguishable from Han Chinese.

As in the former USSR, each of the national minority groups has a 'homeland' – an 'autonomous' unit of local government. At the provincial-level – the immediate sub-provincial level of administration – these non-Han areas are called 'Autonomous Regions' and there are five, one for each of the Tibetans, Uighurs (Xinjiang), Hui (Ningxia), Mongolians, and Zhuang (Guangxi). However, unlike the former USSR, the nationality principle does not generally underlie the determination of administrative units. The remaining twenty-five PRC provinces have boundaries not determined, as were those of the USSR's constituent republics, by a twentieth-century notion of nationality but, as already noted, by traditional patterns of interaction.

Secondly, particularly by comparison with the USSR, the population of China during the first half of the twentieth century was not highly educated, literate, urbanised or politicised. Indeed, there was virtually no tradition of mass politics. All this started to change as the CCP began to mobilise, but even here there have been significant differences with the rise of communism in the Soviet Union. Communist party rule in the PRC resulted from a long struggle for power, based on popular mobilisation for some twenty-eight years, two civil wars and a war against Japan. The CCP consequently had an immediate widespread popularity not shared by many other ruling communist parties, and was regarded as an inherently nationalist force. There may be disenchantment with the CCP, particularly amongst certain sections of the population, such as the intellectuals in the wake of the events of June 1989. However, the CCP's popular base is unlikely to disappear quickly or totally. Particularly in North China the peasantry remain very conscious of being the heirs to the land reform brought by communist forces during the Sino-Japanese War and the successor Civil War against the Nationalists.

Third, and of greatest importance, the CCP has brought improvements in almost everyone's standard of living since 1949, whereas after the Second World War the USSR experienced a declining economic base. Considerable attention has been afforded the high growth rates – in excess of 9 per cent per annum of GDP – achieved in the PRC since 1978 and the start of the programme of reform. Yet from 1949 to 1978 the economy had also grown at 6 per cent of GDP per annum. To be sure, there were years within this period – the end of the Great Leap Forward being the best example – when the economy met severe problems and there was considerable social dislocation and suffering. Nonetheless, over the whole period there were significant improvements in housing, education, health and welfare, as well as economic growth.

The high economic growth rates that have characterised the PRC's economy since 1970 were absent from the USSR before it disappeared. Of course, as already noted, growth has been far from even within the PRC, and it might be thought that there was considerable potential for regional envy and resentment inherent in such a situation. However, the evidence, though varied, tends to other conclusions. In the first place, available studies suggest that resentment occurs not at the level of poor province versus rich province, but within localities, in terms of poor against rich individuals.[9] Moreover, it is far from clear that, as was the case in Western Europe during the early stages of modernisation, but not in Taiwan or Hong Kong, rapid economic growth has increased inequalities. Recent surveys of both Jiangsu and Zhejiang provinces – both admittedly relatively highly urbanised and economically developed – suggest that increased equality has attended their economic growth since 1978.[10]

REGIONALISM AND ECONOMIC INTEGRATION

As was indicated earlier, recent arguments about political disintegration make much of the stimulus provided to provincial autonomy by the economic and financial reforms of the 1980s, and the centre's loss of revenue. Such economic determinism is somewhat crude and of concern not least because the current economic regions are not the traditional provinces. Indeed, it is perhaps misleading even to regard them as regions.

Though administrative practice may lag behind, the areas of economic growth cross not only provincial but also national boundaries. Regional development centred on the Shantou Special Economic Zone is an obvious example, drawing equally from Guangdong and Fujian provinces, and directed at considerable economic integration with Taiwan. Moreover, economic growth is by no means even across a province. Guangdong Province's Pearl River Delta – centred on Shenzhen, Zhuhai, Guangzhou, Zhongshan, Shunde and Dongguan – is the centre of economic growth within the province, but elsewhere its mountain counties in the northeast and northwest are amongst the poorest in the country.

Areas such as the Pearl River Delta, or that centred on the cities of the Lower Yangtze and Shanghai hinterland are perhaps better regarded as poles of economic stimulation with areas of growth emanating from them. These areas of economic growth have (sometimes rapidly) expanding borders, not only into the East Asian economic region but particularly into the rest of China. It has, for example, become clear since 1991 that the economic integration of Hong Kong and Guangdong has generated growth not only throughout Southern China in a series of ever-increasing concentric circles, but also into East and Central China.

In any case, the apparent assumption of a necessary conflict between centre and province, or centre and region, seems fundamentally flawed. This is perhaps the most important lesson from China's history. The general proposition that national and regional identities need not be in conflict but may be complementary is one that provides a useful paradigm for understanding a country of the size and extent of China. There is a clear hierarchy of local integration into the national political culture which the CCP to a large extent has utilised rather than tried to replace.[11] The individual relates first to his or her native place, then the county, province and China as a whole.

To some extent the CCP has always recognised that China's size and diversity presented limits to the uniformity of national policy and campaigns. Local variation in the implementation of national policy was a principle of CCP administration articulated during the era of guerrilla war and carried on well into the pre-Cultural Revolution era. National policy provided the broad goals and outline of implementation, but detailed development was the preserve of local cadres. One consequence of these arrangements was the recognition by CCP leaders that there were, in addition to limits on provincial autonomy (or perhaps better, degrees of manoeuvre), also restrictions on central authority.

Another consequence is a different interpretation of the centre's changing role. A belief that in the Mao-dominated era of the PRC's politics before 1978 the centre was either totalitarian or in some sense all-powerful will necessarily exaggerate the consequences of the centre's reduced role in both government and politics more generally. However, the centre has more options than being everything or nothing. Without in any way minimising the dangers and difficulties inherent in its strategy, the goal and practice of reform has been to transform the centre (and government generally) from immediate involvement in and direction of the economy to macro-economic control.[12]

Particularly during the late 1980s and early 1990s that transformation has caused considerable dislocation and a measure of chaos. However, in some areas of economic activity central control is perhaps even stronger – at least in terms of efficiency, effectiveness and economic impact – than before the start of the reform era. Rather than forecasting political disintegration or doubting that the centre has a role to play as modernisation develops, it seems more sensible to focus on the possible future political roles for the centre in relation to the regions. The experience of other modernising states suggests three somewhat stark options, which may exist in combination. The centre may become the judge of and balance between competing interests, attempting to maintain impartiality. It may, however, have its own economic organisations and interests, and become the leading player amongst a number of smaller, or at least less strategically important economies. Alternatively, it may be neither transcendental, nor active in its own right, but the mechanism for the articulation of regional interests.

Moreover, there can be little doubt that the centre will need to develop new political roles and skills towards the regions as the economy develops. The lure of China's domestic market is as attractive to the fast-developing regions of the PRC as it has been to the world's developed economies. The goal of a fully integrated national market may still be some way off, but it remains a goal.

REGIONALISM IN THE POLITICAL PROCESS

Economic determinism is also misleading as an interpretation of the relationship between centre and region in the PRC, because political rhetoric may not reflect economic reality, partly because of the internal structures and decision-making processes of the CCP. In the first place, the CCP is the framework of all political activity, and in that framework local leaders and national leaders are often the same people wearing different hats. Even where they are not, the image is of a single ruling class, based on vast networks of patron–client relationships.

In the second place, there has been and remains an inherent regional dimension to the policy process. Decision-making – from the conceptualisation of an initiative, through policy formulation to implementation – has remained incremental, experimental and decentralised. In general terms, the CCP has maintained the principle of 'Do the best according to local conditions', born out of its guerrilla experience and a recognition of the large spatial variation in a country the size of China. The centre lays down the broad outline of a policy, with the provinces adopting specific local measures for implementation, often at first on an experimental basis. In the experimental phase, different localities are chosen for the varying conditions that may affect policy implementation.

The whole process allows for considerable variation in policy and local initiative. Initiatives for policy may come from anywhere in the system, though at times it is clear that the transaction costs, and more particularly the opportunity costs of failure, may be high. Consequently, insurance is frequently sought in factional alliances, which frequently serve as a channel for feeding suggestions into the policy process. Certainly, there is every reason to suspect that the selection of 'trial points' and 'experimental plots' is often made with specific policy outcomes in mind. The decision-making process is thus much less straightforwardly an instrument of central control than is usually considered the case from the more totalitarian perspectives on communist party states.

It is quite common to find initiatives floated on a trial basis regionally in order to influence the national decision-making process. Most of the early policy changes of the reform era were introduced in this way, with local leaders, presumably with at the very least the protection of more senior figures in the Political Bureau of the CCP, making the running. Enterprise reforms and the introduction of market forces into management of the state sector were first pioneered by Zhao Ziyang in Sichuan when he was that province's leading party secretary and before he became Premier. Decollectivisation in the countryside, and the introduction of 'responsibility system' for individual households was similarly trialled extensively in Anhui Province by party secretary Wan Li, as with the 'Sichuan Experience', in advance of the Third Plenum of December 1978. Both Zhao Ziyang and Wan Li were at the time closely associated with Deng Xiaoping and others pushing for the reform programme eventually adopted in December 1978.[13] Of necessity, the successful examples of such kite-flying – those which later signalled important policy changes – are better known. However, ever since the establishment of the PRC there have been many examples of this kind of lobbying in practice: sometimes, as in the prelude to the Cultural Revolution,[14] attempting major changes in policies and programmes; but at other times, such as at the Eighth National Party Congress in 1956, simply attempting more modest goals in the articulation of local interest.[15]

One consequent paradox of this particular process of bureaucratic politics is that it is even possible for national policy formulation to follow policy implementation. The most famous occasion when this was the case was in 1958 with the development of People's Communes. For most of the year Mao Zedong and a number of provincial leaders had been promoting the idea of something along the lines of what eventually became known as the People's Commune. Every place Mao visited between February and August 1958 established a People's Commune or its equivalent, before the nomenclature was determined in June. However, the national decision to establish People's Communes was not taken until 5 September. This dynamic aspect of the decision-making process was clearly a large part of the explanation for the rapid success of communisation within a month of the Beidaihe Resolution that formally proposed the establishment of rural people's communes.[16]

When the question of regionalism, or rather criticism of regionalism, is raised by or within the CCP it is sometimes because the centre, or at least part of the centre, is trying to make a political point, rather than because an independent (of the CCP) regionalism has emerged. For example, as a precursor to the Great Leap Forward, when the CCP was about to introduce a higher degree of decentralisation in management of the economy, a rectification campaign against 'political regionalism' was carried out amongst provincial leaders. Education about the purpose and methods of decentralisation, and indeed the programmes of the Great Leap, was the main goal. Resistance to the new policies was characterised as regionalism regardless of its origins.[17] It seems reasonable to assume that a similar dynamic is behind the national leadership's more recent concern with 'localism', and its characterisation and criticism of certain kinds of regional economic activity as the emergence of 'duke economies'.

REGIONALISM AND NEGOTIATION

The consideration of the place of regionalism in the decision-making process provides perspectives on the dynamics of the relationship between centre and region that do not readily or of themselves lend weight to an argument that political disintegration is likely in China. Instead the creative tension between central and local leaders – all of whom are politicians on the national stage – emphasises that there is both negotiation and hard bargaining as China rapidly modernises. Naturally enough sometimes that tension leads to excess, by either side, and there is a need for readjustment. The early 1990s, and particularly the debates on the Eighth Five-year Plan and the Ten-year Programme at the national level, as well as the development of the regions – particularly South China centred on Greater Hong Kong; and East China centred on Shanghai and the cities of its immediate hinterland – provide ample evidence and examples of that interplay between centre and region.

One clear example was the establishment of an open stock exchange in Shenzhen. Before June 1989 there had been much discussion within the PRC of the need to introduce a large-scale capital market, with open trading, exchanges, foreign investment, bonds and equities. Necessarily debate had led to experimentation, with a high degree of activity in a number of cities including Shenzhen, Shenyang, Wuhan and Shanghai. During the second half of 1989, as part of its apparent attempt to recentralise control, central government proclaimed that the PRC's first post-1949 official open stock exchange would commence operations in Shanghai in December 1990. The event was attended by considerable publicity in the official media. However, not to be outdone the Shenzhen Exchange moved from over-the-counter trading to an open exchange, ahead of the Shanghai launch, and clearly without the approval of the central authorities and against some of their wishes. However, it was a move which was rapidly blessed by central government and demonstrates clearly the need to disaggregate the centre as well as the regions. In addition to any conflict between centre and regions, there is competition between the Ministry of Finance, the State Economic Commission, and the Commission for Restructuring the Economy, all of which may have different positions.

A less celebrated example of the bargaining between centre and region concerns foreign investment in Hangzhou during 1991–2. Until the announcement of Deng Xiaoping's 'Journey South' changed the pace of economic development and 'openness' in May–June 1992 there were some relatively severe limitations on foreign investment in the PRC outside the Special Economic Zones. In general, foreign firms were discouraged from investing elsewhere, and there was no provision for land usage rights on long leases. However, between June 1991 and May 1992 some 993 foreign firms invested directly in Hangzhou City, though there was no central or formal provision. Their existence and official approval was publicised after June 1992, once Deng's imprimatur had been firmly placed behind such extensions of policy. Such development highlights the importance of the CCP as the framework of political action. It would seem too coincidental that at the time Zhu Rongji's secretary – Zhao Haikuan – was responsible for economic restructuring in Hangzhou.

An interpretation of the relationship between centre and region in terms of creative tensions and negotiation is further supported by the subsequent history of the planning process on the Eighth Five-year Plan. In effect it seems possible that the establishment of 'duke economies' was a tactic rather than a goal articulated at that time. The planning process was inherently political, with various participants making ambit claims. There was clearly some hard bargaining on a wide range of issues, but at the end of the day an agreement was reached.

CHINA CHANGES SHAPE

Whilst there is considerable evidence of the many ways in which China is changing shape, there is much less to suggest political separatism. As expected, political separatism as opposed to the articulation of localism is only really at issue where there have been independent (of the CCP) movements for national determination in the non-Han areas of Tibet, Xinjiang and Inner Mongolia.

The lack of evidence of separatism is not at all surprising given both the pivotal role of the CCP and the PRC's economic performance since 1978. Indeed, the two are clearly closely related. The CCP has staked its ability to maintain its leading role on both the PRC's economic performance and its ability to keep its nerve. The real test is likely to come later, for both the CCP and political unity, if and when growth slows significantly. The evidence from other modernising societies earlier in the twentieth century, as well as most recently in Eastern Europe, is that movements for regional expression gain support and momentum when economic problems arise rather than during periods of economic growth.[18]

Nonetheless, it is clearly necessary to reinterpret the structures of the Chinese state in a period of relatively rapid economic and social change. The primary concern of this book is the impact of the twin dynamics of China's new regionalism on its domestic politics and international relations. The first and domestic source of this dynamism is the policy changes of the 1980s that have encouraged localised economic growth and the development of localised comparative advantage. The second and external source of dynamism is the increased economic integration of different parts of China with different parts of East, Southeast and Central Asia on its borders. In East Asia, specifically Taiwan and Hong Kong, these dynamics were of course additionally driven by the somewhat sudden late 1980s needs of those economies to restructure.

This chapter and the chapter that follows immediately, on the history of regionalism in China, by John Fitzgerald, provide an overview and set the scene for understanding the impact of China's new regionalism. Three chapters concerned with the political economy of China's new regionalism then follow. Yang Dali examines the impact of policy change and regional growth on relations between centre and region, and on the capacities of central government and political institutions. Anajil Kumar provides a study of trade relations between and amongst the PRC's provincial-level units – municipalities and autonomous regions, as well as provinces – for which detailed statistics were not previously available. Brantly Womack investigates the foreign trade relations of each of the PRC's provincial-level units.

The third, and largest, part of the book contains case studies of China's new economic regions and their interactions with the external (to the PRC) environment. This section is not intended to provide a comprehensive description of China's new regions, or even to be representative, except in the very broadest sense. Rather, each case study was selected because of its particular characteristics.

David Goodman and Feng Chongyi examine Guangdong as Greater

Hong Kong: the first of China's new economic regions where economic integration across the border is already well advanced. Simon Long writes on Fujian, in Southeast China, and particularly its dependency for industrial investment on Taiwan. Ironically the previous military antagonism with Taiwan had acted as a brake on Fujian's economic development. In East Asia, Bruce Jacobs and Hong Lijian examine Shanghai's resurgence and attempt to reclaim its leading role in China's external economic relations, particularly through central sponsorship of the Pudong Zone.

In looking at Northeast China Michael Yahuda highlights the dilemma of reform for an economy dominated by the state sector and heavy industrial development. The conservative outlook of its provinces is hardly surprising, given both their lack of capacity for domestic economic initiatives or opportunity for external economic relations: largely unreformed Russia and North Korea are its immediate neighbours. In Northwest China the Xinjiang Uighur Autonomous Region, discussed by Peter Ferdinand, presents the PRC with a much more radical challenge. Here there is fundamental opposition to the very idea of its inclusion in the PRC, fuelled by developments across the borders in the newly independent Kazakhstan and Kirghizstan. The final case study is of Yunnan Province in Southwest China, by Ingrid d'Hooghe, interesting for the social consequences of its economic integration with the countries to its south and the challenges they present, not least with respect to the slave trade and drug trafficking.

In the final section of the book Gerald Segal's conclusion turns to the wider ramifications of China's new regionalism for international relations. In particular he highlights the consequences for the rest of the world in having to come to terms with the more sophisticated political environment of many, rather than just one, Chinese governments. Political disintegration may not be a distinct possibility, but the need to disaggregate and differentiate political institutions and their decision-making capacities is already very real.

NOTES

1 For a recent example, see Qin Xiangyin and Ni Jianzhong (eds) *Nan Bei Qun Qiu: Zhongguo huibuhui fenlie* [The History of the North versus the South: Will China disintegrate?], Beijing: Renmin Zhongguo chubanshe, 1993.

2 See, for example, the highly publicised report written for the State Council by two 'returned students' who had studied at Yale – Wang Shaoguang and Hu Angang – and published in English as *China's*

State Capacity Report, Shenyang: Liaoning People's Publishing House, 1993.

3 For example: Maria Hsia Chang 'China's Future: Regionalism, Federation, or Disintegration' in *Studies in Comparative Communism* Vol. XXV No. 3, September 1992, p. 211; and W.J.F. Jenner, *The Tyranny of History*, London: Allen Lane, 1992.

4 For a particularly interesting discussion of this matter, see: Athar Hussain and Nicholas Stern, *Economic Reforms and Public Fianance in China*, The Development Economics Research Programme, LSE CP No. 23, June 1992.

5 On 'duke economies' and associated phenomena, see, for example: Shen Liren and Tai Yuanchen 'Woguo "zhuhou jingji" de xingcheng ji chi biduan he genyuan', in *Jingji yanjiu*, No. 3, 1990, p. 12.

6 See, for example: A. Watson and C. Findlay 'The "wool war" in China', in C. Findlay (ed) *Challenges of Economic Reform and Industrial Growth: China's Wool War*, Sydney: Allen and Unwin, 1992.

7 J.B.R. Whitney *China: Area, Administration and Nation-Building*, University of Chicago, Department of Geography Research Paper No. 123, 1970.

8 Allen to Washington, 7 April 1922, *US State Department Papers* 893.00/4405.

9 For example: A. Chan, R. Madsen and J. Unger, *Chen Village under Mao and Deng*, Berkeley: University of California Press, 1992, p. 267 ff.

10 Junhua Wu, 'Economic Growth and Regional Development Strategy in China', in *Japan Research Quarterly*, Vol. 2, No. 3, Summer 1993, p. 31.

11 See, for example: D.J. Solinger, *Regional Government and Political Integration*, Berkeley: University of California Press, 1977.

12 On Kit Tam, 'Reform of China's Banking System', in *The World Economy*, December 1986; and on Kit Tam, 'The Development of China's Financial System', in *The Australian Journal of Chinese Affairs*, No. 17, January 1987, p. 95.

13 'Zhao Ziyang's "Sichuan Experience": Blueprint for a nation', in *Chinese Law and Government*, Spring 1982; S. Shapiro, *Experiment in Sichuan – A Report on Economic Reform*, Beijing: New World Press, 1981; D. Zweig, 'Context and Content in Policy Implementation: Household Contracts and Decollectivisation, 1977–1983', in D. M. Lampton (ed), *Policy Implementation in Post-Mao China*, Berkeley: University of California Press, 1987.

14 R. Baum, *Prelude to Revolution: Mao, the Party, and the Peasant Question, 1962–66*, New York: Columbia University Press, 1975.

15 David S.G. Goodman, 'Provincial Party First Secretaries in National Politics: A Categoric or a Political Group?', in D.S.G. Goodman (ed), *Groups and Politics in the People's Republic of China*, Cardiff: University College Press, 1984, pp. 82–101; S. L. Shirk *The Political Logic of Economic Reform in China*, Berkeley: University of California Press, 1993, p. 149 ff.

16 David S.G. Goodman, *Centre and Province in the People's Republic of China*, Cambridge University Press, 1986, p. 136, Chapter 7, 'Rural People's Communes'.

17 F.C. Teiwes, 'The purge of provincial leaders, 1957–1958', in *The China Quarterly*, No. 27, July 1966.
18 M. Hechter, *Internal Colonialism: The Celtic Fringe in British National Development, 1536–1966*, London: Routledge and Kegan Paul, 1975, provides a particularly stimulating account of these dynamics.

2 'Reports of my death have been greatly exaggerated'

The history of the death of China

John Fitzgerald

It's always necessary to pay attention to history. A long history has its advantages and disadvantages. The history of the United States is short, and perhaps there is some advantage in that, for burdens are lighter and it isn't necessary to remember so many things. We have a long history, which has its advantages, too. If we were to throw out our old traditions, people would call it traitorous. You can't chop off history even if you want to. There's no getting around it. And yet it is really rather troublesome to look back over such a long history.

Mao Zedong, 1956[1]

There is much to be remembered in history, but the legacy of history does not always need to be remembered for its influence to be felt. This is particularly so in China. Inherited patterns of population density, land use, urban settlement and cultural and linguistic differentiation have proven remarkably resilient throughout the late imperial and modern periods. The boundaries of political movements and institutions have also reflected regional and hierarchical patterns, even where political actors have not consciously set out to duplicate them.[2] This should not perhaps surprise us. The Chinese state has either overlain inherited transhistorical structures, like a transparent film over a detailed contour map, or alternatively taken its shape from successive attempts to deny their salience. Either way, there is no more getting around the deep structures of history than there is around remembered history.

The state has been anything but transparent throughout most of the history of the People's Republic. Mao's injunction to follow the example of the Foolish Old Man and 'move the mountain' is an apt metaphor for a regime which recognised few cultural, social, economic or even environmental limits to its wilfulness. Yet even in

Mao's day the deep structures of forgotten histories left their imprint on the urban organisation of the country, on patterns of agriculture, industry and communication and on the social and cultural life of communities across the length and breadth of China. Mao also insisted, with more mummery than sense, that China's six hundred million people were 'first of all destitute and secondly blank', a 'clean sheet of paper' on which he would write 'the newest and most beautiful words.'[3] In fact, however, he confronted in the Chinese people a mountain of memory sufficiently daunting to deter any but the most foolish old man. Mao's metaphor of the page was not meant to be taken literally but intended to signal a determination 'to paste over, rub out or scratch away from the Chinese "page" the countless rich and living traces that the centuries had left on it,' as Simon Leys has observed, 'so that on the "blank" page the Chairman could write his poem.'[4]

The success of a state in promoting economic development in a competitive world system depends, nevertheless, on its capacity to recognise and accommodate itself to what is already inscribed on the page. China needs to build upon rather than obliterate the macro-regional characteristics and the inter-regional and international link-ages indicated by inherited structures. Greater levels of regional differentiation which have emerged since Mao's death, under the reformist regime of Deng Xiaoping, represent a step in this direc-tion. Yet in some quarters the regionalisation of the economy, society and polity has been received with anything but confidence. Instead it appears to threaten the disintegration of China, or, in Chinese terms, to hold out the prospect of the 'death of the state'.

The latest instance is to be found in a report entitled 'Strengthen the central government's leading role amid the shift to a market economy', issued in September 1993. 'In years,' the report predicts, 'at the soonest a few and at the latest between ten and twenty, the country will move from economic collapse to political break-up, ending with its disintegration.'[5] This report, needless to say, does not advocate the disintegration of China; it raises the prospect of China's disintegration only to excite greater interest in maintaining the present regime. And so it has always been. The history of China's imminent disintegration is almost as long as the fabled history of China itself, and is invariably associated with a regime in crisis.

Similar sentiments have been expressed abroad. Indeed few of China's self-appointed saviours who have raised the chorus to 'save the nation' over the course of this century could have put it better than W. J. F. Jenner in his recent book *The Tyranny of History: The*

Roots of China's Crisis: 'The state, people and culture known in English as China are in a profound general crisis,' writes Jenner. 'The very future of China as a unitary state is in question . . .'.[6] Certainly the inflection of Jenner's remark is the reverse of that of China's nationalists. Jenner is daring, if not inviting, the sky to fall in, and few people in China have been so bold. They may have to live with the consequences. The question at issue here, however, is not whether portents of China's immanent collapse should be shunned or welcomed, but whether the crisis of the regime is, as Jenner suggests, a crisis threatening the death of the unitary state or rather a crisis afflicting a particular form of the unitary state in China's 'long history'.

In focusing on something as intangible as the 'thesis of the death of the state' we need to move beyond the transhistorical structures bequeathed by history to speak of history as Mao understood it; that is, with history as memory. To Mao, the rest was bunk. Yet while the structural impediments standing in the way of the revolutionary state were dismissed out of hand, the history of remembered grievances and of cultivated glories served as a rich repository of inspiration. These were, of course, selective memories. The historical memory appropriated by the People's Republic has, until recent years, been a history which ended in 1949 – a history of imperialist aggression, feudal oppression and state disintegration culminating in national reunification and liberation under a Communist Party state. Much happened afterwards, of course, but it appeared to have little bearing on the identity of the subject, China.

A reluctance to remember history can, if allowed to go unchecked, give rise to a dangerous clinical condition. In this respect, the link between national histories and national identities is not unlike the relationship between personal memory and individual identity. Without memory we do not know who we are, it is difficult to make sense of what we are doing, and it is near to impossible to do anything to a purpose. The neurologist Oliver Sacks records the case of a patient who had a clear memory of everything that happened to him until 1945 but lost the capacity to make new memories after that time. When Sacks met him in the early 1980s 'Jimmy' was still convinced that it was 1945. Incapable of remembering anything about him, he was, Sacks records, 'isolated in a single moment of being, with a moat or lacuna of forgetting all about him . . . He is a man without a past (or future), stuck in a constantly changing, meaningless moment.' When his doctors tested Jimmy to discover the cause of the ailment, they were most distressed to learn that they could not find

Jimmy. The patient was barely aware of his loss and could not be made aware because he had suffered not only a loss in himself, but a 'loss *of* himself'.[7]

Had it failed to come to terms with what has happened since 1949, China may well have fallen into a pathological state not unlike that of Jimmy, living constantly in the remote past and incapable of reconstituting its identity in a form capable of equipping it for dealing with the world outside the sanitorium. But with the trauma of the Cultural Revolution and the shock of rediscovering the world beyond China, in the 1970s, the people and the state have begun to remember events which took place after 1949 as part of the history constituting their identity. This new identity has not come easily, crystallising around unassailable memories embedded in private lives and in wider community tragedies which have been painfully dragged out of the darkness into public space, attacked, defended, consolidated and sometimes forced back into privacy. For all the hesitancy and distress that has characterised this collective re-remembering, the process is critical to China's recovery as a viable national community.

This process of historical renegotiation has been taking place, nevertheless, within limits prescribed by a profound memory of 'chaos' attendant on the 'death of the state' which stretches back beyond 1949 and indeed well beyond the republican period into the imperial era. Fear of the death of the state has played a critical part in China's identity as an historical community this century, informing political intention and behaviour much as personal memory informs individual action. In fact memory of the disintegration or death of the state has been invoked with telling effect by all political movements since the middle of the nineteenth century. Fear of the 'death of the state', in other words, has a history of its own which deserves to be remembered, and which perhaps *needs* to be remembered in order to appreciate the rhetorical function of the 'thesis of the death of the state' in contemporary China.

CONTINUITY, UNITY AND LEGITIMACY

China is not just a country with a long history but, as they say in China, a *big* country with a long history. Taken alone, neither its size nor its history is all that remarkable, but the one does generally militate against the other. Rome has a long history but it no longer rules over an extensive empire; the United States is a big country, but has a 'short' history. To be sure, the integrity of the Chinese Empire was favoured more than most by the topography of its borders: the frozen steppes to the north, the deserts to the west, the mountain ranges to the south and the sea-coast to the east all helped to isolate the Chinese Empire from the societies and civilisations at its margins. Yet within the borders of the Empire equally imposing rivers and flood plains, mountain ranges and valleys, highlands and deserts fragmented the realm into isolated regional communites, each with distinctive cultures, languages, and relatively isolated patterns of trade, not unlike those which developed into nation–states in continental Europe.[8] In triumphing over geography *and* history, the Chinese state is unique.

And a triumph it was. Neither Europe nor China were in any sense destined to follow courses mapped out by their geography, but distance and terrain presented formidable obstacles. Julius Caesar and Charlemagne, Charles V and the Hapsburgs, Napoleon and Hitler all tried in effect to emulate the feat of the Chinese Empire, and failed.[9] China itself followed the divided pattern of Europe over the period from the Eastern Chou to the Warring States (771–256 BC), and the states of the ensuing Three Kingdoms (AD 220–280), the Six Dynasties and Ten Kingdoms (226–316), the Northern and Southern Dynasties (317–589), the Five Dynasties (907–960) and the divided Song (1127–1279), all formally approximated the division of Europe into several states without ever succeeding in institutionalising state separatism. Topography was less important to the outcome, in either case, than the relative development of weapons and bureaucracies, in which China had the advantage.[10] But what ultimately distinguished the one from the other was not that China was forever united or Europe perennially divided, but that the Chinese Empire actually survived the transition to the nation–state. In triumphing over geography and history, the Empire established the unitary state as the definitive characteristic of the Chinese nation.[11]

The Chinese state enjoyed a certain advantage over history and geography. Its functionaries kept the office files, and arranged them to greatest advantage in glorifying the achievements and minimising the humiliations of the unitary state. Georg Hegel was moved to note the origins of China's identity as a unitary state in the historical records of the imperial court, and he was inclined to attribute its longevity as a state to the meticulous court records which give China its identity *as* a state. Without a state there is no history, and without a history there is no sense of community: no state, in other words, no nation.[12] China entered the twentieth century as a proto-nation because its state was long accustomed to keeping good records. And twentieth-century custodians of the record, as Mao intimated in 1956, have been reluctant to surrender any of the advantages which such a 'long history' confers.

Court diarists and historians played an important part in eliding some of the more glaring discontinuities in the history of China and, more remarkably still, succeeded in associating all that was continuous in China's history with one of its discontinuous features: the unitary imperial state. The chief function of the court historian was to highlight the genealogy of political legitimacy which was thought to run, like a golden thread, through the matted history of the rise and fall of dynastic houses.[13] In the course of his duty, the historian was obliged to arbitrate among rival claimants to the throne, and thereby establish continuity of succession from the founding emperors of China right up to the reign of the incumbent emperor. The problem of historical continuity was at one level a problem of 'calendar making', as John Fincher has noted, but it was much more besides.[14] In compiling his calendar, the court historian conferred continuity upon the chaos of history and legitimacy upon his patron. Significantly, the principles which he devised for asserting the continuity of the Empire were identical to those which established the legitimacy of its rulers.

The big question was how to accommodate awkward periods of disunity within a uniformly legitimating system of succession.[15] Up to the Song period, at least, the principles conferring continuity and legitimation were derived from the ethical and political considerations which reflected most favourably upon the incumbent imperial house. They varied accordingly. In the Song, however, the prominent scholar and statesman Ouyang Xiu proposed that periods of disunity should be omitted from the line of legitimate succession altogether. The unity of the state took precedence over continuity of succession. Periods of disunity, he argued, were intervening blanks in the history of a state which was constantly striving to reconstitute itself as a unitary state. They should be left out of history, or at best recognised as no more than lacunae in the history of the unitary state.[16]

Ouyang Xiu's reformulation assisted in redefining the concept of political legitimacy to emphasise the principle of unification: the preservation of *unity* established legitimacy and in the absence of unity there may be no legitimacy at all.[17] The title of the essays in which Ouyang Xiu set out these principles, *On Legitimate Succession*, embraces a term which was at the centre of the debate on the problem of legitimacy in the late Empire, *zhengtong* ('legitimate succession').[18] The word has a long history of its own, dating back to the Gong-yang commentary on *The Spring and Autumn Annals*, but

Ouyang Xiu modified earlier interpretations to lend greater emphasis to the ideal of state unity. In earlier texts, the second syllable of *zhengtong* was generally read to mean 'system'; but it can also mean 'unification', and this is the sense in which Ouyang Xiu employed the term.[19] He wished to stress the relationship between 'rectitude' (*zheng*) and 'unification' (*tong*) in the word for 'legitimate succession' in ways often overlooked in earlier commentary. And on his new reading, rulers who succeeded in unifying the imperium, irrespective of the means to which they had resort, were to be counted legitimate rulers of China. A little 'rectitude' would certainly not go astray, but rectitude was no longer the *sine qua non* of legitimacy.[20] Perhaps linking legitimacy to unification of the imperium did not mark a radical departure from practice. In fact Ouyang Xiu seems to have done little more than make a virtue of necessity: Han usurpers and invading 'barbarians', peasant rebels and enfeoffed nobles all competed on an equal footing when it came to seizing the throne, and all were as inclined to claim legitimacy, if they won, as they were obliged to concede legitimacy if they lost. Nevertheless Ouyang Xiu set out the relationship between historical continuity, state unity and political legitimacy with such simple clarity that his principle served as the foundation for the official historiography of the late Empire.

In the early Republic, the aging but still brilliant scholar Liang Qichao attempted to apply the term *zhengtong* to the unity and continuity of the Chinese nation, rather than to the political unity of the imperium.[21] Artfully contrived though the claims of continuity may have been between different dynastic houses and individual rulers, over two thousand years of history, they pale in comparision with the assertion of continuity between the Chinese Empire and the kind of political nationalism Liang had in mind. The two are as different as chalk and cheese. The China of history was an empire, not a nation–state, and it was held together by the wedding of internal differentiation with formal unity. That is, it consisted of a series of distinct vertical communities within large regional blocs which were integrated internally by ties of custom and commerce, which were associated with one another through common ritual practices and a common textual tradition, and which were bound to the state through the working of the imperial bureaucracy and the placement of imperial garrisons. The state insisted upon a high degree of formal similarity in its bureaucratic procedures and ritual practices, not because it feared internal differentiation, but out of fear that *un*differentiated patterns of heterodox belief could at any time sweep across communities and override the barriers of local differentiation which

served to contain them.[22] The Empire tolerated variety among localities because it feared mass horizontal communication of the kind we
now associate with political nationalism.[23]

When the Empire collapsed, in 1912, the people spread out over the
realm were still as divided as the physical landscape, split by mountain
ranges on three sides and sliced down the middle by vast river systems.
Within and between these geographical divisions communities were
separated by local and regional loyalties, by kinship, ethnicity, language and custom. In imperial times this diversity had been celebrated
in common subjection to an imperial state which governed 'all under
Heaven'. In the Republic, however, the differences celebrated by the
phrase 'all under Heaven' read as a catalogue of nationalist night-
mares. The twang of local dialect and the colour of local custom, long
considered quaint and picturesque under the Empire, now seemed
particularist and served to remind nationalists of the internal divisions
and backwardness of their nation. Ethno-linguistic differences were
viewed with suspicion; communities founded upon ties of patriarchal
kinship were branded as 'feudal'; and national educational programmes were devised to maximise the possibility of mass communication and minimise the scope for local exclusion.[24] The enemies of
nationalism in China were invariably identified by their local attach-
ments: 'local bullies', 'local patois', 'regionalism' and clanism.[25]

The nationalist movement put forward a range of new horizontal
communities to smash particularist barriers and bring the 'people'
together for social and political mobilisation. Nationalists employed
hyper-national categories like 'citizen', 'race', 'masses', 'class', and
'youth', 'men' and 'women' to supplant father, son and emperor, and
they promoted identification with the nation in place of ethnic, sub-
ethnic or native-place affiliation. All who dwelt within the borders of
the old Empire were to be made to think of themselves as members of
the Chinese 'race', all who worked the Loess plains of the Yellow
River, the paddies of the Yangtze Valley and the sugar plantations of
south China were to be made conscious of their status as 'Chinese
peasants', and the many soldiers who tramped across the land under a
hundred standards and speaking as many tongues were each and
every one to count themselves 'citizens' of a Chinese Republic.
This was the stuff of dreams. Yet nationalists believed it was not
they, but China, which was dreaming. The residue of empire was still
only a potential nation or, as nationalists preferred to put it, a
'sleeping' nation in need of awakening by nationalism itself.[26]

The problem was not just one of persistent local cultures. With the
establishment of the Republic, the mountains and rivers of the Empire

divided the polity as well. The first President, General Yuan Shikai, failed to recapture the loyalty of the provincial elites which had declared their independence of the Empire and shortly after he died, in 1916, Defenders of the Original Constitution gathered south of the Hunan–Guangdong mountains to set up a rival republican administration in Guangzhou. In 1917 these patriots went to war to 'protect the constitution' and ushered in a decade of civil war between great northern and southern military alliances and among the allies in each camp. When the Nationalists came to power, in 1928, they exercised control over just five of China's provinces, and, although they managed to extend their reach over the following decade, their gains were eliminated when the Imperial Army of Japan invaded central and southern China in 1937. In fact the Nationalists never managed to govern all of China, as a unitary state, and yet to this day they have not given up trying. Such persistence is worth noting on two counts. First, it reminds us that there has barely been a moment since the fall of the Empire when the people of China have not been invited to adjudicate among rival (and absolute) claimants to political legitimacy. Second, it reminds us that none of these regionally-based governments has ever been content to govern in the name of its region alone. The legitimating ideal of the unitary state as been upheld in each and every period by the reluctance of any of the rival governments to abandon the titles of 'central' or 'national', or to confine its ambitions to the territory effectively under its control. Abandoning the pretence of state unity (however absurd) means abandoning all claim to legitimacy. If anything, political divisions have reinforced rather than undermined the ideal of a single nation brought together under a unitary state.[27]

Since nations do not evolve naturally, as it were, from imperial states and kingdoms, the assertion of historical continuity in the face of the nationalist rupture must always entail imagination and a measure of artifice. This was Liang Qichao's objective in applying the term *zhengtong* to the nation, rather than to the state. But pasting over historical ruptures is far too important a task to leave to scholars and historians; historical consciousness, as George Mosse observed, is the very foundation of the nation.[28] Much of the work is done far from the archives – in fashion houses and museums, in engineering workshops and monumental spaces, in the press and public education, and in anthems, flags and impressive public rituals. Together these effect a fundamental change, in Benedict Anderson's words, 'in modes of apprehending the world which, more than anything else, [make] it possible to "think" the nation.'[29]

Historians nevertheless have their part to play, for the more modern the nationalist aspiration, the more it needs to mobilise authenticated tradition in its support. Tradition may well yield to traditionalism, as Joseph Levenson has suggested, but traditionalism also revives an interest in the study of the past. To the extent that Chinese nationalist thought was fundamentally an historical *attitude*, it required modern historians to expose 'false' histories and reveal the 'true' face of the nation, presumed to have been long suppressed by the fabrication and dissemination of arcane traditional scholarship.

Here China's new historians were caught between a rock and a hard place. On the one hand they sought to escape the tyranny of traditional historical scholarship, but on the other they were hard-pressed to preserve the historical continuity on which national identity is founded.[30] Their solution lay not in a retreat from the 'tyranny of history' but in a revolution in historical scholarship. One of the pioneers of the New History, Gu Jiegang, announced that what he proposed to do with history was: 'a great act of destruction, but without it our nation will not find a viable path. Our acts of destruction are not cruel activities; we are only restoring these various things to their historical position.'[31]

The new science of history was at once 'an act of destruction' and an act of restoration, in effect destroying the hold of the past by restoring its artifacts to the museum, where modern men and women could gaze and wonder at how far they had advanced beyond their ancestors. While Gu Jiegang and his colleagues exposed the myths and fabrications of earlier scholarship, they rummaged through unorthodox histories and minor schools of philosophy to establish indigenous precedents for progress and inventiveness, egalitarian ethics and responsible government, vitality and adventurousness, and all of the other imagined qualities of a nation in want of a past.[32] History was not only a tyrant, but a liberator.

Twentieth-century historians have tended to follow court archivists and political philosophers in tracing the integration and disintegration of the unitary state as the unifying theme of China's history.[33] This coincidence is partly explained by the nature of the historical enterprise and the identity of the historical subject: the proper object of study for China's 'scientific' historians appeared to be the nation–state simply because it was assumed to be the natural unit of historical development.[34] And if 'China' was to be taken as the subject of history, then periods of national disunity once again appeared, not unreasonably, as aberrations from the subject at hand. Still, the assumption that the disaggregation of China deserved study chiefly as a study of imperial or national disintegration rather than as a study of the integration of other constituent communities – or indeed the emergence of entirely new forms of continuity altogether – does give a particular momentum to China's history as the history of a unitary state.[35] This, too, is a theme which has its origins in the Chinese textual tradition.[36]

THE DEATH OF THE STATE

W.J.F. Jenner traces the roots of China's crisis to the 'tyranny' of its history, and certainly the historiography of China is not to be distinguished easily from the legitimating ideology of the unitary state. The establishment of state unity and the assertion of historical continuity have, we noted, served as the two legitimating principles of widely differing state formations from one epoch to the next. Yet in ascribing particular characteristics to the unitary historical state, nationalists and historians have tended to conflate three quite distinct phenomena with the general ideal. First, the unitary state has been implicitly identified with particular state formations and regimes; second, it has come to be associated with a powerful central state; and third, it has been conflated with the idea of a uniform national people. Political competition between absolute monarchists and constitutionalists, reformers and revolutionaries, federalists and centralists, and among Nationalists, liberals and Communists was endlessly enlivened by the common knowledge that they all were engaged in a battle much grander than a partisan struggle to seize state power. They were competing to give particular form to a common ideal of the unitary state, and to give a definitive shape to their nation. In 'saving' the country, they would manufacture China both as a nation and as a state. Although contingent on the ideal of the unitary state, the nation and state which they succeeded in creating were never more than contingent variables. And as the legitimating principle of each particular state, the ideal of the unitary state has survived each of their particular 'crises'.

State and Regime

While nationalists have rarely refrained from boasting of China's long and glorious history, neither have they been loathe to issue dire warnings that this history might come to an abrupt and inglorious end at any moment. These are two refrains of a single melody. The phrase 'death of the state' conveys an image of China disappearing from the face of the earth, and connotes as well, morbid fears of territorial dispossession, cultural alienation and racial genocide. Similarly, its rhetorical counterpart to 'save the state' suggests the salvation of the people and culture of China as well as the survival of the state. Both terms have enjoyed a prominent place in the memorials of nineteenth-century reformers, in the cultural jeremiads of May Fourth activists and in the songs and wall posters of Nationalist and Communist revolutionaries. Nationalists of every persuasion shouted that the sky was about to fall in so that they might rush in and demand first place among those queuing and jostling to hold it up.

Nor are predictions of China's imminent demise simply a twentieth-century phenomenon. In the crisis brought on by British and French military pressure in the mid-nineteenth century, the eminent Confucian scholar Yu Yue warned that 'the name of China' and the 'universe as we know it' would come to an end if the imperial government continued to maintain relations with the foreign powers.[37] Some foreign observers defined the crisis afflicting the Qing as a crisis of the unitary state itself. In 1899, Lord Charles Beresford published his findings on the 'present commerce, currency, waterways, armies, railways, politics and future prospects' of China under the title *The Break-up of China*, assuming that portents of the end of empire foretold the end of China itself.[38] Neither was entirely wrong. Within half a century of Yu Yue's prediction, the Celestial Empire had disappeared and the emperor could no longer claim with any credibility to be the Son of Heaven. But China survived, because the revolutionary nationalists who strove to bring down the Empire contested the claim of Confucian scholars that the history, the scholarship and the future of the nation all rested in their hands. It rested, instead, with revolutionary nationalists.

'If our nation's antiquity and our people's historical record come to an end in my hands,' wrote the radical racist Zhang Binglin in 1903, 'this will be my crime to bear.'[39] Sun Yatsen spoke for his Nationalist Party in warning that 'if China perishes the guilt will be on our own heads and we shall be the world's great sinners.'[40] Both worked to bring down the Empire, but neither had any intention of killing off China. Yet revolutionary nationalists differed from their enemies (and among themselves) on what they understood by the term 'China': they differed in their understanding of its historical pedigree, in their assessment of its essential character, in their differing perspectives on the forces threatening the state, and in their widely varying rememedies for its salvation. But in every case, the remedy involved identifying their own partisan movements with China as a nation and as a state. Needless to say, the details of China's long history have never seemed quite as important to nationalists as they have to more pedantic historians. Mao Zedong claimed four thousand years of history for China, Chiang Kaishek five thousand and Sun Yatsen, when pressed, was inclined to push the point to six thousand years. But this was a minor point of difference: what seems to have mattered most was the contrast between a vague dream of China's longevity and a vivid nightmare of its imminent demise. On this point, at least, the truly significant differences among China's nationalists are to be identified not by their varying estimates of the age of their nation but in their estimates of what exactly was under threat and how close it had come to death, in their competing identifications of the forces arrayed against it and in their implicit association of their own particular fortunes with the fate of the nation as a whole – all under the rubric of the 'death of the state'.

What distinguished Sun Yatsen and republican revolutionaries from imperial reformers – all of whom feared 'death of the state' – was the tendency on the part of revolutionaries to qualify the principle of state unity with the axiom of racial sovereignty. In the view of Sun Yatsen, the Qing state was not authentic China at all, as Yu Yue had imagined, but an historical aberration. China had been dead for the past two and a half centuries, not because it was in any sense disunited but because it had fallen into the hands of the alien Manchus. So at the founding ceremony of the Republic on 15 February, 1912, Sun Yatsen proceeded under military escort with members of his cabinet and other high officials to the sepulchre of the Founding Emperor of the Ming, in the hills skirting Nanjing, to announce that after a lapse of almost three centuries China had finally been restored unto itself. With the birth of the Republic, China was thought to have been resurrected from the grave.[41]

Still China was not safe. In later years, Sun Yatsen identified 'the law of natural selection' as the chief historical force threatening the nation. On this point China had done creditably well:

From ancient times, the increase and decrease of population has played a large part in the rise and fall of nations. This is the law of natural selection. Since mankind has not been able to resist the forces of natural selection, many ancient and famous nations have disappeared without trace. Our Chinese nation is one also of great antiquity, with four thousand years of authentic history, and so at least five or six thousand years of actual existence . . . we have enjoyed the blessings of Nature in greater measure than any other nation, so that through four millenniums of natural experiences, human movements, and varied changes we see our civilization only advancing and our nation free from decay.[42]

But Sun's optimism had its limits. The 'blessing of nature' offered a flimsy guarantee in an age when humankind had learned to master the forces of nature. So, no sooner had Sun conceded that China had been mercifully spared by the forces of natural selection, than he attacked the 'optimists' who fondly imagined that China was destined to survive the new forces now arrayed against it. 'Because the Chinese nation has survived innumerable disasters in the past, [optimists] hold that the nation cannot perish in the future, come what may.'[43] He dismissed such wishful thinking as 'misguided'. Speaking in 1924, near the end of his own life, he announced that the nation had little more than a decade of life left in it: 'China, if she were affected only by natural selection, might hold together another century; but if she is to be crushed by political and economic power, she will hardly last ten years more.'[44]

In *China's Destiny* (1947), Chiang Kaishek elaborated upon Sun Yatsen's model of the nation as an historically united and continuous race of people and, like Sun, compared its longevity more than favourably with those of all other nations. 'Five thousand years have passed since the founding of our Chunghua (Chinese) nation upon the mainland of Asia,' he announced. 'But while other nations equally ancient have become mere historical vestiges, China's life still goes splendidly on.'[45] Chiang also felt that China's history might soon come to an end, but he parted company with Sun in identifying the chief force threatening the nation. China was no longer 'crushed' by foreign political and economic power but subverted by Chiang's enemies in the communist movement. The communists, Chiang counselled, 'can never have any sense of loyalty to their own country: they are devoid of patriotism or national consciousness.'[46] In view of the communists' propensity to attack 'their own people', any concession to the communists yielded the fundamental integrity of the nation. In Chiang's reckoning, a communist China was not an alternative to national disintegration, but was nothing less than the extinction of China itself.

Mao Zedong, writing in 1939, was happy to concede a comparable lifespan for the nation, but in referring to the threat facing China he identified different historical forces again. Race was a minor category in his calculus. All the same, the longevity of China's history impressed him no less than Sun or Chiang Kaishek. 'China has one of the oldest civilizations in the world; she has a recorded history of nearly 4,000 years,' Mao noted. '[T]he Chinese nation has a glorious revolutionary tradition and a spendid historical heritage.' The historical heritage to which he referred was not, however, a tradition of racial struggle for survival but a tradition of class struggle for supremacy.[47] So although Mao shared the general fear of 'death of the state', he did so on grounds quite distinct from those of his erstwhile Nationalist colleagues. For a start, the inherited social formation meant that China would fall short of its manifest destiny as a highly developed economy and society:

> Although China is a great nation and although she is a vast country with an immense population, a long history, a rich revolutionary tradition and a splendid historical heritage, her economic, political and cultural development was sluggish for a long time after the transition from slave to feudal society.[48]

If this trend were to continue, Mao went on, China would face extinction: the nation was under threat from the combined forces of feudalism and imperialism which were working together to compromise the sovereignty of the state and to limit its capacity for resistance. Foreign imperialists, aided and abetted by domestic feudal forces, were seizing control of China's ports, customs and communications; they were monopolising finance and capital, exploiting labour, impoverishing the people and poisoning the minds of the young. Only the party of the proletariat, with the assistance of the organised peasant masses, could restore the country to its rightful place in history.[49]

The rhetoric of state survival served each regime well in its efforts to identify its own fate with that of the nation in the period of revolutionary struggle. And after the seizure of state power, the imminent collapse of each regime has been assumed by its supporters to entail the end of China as a civilisation and as a unitary state. Once the Nationalist Party had grafted itself onto the state, in 1928, it continued to face serious challenge from within and from without, and as their fortunes waxed and waned the heirs of Sun Yatsen insisted that China was drawing perilously close to extinction. In 1943, President Chiang Kaishek echoed Yu Yue's fears in linking the name of China with the Nationalist state:

> Without the Kuomintang there would be no China. In a word, China's destiny is entrusted to the Kuomintang. If the Kuomintang Revolution should fail, China as a nation would have nothing to

rely upon . . . The name of the Chinese Republic would disappear altogether from the map of the world.[50]

In 1949 the name of the Chinese Republic disappeared from all but a very small corner of the globe and yet the name of China was not deleted from the map. In place of the Republic of China stood the People's Republic, a New China proclaimed to be more vital than ever. 'China,' Mao Zedong announced to his Political Consultative Conference in 1949, 'has stood up!'[51] A popular song captured the mood of the moment: 'Without the Communist Party there would be no New China'. On Taiwan, Chiang Kaishek remained sceptical that China only came into its own with the collapse of the Nationalist state, and to his death maintained that China survived only on the small Republican enclave off the coast. Like the old China under the Manchus, China under the communists lay asleep on the mainland awaiting its own 'Glorious Recovery'.

The single-party regimes on the mainland and Taiwan have both come under challenge in recent times, and communist and Nationalist functionaries have begun to repeat the refrain that China's survival hinges on their own. China, it is said, must fall with the Communist Party because only under communist leadership can the nation stand on its own two feet. The heavy burden of history now appears to rest on the shoulders of the Communist Party, which is responsible not only for keeping the flame of scientific socialism alive following the collapse of the Soviet Union (many would count this a lesser burden) but also, more pointedly, for ensuring the unbroken continuity of China's history as unitary state.[52] Similar fears have been raised on Taiwan, where the Nationalist Party is struggling to retain its position as the dominant party in an emerging multi-party system. In October 1993, the Minister of the Interior warned that a forthcoming electoral contest was not only a challenge to Nationalist Party rule but 'also a fight to protect the name of the Republic of China'.[53] Without the Nationalists, as Chiang Kaishek indicated in 1943, there would be no China, even no Taiwan.

Every age has its doomsayers, and, were it not for the consistency with which these dire predictions have been repeated, we might dismiss each of them as a misplaced or mistaken fear on the part of partisan political factions with a clear stake in identifying their own fates with the fate of their country. Given the partisan identification of the Republic of China and People's Republic, as single-party states, this is perhaps not surprising. Yet China, we can confidently say, survived the collapse of empire and the dissolution of the Republic, and certainly survived the retreat of the Nationalists to Taiwan. Whether it flourished is another matter. The significance of such persistent remarks about the nature of the threat to China lies elsewhere – in what they reveal about the idea of China itself. The idea of China is implicitly identified with the ideal of the unitary state, and the unitary state itself is conflated with each successive state formation and ultimately with the particular parties which govern in its name.

And yet the term 'state', in the phrase 'death of the state', is not to be identified with a particular regime except to make a partisan political statement. In fact, as Liang Qichao discovered, it could take any form at all consistent with the attainment of state unity. Liang Qichao was perhaps the first among China's nationalists to highlight the possibility that the state might disappear under the onslaught of foreign imperialism; he was certainly the first to give this idea prominence in his political philosophy.[54] Other reformers were concerned about corruption and waste at court; other nationalists were eager to usurp the power of the alien Manchu dynasty. But Liang focused his attention on preserving the unitary state *as such*. Employing the principle of 'Reason of State', he came to attribute a higher value to the survival of the unitary state than either the safety of the sovereign or the preservation of time-honoured customs, indeed even higher than the well-being of the people. Any kind of state would do for his purpose, 'irrespective of its moral and ideological consequences' (in Hao Chang's words), so long as it served to forestall the imminent death of the state.[55] Once Liang had accepted the ideal of the unitary state as the supreme political value, he began to evaluate different kinds of state formation in a systematic attempt to find the one best suited to preserving his ideal of the continuous unitary state. Although he ultimately came out on the side of constitutional monarchy, Liang was not deeply committed to any particular form of the state at all – to imperial absolutism, constitutional monarchism, republicanism or state socialism – except in so far as it offered a reasonable prospect of forestalling the 'death of the state'.

After the overthrow of the Manchu dynasty, Sun Yatsen came around to a position closer to that of Liang Qichao and began to target foreign imperialism as the gravest danger facing China. In his valedictory lectures on the Three Principles of the People in 1924, we noted, Sun continued to equate the death of the state with the disappearance of the 'race' but attributed the imminent death of the pair of them to the prospect of unimpeded imperialist intervention in China.[56] The survival of the nation then appeared to depend on the capacity of the state to adapt to the new and hostile environment of international imperialism. To this end, Sun turned for help to Lenin, and to China's Leninists.

Yet the Leninists had an altogether different notion of what the death of the state might entail, because they held a distinctive view of the nation itself. In Li Dazhao's estimation, the prospect of losing the state did not appear to threaten racial genocide but involved instead a grave risk of loss of territory, cohesion and national identity.[57] Nevertheless, the prospect of the death of the state filled him with a comparable sense of dread. Li cited in illustration of 'death of the state' the case of the Jews – 'a lost people who dream about recovering their country' – as fair warning of the fate in store for the Chinese people should they fail to preserve their state. Like Liang and Sun, Li Dazhao identified the continuity of the unitary state with the continued existence of 'China' and the welfare of the 'Chinese people'.

Li had only recently expressed his dread of 'death of the state' when his friend Chen Duxiu published an article on the subject in 1913. Chen's comments alarmed Li Dazhao. A particular state which failed to inspire patriotism was, in his estimation, not a state at all. Chen turned for illustration to the states of Europe and America where the state was 'an organisation whose members cooperate in the search for the security and happiness of the citizens' and for which all citizens felt corresponding love and respect. Such a state had never been known in China, so there were few patriots; or, rather, since there were so few patriots in China there was no *state* to speak of:

> Once the meaning of the state has been cleared up, one is able to say that we Chinese are not patriots. One can even say that there have never been as yet any patriots among us; one can even go so far as to say that we Chinese have never as yet set up a state.[58]

A particular state which failed to inspire patriotism failed to qualify for recognition as a state, in Chen's view, because a true state was one which inspired a national people to love their state and respond to its demands without demur. From these reflections, Chen Duxiu derived the radical conclusion that the collapse of the Republican state, as it was presently constituted, would be a matter of little concern to those who professed concern for 'death of the state'. In fact it was not a 'state' at all, and it was not worth worrying about it: when a state does not 'defend the rights of the people' nor 'increase the happiness of the people . . . it is neither glorious to maintain one's state nor regrettable to lose it.'[59] After settling their differences and arriving at a mutual agreement to create a more ideal state, Chen Duxiu and Li Dazhao cooperated in founding the Communist Party of China. Their perfect state was to be a highly-centralised, single-party authoritarian state, built on the model of the vanguard party of Lenin. This would be a state indeed.

Powerful centralised state

This brings us to the second point of conflation between the universal ideal of the unitary state and more particular ideas of the state. In all strains of nationalist thought this century, the unitary state has been identified implicitly with a strong state and, in more dominant strains, with a highly centralised state. There is of course no necessary correlation between unity, centralisation and strength. The immense power and exemplary authority of the United States of America (in its admittedly short history) has been enhanced by federalism and the retention of significant powers by its constituent states. This was not lost on China's nationalists. On a visit to the USA in 1903, Liang Qichao was impressed by the vitality of the federal polity in the country, the strength of American industry and the wealth of its more prominent financiers. But he was not convinced that the federalism he witnessed in the United States – nor for that matter its liberalism – should be adopted for use in China. In the first place, he argued, the political system in the United States was grounded in tenacious traditions of local self-government which were without parallel in China. Equally significantly, Liang was inclined to the belief that all states, including the USA, were tending towards higher degrees of centralisation which would eventually spell the end of liberalism and federalism universally.[60] In any case, Liang's thinking on centralisation and federation was directed toward establishing a *strong* state and all of his calculations on the most appropriate form of the state were directed to this end. This concern he shared with many nationalists whom he counted his rivals.[61]

The call for a strong state resounded widely among reformers and revolutionaries, including those who promoted a centralist model of the state as well as provincial elites favouring a high degree of regional autonomy.[62] The appeal of the strong state may be traced to the precarious situation in which the imperial state found itself, in the mid-nineteenth century, in meeting increasing burdens of domestic expenditure and paying weighty foreign indemnities. These burdens encouraged state functionaries to make new demands on behalf of the state itself. But the attraction of the strong state is to be found equally in the mixed responses to these new state demands in elite society, and to elite demands for the state to assist in restoring order and in 'modernising' society.[63] The 'New Policies' of administrative and fiscal reform introduced over the last decade of Qing rule, along with associated initiatives in education, industry and communications, offered clear signals of this new determination on the part of the state to extend its reach and its capacity well in advance of the more interventionist states which emerged some decades later, under Nationalist and Communist party rule.

By the 1920s and 1930s, expectations of the state ran higher still. Among the educated youth of China, it was widely expected that the state should rescue the nation from imperialists and warlords, liberate slave-girls, outlaw concubinage, legislate better conditions for labour, educate citizens in public ethics and improve public hygiene in the streets. A state concerned to eliminate spitting, or to improve the lot of the Chinese people, could well legislate for such changes; but only a very powerful and intrusive one could hope to enforce them. Few nationalists thought to ask, as one foreign missionary recalled, 'whether a government would be sufficiently capable, honest, and enlightened to be entrusted with any large measure of state control.'[64] But the missionaries had only themselves to blame. China's young nationalists bore witness to an immense range of missionary initiatives in fields they wished to reserve for themselves: in promoting public health and hygiene, in championing language reform and popular education, and in emancipating women and caring for the socially disadvantaged. Missionary demands for better urban planning, more reliable fresh water supplies, improved sanitation and waste disposal systems, for more public schools and modern hospitals also anticipated, in the aggregate, a new and expanded role for the state which came to be spelled out in Nationalist and Communist ideology. The state summoned up by these expectations was nationalist, and hence jealous of its own autonomy, and was so thoroughly rationalist that it could hardly countenance 'superstition' of the kind which Christian missionaries professed.[65] There was an alternative anarchist discourse, Arif Dirlik reminds us, at every point along this route to statism.[66] Yet what seems to have distinguished the anarchists from statist radicals was a simple conviction that no government *would* be sufficiently capable, honest and enlightened to be entrusted with the immense burden of transforming society in the direction in which they all sought to push it.

Advocacy of a strong central state was not initially counted inconsistent with the assertion of individual freedoms, for there was little sense of contradiction between the demands of personal liberation and the wider requirements of state-building. The larger ethical question of the relationship between the individual and the community, in planning for the 'good society', was rarely raised in isolation from the political problem of mobilising society in support of the state. In the New Culture Movement, for example, radical intellectuals called upon their compatriots to free themselves from the patriarchal bonds of 'feudal' society in the belief that personal liberation was the first step on the long path to 'saving the state'. At the same time, they thought it an obligation upon the modern state to liberate the individual from all forms of social and political oppression in pursuit of its own legitimate ends.[67] After the movement split into mass-democratic and liberal democratic wings, in the early 1920s, the liberals remained true to their convictions in asserting the social context of their individualism. 'Once you have independent men and women,' wrote Hu Shi, 'you will naturally create a good society.'[68] In time, however, the mass democrats moved on to assert the primacy of collective solidarity in creating the good society and, not incidentally, to favour a centralist model of the state over a federal one.

Advocates of a strong central state came to blows with liberals in an ideological dispute on the merits of federalism in 1922, and they gained an unassailable political advantage in the Nationalist Revolution of the late 1920s. By June 1922, the federalist movement had gained considerable support from leading liberal intellectuals, including Hu Shi, and received additional momentum from provincial military and political leaders in Hunan, Yunnan and Guangdong provinces. But once support for federalism began to assume the dimensions of a national movement, leading members of the Communist Party mounted the public platform to debate the merits of federal and centralist models of state organisation. First, they argued that federalism was nothing more than a code for warlord separatism.[69] The treachery of warlords had become an article of faith in Communist and Nationalist circles in the aftermath of Governor Chen Jiongming's 'betrayal' of Sun Yatsen in June 1922, so the simplest way to slander the federalist movement was to show that warlords like Chen Jiongming were keen on it.[70] More significant, at least for the subsequent development of nationalist rhetoric, was deployment of the term 'feudalism' to characterise both warlords and the federalist movement.[71] If feudalism was the basic problem confronting the modern nation, it followed that federalism under warlord sponsorship was just one more enemy to be overcome along with all other vestiges of 'the old forces of feudalism' in the Nationalist Revolution. Needless to say, warlords such as Chen Jiongming owned few estates, kept no serfs in bondage and generally presented themselves as the most forward-thinking provincial rulers in China's long history. In their own estimation, they represented progressive federal forces, not ancient feudal ones. But for the communists, the relative merits of a federalist or centralist system of rule were evaluated entirely within the framework of lingering 'feudal forces'.

Another line of argument against federalism focused on the character of the Chinese nation. Twentieth-century nationalists resorted to essentialist characterisations of the nation in their efforts to deny that there were significant categories of difference dividing the country – except perhaps for differences of social class – which might be appropriately represented under a federal system of government. Concern among Nationalists and Communists to eliminate the remnants of China's 'feudal' past then extended well beyond the limited political struggle against warlords. While warlords like Chen Jiongming were targeted for dividing the country, so, too, were all other emblems of cultural, social and economic particularism. Communist Party General Secretary Chen Duxiu was not content to dismiss federalism as merely a warlord plot, and mounted a range of secondary arguments to explain why there would be little scope for introducing federalism in China even if there were no warlords at all. These arguments derived from an assertion of the fundamental unity of the 'Chinese people'.[72] His ideal of unity was highly contrived, but no more so than that of the federalists he condemned. In fact proponents of a federal system rarely based their case for provincial self-government on the particularist grounds which centralising nationalists set out to condemn. Even distinctive local languages and customs did not feature prominently in the arguments of federalists, who mounted their case not as an alternative to the ideal of a unified Chinese nation but as an alternative reading of national unity. Provincial autonomy with a federal system was conceived not as an end in itself but as a prelude to 'the independence of all China'.[73]

Uniform national people

Mention of the unity of the 'Chinese people' in the debate on federalism brings us to the third point of conflation: assimilating the ideal of the unitary state with the idea of a uniform national people. The federalist debate aside, the first and most noticeable effect of identifying China with a unitary state, and then with particular state formations, has been to diminish the significance of China *as a nation* in elite nationalist thought. Fang Lizhi recalls:

> I remember in my younger days joining in on the criticism of our poor old teachers, who would always defend themselves by saying 'At least I'm patriotic; at least I love my country.' Our standard reply was 'But what country do you love? A communist country? or a Kuomintang country?' Of course what we were implying was that they weren't really patriotic at all. In this context, patriotism obviously does not mean loving your native place, your rivers, your soil, your cities; it means loving the state.[74]

Even in Fang Lizhi's recollection, the state is conflated with particular state formations in the form of the Communist and Nationalist party-states, and the intermediate stage in the transition from love of the state to love of a particular regime is elided in the juxtaposition of regime against the nativist symbols of family and place. In fact the native places, the rivers, the soil and the cities of China had yielded to an ideal of the unitary central state in the rhetoric of nationalism long before the Communists came to power. Only after nationalism had begun to focus on the survival of the state, and patriotism had been conceived as love of the state, was it possible to choose between loving a 'communist country' or a 'Kuomintang' one, or to relegate native place, rivers, earth and cities to the background of nationalist concerns. Primordial sentiments focusing on family and locality were consistently subordinated to a rational, statist iconography of national belongingness by Communists and Nationalists alike. The political struggle to remake China as a unitary state, and to capture the state for a particular state formation, relegated memories of affective community to the realm of the irrational and the pre-modern, and reduced the people of China to a functional desideratum of national state-building. The 'Chinese people' came to be imagined as neither more nor less than the mass referent of the state which purported to represent them.

All models of the unitary state put forward in China this century have embraced the principle of representative national government, in one form or another. This may seem so obvious as to require little elaboration. There is barely a republican state in the world which has not claimed to 'represent the nation' and all nationalists in China, centralist or not, have professed to speak on behalf of the national people. The idea of state representation is, nevertheless, quite a radical proposition in its own right, with far-reaching ramifications for the transformation of an old imperial state such as China into a modern 'national' one.

In the first place, the idea of representation implies the existence of a Chinese nation which is in need of representing, and not just the existence of a unitary state which happens to be in need of preservation. Few emperors had ever lost a night's sleep wondering whether they had adequately 'represented' the people over the days gone by, but China's nationalists seem to have fretted fitfully. The idea of representation also meant that disputes among China's nationalists over the form, or constitution, of the state had its corollary in debate over the form of the nation each state was held to 'represent'. Among centralising nationalists, a parallel problem to the want of a central state (which they would supply) was the want of a suitable body of people to represent (which they would 'awaken'). Liang Qichao promoted the ideal of a 'new citizen'; Sun Yatsen and Chiang Kaishek held dear to the notion of a mono-racial community; and Mao Zedong asserted the existence of revolutionary masses. But all knew full well that there were no such creatures in existence before they themselves set about awakening them. In addition to manufacturing a unitary state, each state movement was faced with the awesome task of bringing their idealized communities into existence by awakening the people as a rational national community. Only then could they be adequately represented.

Elsewhere, the development of representative government has been closely associated with the the development of civil society and the 'public sphere'.[75] In China, too, early experiments in local and provincial representative government were grafted on to the foundations of public associations and public opinion at the local level in the villages, county towns and provincial centres of the late Empire. Whether the local institutions of the period properly qualify for the historical category of 'civil society' remains a moot point, but they certainly generated a lively public sphere at the local level.[76] Local identity took shape in an expanding urban culture situated at the junction between the private world of the household and the lineage, and the official world of the imperial state. And it was here, in the public sphere at local and provincial levels, that the imperial state itself undertook the earliest experiments in representative government.

The institution of public opinion had a longer history still in the administration of the Empire. In a recent article, William Rowe has suggested that the origins of public opinion are to be found in the administrative practice of local officials who customarily consulted with local notables before implementing imperial policy.[77] This argument is confirmed by the observations of a contemporay observer,

Naitô Konan, on the development of provincial assemblies in the late Qing. 'Contrary to what one might expect,' he observed, 'China is first and foremost a nation of public opinion.'[78] Naitô traced the strength of the institutions of public opinion to the common practice of imperial regents in making and confirming the appointment of local officials:

> 'Public opinion' is an expression of Chinese origin, and in China emphasis is placed upon one's reputation among the masses. When the emperor would question the quality of the local officialdom, he would first listen to whether their reputation was regarded as good or bad. He did not care much whether or not an official had accomplished anything. There was nothing a local Chinese official was likely to be able to accomplish in three or four years at a post, and in any case the emphasis was placed on one's reputation. If someone were said to be 'shengming hao', it meant that he was a good official.[79]

On the basis of hardy indigenous precedent for the institution of public opinion, Naitô concluded that China was ripe for representative constitutional government.[80]

A state claiming to represent the many and varied communities of China could not, however, take the form of a highly *centralised* polity without first co-opting local public opinion, or alternatively reconstituting local communities *ab initio*. The late imperial and early republican states both attempted to co-opt local public opinion through an articulated system of representative assemblies reaching from county level, to the province and ultimately to the national state. Revolutionary nationalists preferred the second option of reconstituting local communities so that local public opinion no longer featured prominently in the public life of the nation. The turning point came with the New Culture and May Fourth Movements of the late 1910s and early 1920s, when youthful activists were persuaded to 'go among the people' and transform the patriarchal 'feudal' culture of Old China. Among the feudal targets of the movement was the venerable institution of elite 'public opinion'.

From the time of the May Fourth Movement, when a national forum of public opinion was just beginning to take form, advocates of the New Culture turned upon public opinion with a vengeance. May Fourth magazines held the 'common people' and the 'masses' in inordinately high esteem, but they generally counted public opinion an enemy of New Culture, a domain of prejudice and superstition and a cover for sectional interests seeking to gain hegemony over the direction of public life.[81] Their contemptuous attitude strikes an interesting contrast to the more cautious judgement of parliamentary factions and the broadsheet newspapers of the period, which rarely exalted the masses and yet took public opinion very seriously indeed. In this respect, the centralising nationalists of the Nationalist and Communist parties correctly trace their paternity to the mass activists of the May Fourth Movement, for they, too, counted public opinion an obstacle to the development of mass representative politics.

At the local level, independent community associations presented obstacles to the inroads of the centralising state, and at the national level – or at least in the major metropolitan centres – independent public associations and newspapers raised voices out of chorus with the disciplined mass propaganda of the party-state.[82] Under the Nationalists they were 'partified'; under the Communists they were eliminated ruthlessly. In the event, advocates of a highly centralised state were obliged to manufacture a national people in place of particularist local ones, and to eliminate alternative liberal models of national community so that they might 'represent' a more uniformly disciplined national people, roughly corresponding to the central state which represented them. For local and national public opinion they substituted pedagogical mass instruction, and for public associations they substituted the state itself.

CONCLUSION

To Louis XIV's 'I am the state', Mao Zedong proclaimed 'I am the People'. But a people is not identical to a state, let alone a particular regime, nor can a state substitute for a nation without collapsing under the weight of its own presumption. For a start, it is not the state alone which has kept China together throughout its long (and burdensome) history. Although the modern phenomenon of the 'people' may be an invention of the state, the differences which separate communities in China have long been mediated by a common agreement that they happen to belong together. People who live in China have a long history of their own, preserved not in court records but in immense repositories of cultural memory captured in story and song, festival and ritual, street news and, today, on television and film. The search for an alternative community-consciousness in this storehouse of collective memory need not be a celebration of alterity, as memories preserved in the dark and circulated in private have a way of growing into surreal shapes which arouse bizarre

expections and feed fratricidal dreams of revenge.[83] Awareness of
this suppressed side of history generates fear of freedom no less than
fear of repression. Yet neither does it mean abandoning history,
altogether, as a 'tyrant'.

Jenner's argument in *The Tyranny of History* highlights the art and
artifice which have gone into fabricating the ideology of the unitary
state. In this respect, *The Tyranny of History* might well be compared
with Harrison Salisbury's *The Coming War between Russia and
China*, published in 1969. The fact that conflict between China and
the Soviet Union in the 1960s did not erupt into war in no way
diminishes the heightened tensions to which Salisbury wished to
draw attention. Similarly, Jenner's argument is not to be evaluted,
one way or the other, by whether or not China disintegrates under the
weight of its past history or its present statist ideology. Neither book
is to be tested by the reliability of its predictions but by the way it
draws attention to trends which might otherwise escape attention. The
general crisis of the state, and the fragility of its legitimating symbols,
invites us to reflect on the function of unity, centrality and history in
relation to the legitimacy of the regime, and more generally the
unitary state, in China today.

Widespread support for the ideal of the unitary state may well
continue to prop up the present regime, and not simply in consequence of popular ignorance or of state propaganda. People in China
are no longer prisoners of their past in the sense that they were two or
three decades ago, cut off from international news and isolated from
global trends. Yet with each soundbite of wealth and freedom that
travels over the international airwaves comes a corresponding image
of the disintegration of the the former Soviet Union or of the former
Yugoslavia's slide into genocide. A regime can lose its legitimacy
and still maintain the momentum of its authority when it appears
better than some alternatives on offer.[84] The performance of any
regime is still likely to be measured by the time-honoured criterion
of how well it forestalls the disintegration of the unitary state, for the
history of the unitary state is grounded, not in simple strategies of
deception, but in a widespread and perfectly reasonable belief that the
disintegration of the unitary state is more likely to invite chaos into
the life of the nation than to usher in a redemptive communitarian
lifestyle. It is perhaps for this reason that twentieth-century political
leaders have learned that there are as many advantages to holding out
the prospect of China's disintegration – or the 'death of the state' – as
there are in celebrating its 'long history'.

The history of the 'death of the state' nevertheless warns us against confusing the crisis of a regime with a crisis of the unitary state itself. As a general rule, political actors who announce the end of history tend to have a rather grandiose view of their own place in history and to cherish an exaggerated impression of the role of the state. A more prosaic view of the state – as a mundane and necessarily imperfect institution, set up to do a limited job of work, and distinct from any particular regime – is less likely to lead to the conclusion that the death of a particular regime means the end of history. Indeed, peeling away the encrustations which have built up around the ideal of the unitary state reveals a far more modest ideal of unity than many of the states which have tried to put it into effect would have us believe: a unitary state is no more than a single state system, acknowledging one legitimate centre, and recognised internationally as the legitimate government of the territories which it claims for itself. We can, I believe, dismiss the claim that China is about to fall apart (or alternately *ought to* fall apart) simply because the present state has failed to realise far more grandiose ambitions than these. We can, in sum, begin to contemplate alternative models of community and state which are less rigidly constituted or highly-centralised than those which have been in place since 1928.

Paradoxically, the regime itself may well present the gravest danger to the unity of the state, to a far greater degree than other 'traditional' sources of fracture in the geography, culture, language, local society and regional economies of China. The People's Republic is not just a centralist state but a single-party state, and the effectiveness of the central government is heavily dependent on the vitality and discipline of the Communist Party. Franz Schurmann asked, many years ago, whether the system of state organisation set up by communist parties could function without the guiding hand of the party, and answered that it could not. The party was 'the keystone of the whole structure.'[85] As the party withers away, so must the legitimacy of the state. True, party functionaries are not easily distinguished from the bureaucratic and entrepreneurial functions which they are called upon to perform, but these functions cannot be performed without a legitimating party authority, and as party centre loses its capacity to discipline its members the state loses its capacity to function *as* a state. Admittedly the central policing apparatus is highly repressive, but it can no longer co-opt other state and social institutions to do its bidding with the confidence that they will respond with any enthusiasm. And the collapse of key institutions in the network of social organisation which linked state and society together – including the commune, the brigade and to some extent the urban *danwei* – has exposed the limited reach of central state institutions at the local level in the post-reform period. Along with the party, customary instruments of co-option and institutional levers of coercion have lost much of their credibility, and with it their effectiveness.

Conversely, the state may be strengthened by weakening its direct control over local communities and capitalising on the given strengths and specialities of regions as these have been bequeathed by history. At any rate the centre needs the regions. Without voluntary local assistance it cannot exercise budgetary discipline over provincial governments and agencies, it cannot retain control over credit to the many collective enterprises which are emerging in the coastal regions, it cannot contain the present demographic explosion, keep internal migration within manageable limits, check festering inland grievances or maintain even a semblance of social coherence in the straitened financial circumstances and ideological vacuum left by the collapse of the centrally-planned economy. Beijing has to do much more than issue central commands to cope with these problems; it needs to negotiate.[86]

The regions also need the centre. The local party-state nexus may be reluctant to admit central interference in its affairs, but the centre remains an important focus of unity because it provides the only assurance that competition for resources, markets and political advantage among localities, provinces and regions will not get out of hand. The most dynamic counties and the least responsive local governments may yet prove to be Beijing's salvation. Seen from Nanhai and Shunde, Wuxi and Wenzhou, Beijing is beginning to resemble the symbolic political centres of old which set out in their ritual practices the principles for state organisation and behaviour throughout the realm without closely policing their compliance.

Admittedly, signs to date are not all that encouraging. Beijing persists in branding moves towards greater provincial and local autonomy as 'feudal', taking all too little account of the transformation which China and the world have undergone over the past six or seven decades. In the twentieth century, the word 'feudal' has had little meaning except as a term of abuse, and the distinctive features of the early Republic which brought the fury of Nationalist and Communist revolutionaries down upon the heads of warlords and 'feudal forces' no longer apply. Even the appearance of inter-provincial rivalries is easily overstated, as highly-publicised instances of armed patrols monitoring and controlling the flow of goods in and out of the provinces are more than offset by the increasing complexity and intensity of inter-provincial co-operation. With respect to central–provincial relations, it would appear that the champions of provincial and local autonomy are to be counted among those most concerned to maintain a stable (if weak) central regime in order to pursue their development programmes with minimum disruption.

Perhaps the gravest danger to both the unitary state and the regime is Beijing's insistence on asserting a degree of formal control which is no longer consistent with its real power and authority. Should the centre prove insufficiently elastic in its response to those who seek a higher measure of autonomy, then it courts the danger of compelling regional leaders to express their demands in the rhetoric of provincial separatism. But this is a measure of last resort – even in the warlord politics of the Republic, local autonomy was never counted inconsistent with national integration. The demands of China's local and regional leaders today are also consonant with the unity of the nation and the state. Whether they prove to be consistent in practice is something which Beijing, the localities and the regions must decide for themselves, together.

NOTES

I should like to thank Antonia Finnane, John Israel, G. William Skinner and the editors for their stimulating comments and suggestions.

1 Mao Zedong, 'Talk with Music Workers', 24 August 1956. In John K. Leung and Michael Y.M. Kau, *The Writings of Mao Zedong, 1949–1976, Volume II, January 1956–December 1957*, Armonk, New York: M.E. Sharp, 1992, pp. 94–108, esp. p. 100.
2 Study of the macroregional organisation of China's society and economy was pioneered by G. William Skinner. See G. William Skinner, ed, *The City in Late Imperial China*, Stanford: Stanford University Press, 1977. The social, cultural and political implications of China's macroregional organisation are explored in: Susan Naquin and Evelyn Rawski, *Chinese Society in the Eighteenth Century*, New Haven: Yale University Press, 1987; David Johnson, Andrew Nathan and Evelyn Rawski, eds, *Popular Culture in Late Imperial China*, Berkeley and Los Angeles: University of California Press, 1985; and R. Keith Schoppa, *Chinese Elites and Political Change: Zhejiang Province in the Early Twentieth Century*, Cambridge, Mass.: Harvard University Press, 1982.
3 Mao Wrote: 'China's six hundred million people have two remarkable peculiarities; they are, first of all, poor, and secondly, blank. That may seem like a bad thing, but it is really a good thing. Poor people want change, want to do things, want revolution. A clean sheet of paper has no blotches and so the newest and most beautiful words can be written on it, the newest and most beautiful pictures can be painted on it.' This was

written, appropriately, for the inaugural issue of the flagship propaganda journal, *Red Flag*, on 15 April 1958. Extracted and translated in Stuart R. Schram, *The Political Thought of Mao Tse-tung*. Revised and enlarged edition, Harmondsworth: Penguin Books, 1969, p. 352.

4 Simon Leys, *The Chairman's New Clothes: Mao and the Cultural Revolution*. Translated by Carol Appleyard and Patrick Good, London: Allison and Busby, 1977, pp. 15–21.

5 Agence France Press Report, 21 September 1993.

6 W. J. F. Jenner, *The Tyranny of History: The Roots of China's Crisis*, Harmondsworth: Allen Lane Penguin Books, 1992, p. 1.

7 Oliver Sacks, *The Man Who Mistook His Wife for a Hat*, London: Picador, 1986, pp. 28–34.

8 Charles O. Hucker, *China's Imperial Past: An Introduction to Chinese History and Culture*, Stanford: Stanford University Press, 1973, pp. 1–6.

9 Karl Bünger, 'Concluding remarks on two aspects of the Chinese unitary state as compared with the European state system', in S.R. Schram, ed, *Foundations and Limits of State Power in China*, London: School of Oriental and African Studies, 1987, pp. 313–23.

10 See Geoffrey Barraclough, *Turning Points in World History*, London: Thames and Hudson, 1977; and Karl Bünger, 'Concluding remarks', pp. 313–23.

11 Arguments for and against the role of geography in determining China's history are canvassed in Andrew L. March, *The Idea of China: Myth and Theory in Geographic Thought*, Melbourne: Wren Publishing, 1974.

12 Georg Wilhelm Friedrich Hegel, *The Philosophy of History*. Translated by J. Sibree, New York: Willey Book Co., 1944, p. 161. Hegel also insisted that China was nothing more than a state; *ibid*. Compare Schlegel's roughly contemporary comment: 'In China, before the introduction of the Indian religion of Buddha . . . the state is all in all'. See Frederick Von Schlegel, *The Philosophy of History*, Translated by J.B. Robertson, London: Henry G. Bohn, 1847, p. 124.

13 The many functions of court diarists and historians, and the bureaucratic apparatus for the compilation of official history in the Tang Dynasty, are detailed in Denis Twitchett, *The Writing of Official History Under the Tang*, Cambridge: Cambridge University Press, 1992. Twichett notes that the legitimating function of the histories was accentuated at periods of crisis in the line of succession, *ibid.*, pp. 120, 160.

14 John Fincher, 'China as a Race, Culture, and Nation: Notes on Fang Hsiao-ju's Discussion of Dynastic Legitimacy', in David C. Buxbaum and Frederick W. Mote, eds, *Transition and Permanence: Chinese History and Culture: A Festschrift in Honor of Dr. Hsiao Kung-Ch'üan*, Hong Kong: Cathay Press, 1972, p. 60.

15 The first important English-language study of this problem in orthodox Confucian historiography (and in the history of the fragmentation of empire) is Wang Gungwu's classic work, *The Structure of Power in North China During the Five Dynasties*, Kuala Lumpur: University of Malaya Press, 1963.

16 Chan Hok-lam, *Legitimation in Imperial China: Discussions under the Jurchen-Chin Dynasty (1115–1234)*, Seattle: University of Washington Press, 1984, pp. 38–9; Fincher, 'China as a Race', pp. 60–61.

17 Ouyang Xiu did not insist that unity of the realm should serve as an exclusive principle of legitimation. Rulers might base their claim to legitimacy on 'rectitude' (*zheng*) alone – just as they might on unification alone. Illegitimacy was indicated by the absence of both. Chan Hok-lam, *Legitimation in Imperial China*, p. 39.

18 Ouyang Xiu's work was entitled *Zhengtong lun* (On Right and Unity). In earlier use, the term was something of an oxymoron marking the tension between power based on right and power based on might. Ouyang Xiu's reformulation never quite escaped this ambivalence. The term *zhengtong* is to be found in popular literature of the late imperial period as well state-sponsored histories from much earlier times. Its place in debates on imperial statescraft is discussed in Chan Hok-lam, *Legitimation in Imperial China*, and Howard J. Weschler, *Offerings of Jade and Silk: Ritual and Symbol in the Legitimation of the Tang Dyasty*, New Haven: Yale University Press, 1985. In literature, the term *zhengtong* is often framed within a Daoist cosmology of waxing and waning. See, for example, the preface to a mid-seventeenth century edition of Luo Guangzhong's *Sanguo yanyi* (Romance of the Three Kingdoms), by Mao Zonggang: 'They say the momentum of history was ever thus; the empire, long divided, must unite; long united, must divide'. *Three Kingdoms: China's Epic Drama*, translated by Moss Roberts, New York: Pantheon Books, 1976, p. 1. I wish to thank Anne McLaren for bringing this to my attention.

19 Chan Hok-lam, *Legitimation in Imperial China*, p. 21.

20 Chan Hok-lam, *Legitimation in Imperial China*, p. 39; Fincher, 'China as a Race', pp. 60–61.

21 Chan Hok-lam, *Legitimation in Imperial China*, p. 133.

22 Even rumours of unorthodox movements – spread inadvertently through the agency of wandering beggars and transient monks – could incite a fierce imperial reaction. One such case is closely examined in Philip Kuhn, *Soulstealers: The Chinese Sorcery Scare of 1768*, Cambridge, Mass.: Harvard University Press, 1990. Kuhn concludes 'Chinese culture was unified but not homogeneous. That, I think, is why there could occur a society-wide experience such as the soul-stealing crisis, even while different social groups represented that experience in different ways'; *ibid.*, p. 223. Similarity in orthodox (and heterodox) ritual forms throughout the Empire in fact disguised a variety of local interpretations. In approved cults, differences were counted of little consequence so long as formal similarities were observed. See Prasenjit Duara, 'Superscribing symbols: The myth of Guandi, Chinese god of war', *Journal of Asian Studies*, 47:4, November 1988; pp. 778–95.

23 Note Joseph Levenson's brilliant evocation of this paradox: under the Empire, the pattern was local uniformity and regional diversity; under the nation, the pattern is one of local diversity and regional uniformity. Joseph Levenson, 'The Province, the Nation and the World: The Problem of Chinese Identity', in Levenson, ed., *Modern China: An Interpretive Anthology*, New York: Macmillan, 1971, p. 57.

24 See John De Francis, *Nationalism and Language Reform in China*, Princeton: Princeton University Press, 1950.

25 Historians of China often seem to share this disdain in their use of the

term 'localism' (*difangzhuyi*) to describe behaviour resistant to national integration on terms unfavourable to the locality. A useful comparson may be drawn with German history and historiography. See Irmline Veit-Brause, 'Particularism: A paradox of cultural nationalism?', in J.C. Eade, ed, *Romantic Nationalism in Europe*, Canberra: Humanities Research Centre ANU, 1983, pp. 33–46.

26 Sun Yatsen frequently employed the metaphor of the sleeping nation: 'Since our subjugation by the Manchus our four hundred millions have been asleep, our ancient morality has been asleep, our ancient learning has been asleep.' Sun Yatsen, *San Min Chu I, The Three Principles of the People*, trans. by Frank W. Price, ed. by L.T. Chen, Chungking: Ministry of Information, 1943, p. 133.

27 The political, social and cultural divisions of post-imperial China were far from reassuring to nationalists, who often remarked that there was neither national unity nor 'real nationalism' among their fellow 'nationals' and that this want of nationalism largely accounted for the political division of the state. But such observations were never intended to suggest that the nation was a fiction. To the contrary, they implied that the truth of the nation had yet to be revealed to the people of China. See Sun Yatsen, *San Min Chu I.*

28 George L. Mosse, 'Mass Politics and the Political Liturgy of Nationalism', in Eugene Kamenka, ed, *Nationalism: The Nature and Evolution of an Idea*, Canberra: Australian National University Press, 1973, pp. 39–54, esp. p. 40.

29 Benedict Anderson, *Imagined Communities: Reflections on the Origin and Spread of Nationalism*, London: Verso, 1983, p. 28.

30 Laurence A. Schneider, *Ku Chieh-kang and China's New History: Nationalism and the Quest for Alternative Traditions*, Berkeley, Los Angeles and London: University of California Press, 1971, p. 3.

31 Schneider, *Ku Chieh-kang*, pp. 60–61.

32 Schneider, *Ku Chieh-kang*, pp. 12–15, and *passim*.

33 See, for example, Charles Hucker 'China's history was, among other things, a long struggle to gain and recurringly to regain political unity.' Charles O. Hucker, *China's Imperial Past*, p. 16.

34 See Joseph Levenson, 'The Province, the Nation and the World', p. 57.

35 This mode of apprehending China in history even locates 'China' at a point logically prior to its own development as a unitary state. See Antonia Finnane, 'Internal Colonialism and the Chinese City: The Case of Yangzhou', paper presented to the Annual Conference of the Association for Asian Studies, Washington, 1989, p. 3.

36 All histories of China, including English-language historiography, owe a considerable debt to the textual tradition generated by the unitary state. When one outside scholar, Ira Lapidus (an historian of Islam and the Middle East) was invited to cast a comparative eye over Western scholarship of the Chinese Empire he found that it mirrored the Chinese textual tradition to a high degree in its coherence, its hierarchies, its points of symmetry, even indeed in its contradictions. Ira Lapidus, 'Hierarchies and Networks: A Comparison of Chinese and Islamic Societies', in Frederick Wakeman Jr. and Carolyn Grant, eds, *Conflict and Control in Late Imperial China*, Berkeley and Los Angeles: University of

54   John Fitzgerald

California Press, 1975, pp. 26–42. There are signs of new directions in cultural and social history to which this judgement would clearly not apply. In social history, recent attempts to apply the concepts of public sphere and civil society to state–society relations (and to displace the earlier paradigm of 'conflict and control') mark a significant departure from Chinese and Western scholarship on China's late imperial history. Much of this literature is covered in 'Symposium: "public sphere"/ "civil society" in China?', *Modern China*, 19:2 April 1993. For an overview of other recent work in socio-economic and cultural studies, see Evelyn S. Rawski, 'Research themes in Ming–Qing socioeconomic history – the state of the field', *Journal of Asian Studies*, 50:1 (February 1991), pp. 84–111. For all its theoretical sophistication, the emphasis of recent scholarship tends in much the same direction as earlier work on the political integration of the Empire, in attempting to measure the degree of social and cultural integration in the late imperial period as a general measure of progress. See Susan Naquin and Evelyn Rawski, *Chinese Society in the Eighteenth Century*, and David Johnson, Andrew Nathan and Evelyn Rawski, eds, *Popular Culture in Late Imperial China*.

37 Translated in Dun J Li, ed, *China in Transition 1517–1911*, New York: Van Nostrand Reinhold Co., 1989, pp. 163–5.
38 Lord Charles Beresford, *The Break-Up of China, with an Account of its Present Commerce, Currency, Waterways, Armies, Railways, Politics and Future Prospects*, London and New York: Harper & Brothers, 1899.
39 Cited in Shimada Kenji, *Pioneer of the Chinese Revolution: Zhang Binglin and Confucianism*, trans. by Jousha A. Fogel, Stanford: Stanford University Press, 1990, p. 19.
40 Sun Yatsen, *San Min Chu I*, p. 75.
41 Sun added: 'I have heard say that triumphs of tartar savages over our China were destined never to last longer than a hundred years. But the reign of these Manchus endured unto double, aye, unto treble, that period. Yet Providence knows the appointed hour, and the moment comes at last. We are initiating the example to Eastern Asia of a Republican form of government.' Translated in James Cantlie and C. Sheridan Jones, *Sun Yat Sen and the Awakening of China*, 2nd edn, London: Jarrold & Sons, n.d., pp. 161–2.
42 Sun Yatsen, *San Min Chu I*, pp. 29–30.
43 Sun Yatsen, *San Min Chu I*, p. 30.
44 Sun Yatsen, *San Min Chu I*, p. 32.
45 Chiang Kaishek, *China's Destiny*. First published 1943. Trans. Wang Chung-hui, New York: The Macmillan Company, 1947, p. 3. In fact Chiang did not author this work; he 'approved' of its publication under his own name.
46 Chiang Kaishek, *Soviet Russia in China*, rev. ed., New York: Farr, Strauss and Cudahy, 1968, pp. 88–89. Emphasis added.
47 Mao Zedong, 'The Chinese Revolution and the Chinese Communist Party' (December 1939), in *Selected Works of Mao Tse-tung*, Beijing: Foreign Languages Press, 1967, 4 Vols, II, pp. 305–34, esp. pp. 306–7. Mao did not draft the chapter from which this quotation is taken, although (like Chiang Kaishek above) he did approve its revision.

48 Mao Zedong, 'The Chinese Revolution and the Chinese Communist Party', p. 307.
49 Mao Zedong, 'The Chinese Revolution and the Chinese Communist Party', *passim*.
50 Chiang Kaishek, *China's Destiny*, p. 220.
51 Mao Zedong, 'The Chinese people have stood up' (Zhongguo renmin zhanqilai le), in *Mao Zedong xuanji*, Beijing: Renmin chubanshe, 1977, 5 vol, v, pp. 3–7.
52 See Tang Tsou, 'Marxism, the Leninist party, the masses, and the citizens in the rebuilding of the Chinese state', in S.R. Schram, ed, *Foundations and Limits of State Power in China*, pp. 257–8.
53 Minister of the Interior Wu Po-hsiung, cited in *The Far Eastern Economic Review*, 14 October 1993, p. 20.
54 Hao Chang, *Liang Ch'i-ch'ao and Intellectual Transition in China, 1890–1907*, Cambridge, Mass.: Harvard University Press, 1971, pp. 164–6.
55 Hao Chang, *Liang Ch'i-ch'ao*, p. 255. Hao Chang offers a brilliant survey and analysis of Liang's use of the concept of Reason of State; *ibid*, pp. 255–9.
56 Sun Yatsen, *San Min Chu I*, pp. 12, 38, 75.
57 Maurice Meisner, *Li Ta-chao and the Origins of Chinese Marxism*, New York: Atheneum, 1974, p. 19.
58 Chen Duxiu, 'Patriotism and consciousness of self', *Jiayin zazhi*, 1:4, 10 November 1914, excerpted and translated in Hélène Carrère d'Encausse and Stuart R. Schram, *Marxism and Asia, An Introduction with Readings*, London: Allen Lane/Penguin Books, 1969, pp. 204–8, from which this quote has been adapted.
59 Chen Duxiu, 'Patriotism and consciousness of self', adapted from *ibid.*, p. 206.
60 Hao Chang, *Liang Ch'i-ch'ao* pp. 241–2.
61 It is true that at one stage, early in his career, Sun Yatsen advocated something which he called federalism, but his preferred model was of a federation of counties under a central government; this is best understood as a modified form of centralism rather than a variant of federalism. See Li Dajia, *Minguo chu nian de liansheng zizhi yundong*, Taipei: Kongwenguan, 1986, pp. 144–5, cited in Prasenjit Duara, 'Provincial narratives of the nation: centralism and federalism in Republican China', unpublished paper (1991), p. 30.
62 See Philip Kuhn, 'Civil society and constitutional development', paper prepared for the American–European Symposium on State vs. Society in East Asian Tradition, Paris, 1991. Cited in Frederick Wakeman, 'The civil society and public sphere debate', *Modern China*, 19:2, April 1993, pp. 108–38.
63 The development of the late Qing state clearly opened up new areas of contest between the staff and local elites, as well as expanding the notional role of the state in elite thought. This is one of the paradoxes represented in the 'irony' of the Chinese revolution. See, for example, Mary C. Wright, ed, *China in Revolution: The First Phase, 1900–1913*, New Haven: Yale University Press, 1968; also Mary Backus Rankin, 'Some observations on a Chinese public sphere', *Modern China*, 19:2, April 1993, pp. 158–82. Rankin here astutely notes the 'rise of a

European-like conflict between a centralizing reformist state and politi-
cized elites outside it', a transformation which eventually destroyed both
the Imperial state and the local elites which it was attempting to co-opt in
the process of reforming itself.

64 John Foster, *Chinese Realities*, London: Church Missionary Society,
1928, p. 80.
65 See Yip Ka-che, *Religion, Nationalism and Chinese Students: The Anti-
Christian Movement of 1922–1927*, Bellingham: Washington University,
1980; and Jesse Gregory Lutz, *Chinese Politics and Christian Missions:
The Anti-Christian Movements of 1920–1928*, Notre-Dame: Cross Roads
Books, 1988.
66 Arif Dirlik, *Anarchism in the Chinese Revolution*, Berkeley and Los
Angeles: University of California Press, 1991; and Ming K. Chan
and Arif Kirlik, *Schools into Fields and Factories: Anarchists, the
Guomindang, and the National Labour University in Shanghai, 1927–
1932*, Durham and London: Duke University Press, 1992.
67 The group of intellectuals associated with New Tide (*Xin chao*) magazine, including Luo Jialun, Fu Sinian and Gu Jiegang, dwelt closely on
this problem. See Schneider, *Ku Chieh-kang*, p. 28.
68 Cited in Elisabeth Eide, 'Optimistic and Disillusioned Noras on the
Chinese Literary Scene, 1919–1940', in Anna Gertslacher, Ruth Keen,
Wolfgang Kubin, Margit Miosga and Jenny Schon, eds, *Women and
Literature in China*, Bochum: Studienverlag Brockmeyer, 1985,
pp. 193–222, esp. p. 199.
69 'The source of chaos in China's present political situation,' complained
Chen, 'is militarist separatism.' Chen Duxiu 'Liansheng zizhi yu
Zhongguo zhenxiang' (Federalism and China's political situation),
Xiangdao, 1, 13 Sept 1922, p. 2. So too Cai Hesen: 'The source of
chaos in Chinese politics is, of course, the warlords.' [Cai] Hesen,
'Wuli tongyi yu liansheng zizhi: junfa zhuanzheng yu junfa geju'
(Military reunification and federalism: World dictatorship and warlord
separatism), *Xiangdao*, 2, 20 September 1922, p. 15.
70 Recent talk of federal self-government arises not from the needs of the
people but from the leadership of the warlords of Hunan, Guangdong and
Yunnan Provinces.' Chen Duxiu *'Liansheng zizhi'*, p. 2.
71 [Cai] Hesen, 'Wuli tongyi', p. 14.
72 Chen Duxiu argued that federalism was best suited to countries with
regionally differentiated economies, languages, religions and cultures.
This was not the case with China, one country housing a single 'Chinese
people' (*Zhonghua minzu*) within a uniform socio-economic system. As
China's economy was subject to the universal laws of history, the
nation's million-strong industrial proletariat supplied the historical fixa-
tive to bond their four hundred million compatriots into one. Chen Duxiu
'Liansheng zizhi', p. 2. Cai Hesen went a step further in arguing that
political differences between north and south, or between liberal and
mass democrats, were at base differences between social classes. Hence
'class warfare' (*jieji zhanzheng*) would ultimately supply a force for
unity sufficient to overcome all regional differences. [Cai] Hesen,
'Wuli tongyi', p. 14.
73 Guangdong was the subject of the most radical expression of 'separatist'

rhetoric published in the late Empire, Ou Qujia's *New Guangdong*, which proposed greater provincial autonomy within a national Chinese federation. It fell short of mounting a case for Guangdong nationalism. Ou promoted the ideals of self-government, self-management of resources and 'independence' for Guangdong on the understanding that 'the people of Guangdong are truly the masters of Guangdong'. Still, it was Ou who considered greater provincial independence as a prelude to 'the independence of all China'. Ou believed China as a whole stood to profit from greater competition among relatively independent provinces. See Duara, 'Provincial narratives', pp. 9–10.

74 Fang Lizhi, 'On patriotism and global citizenship', speech of 25 February 1989, Beijing. Transcribed by G.K. Sun, translated by James H. Williams, in George Hicks, ed, *The Broken Mirror: China after Tiananmen*, Harlow, Essex: Longman, 1990, pp. xxi–xxv.

75 In the field of China studies, this research has been stimulated by interest in the work of Jurgen Habermas, most notably *The Structural Transformation of the Public Sphere: An Enquiry into a Category of Bourgeois Society*, Cambridge, Mass.: MIT Press, 1989.

76 William Rowe argues that there was indeed a 'public sphere' in late imperial China, although not necessarily a 'civil society' (for which there is still no agreed term in Chinese). Either way, Rowe is 'fully convinced' that there was an expanding urban bourgeois culture in late imperial China. William T. Rowe, 'The problem of "civil society" in late imperial China', *Modern China*, 19:2, April 1993, pp. 139–57. This issue is taken up by other contributors to the same volume.

77 Rowe, 'The problem of "civil society" in late imperial China'.

78 Naitô Konan, 'Constitutional Government in China', in Joshua A. Fogel, edited and translated, 'Naitô Konan and the Development of the Conception of Modernity in Chinese History', *Chinese Studies in History*, 17, Fall 1983, pp. 61–87, esp. pp. 69–70.

79 Naitô Konan, *ibid.*, esp. pp. 68–9. This impressionistic account of the system of personnel evaluation in the late Empire needs to be qualified, however, by reference to the more complex formal procedures which were in place. See Kuhn, *Soulstealers*, Chapter 9, *passim*.

80 Naitô Konan, 'Constitutional Government in China', pp. 69–70.

81 See, for example, the editorial by Hua Zhou, in the Nationalist Party newspaper supplement, *Juewu* (Awakening), 9 September 1920.

82 The Nationalists' relations with the Shanghai bourgeoisie has been the subject of a lively debate in Western scholarship on China. See Lloyd E. Eastman, *The Abortive Revolution: China Under Nationalist Rule 1927–1937*, Cambridge, Mass.: Harvard University Press, 1974; Parks M. Coble Jr., *The Shanghai Capitalists and the Nationalist Government 1927–1937*, Cambridge, Mass.: Council on East Asian Studies, Harvard University, 1980; Joseph Fewsmith, *Party, State and Local Elites in Republican China: Merchant Organization and Politics in Shanghai, 1890–1930*, Honolulu: University of Hawaii Press, 1985; Tim Wright, 'The Nationalist state and regulations of Chinese industry during the Nanjing decade: Competition and control in coal mining', in David Pong and Edmund Fung, eds, *Ideal and Reality: Social and Political Change in Modern China, 1860–1949*, Lanham: University Press of

58   *John Fitzgerald*

America, 1985, pp. 127–83. The Nationalists' relations with the inde-
pendent press of Shanghai are discussed in Terry Narramore, 'The
Nationalists and the daily press: The case of *Shenbao*, 1927–1934', in
John Fitzgerald, ed, *The Nationalists and Chinese Society, 1923–1937: A
Symposium*, Melbourne: Melbourne History Monographs, 1989.

83   Richard Madsen warns against assuming that newly emerging (or
revived) social organisations which are presently weakening state control in China are in fact contributing to the development of a democratic
public sphere. They may do, but they may also be leading to 'chaotic
fragmentation of society'. The answer to the question is to be found in a
new kind of research agenda. Richard Madsen, 'The public sphere, civil
society and moral community: A research agenda for contemporary
China studies', in *Modern China*, 19:2, April 1993, pp. 183–98.

84   As Madsen notes, 'it appears to be the fear of just such chaotic conflict
that for the time being seems to keep Chinese society from widely
supporting the overthrow of its regime, even though the regime seems
to have largely lost its legitimacy, among the urban population at least.'
Madsen, 'The public sphere, civil society and moral community', p. 195.
On the general question of legitimacy see David S. Goodman, 'Democracy, interest and virtue: The search for legitimacy in the People's
Republic of China', in S.R. Schram, ed, *Foundations and Limits of State
Power in China*, London: School of Oriental and African Studies, 1987,
pp. 291–312.

85   Franz Schurmann, *Ideology and Organization in Communist China*, 2
edn, Berkeley and Los Angeles: University of California Press, 1968,
p. 105.

86   The transition to negotiation has, it seems, already begun. See Suisheng
Zhao, 'From Coercion to Negotiation: The Changing Central–Local
Economic Relationship in Mainland China', *Issues and Studies*, 28:10,
October 1992, pp. 1–22.

3 Reform and the restructuring of central–local relations

Dali L. Yang

For observers of China, 1993 may very well be remembered as the year of the 'China miracle'. Bedazzled by China's star economic performance, virtually every business or public affairs publication hopped on to the bandwagon of remaking China's image from that of pariah of the international community to that of a giant reawakening. Amid all the fashionable talk (and lingering disbelief) about the rise of China, however, the question persists about the centre's ability to hold China together, especially after Deng Xiaoping's death. Those who raise this question point to the growing economic resources going to the provinces and the power vacuum Deng's departure may leave behind.

In this chapter, the impact of the reforms on relations between the centre and the provinces is examined in order to gain a better under-standing of the centrifugal forces swirling in the Chinese polity. The discussion will consist of two main parts. First, data is presented on the extractive capacity of the Chinese state in order to examine how the economic reforms have affected the power of the state and, within the state, that of the centre and the crucial relationship between centre and localities. The usual measures of the weakening of the centre, focusing on the fiscal dimension of central–provincial relations, fall short of capturing the complexities of that dynamic relationship. Secondly, the evolution of central–local relations is discussed, with special attention to the politics of fiscal rationalisation at the third plenary session of the fourteenth Party Central Committee held in late 1993. It is suggested that the adoption of sweeping fiscal reforms at the plenum may be a watershed in central–local relations.

THE EXTRACTIVE CAPACITY OF THE CHINESE STATE IN HISTORICAL AND COMPARATIVE PERSPECTIVE

'The revenue of the state is the state,' Edmund Burke wrote in his *Reflections on the Revolution in France*.[1] Burke may sound exaggerated, but there can be no doubt that revenue generation is of fundamental importance to the survival and operation of the apparatuses of a state. In the case of China, Zelin has argued that the enervation of the Chinese imperial regime in the nineteenth century was first of all due to a lack of means, since the Chinese state was hampered by a predominantly agrarian economy and inadequate tax collection capability.[2]

What about contemporary China? To better understand the changes in central–local relations in contemporary China, the extractive capacity of the Chinese state is considered here. This immediately raises two issues: (1) how the concept of the state is defined and (2) how the extractive capacity of the state is to be measured. At the broad theoretical level, one can agree with Max Weber that states are compulsory associations claiming control over territories and the people within them. In practice, the state apparatus in China is defined to include *both* central and local governments, even though as will be discussed later the centre and localities may work at cross purposes. The extractive capacity (E) of the state is the ratio of the government revenue to gross national product.

The consolidated general government revenue includes the revenues *and* extra-budgetary funds of both central *and* local governments. Since GNP figures are not available for all years, two indices have been computed, one based on national income figures for the 1952–91 period and the other based on GNP figures for 1978–91. The resulting indices of state extractive capacity over 1952–91 are shown in Figure 3.1.[3]

For the 1952–91 period, the extractive capacity index calculated on the basis of national income averaged just under 41.5 per cent. For most of these four decades, the fluctuations in the index were clearly related to shifts in the rates of economic growth. It rose steadily after the Communist takeover and with the imposition of the command economy, culminating in a plateau of 56.6 per cent in 1960 during the Great Leap Forward but plunged back to 41.5 per cent as the Leap collapsed. The turmoil during the Cultural Revolution led to another dip after 1966. After Mao's death and with Hua Guofeng's Great Leap Outward, the index rose to another top in 1978 (48.7 per cent)

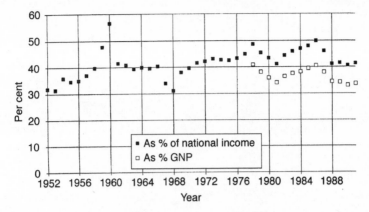

Figure 3.1 State revenue as percentage of national income
Source: Ministry of Finance, *Zhongguo caizheng tongji* (China finance statistics)
(Beijing: Kexue chubanshe 1992), pp. 319–20.

but dropped back to 41 per cent in 1981 as an economic adjustment
programme took effect. Steady double-digit growth rates thereafter
under the reforms saw the index to another peak at 50 per cent in
1986. In the next two years, however, the index dropped back to
around 41 per cent as enterprise contracting spread and the economy
fluctuated amid an austerity programme (1988–90). Nevertheless, in
spite of the recent pullback, the index based on national income has
remained at its historical average. The index of state extractive
capacity calculated on the basis of GNP tells a parallel story, but at
a lower level and for a shorter time period. Thus, from a historical
perspective, the extractive capacity of the Chinese state had not
suffered a significant decline, in spite of the realignment of fiscal
resources between the centre and the localities which will be
discussed later.

Yet what if we compare China with other countries? Owing to data
availability, comparability, and selection bias, such comparisons
present a thorny problem and should be interpreted with caution.
Table 3.1 presents data on relative state extractive capacity from
ten large market economies at various economic development levels
(Japan is not included owing to data unavailability). It is known that
the level of extractive capacity for all countries tends to rise as the
level of income rises (Brazil is a major anomaly). As of the late
1980s, China's consolidated government revenue as a percentage of
GNP was about 33 per cent.[4] This was slightly lower than the level
achieved in the US, but considerably higher than those for Indonesia,

Table 3.1 Consolidated general government revenue as percentage of GDP, international comparisons.

Country	Year	Mid-year population (millions)	Consolidated general government revenue as % of GDP
Indonesia	1989	179.2	17.1
India	1987	785.2	20.5
Mexico	1987	81.2	20.6
USA	1989	246.8	34.6
Australia	1990	17	37.2
Canada	1989	26.2	40.3
UK	1989	57.2	41.4
Germany	1990	62.1 (1989)	44.5
France	1990	56.4	46.3
Brazil	1989	147.4	96.7

Source: International Monetary Fund, Government Finance Statistics Yearbook 1991 (Washington D.C.: IMF 1991).
* *Data on Japan are not available.*

India and Mexico, even though Mexico and Indonesia had higher per capita income levels than China.[5] In short, we may conclude that, even though China had much lower income levels, its relative extractive capacity as of the late 1980s and early 1990s stood roughly midway between the developed and the developing economies. In comparative terms, the extractive capacity of the Chinese state may not be super-strong, but it cannot be characterised as weak or feeble.[6]

FISCAL DECENTRALISATION

While Burke emphasised the importance of revenue extraction to the state, he was nevertheless not in favour of an over-concentration of resources in the hands of the state but called for a balance between public and private. He believed that such a balance was crucial to the prosperity of both the state and the nation comprised of private individuals.[7] In China, the same concerns expressed by Burke have animated a debate framed in terms of centralisation vs decentralisation for centuries.[8] The establishment of a command economy under CCP leadership accentuated the challenges of balancing local initiatives and central control.[9] In consequence, inter-governmental and especially central–provincial relations in the PRC have undergone a series of twists and turns.

Given the crucial role of resource allocation in a command

economy, scholars have paid special attention to changes in central–provincial fiscal relations both in the command economy and since the start of the post-Mao reforms.[10] It is generally recognised that fiscal decentralisation has been one of the defining characteristics of the post-Mao reforms, even though it represents only one aspect of the changing central–local relations.

The realignment of fiscal resources between centre and localities

There is no need to repeat the extensive discussions of the changing fiscal mechanisms that have led to the decentralisation of fiscal resources in post-Mao China, especially since the widespread adoption of central–provincial revenue-sharing contracts (hereafter fiscal contracting) in 1980.[11] One point worth keeping in mind, however, was that the devolution of resources and decision-making power to local governments and enterprises was initially intended by the Chinese leadership to stimulate the initiatives of localities. In other words, the nature of the fiscal reforms leads us to expect that the share of resources directly controlled by the central government would decline over time. Nevertheless, dramatic changes in other aspects of the economic system, especially the erosion of the state enterprise sector caused by the entry of competitors, have compounded the effect of the shifting fiscal arrangements and may have led to a far more precipitous (relative) decline in central control over resources than anticipated.

Budgetary revenues and expenditures

Table 3.2 presents data on the *relative* distribution of budgetary resources between central and local governments. On the revenue side, it is apparent that after significant reductions in the 1970s, the central government's share of the budget revenue has steadily increased over the post-Mao period, doubling from just above 20 per cent in 1981 to around 39 per cent in the late 1980s and early 1990s.[12]

The relative share of budget revenues says precious little, however, about central–local fiscal relations. This is due to a fact which has been commonly neglected by studies of China's fiscal revenues: the budget revenue figures released by the Chinese government *only* indicate who collected the revenues but not who had claims over the revenues collected. In other words, as noted in statistical yearbooks published by the State Statistical Bureau, they 'are *not* the figures [of

Table 3.2 Budgetary revenues and expenditures in China, 1953–1991.

	Budgetary Revenue					Budgetary Expenditure				
	Total	Centre	Central %	Localities	Local %	Total	Centre	Central %	Localities	Local %
1953–57	135.49	61.52	45.41	73.97	54.59	134.57	99.73	74.11	34.84	25.89
1958–62	211.66	48.04	22.70	163.62	77.30	228.87	110.16	48.13	118.71	51.87
1963–65	121.51	33.58	27.64	87.93	72.36	120.5	71.89	59.66	48.61	40.34
1966–70	252.9	79.01	31.24	173.89	68.76	251.85	153.8	61.07	98.05	38.93
1971–75	391.97	57.64	14.71	334.33	85.29	391.94	212.51	54.22	179.43	45.78
1976–80	496.07	77.45	15.61	418.61	84.39	524.74	259.02	49.36	265.72	50.64
1981–85	683.07	208.76	30.56	474.31	69.44	695.2	339.51	48.84	355.68	51.16
1981	108.95	22.47	20.62	86.47	79.37	111.5	60.22	54.01	51.28	45.99
1982	112.4	25.85	23.00	86.55	77.00	115.33	57.51	49.87	57.82	50.13
1983	124.9	37.2	29.78	87.7	70.22	129.25	64.25	49.71	64.99	50.28
1984	150.19	52.45	34.92	97.74	65.08	154.64	73.87	47.77	80.77	52.23
1985	186.64	70.79	37.93	115.85	62.07	184.48	83.65	45.34	100.82	54.65
1986–90	1351.77	534.14	39.51	817.62	60.49	1397.83	553.26	39.58	844.57	60.42
1986	226.03	91.67	40.56	134.36	59.44	233.08	96.23	41.29	136.86	58.72
1987	236.89	90.58	38.24	146.31	61.76	244.85	103.19	42.14	141.66	57.86
1988	262.8	104.55	39.78	158.25	60.22	270.66	106.04	39.18	164.62	60.82
1989	294.79	110.55	37.50	184.24	62.50	304.02	110.52	36.35	193.5	63.65
1990	331.26	136.79	41.29	194.47	58.71	345.22	137.28	39.77	207.94	60.23
1991	361.09	139.97	38.76	221.12	61.24	381.36	151.77	39.80	229.58	60.20

Source: Zhongguo tongji nianjian 1992 (Statistical yearbook of China 1992), p. 227

revenues going to centre and localities respectively] calculated on the basis of fiscal arrangements.'[13]

On the expenditure side, the trend is clearer. The central government's share of budgetary expenditures has declined from about 50 per cent at the start of the post-Mao reforms to just under 40 per cent in 1991. For two reasons, however, too much should not be attributed to this 10 percentage point decline. First, as already mentioned, since fiscal decentralisation has been part of the reform agenda, some decline in the centre's share of budgetary expenditures may be expected in any case, even though the 10-point drop may be larger than the central leadership had anticipated (but no one really knows because no official targets were issued). Secondly, China has had a unitary consolidated budget management system and, until the fiscal reforms announced at the end of 1993 are implemented, will continue to do so. This means that even though the share of budgetary expenditures being spent by local administrations has increased, these expenditures must still be included into the unified state budget plans and subjected to the supervision of the central government. Indeed, through a detailed examination of the fiscal responsibilities facing the centre and localities respectively, Christine Wong has concluded that 'the present division of responsibilities is extremely unfavorable for local budgetary reductions, since fiscal reforms have not altered the traditional roles whereby the central government managed and financed the economic development program while leaving the chores of day-to-day public administration to local governments.'[14]

Nevertheless, it must be admitted (and it is also well known) that as reforms progressed, the government budget as a share of national income has significantly shrank from just under 40 per cent at the start of the reforms to under 20 per cent as of the early 1990s. Again, however, this fact alone does not necessitate that the reduced share alone significantly reduced the capacity of the central government to manage the economy. As will be discussed later, a government's capacity to manage the economy depends not only on the amount of resources it directly controls but also, in the case of an economy becoming more and more market-oriented, on whether it possesses the appropriate economic institutions for undertaking such management.

The expansion of extra-budgetary funds

Another key indicator of the degree of centralization or decentralization in China's economy is the proportion of public sector

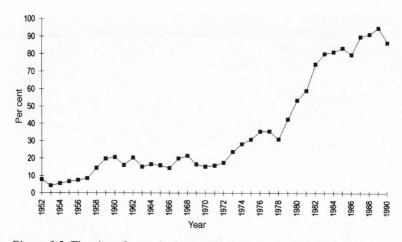

Figure 3.2 The rise of extra-budgetary funds: extra-budget funds as percentage of state budget revenue
Source: State Statistical Bureau, *Zhongguo tongji nianjian 1992* (Statistical yearbook of China 1992) (Beijing: Zhongguo tongji chubanshe, 1992), p. 228.

extra-budgetary funds. By definition, these funds are not formally included in the consolidated state budget and therefore are not subjected to as stringent central control as budgetary expenditures.

Figure 3.2 plots the historical rise of extra-budgetary funds as a percentage of the state budget revenue (hereafter the E-ratio).[15] The first rise of the E-ratio coincided with the Great Leap Forward and the decentralization that it entailed. With the collapse of the Leap into the Great Leap Famine and the subsequent economic readjustment, extra-budgetary funds were also reined in. During the turmoil of the Cultural Revolution, the E-ratio saw another short-lived rise. In the 1970s, with the drastic devolution of central enterprises to provincial governments, the share of budget revenues collected by the centre was halved from the level of the 1960s (see Table 3.1). In the meantime, the allocation of depreciation funds and other funds, as well as diversion of budget revenues, more than doubled the E-ratio. The cumulative effect of these developments and the policy of allowing state enterprises to retain a certain amount of profits under the reforms led to a more rapid rise in the E-ratio (while the central budget revenue ratio doubled in the first half of the 1980s). By the end of the 1980s, it had reached about 90 per cent.

Has the expansion of extra-budgetary funds led to the weakening of the central government relative to local governments? The available data indicate an ambiguous answer. Figure 3.3 presents the distribution of extra-budgetary funds among three groups: state enterprises, institutions, and local governments. The biggest chunk of the extra-budgetary funds belongs to state enterprises and their supervisory agencies; these funds are made up of retained profits and depreciation funds, each contributing about half.[16] Surprisingly, the share accounted for by local governments has been steadily declining since at least the early 1970s and by the end of the 1980s it stood at a mere two per cent of the total. In this context, it would apparently be difficult to conclude that the rapid expansion of extra-budgetary funds has empowered local governments vis-à-vis the centre.[17]

One author has nevertheless suggested that the two per cent figure understates the influence of local governments because 'local governments have no difficulty encroaching on the resources of the enterprises under their jurisdictions' through a variety of levies.[18] While it is clear that local authorities do have substantial influence over the behaviour of enterprises, for at least four reasons the argument is one-sided. First, the imposition of various levies reflects as much on the influence of local governments as on their difficult fiscal situation, because, as Gordon White, Christine Wong and others have pointed out, local governments have experienced as many budgetary difficulties as the centre.[19] Secondly, the centre has also tapped into the growing extra-budgetary funds. Since 1983, it has imposed taxes on

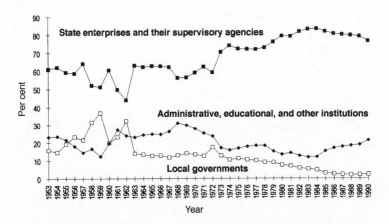

Figure 3.3 Inter-temporal distribution of extra-budgetary funds
Source: State Statistical Bureau, *Zhongguo tongji nianjian 1992* (Statistical yearbook of China 1992) (Beijing: Zhongguo tongji chubanshe, 1992), p. 228.

extra-budgetary receipts and extra-budgetary construction. These two tax items rose from 9.5 billion *yuan* in 1983 to 24.4 billion *yuan* in 1991; these amounted to 6.2 and 7.2 per cent respectively of the consolidated government revenue.[20] Thirdly, it should be emphasised that much of the extrabudgetary funds are collected through specially authorised levies and targeted for specific purposes, such as road maintenance, industrial renovation and repair, energy development, and science and technology. In consequence, much of the extra-budgetary funds cannot be spent at will and Chinese authorities stress that the use of these funds 'should also be subject to planning and supervision'.[21] It is true that agencies, institutions, enterprises and local governments enjoy considerable discretion in using the extra-budgetary funds under their control and are also known to use evasive tactics to shift funds earmarked for one purpose to other uses. Part of this autonomy is the intended outcome of the reforms. Even though the autonomy may now be perceived as to have exceeded the original intent of the reformers, it should not be exaggerated. Finally, even if the local share of funds had expanded far more than that of the centre, we should not jump to the conclusion that all localities gained at the expense of the centre. It is likely that some localities had gained more than other localities and that some localities might actually have seen their share of resources decline. While the actual changes in the share of resources are subject to empirical investigation, the unevenness of such changes suggests that it may be unwarranted to categorically speak of either the centre losing power or the localities gaining it. Instead, the localities are not a unified block and they are subject to political cleavages, which the centre might exploit.

To sum up, there is a need to be careful and to distinguish between the state and the centre. The data presented suggest that while the extractive capacity of the Chinese state (vis-à-vis the economy and society) has declined, that decline is not precipitous. Moreover, the analysis of data on budgetary and extra-budgetary resources does not provide conclusive evidence of a declining centre within the Chinese state. Table 3.3 presents official figures on the relative distribution of central and local government expenditures over the 1982–90 period.[22] Overall, the central share of both budgetary and extra-budgetary expenditures has shown a decline of 3 percentage points. This and the other data presented so far may be cause for some concern, but they do not point unambiguously to a crisis, though they have been widely interpreted as a crisis by both Chinese and Western scholars. Instead, as is conventional wisdom, complex organisations change only slowly. As will be discussed later, the

Table 3.3 Percentage shares of central and local government expenditure in China, 1982–1990

Year	(I) Budgetary funds Centre %	Localities %	(II) Extra-budgetary Centre %	Localities %	(III) = (I) + (II) Centre %	Localities %
1982	49.87	50.13	30.91	69.09	42.49	57.51
1983	49.71	50.28	34.30	65.70	43.48	56.51
1984	47.77	52.23	37.70	62.30	43.55	56.45
1985	45.34	54.65	40.88	59.12	43.44	56.56
1986	41.29	58.72	40.61	59.39	41.01	58.99
1987	42.14	57.86	40.29	59.71	41.35	58.65
1988	39.18	60.82	39.29	60.71	39.23	60.77
1989	36.35	63.65	38.99	61.01	37.54	62.46
1990	39.77	60.23	38.33	61.67	39.14	60.86

Source: *Zhongguo tongji nianjian 1992* (Statistical yearbook of China 1992), p. 227

perception of crisis was a reflection of the centre's temporary difficulties in matching revenue with expenditure and in building institutions suited to an increasingly market-oriented economy.

Shifting revenue base, budget deficits

It is now common knowledge that China's dynamic economic growth over the reform period has been fuelled by the dramatic expansion of the non-state sectors, including rural enterprises, ventures associated with foreign capital and private firms. The shift in the ownership structure of the economy has also meant a shift in the taxation structure for the Chinese state. As Figure 3.4 shows, whereas the share of the state revenue accounted for by state enterprises has steadily declined (left scale), those of other types of ownership have expanded (right scale).

In the command economy, the Chinese state had relied on taxing state enterprises as its main source of revenue, and other types of ownership were either suppressed or were relegated to subsidiary status. This institutional set-up allowed the Chinese state to extract revenue with a minimal revenue extraction apparatus. Ironically, while the rise of non-state firms has contributed to China's dynamic economic performance, the entry of and competition from these firms has brought down the level of profits enjoyed by the state-owned enterprises, thus undermining the traditional tax base of the Chinese state.[23] In the meantime, the diversification of the Chinese economy into various forms of ownership has meant that it is outmoded for the

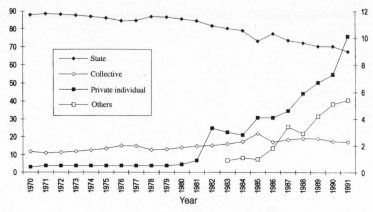

Figure 3.4 Sources of state revenue by ownership (Total = 100)
Source: Ministry of Finance, *Zhongguo caizheng tongji* (China finance statistics)
(Beijing: Kexue chubanshe 1992), pp. 26–7.

state to depend on taxing state enterprises. Yet reform of the tax
administration in terms of both manpower and techniques has lagged
behind changes in the economic structure.[24] Thus, Barry Naughton
concluded that the decline in the relative importance of the state
budgetary revenue

> is not being caused by a generalized deterioration in central
> government power but rather by the collapse of a specific fiscal
> mechanism. The breakdown of the traditional system of revenue
> mobilization under conditions in which no replacement taxation
> system has been created has caused a chronic fiscal crisis.[25]

To the extent that local authorities have been given discretionary
power to adjust the tax rates for enterprises under their jurisdiction,
this has added to the budget woes at the centre.

Unfortunately for the central government, this development has
occurred when the centre sought to introduce reforms in various
policy arenas and needed funds to compensate the losers out of
considerations of political stability and social equity. The most
obvious item was consumer price subsidy, which amounted to
32.15 billion *yuan* in 1992 or 7.3 per cent of total expenditure.
While the government raised agricultural procurement prices to
stimulate agricultural production, it simultaneously paid out subsidies to urban residents when staple grain sales prices were increased.

Such subsidies (and other benefits provided for workers in loss-making state enterprises) were used to secure urban stability. In short, because the government has not been able to streamline its obligations in line with the slower-growing revenue stream, the government budget deficit has widened significantly both in absolute terms and as a percentage of revenue.[26] So far the state has financed its deficit by domestic and international borrowing as well as borrowing from the central bank (currency creation). In 1992, domestic borrowing was 45.53 billion, international borrowing 21.22 billion, and the rest, 20.64 billion, came from the central bank. In addition, local governments were ordered to take care of 3.11 billion *yuan* in unanticipated local government budget deficits. Excluding the 3.11 billion, in 1992 the centre had to deal with a total of 87.4 billion *yuan* in budget deficit, which was equal to 19.7 per cent of total expenditures.[27]

Decline of central control over investment

In socialist command economies, the most important macro-economic mechanism planners employed was investment planning. Through their control over investment, planners targeted capital goods (heavy) industries and promoted the development of particular regions. Even in reformist models such as the market socialism proposed by Oscar Lange, socialist planners would still retain control over new investment. In the West, control over the flow of investment has shaped and reshaped the industrial landscape, with significant geopolitical implications.[28]

In China, however, waves of decentralisation gradually shifted control over investment from the centre to local governments even prior to the post-Mao reforms. But, as Barry Naughton has argued forcefully, the decline in the proportion of centrally-controlled fixed investment has been the 'single most striking, consistent change in the Chinese economy since 1978.'[29] Similar stories can be told of other aspects of the central control over investment resources. As can be seen from Figure 3.5, the share of total investment accounted for by state budgetary investment has been in decline ever since the end of the First Five-year Plan in 1957; by 1991, it stood at around 10 per cent.

The factors which contributed to the decline of the share of the government budget as a share of national income are also the factors leading to the reduction in the central share of investment, namely decentralisation and the expansion of non-state sectors. From the

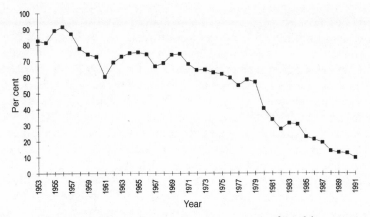

Figure 3.5 State budgetary investment as percentage of total investment
Source: State Statistical Bureau, *Zhongguo tongji nianjian 1992* (Statistical yearbook
of China 1992) (Beijing: Zhongguo tongji chubanshe, 1992), p. 149.

perspective of a command economy that rested on central control
over investment, by definition the decline of central control over
investment has clearly undermined the centre's capacity to control
and manage the economy.

From the perspective of a market economy, however, the decline in
the proportion of investment controlled by the central government
permits the allocation of scarce resources by decentralised economic
agents which may enhance the efficiency of investment. While
economists from Adam Smith to the members of the President's
Council of Economic Advisers have prescribed many functions a
government ought to perform in a capitalist economy, making
detailed investment decisions is not one of them. In this sense, the
decline in the central share of investment is a sign of success of
China's transition from the command economy.

Nevertheless, a government is charged with the economic tasks of
providing macro-economic stability and making prudent policies that
enhance economic growth (there may also have been other objectives
such as equitable income distribution). Whereas the Chinese government has largely lost its traditional tool of macro-economic control
through direct control over investment, it does not yet possess a set of
economic institutions for macro-economic control suitable for a
market economy. To use a hackneyed phrase, China is caught
between plan and market.[30]

A first cut on the problem of central–local relations in contemporary China easily focused on the fiscal dimension of that relationship because of the availability of fiscal data. On the basis of the information and data presented so far, what inferences can be drawn about central–local, particularly central–provincial relations in China? First, overall it does appear that the role of the centre in the Chinese economy has been reduced over the reform period. In particular, because the amount of the resources – especially investment – directly controlled by the centre has declined significantly, it has become more difficult for the centre to exercise macro-economic control by pulling the investment levers. Second, persistent budget deficits have also constrained the central government since its capacity to deal with the deficit through currency issue and borrowing has declined owing to growing debt repayment and the political costs of high inflation.

The implications of these developments for central–local relations are not clear-cut, however. To be sure, the share of tangible resources directly controlled by the centre has decreased vis-à-vis that of the provinces. In this respect, the conventional wisdom that the provincial authorities have gained room for financial manoeuvre appears correct.[31] Yet central–local relations are not and should not be construed as a zero-sum game. As already noted local governments have also been under financial pressure; all provinces have not gained equally, some have in fact found it harder to keep up with others. Moreover, the macro-economic problems that have resulted as a corollary of all these developments do not just undermine the centre's legitimacy but also expose economies in the provinces to various adverse currents, though some provinces along the coast have been able to weather such adversities more resiliently than others (such as the traditional core provinces for heavy industry). In other words, the fiscal developments have led to the undersupply of a crucial public good – macro-economic stability. Difficulties in these respects may be remedied through improvement of the fiscal and taxation system and of the financial system (such as the establishment of a central banking system). From this perspective, the economic instabilities facing the Chinese government are to a great extent due to the obsolescence of traditional planning tools as well as the limited nature of fiscal and financial reforms.

The distribution of fiscal resources is only one indicator of evolving intergovernmental relations. Perhaps equally important is the centre's control over personnel appointment at the provincial level. Moreover, central authorities enjoy various other prerogatives; they can, for example, constrain provincial expenditures through bank disbursement regulations.[32] In addition, central leaders enjoy important procedural and organisational advantages if they negotiate with provincial leaders. Unfortunately, these other factors, unlike the control of fiscal resources, are very difficult to measure in precise terms.

Thus, it is important not to conflate central control over resources with the highly ambiguous concept of state capacity. If the power of the centre vis-à-vis the localities is defined as the centre's capacity to influence the economic behaviour of localities, then there is a need to examine not only the distribution of fiscal resources but more fundamentally the relative distribution of power that may redefine the relative distribution of fiscal resources. Central and provincial authorities may actually possess much more power than they have actually used and, in the absence of accurate measurements of such latent power, then *a priori* there is a significant element of uncertainty in assessing central–local relations. It is difficult to differentiate between the case of the centre choosing *not* to exercise its prerogatives and the centre being *unable* to do so. In other words, until the centre tries to exercise its power vis-à-vis the provinces and fails, it is not possible to conclude that the centre has lost control over the provinces.

THE POLITICS OF FISCAL RATIONALISATION

By the late 1980s, China's fiscal system exhibited features common to the majority of developing countries. In these countries

> [the] budget deficits have been financed to an excessive extent by money creation and borrowing abroad with consequent inflation and foreign debt problems. In principle, the deficit problem could be resolved by cutting expenditure and raising charges for services. But, with realistic allowances for expenditure economies and nontax revenue, it seems clear that many countries will need to increase tax revenue.[33]

As discussed earlier, China's fiscal problems stem from a fundamental disjuncture between a set of economic institutions that worked in a command economy and an economy that is becoming more and more market-oriented. Furthermore, while the fiscal contracting system gave localities powerful incentives to encourage economic expansion, it limited the fiscal benefits the centre might receive from an expanding economy. Since at least 1987, the central leadership, especially fiscal conservatives such as Chen Yun and Yao Yilin, had been concerned about the growing budget deficits and wanted to change the particularistic fiscal contracting system to one of separate tax systems for centre and localities in order to both rationalise the fiscal structure and raise the centre's share of revenue. The attempts to rationalise the fiscal system met with much resistance, however, and were not implemented before 1993. Why did the delay in fiscal rationalisation occur? What does this say about the evolution of central–provincial relations in China? Was it a symptom of the centre becoming too feeble?

In her ambitious book *The Political Logic of Economic Reform in China*, Susan Shirk offered an explanation for the delay in fiscal rationalisation. According to Shirk, these centralising efforts failed even during a period of conservative resurgence at the top because 'fiscal policies were constrained by provincial preferences and the political incentives of succession contenders to play to the provinces.'[34] In particular, contenders in the politics of succession offered particularistic contracts to the provinces in order to broaden their base of political support. In consequence, according to Shirk, despite the fact that Li Peng owed political patronage to conservatives such as Chen Yun, once he became premier in 1988, Li Peng also became reluctant to antagonise provincial leaders. While Li Peng initially sought to have the provinces remit more revenue to the central government, he backed down in 1990 in the face of strong provincial opposition. Instead, Li Peng came up with 'a package of particularistic giveaways that enabled him to claim credit with provincial officials,' presumably to bolster his chances of surviving the political succession.[35] As a result, fiscal contracting was retained and the centre continued to feel the fiscal pressures, which had been made especially acute by the much slower economic growth during 1989–91.

By 1993, however, the dynamics of political succession has presumably intensified as the age of Deng Xiaoping and his cohort inexorably advanced and their health further deteriorated.[36] Therefore, following Shirk's logic, one would expect China's central leaders, especially President and General Secretary Jiang Zemin, at least to continue with the particularistic fiscal arrangements if not give out more pork barrels of their own. Instead, as will be discussed later, there has been a strong push for fiscal rationalisation at the Third Plenum of the Fourteenth Party Central Committee. Put simply, the main document of the plenum enshrined systematic fiscal and tax reforms which would both rationalise the tax system and sharply increase the centre's share of the revenue over a period of time. Clearly this train of events cannot be readily accounted for by the mechanisms identified by Shirk.

While he did not specifically write on China, Richard Goode, a long-time IMF adviser on tax reforms in developing countries, has provided an alternative, more eclectic, and ultimately superior perspective on China's delayed fiscal rationalisation. For Goode, attempts to raise revenue are hampered by intellectual or analytical difficulties, political obstacles, bad advice, and administrative and compliance weaknesses. While easy to adumbrate intellectually by various experts and advisers, systematic tax reform is especially unlikely to be accepted and carried out because of the multifarious interests it affects. Invoking the terminology of Albert Hirschman, Goode suggests that 'systematic tax reform may generally be classified as a "chosen" problem selected by policy makers for attention rather than a "pressing" problem forced on the policy makers by the pressure of interested or injured groups. The pressing problems are likely to be given priority.'[37] Government leaders are most likely to first choose the path of least resistance by financing budget deficits through money creation or borrowing. When tolerance of inflation and opportunities for borrowing abroad have diminished, however, political leaders would begin to perceive the need to strengthen the tax system in order to satisfy expenditure demands. Frequently, it was perceptions of fiscal crises that have served to 'concentrate the minds of government leaders and make them more receptive to new measures.'[38] Even then, fiscal rationalisation is neither inevitable nor guaranteed and its adoption and implementation demand effective political leadership.

The changing diagnosis of China's fiscal problems

Analytically, Chinese economists-cum-policy advisers recognised the potential pitfalls of fiscal decentralisation soon after it was launched in the early 1980s, although they turned their attention to other more pressing issues soon thereafter. Take the example of Xue Muqiao, editor-in-chief of the authoritative *Chinese Economic Yearbook* and a senior (and mainstream) statesman as far as Chinese economic policy is concerned.[39] Shortly after the post-Mao wave of fiscal decentralisation was launched amid an economic readjustment programme, Xue expounded in the first *Yearbook* of 1981 that the unitary fiscal system encouraged waste and stifled local initiative. He supported the introduction of fiscal decentralisation to local governments and enterprises and the accountability it entailed. But Xue also warned that miscalculation in carrying out decentralisation may also be counterproductive. In particular, he argued that the decentralisation was too sudden and local governments and enterprises were given resources at the expense of the centre, thus impairing the centre's macro-economic readjustment policy (the centre in 1981 issued treasury bonds in order to absorb funds in society).[40] The next year (1982), Xue had become more worried about the rising budget deficits as a major source of inflationary pressures and called for balancing the budget. He was especially concerned about the centre's shrinking share of resources which had forced the centre to 'borrow' from localities. For him, while fiscal decentralisation stimulated local initiatives, it also led to excessive and duplicative investment and local protectionism, which he blamed on the lack of complementary reforms. In a comment that anticipated the rhetoric for fiscal rationalisation by a full decade, Xue stated that

> budget revenue used to be about one third of national income, but last year (1981) it dropped to 26 per cent, which is far lower than those of the Soviet Union and East Europe, and even lower than those of capitalist countries (more than 30 per cent), and the trend seems to be going lower still.[41]

As the economy shifted into high gear over 1983–88, Xue's earlier concern about the impact of fiscal decentralisation receded. This appears to reflect the general concerns of the economics field in China. Indeed, in the index to Robert Hsu's *Economic Theories in China, 1979–1988*, there was only one entry on the 'fiscal contract responsibility system', and none on 'finance' and 'deficits'.[42] In 1984, Xue Muqiao did mention the budget deficit and the 'considerable difficulties' it caused the state treasury in the form of increased borrowing and currency issue. Nevertheless, Xue concluded that the fiscal difficulties were temporary and not difficult to deal with in an expanding economy with a growing pool of savings.[43] Instead of preaching stringency, Xue shifted his attention to the construction of macro-economic institutions suitable to an increasingly market-oriented economy, since the old tools which revolved around the administrative allocation of fixed assets investment have become obsolescent. He especially called for strengthening monetary policy with a real central bank to complement fiscal policy. However, ever the pragmatist, he admitted that the construction of new institutions and a complementary legal framework would take time and temporary macro-economic difficulties were in consequence inevitable.[44]

In short, the evolution of Xue's thinking on fiscal and macro-economic issues dovetailed developments in China's fiscal reforms. Most importantly, it is clear that Xue recognised the pitfalls of fiscal decentralisation, as would an array of China's leading economists (including Liu Guoguang, Dong Fureng, Wu Jinglian and Dai Yuanchen) in the late 1980s.[45] Moreover, it is hardly surprising that the Ministry of Finance was the leading institutional advocate for fiscal rationalisation as it sought to bring greater order into the financial system and strengthen the centre's balance-sheet.[46] Yet these arguments had no immediate impact on policy in the 1980s; indeed, the centre institutionalised fiscal contracting in 1988. Instead of raising revenue through taxes, the centre also gradually gave localities even more leeway in setting tax rates for enterprises under their jurisdiction and financed its deficits through borrowing and credit creation. As a result, as Shirk has documented in her book, attempts to change the contracting system in the 1980s fizzled out.

In 1989, the cash-strapped central government had to extract additional contributions from the provinces. For example, Deng Xiaoping negotiated 2.5 billion *yuan* from Shanghai in early 1989.[47] The fiscal problems in the context of an economic austerity programme and political crisis led to an outpouring of arguments for fiscal reforms. Xue Muqiao, for example, returned to his earlier concern about fiscal decentralisation. At a meeting of the Central Finance and Economy Leadership Group held in April 1989, he argued against local interests and forcefully advocated abolishing the fiscal contracting system which had become a major cause of macro-economic problems.[48] He was in favour of shifting to a tax assignment system.[49] In the aftermath of the political crackdown of 1989, premier Li Peng in 1990 sought to rationalise the fiscal system in order to relieve the fiscal pressures on the centre but failed. In contrast to Shirk's argument, it appears that the centre's efforts to rationalise the fiscal system faltered for at least two major reasons. First, in the context of the economic and political turmoil that prevailed in 1988–90 and (was perceived to have) threatened the regime's legitimacy and in light of the volatile changes in East Europe and the Soviet Union, China's central leaders were probably timid about making major changes in the system because such moves were inherently risky.[50] Secondly, the economic slowdown that resulted from the austerity programme not only lowered people's expectations but also put a damper on the expansion of both local and central revenue. In consequence, local efforts to keep what they already had were more intense than if the economy was booming, and therefore it was more difficult for the centre to negotiate for a greater share of the revenue.[51]

Yet the delay in revamping the fiscal system and the continuing rise in the budget deficit fuelled a lively discussion on China's fiscal problems, providing the intellectual impetus for fiscal rationalisation.[52] An imperfect but useful indication of the growing attention to fiscal issues can be seen from the contents of *Economic Research*, China's leading monthly journal of economics. Of the 146 articles published in that journal in 1988, only one article touched on fiscal issues, and it was an abstract discussion of the type of fiscal system to be built in China.[53] In 1989, two articles confronted China's fiscal problems head on, and both called for raising the ratio of revenue to national income.[54] In 1990, the number of articles rose to five that dwelled either on the highly controversial issue of decentralisation of power to localities or on China's fiscal dilemmas and continued the debate on the declining ratio of revenue to national income that was started in December 1989.[55] The debate about the declining ratio of fiscal revenue to national income continued over 1991–92 and beyond, but by then the case for fiscal rationalisation was already made.[56] Writing on the growing budget deficits and other associated problems, Chen Yuan, a deputy director of the People's Bank of China and the son of conservative patriarch Chen Yun, warned in 1991 that the decline of central revenue as a share of national income might lead to 'the further loss of economic control and [even] economic disintegration.'[57]

In his *The Rhetoric of Reaction*, Albert Hirschman mapped out the rhetorical tricks both reactionaries and reformers have used throughout history to justify their causes. One major device employed by reformers is what Hirschman calls the imminent-danger thesis, that is, if something is not immediately undertaken, then society might be faced with some sort of deadly threat, such as social dissolution.[58] The argument by Chen Yuan clearly belonged to this genre. With the relaxation of political atmosphere following Deng Xiaoping's southern tour in early 1992, those who argued that China faced a major fiscal crisis and advocated rationalisation of the fiscal system felt freer and their portrayal of China's dangers from fiscal decline reached a crescendo in 1993, in anticipation of the Third Plenum of the Fourteenth Central Committee. Typically, the argument was made with abundant references to economic figures, as the following example in the *Economic Daily* illustrates.[59] Fiscal and taxation reforms are necessary for building a market economy, crucial to strengthening macro-economic control, and fundamental to resolving the fiscal dilemmas facing the central government. Symptomatic of the centre's fiscal problems is the rising budget deficit, which according to official calculations rose from 2.55 billion in 1981 to 23.749 billion *yuan* in 1992. Yet following international accounting practices, the fiscal deficit for 1992 was actually 90.5 billion yuan, or 3.8 per cent of GNP, which the author claimed to be higher than the average for Western industrialised countries. According to the author, the pressures of debt payment (43.68 billion in 1992) have undermined investment in education, science and technology, public health, defence, agriculture and infrastructure and weakened the centre's ability to provide macro-economic stability, deal with social inequality and regional disparities, and implement much-needed reform measures. Therefore, it is imperative to carry out fiscal reforms.

In a few cases, the authors of these arguments went on to spell out the political implications of China's fiscal problems. As one eye-catching internal Chinese report speculated: 'If a "political strongman" [read Deng] dies, it is possible that a situation like post-Tito Yugoslavia will emerge.' According to this report, 'In years, at the soonest a few and at the latest between 10 and 20, the country will move from economic collapse to political breakup, ending with its disintegration.'[60] Separately, a co-author of the above study wrote in English that the erosion of the central government's hold over financial resources has implied that 'the central state has lost its battle over the control of crucial political resources to competing local governments.'[61]

Outside China, the argument about the dangers of regional disintegration arising from the decentralisation of economic resources also appeared to have attained hegemony among commentators on Chinese developments. The World Bank, which had been a strong voice for decentralisation, became a major advocate for macro-economic control and for the centralisation of power in some areas, including fiscal reforms. The Bank was worried about the precipitous drop in central revenue as a percentage of GDP which had occurred with economic decentralisation.[62] A report of 6 November, 1993 in *The Economist* carried the title 'China – Can the Center Hold?' and suggested that the centre may be wobbling, lacking the courage to stand up to the boom provinces. In his *The Rise of China*, William H. Overholt wrote that the failure to mobilise sufficient revenues has historically been a key reason for the downfall of China's regimes and argued that China must solve the central government's tax problem which is caused by the decentralisation of resources to the provinces.[63] The Tofflers, futurists and self-styled China-aficionados, were even more straightforward:

> [The new elites in prosperous coastal provinces] are already thumbing their collective nose at economic edicts from Beijing's central government. How long before they decide they will no longer tolerate Beijing's political interference and refuse to contribute the funds needed by the central government to improve rural conditions or to put down agrarian unrest? Unless Beijing grants them complete freedom of financial and political action, one can imagine the new elites insisting on independence or some facsimile of it – a step that could tear China apart and trigger civil war.'[64]

While the reform of the fiscal reforms is ultimately a political decision, the near unanimity with which analysts both in China and abroad dissected China's fiscal problems undoubtedly contributed to the efforts by the Chinese leadership to push for fiscal reforms at the Third Plenum of the Fourteenth Central Committee held in late 1993.[65]

The Third Plenum and fiscal restructuring

The Third Plenum of the Fourteenth Central Committee unveiled an ambitious agenda geared toward transforming the Chinese economy into a *market* economy by the end of this century.[66] Even though much remains to be ironed out over the coming months or even years, and even if the agenda is only partially implemented, the plenum decision deserves careful examination for its fundamental implications for central–local relations. In addition, overhauls of the banking and fiscal systems should give the centre more sophisticated tools to adjust the economy.

According to the plenum decision, the government should withdraw from direct involvement in enterprise management. Instead, 'Government functions in economic management consist mainly of devising and implementing macro-economic control policies, appropriate construction of infrastructure facilities and creation of a favorable environment for economic development' [Art. 16]. Macro-economic control should rely primarily on market-oriented monetary and fiscal policies. This calls for the establishment of appropriate institutions such as a central bank which must not be simply the government's cashier but should actively monitor and regulate money supply. Thus the plenum declared that the government will in the near future 'take significant steps in the reform of the systems of taxation, financing, investment and planning, and establish a mechanism in which planning, banking and public finance are co-ordinated and mutually check each other while strengthening the overall coordination of economic operations' [Art. 17].

Of the major reforms, the reform of the fiscal and taxation systems bears directly on central–local relations. As spelt out in Article 18 of the plenum decision, reform in this area is intended to demarcate the tax control boundaries of local and central government and strengthen central government revenue. This means 'changing from the current fiscal contractual responsibility system of local authorities to a tax assignment system on the basis of a rational division of power between central and local authorities, and establishing separated central and local taxation systems.'[67] Though the full implications of the tax overhaul and fiscal restructuring may take years to be fully understood, the Chinese leadership hoped that the reform would 'gradually increase the per centage of fiscal income in the gross national product (GNP) and rationally determine the proportion between central and local fiscal income.' According to vice-minister of finance Xiang Huaicheng, the centre's share of state revenue should reach at least 60 per cent, with 40 per cent as central expenditure and 20 per cent as transfer grants to local governments.[68] In time, this would not only allow the centre to reduce the soaring budget deficits and have more resources for macro-economic control but would strengthen its regional development policy implementation through transfer payments in order to 'support the development of economically underdeveloped regions and the transformation of the old industrial bases.' Before the age of abundance dawns, however, the plenum called for strict controls over fiscal deficits and, when these cannot be avoided, they should be financed 'by issuing long and short-term government bonds rather than by overdrafts from the bank' [Art. 18].

Yet even with full implementation of the fiscal reforms, China's fiscal system will never again be as centralised as it was during the heyday of Maoism. The centre recognises the need not only to have local initiatives, given China's size and diversity, but also to coordinate them and rationally delineate the powers of the central and local authorities over economic administration. It is recognised that the control of economic resources alone is not enough. Thus in Article 21 the centre vigorously asserted its prerogatives over macro-economic management:

Powers of macro-economic control, which include power over the issuance of currency, the determination of benchmark interest rates, regulation of exchange rates and readjustment of the rates of major tax items, must be concentrated in the hands of the central government. This is necessary for maintaining the balance of economic aggregates, optimizing the economic structure and unifying the national market. [Art. 22]

What accounts for the formal adoption of sweeping fiscal and tax reforms in 1993? To answer this question requires understanding of the rapidly shifting macro-political context in China. Whereas the attempt by the Li Peng administration to rationalise the fiscal system fizzled out in 1990 amid multiple political jitters, by 1992 the psychology of the political participants had shifted with the re-ignition of the engine of economic growth. By now the central leaders had largely steadied their nerves, which had been rattled by the turmoil of summer 1989 and the shockwaves from the collapse of communist regimes in the Soviet Union and East Europe. In the meantime, an unintended but nonetheless striking impact of the 1988–90 austerity programme was to expose the weakening founda-tions of China's fiscal system and, as was discussed a little earlier, help foster a perception of fiscal crisis and a virtually unanimous intellectual atmosphere for rationalising the fiscal system. Among the leadership, the concern about the rising budget deficit had become so acute that the National People's Congress, in partnership with the Ministry of Finance, was actively considering the passage of a Budget Implementation Law, which would demand that deficits be avoided in both central public expenditures and local budgets.[69]

Against this background, instead of compelling potential succes-sors to dole out pork and compete with each other, as Shirk would have predicted, the impending political succession appeared to have imparted a growing sense of urgency in rebuilding the fiscal founda-tions for the central government.[70] In the words of one commentator: 'A key lesson that Mr Deng learned from the dissolution of the Communist parties of the former Eastern bloc was their failure to control the purse-strings'. Thus Deng Xiaoping's personal agenda for [the Third Plenum of 1993] was to bolster the political and economic powers of the Party Center and to ensure that his anointed successor, President Jiang Zemin, can then hold the fort after [Deng's] rendez-vous with Marx.'[71] As it turned out, all three leaders with respons-ibility for the economy – president Jiang Zemin, premier Li Peng, and vice-premier Zhu Rongji – chose to push for sweeping fiscal reforms.

While premier Li Peng, who was unable to push through the fiscal reforms in 1990 and appeared to remain committed to them, was on sick leave, the initial document was drafted under the supervision of Zhu Rongji. President Jiang Zemin then further expanded the scope of the reforms included in the document and reportedly decided to make the programme 'a grand social systems project for the establishment of a new economic structure'.[72]

Besides the succession factor, the macro-economic difficulties encountered by the Chinese government throughout 1992 and the limited success the Chinese leadership had with reining in economic overheating in 1993 also helped convince the top leadership that speedy and fundamental changes were necessary to deal with the structural problems facing the Chinese economy.[73] Meanwhile, with expectations of brighter economic prospects, local officials appeared to be more willing to make concessions.[74] Any fundamental restructuring of central–local fiscal relations must involve compromise and accommodation between centre and localities; it would be wrong to interpret this dynamic relationship as zero-sum. The fiscal restructuring of 1993 was no exception. Right through the November plenary meeting of the Party Central Committee, there were reports based on sources within the Chinese government that the plan to produce a new tax structure strengthening the central government's fiscal foundations had been 'shelved because of provincial opposition', leaving 'the thorny issue of relations between the central government and the provinces' unresolved.[75] In reality, the central leadership chose to focus on rebuilding the fiscal foundations of the central government on which the survival of the system ultimately rested, even though this meant displeasing some provincial and ministerial officials. To be sure, there was compromise in which the provinces were allowed to keep what they already had and only had to share with the centre more of the added revenue stream in the future. Over the long run, however, subject to the implementation of the reforms, the centre expects to gain greater capacity to manage China's economy.

Factors favouring the centre

It is instructive to examine the factors which made it possible for the central leadership to bring sub-national officials onto the bandwagon of fiscal reform. Three factors are especially important. First, there is a powerful Party norm against factionalism or the building of open alliances or blocs on specific policy issues. Thus organisationally, local officials can rarely present a united front against the centre. Even if each of the sub-national officials had come to the conclusion that fiscal rationalisation would be less advantageous to them, some of them might still be willing to agree with the centre in order to curry political favour or obtain some other political goods. For a lower-ranked local official sitting face-to-face with a top-ranked central leader who has great resources and sanctions, such temptation may be especially strong. Jiang Zemin and Zhu Rongji made extensive trips to the provinces to convince individual local officials to accept the new tax and fiscal arrangements. One analyst even commented that vice-premier Zhu Rongji had one-on-one sessions with the local chieftains because 'Mr Zhu dared not call a large meeting of the "warlords" lest the latter gang up on him.'[76]

Secondly, since the fiscal reforms would promote a sounder macro-economic environment, their effect potentially would benefit all the localities. Because macro-economic stability is a public good, however, each of the local players has incentives to contribute as little as possible while still enjoying the benefits of the public good to be produced. But the impact of the fiscal reforms in terms of macro-economic stability and regional policy will have a differential impact on different localities. To begin with, all other things being equal and assuming an integrated economy, a high growth and high inflation environment mean that faster-growing areas export inflation to areas that grow more slowly. In other words, interior officials would like the centre to do more to establish macro-economic order. Moreover, because fiscal reforms would also potentially put more resources in the hands of the centre, it appears that many officials in the poorer interior would also welcome them more than officials in richer coastal provinces. The centre could count on such regional cleavages in seeking support for fiscal reforms.

Cleavages among local officials can also be found within certain provincial administrations. It is a well-known fact that the party secretary and provincial governor within a single provincial unit compete against each other, and a number of the personnel changes in recent years were made to reduce such internal tensions within provincial administrations.[77] The lack of political cohesion within a locality has tended to undermine the locality's degree of autonomy and administrative efficiency and invite central intervention.

Thirdly, central leaders possess powerful resources and sanctions in dealing with sub-national officials. Of course, party norms and discipline have declined under the reforms and the legitimacy of party rule has been severely eroded by abuses of power, especially the widespread incidence of corruption. Nevertheless, the Party centre continues to possess powerful resources vis-à-vis subnational officials. The most important of the sanctions is the power of appointment and removal of provincial-level leaders through the nomenklatura system.[78] The CCP has from time to time transferred provincial leaders laterally in order to avoid their becoming too attached to parochial local interests, even though most provincial leaders now tend to be natives or to have worked for extensive periods in the province of their appointment. On fundamental issues, those local cadres who stick their necks out against the centre may see their power reduced. Thus it is hardly surprising that in preparation for the Central Committee plenum of November 1993, the Party Centre rotated and retired a significant number of provincial party secretaries and governors and that 'quite a few regional politicians were dumped for rubbing up Beijing the wrong way'.[79] The most prominent case occurred in Jiangsu, China's richest province, where Zhu Rongji reportedly had heated arguments with Shen Daren and Chen Huanyou about the shape of the fiscal reforms. This was believed to have been a major reason why She Daren lost his job as Jiangsu party secretary in October 1993.[80]

In view of the three factors identified here, the central leadership may be expected to take a two-pronged approach to secure the cooperation of local officials. (1) Display unity; demonstrate resolve by removing recalcitrant local officials if necessary. (2) Divide and rule. This may be divided into two aspects: (a) negotiate with local officials individually; (b) target potential local resisters, especially those who are known to seek greater local autonomy, and persuade them publicly to support the centre early, thus providing cues to officials in other localities suggesting the desirability of jumping on to the policy bandwagon.

Besides following tactics 1 and 2a, the central leadership also applied tactic 2b. In the early 1980s, Guangdong entered into a fiscal arrangement with the centre whereby Guangdong remitted 1.17 billion *yuan* per year to the centre and retained the rest. This arrangement was adopted because at the time Guangdong was relatively backward (especially compared to Shanghai, which remitted ten times as much to the centre), had been starved of central investment throughout the Maoist era because it was on the military front, and was encouraged to experiment with the reforms. However, after a decade of buoyant growth, Guangdong became the focus of jealousy by provinces that had been on other types of fiscal arrangement, especially Shanghai. Speculation has been rife about Guangdong's growing autonomy. In reality Guangdong had in the meantime increased the amount of money it handed over to the centre. In 1990, for example, Guangdong remitted 3.83 billion *yuan* to the central treasury. In addition, while at the beginning of the reforms enterprises in Guangdong under the jurisdiction of the centre provided only 0.44 billion *yuan* to the centre, in 1990 they remitted 10.96 billion.[81] Altogether, Guangdong by the early 1990s was contributing just as much to the central treasury as did Shanghai.[82]

In preparing for the Third Plenum of 1993, central leaders apparently targeted Guangdong to provide an example for other localities. While Guangdong leaders Xie Fei and Zhu Senlin are well-known for towing the centre's line, they reportedly were reluctant at first to meet the tax demands made by Zhu Rongji. Nevertheless, they agreed to the new plan when president Jiang Zemin met with them face-to-face.[83] At the plenum, Zhu Rongji reportedly praised Guangdong for having 'played a great leading role in the current financial and banking structural reform, and that it was the model for submission by the part to the whole.'[84]

Drawing on its organisational advantages and significant political resources, the centre was able to obtain formal agreement for a programme for fiscal rationalisation at the Third Plenum of 1993. In the process of negotiations, however, the centre compromised with local interests. In fact, the central–local negotiations took place with the understanding on both sides that neither excessive centralisation nor excessive decentralisation was desirable. Thus president Jiang Zemin pointed out that while central authorities must persevere with the fiscal reforms, 'there should not be excessively big changes in the balance and distribution of interests between the center and the localities, or in the relationship in the apportionment [of profits] between the state and enterprises.'[85] During the Third Plenum, Jiang reportedly stated that 'the central authorities must take local authorities' difficulties into consideration, while the latter must foster awareness of keeping the situation as a whole in mind and must define the principle of the whole caring for the part and the part submitting to the whole.'[86]

The grand bargain that resulted from the Third Plenum reflected the reciprocal interests of the centre and the provinces.[87] The centre – in a concession – allowed the affected parties (including taxpayers and enterprises, for that matter) to keep all the money they already received, but in the future the centre would expect to receive more of the increased revenues, thus boosting the share of central revenue as a percentage of GNP over a period of time rather than immediately.[88]

In the words of finance minister Liu Zhongli: 'The tax burdens of enterprises as a whole will remain basically unchanged, and the interests of localities will be guaranteed.'[89] Likewise Vice Finance Minister Jin Renqing pledged that 'the vested interests of these [coastal] provinces will be protected' and that the fiscal reform 'won't dampen their incentives' to expand their economies.[90] The centre's strategy is not to redivide the existing pie but to capture more of the growing part of the pie through a realignment of revenue base and through a broadening of the taxation base.

The corollary of the grand bargain between centre and provinces is that, since revenue expansion crucially depends on vigorous economic growth and that revenue would slump in an economic slow-down, the centre has every incentive to keep the economy humming along rather than slam hard on the brakes as it did in 1989–90. This partly explains why the macro-economic adjustment measures of 1993, which started in June, were rapidly eased ahead of the central committee plenary meeting in November. In short, the grand bargain implies an inflationary bias for China's economic policy. Indeed, although in mid-1993 the Chinese leadership launched a macro-economic adjustment programme, by September they had turned to promoting high-speed growth in preparation for the Third Plenum, since economic boom would soften local opposition to redistributive reforms. Some of China's most zealous reformers reportedly contended that economic growth must be kept high and unemployment kept to a minimum in order to overcome political resistance to the reforms from entrenched interests.[91] In fact, while vice-premier Zhu Rongji presided over the macro-economic adjustment programme, it was he who began the shift from austerity to high growth in late September when state-owned enterprises and other businesses complained bitterly.[92] Not surprisingly, this came at a time when Zhu was intensively drumming up support for the Third Plenum decisions.

Assuming that extremely high growth is unsustainable, then the short-term effect of the grand bargain may be to accentuate such hyper-growth. With growing inflation, declining financial confidence, and other sources of instability, however, this short-term effect of growth at all costs may increase the likelihood that a severe economic retrenchment will eventually occur when the government is forced to take harsh austerity measures. In other words, the grand bargain may have the unintended result of increasing the magnitude of China's economic swings, which may in turn increase the chances of major social unrest. Indeed, the easing of the economic readjustment programme prior to the Third Plenum led Zhu Rongji to concede at year-end that economic overheating had not yet been controlled.[93] In the meantime, in the aftermath of the plenum, anticipations that the tax reforms would lead to higher prices led to panic buying of electronic goods and staple goods and further fuelled the rapid price inflation at the year-end. Grain prices soared more than 30 per cent in various parts of the coastal region even though the 1993 grain harvest was a good one. And the government was forced to intervene and reintroduce price controls for food items in Beijing and several other cities.[94] The grand bargain also puts the burden of uncertainty squarely on the centre. Whereas the aim of the fiscal rationalisation is to increase the share of revenue the centre receives, there is no guarantee that the far-reaching institutional changes can be implemented according to plan and, if so, they will meet the specified revenue goals.

CONCLUSIONS

As China confronts a future without Deng, a recurrent question about the future of Chinese politics is whether the centre can hold itself against the centrifugal forces. In spite of having presided over an outstanding record of economic growth over the last fifteen years, the Chinese leadership in the post-communist world order face multi-faceted challenges, including ethnic tensions, fears of military intervention, societal disaffection, as well as accidental events such as the order of deaths of the patriarchs.

It would seem that though the share of fiscal resources under the direct control of the centre has declined since the mid-1980s and that the Chinese economy has suffered from bouts of macro-economic instabilities, these should not be interpreted to mean that the centre has inexorably lost control over resources. Leaving aside the point that the centre and localities are not necessarily engaged in a zero-sum game and that local governments do not constitute a solid block, it is quite crude to use the relative distribution of fiscal resources as *the* indicator of the relative power of centre vs. localities, since they fail to capture the political dimension of resource distribution between centre and localities.

Of course, should the changing pattern of relative resource distribution between the centre and localities become permanent, then it would certainly signal a major realignment of power between them. However, there is no reason to believe a temporary drop in the centre's share of resources is a permanent drop. It can be argued that those who emphasised the diabolic consequences of China's fiscal crisis have helped to concentrate the attention of the central leadership, thus providing the intellectual impetus for the adoption of systematic fiscal reforms in late 1993 intended to readjust the distribution of resources between the centre and localities.

To be sure, the implementation of the fiscal and other reforms is fraught with uncertainties, since there will not only be administrative leakage but the full implications of the reforms cannot be accurately predicted.[95] In fact, the stipulation that the local revenue base for the future will be based on the 1993 revenue figures prompted local governments to collect as much revenue as possible in 1993, in some places even collecting part of the 1994 revenue to count as 1993 revenue.

China is going through a set of fundamental transformations. In the short run, rapid economic growth and apparent prosperity may legitimise the regime and divert attention from demands for the formal trappings of political participation. The rhetoric of disintegration, fragmentation, and warlordism as well as international pressures may serve as justification for continuing authoritarian rule. Yet either because of economic crises or because of the achievement of economic prosperity, growth under authoritarian rule cannot be sustained indefinitely. Sometime in the future, the Chinese will have to grapple with the constitutional issue of how to reconstitute political power and authority on sounder moral foundations.

NOTES

1 Edmund Burke, *Reflections on the Revolution in France*, edited by Connor C. O'Brien (Harmondsworth: Penguin Books, 1969), p. 351.
2 Madeleine Zelin, *The Magistrate's Tale: Rationalizing Fiscal Reform in Eighteenth-Century Ch'ing China* (Berkeley: University of California Press, 1984).
3 Unless otherwise indicated, fiscal data for this study come from Ministry of Finance, *Zhongguo caizheng tongji 1950–1991* (China finance statistics, 1950–1991) (Beijing: Kexue chubanshe, 1992). The data for Figure 3.1 come from this volume, pp. 319–320 and State Statistical Bureau, *Zhongguo tongji nianjian 1992* (Statistical yearbook of China 1992, hereafter *ZGTJNJ 1992*), pp. 31–32. Foreign borrowing has been excluded from budgetary revenues.
4 For the sake of comparison, I assume here that GNP and GDP figures are roughly the same in the case of China.
5 A recent survey by *The Economist* (25 December 1993, p. 39) had the following estimate of total tax as percentage of GDP in 1991: Brazil (75), Sweden (50), Hungary (50), China (45), Russia (40), France (41), Germany (39), Canada (36), Britain (36), Japan (30), United States (27), Australia (27), Mexico (18), South Korea (16), India (14).

6 Compared with other formerly socialist economies, China's extractive capacity was always much lower. The ratios of fiscal expenditure as a percentage of national income were as follows for 1975, 1980 and 1983 respectively: China (32.8, 32.9, 27.3), USSR (59.0, 63.7, 64.6); Poland (52.0, 62.6, 44.8); Hungary (79.8, 73.3, 74.5); Bulgaria (64.3, 64.4, 71.1). This comparison suggests that as far as state extractive capacity is concerned, it is not 'the more, the merrier'. Indeed, one suspects that China's lower state extractive capacity partly explains why the Chinese reforms have been more dynamic than in the other countries. The data used here are taken from Zhang Fengbo, ed., *Zhongguo hongguan jingji jiegou yu zhengce* (China's macroeconomic structure and policies) (Beijing: Zhongguo caizheng jingji chubanshe, 1988), p. 158.

7 See, for example, p. 352 of *Reflections on the Revolution in France*: 'the prosperity and improvement of nations has generally increased with the increase of their revenues; and they will both continue to grow and flourish, as long as the balance between what is left to strengthen the efforts of individuals, and what is collected for the common efforts of the state, bear to each other a due reciprocal proportion, and are kept in a close correspondence and communication.'

8 For summary discussions of these issues, see Etienne Balazs, *Political Theory and Administrative Reality in Traditional China* (London: School of Oriental and African Studies, University of London, 1965); Min Tu-ki, *National Polity and Local Power: The Transformation of Late Imperial China*, edited by Philip Kuhn and Timothy Brook (Cambridge, MA: Council on East Asian Studies/Harvard University and the Harvard–Yenching Institute, 1989), chapter 4.

9 For Mao's discussion of the relationship between the centre and the regions in his 'On the Ten Great Relationships', see Stuart Schram, ed., *Chairman Mao Talks to the People* (New York: Pantheon, 1974), pp. 71–73.

10 See Nicholas Lardy, 'Centralization and Decentralization in China's Fiscal Management', *China Quarterly*, no. 61 (March 1975), pp. 26–60; Audrey Donnithorne, 'Centre-Provincial Economic Relations in China', *Contemporary China Papers*, no. 16 (Canberra: Contemporary China Centre, Australian National University, 1981); Michel Oksenberg and James Tong, 'The Evolution of Central–Provincial Fiscal Relations in China, 1971–1984: The Formal System', *China Quarterly*, no. 125 (March 1991), pp. 1–32; Christine Wong, 'Central–Local Relations in an Era of Fiscal Decline: The Paradox of Fiscal Decentralisation in Post-Mao China', *China Quarterly*, no. 128 (December 1991), pp. 691–715; and Jia Hao and Lin Zhimin, eds, *Changing Central–Local Relations in China: Reform and State Capacity* (Boulder, CO: Westview Press, 1994). For Chinese studies, see especially *Dangdai Zhongguo caizheng* (Contemporary China's finance) (Beijing: Zhongguo shehui kexue chubanshe, 1988), two volumes.

11 See especially Oksenberg and Tong, 'The Evolution of Central–Provincial Fiscal Relations in China, 1971–1984', and World Bank, *China: Revenue Mobilization and Tax Policy* (Washington, D.C.: The World Bank, 1990).

12 Contrast this trend with Wang Shaoguang, 'Central–Local Fiscal Politics in China', in Jia Hao and Lin Zhimin, eds, *Changing Central–Local*

92   *Dali Yang*

Relations in China, p. 98. Note also that the pattern of relative shares does not change much if we reconstruct the revenues by excluding government borrowing. See Christine Wong, 'Central–Local Relations in an Era of Fiscal Decline', p. 700.

13 For example, State Statistical Bureau, *ZGTJNJ 1992*, p. 227.

14 Christine Wong, 'Central–Local Relations in an Era of Fiscal Decline', p. 704.

15 The source of data for figures 3.1 and 3.2 is *ZGTJNJ 1992*, p. 228. Foreign borrowing has been excluded from state budget revenue.

16 Deng Yingtao, Yao Gang, Xu Xiaobo and Xue Yuwei, *Zhongguo yusuanwai zijin fenxi* (An analysis of extra-budgetary funds in China) (Beijing: Zhongguo renmin daxue chubanshe, 1990), p. 23.

17 The dispersion of extra-budgetary funds has contributed to China's macro-economic difficulties in recent years not because of these funds *per se* but because of the lack of adequate institutions for macro-economic control in an increasingly market-oriented economy. Local governments are to blame only to the extent that they obstructed the construction and operation of such institutions.

18 Wang Shaoguang, 'Central–Local Fiscal Politics in China', p. 99.

19 Cited in Barry Naughton, 'Implications of the State Monopoly Over Industry and its Relaxation' *Modern China*, vol. 18, no. 1 (January 1992), p. 40. note 8.

20 Calculated from World Bank, *China: Reform and the Role of the Plan in the 1990s* (Washington, D.C.: The World Bank, 1992), p. 239.

21 State Statistical Bureau, *ZGTJNJ 1992*, p. 231.

22 Data on other years are presently unavailable.

23 Barry Naughton, 'Implications of the State Monopoly over Industry and its Relaxation', *Modern China*, vol. 18, no. 1 (January 1992), pp. 14–41; on the regional implications of this system, see Dali L. Yang, 'Reforms, Resources, and Regional Cleavages: The Political Economy of Coast-Interior Cleavages in China', *Issues and Studies*, vol. 27, no. 9 (September 1991), pp. 43–69; for an overall description of the Chinese taxation arrangements up to the late 1980s, see Jinyan Li, *Taxation in the People's Republic of China* (New York: Praeger, 1991).

24 The non-state businesses tend to be smaller than state enterprises and thus require more administrative effort to tax. As befitting any developing country, tax evasion has become a particularly vexing problem.

25 Barry Naughton, 'Implications of the State Monopoly over Industry and its Relaxation', p. 33.

26 For an analysis of the budget, see Christine Wong, 'Central–Local Relations in an Era of Fiscal Decline'.

27 The budget figures are from Liu Zhongli, 'Guanyu 1992 nian guojia yusuan zhixing qingkuang he 1993 nian guojia yusuan cao'an de baogao' (Report on the implementation of the 1992 state budget and the draft 1993 state budget), *Xinhua yuebao* (New China monthly), no. 4 (1993), pp. 29–30.

28 See Ann Markusen, Peter Hall, Scott Campbell and Sabina Deitrick, *The Rise of the Gunbelt: The Military Remapping of Industrial America* (New York: Oxford University Press, 1991).

29 Barry Naughton, 'The Decline of Central Control over Investment in

Post-Mao China', in David Lampton, ed., *Policy Implementation in Post-Mao China* (Berkeley: University of California Press, 1987), pp. 57–79, quote on 51.

30 Space limit does not permit me to elaborate. For a more extended treatment, see Dali L. Yang, 'Policy Credibility and Macroeconomic Control in China', paper delivered at the American Political Science Association Annual Meeting, The Washington Hilton, September 2–5, 1993

31 Peter Ferdinand, 'The Economic and Financial Dimension', in David S.G. Goodman, ed., *China's Regional Development* (London: Routledge, 1989), p. 38.

32 Michael Oksenberg and James Tong, 'The Evolution of Central–Provincial Fiscal Relations in China, 1971–1984', p. 3.

33 Richard Goode, 'Obstacles to Tax Reform in Developing Countries', in Richard Bird and Oliver Oldman, eds., *Taxation in Developing Countries*, 4th edn (Baltimore: Johns Hopkins University Press, 1990), p. 121; for a classic discussion of this and related issues, see W. Arthur Lewis, *Theory of Economic Growth* (London: Allen & Unwin, 1955).

34 Susan Shirk, *The Political Logic of Economic Reform in China*, (Berkeley: University of California Press, 1993), p. 191.

35 *Ibid.*, p. 192.

36 Deng turned 89 in 1993. The life expectancy at birth in China as of 1991 was 69.

37 Richard Goode, 'Obstacles to Tax Reform in Developing Countries', p. 124.

38 *Ibid.*, p. 128.

39 These essays are collected in Xue Muqiao, *Bashi niandai de zhongguo jingji* (The Chinese economy in the 1980s) (Beijing: Jingji guanli chuanshe, 1992). Unless otherwise noted, all references to Xue's writings in this section are to this volume.

40 *ibid.*, pp. 13–14.

41 *ibid.*, pp. 24–26, quote on 24.

42 Cambridge: Cambridge University Press, 1991.

43 Xue Muqiao, *Bashi niandai de zhongguo jingji*, p. 36.

44 *Ibid.*, pp. 51, 59, 65–67, 81, 84.

45 Shi Xiaomin and Liu Jirui, 'Jingji xuejia shouxian yao zunzhong lishi he shishi' (Economists should first of all respect history and facts), *Jingji yanjiu* (Economic research), no. 2 (1989), p. 12.

46 David Bachman, 'The Ministry of Finance and Chinese Politics', *Pacific Affairs*, vol. 62, no. 2 (Summer 1989), pp. 167–87, esp. 178–79.

47 Zheng Yi, *Zhu Rongji pingzhuan* (A biography of Zhu Rongji) (Hong Kong: Mingchuang chubanshe, 1992), pp. 179–80.

48 Xue Muqiao, *Lun Zhongguo jingji tizhi gaige* (On reforming China's economic system) (Tianjin: Tianjin renmin chubanshe, 1990), pp. 420–24.

49 Xue Muqiao, *Bashi niandai de zhongguo jingji*, pp. 91–92.

50 In a number of areas such as currency and price reforms, the economic conditions for reform were excellent but Chinese leaders were clearly afraid of major moves and later regretted the missed opportunities. At the time, the official and black-market currency exchange rates were converging and inflation was falling partly owing to the austerity programme

and partly owing to the impact of the military crackdown on consumer expectations.

51 Cf. Robert Delfs, 'Saying No to Peking', *Far Eastern Economic Review*, April 4, 1991, pp. 21–22.

52 For an overview of the Chinese debate on fiscal issues, see Lu Dongtao and Xu Yan, *Gaige lilun fengyun lu* (Storms over reform theories) (Beijing: Beijing yanshan chubanshe, 1993), pp. 250–87.

53 Zhang Zhenbin, 'Chongjian yi shangpin jingji wei jichu de caizheng tizhi' (Reconstruct the fiscal system on the basis of a commodity economy), *Jingji yanjiu*, no. 10 (1988), pp. 27–31.

54 Zhang Zhenbin, 'Zhongguo tonghuo pengzhang de caizheng fenzi' (A fiscal analysis of China's inflation), *Jingji yanjiu*, no. 5 (1989), pp. 41–45; Wang Shouchun, Zhang Guoping and Li Changyu, 'Zouzhu dierci digu: caizheng shoulu zhan guomin shoulu bizhong xiadie wenti de yanjiu' (Out of the second trough: a study of the decline of fiscal revenue as a ratio of national income), *Jingji yanjiu*, no. 12 (1989), pp. 37–43.

55 Shen Liren and Dai Yuanchen, 'Woguo "zhuhou jingji" de xingcheng jiqi biduan he genyuan' (The formation, adverse consequences, and roots of 'duke-style economies' in our country), *Jingji yanjiu*, no. 3 (1990), pp. 12–20; Wu Minyi, 'Guanyu difang zhengfu xingwei de ruogan sikao' (Reflections on local government behaviour), *Jingji yanjiu*, no. 7 (1990), pp. 56–60; Wang Xuefeng, 'Ye tan caizheng shoulu zhan guomin shoulu bizhong xiajiang wenti' (Another look at the declining ratio of fiscal revenue to national income), *Jingji yanjiu*, no. 4 (1990), pp. 51–53; Wu Zhengrong, 'Guanyu caizheng shoulu zhan guomin shoulu de bizhong wenti' (On the ratio of fiscal revenue to national income), *Jingji yanjiu*, no. 12 (1990), pp. 42–45; Zhang Jun, 'Lun woguo xian jieduan de caizheng kunjing' (On the fiscal dilemmas faced by contemporary China), *Jingji yanjiu*, no. 12 (1990), pp. 46–50.

56 For book-length discussions of the need for fiscal reforms, see Han Yingjie, Du Lingfeng and Yang Xiuqin, eds, *Zhongguo xianxing shuishou zhidu* (China's current taxation system) (Beijing: Zhongguo renmin daxue chubanshe, 1989); Liu Guoguang, *Gaige, wending, fazhan* (Reform, stability and development) (Beijing: Jingji guanli chubanshe, 1991); Song Xinzhong, ed., *Zhongguo caizheng tizhi gaige yanjiu* (Studies on the reform of China's fiscal system) (Beijing: Zhongguo caizheng jingji chubanshe, 1992); Wang Shaofei, ed., *Jiushi niandai Zhongguo shuizhi gaige shexiang* (Tentative plans for reforming China's tax system in the 1990s) (Beijing: Zhongguo caizheng jingji chubanshe, 1990); Zhou Xiaochuan and Yang Zhigang, *Zhongguo caishui tizhi de wenti yu chulu* (Problems in China's fiscal and taxation system and their solutions) (Tianjin: Tianjin renmin chubanshe, 1992); Zhang Zhuoyuan and Huang Fanzhang, eds, *Zhongguo shinian jingi gaige lilun tansuo* (Theoretical explorations into China's ten-year economic reform) (Beijing: Zhongguo jihua chubanshe, 1991), esp. pp. 197–212.

57 Chen Yuan, 'Woguo jingji de shenceng wenti he xuanze (gangyao)' (The deep problems and choices of our country's economy), *Jingji yanjiu*, no. 4 (1991), pp. 18–26, quote on p. 18.

58 Cambridge, MA: Harvard University Press, 1991.

59 Wang Xingyi, 'Caishui gaige shi zai bixing' (Reforms of finance and taxation are imperative), *Jingji ribao*, September 4, 1993, pp. 1–2.

60 Wang Shoguang and Hu Angang, 'Strengthening Central Government's Leading Role amid the Shift to a Market Economy'. Quote from report by AFP, September 20, 1993, FBIS-CHI-93-180, September 10, 1993, p. 19. For an openly published version of this study, see Wang Shaoguang and Hu Angang, 'Zhongguo zhengfu jiqu mengli de xiajiang jiqi houguo' (The decline of the Chinese government's extractive capacity and its consequences), *Ershiyi shiji* (Twenty-first century), no. 21 (February 1994), pp. 5–14. I have contributed a critique in the same issue. See also Shuangyi, 'Xuezhe xiance, quanzhe juece' (Scholars propose, power-holders decide), *Zhongguo shibao zhoukan* (China Times Weekly), 17 October 1993, pp. 16–18.

The above view is also found in a review by Gerald Segal of a biography of Deng Xiaoping for *The Economist* (30 October 1993, p. 104): 'Mr. Deng will soon pass on to meet Marx and Mao in the communist heaven. As is commonly the case with great and ruthless leaders, he leaves no one with real authority to govern the country. In the absence of a strong successor, China may well slip back to the fragmentation and chaos of Mr Deng's early years [i.e. the early 20th century].'

In his November speech in Hong Kong, George Bush also referred to this view (and argued against it): 'Some see a China torn by internal divisions – with region pitted against region – something that in my view would be disastrous – divided as it was in the 1920s, the 1850s, way back before then.' This suggests that the disintegration view is a common refrain among the policy elites in the US. Richard Vines, 'China's New Rich Bring Change', *South China Morning Post*, 20 November 1993, p. 3.

For report on the views of the dissident Yan Jiaqi, who pointed to the possibility of civil war after the death of Deng Xiaoping, see Zhang Weiguo, 'Jiang "Faces Challenge of Civil War after Deng"' *South China Morning Post*, 7 December 1993.

61 Wang Shaoguang, 'Central–Local Fiscal Politics in China', p. 92.

62 'China – Can the Centre Hold?' *The Economist*, 6 November 1993, p. 32.

63 William H. Overholt, *The Rise of China* (New York: Norton, 1993).

64 Alvin Toffler and Heidi Toffler, *War and Anti-War: Survival at the Dawn of the 21st Century* (New York: Little Brown and Company, 1993), p. 214. While he termed it a 'realistic possibility that China will be able to sustain its boom for decades to come', Nicholas Kristof, former Beijing Bureau Chief for *The New York Times*, suggested that '[m]ilitary coups, chaos and even civil war are all possibilities in China over the next dozen years'. Nicholas Kristof, 'The Rise of China', *Foreign Affairs*, vol. 72, no. 5 (November 1993), p. 60.

65 On the importance of such intellectual arguments for reforms in other countries, see John Williamson, ed., *The Political Economy of Policy Reform* (Washington, D.C.: Institute for International Economics, 1994).

66 All references to the Plenum decision shall be to 'Decision of the CPC Central Committee on Issues Concerning the Establishment of a Socialist Market Economic Structure (14 November 1993)', *China Daily* (Supplement), 17 November 1993.

67 According to the Plenum decision (Art. 18) and the Ministry of Finance

96   *Dali Yang*

[*ibid.*], the major taxes and responsibilities shall be allocated as follows. The central government is responsible for funding national defence, diplomacy, armed police, key state projects, the national deficit and governmental administrative departments, while other expenditures shall be the responsibility of local governments. Central revenue will come from tariffs, a consumption tax collected by customs, value-added taxes and (nationally-based) business taxes. Taxes collected by local governments include business tax, income tax of local enterprises and a personal income tax. Taxes shared by both central and local governments include the value-added tax (3:1), securities trading tax (1:1) and natural resources tax (TBA). In other words, the centre will rely on indirect taxes, leaving the politically hazardous and administratively cumbersome personal income tax to local authorities. Moreover, it appears that some extra-budgetary revenue will likely be refined as budgetary revenue for local authorities.

68 'Tax Reform Aims to Direct Revenue to State Coffers', *China Daily*, 25 November 1993, p. 4.
69 'Budget Implementation Law Deliberated', Xinhua in English, 22 October 1993 FBIS-CHI-93–203, 22 October 1993, p. 19.
70 Cf. 'Central Leadership Moving to "Bolster" Power', *South China Morning Post*, 2 November 1993, p. 1, FBIS-CHI-93-210, 2 November 1993, pp. 30–31.
71 Willy Wo-Lap Lam, 'Plenum's Push for Growth Masks a Power Scramble', *South China Morning Post*, 20 November 1993, p. 11.
72 For more details about the process that led to making the Third Plenum document such an ambitious programme, see Zou Aiguo and Zheng Qingdong, 'Maixiang xinshiji de hongwei gangling' (A monumental blueprint for the new century), *RMRB*, overseas ed., 23 December 1993, pp. 1 and 3; Huang Yao-hua, 'Third Plenary Session of 14th CPC Central Committee to be Moved up to November', *Lien Ho Pao*, 5 October 1993, p. 10, FBIS-CHI-93-191, 5 October 1993, p. 19; Chen Chien-ping, 'Inside Story of Drafting Third Plenary Session's Decision', *Wen Wei Po*, 24 November 1993, p. 2, FBIS-CHI-93-228, 30 November 1993, pp. 21–22; for the positions of liberal economist/policy-makers, see Willy Wo-lap Lam, ' "Ferocious Debate" Over Economic Reforms', *South China Morning Post*, 19 October 1993, p. 7, FBIS-CHI-93-200, 19 October 1993, pp. 10–11.
73 Julia Leung and Kathy Chen, 'China Endorses Swift Market Reform, Signals Privatisation', *Dow Jones News*, 15 November 1993; for a discussion of the political economy of macroeconomic adjustment, with special references to 1993, see Dali Yang, 'Policy Credibility and Macroeconomic Control in China'.
74 For writings on Chinese bureaucratic politics, see Kenneth Lieberthal and Michel Oksenberg, *Policy Making in China: Leaders, Structures, and Processes* (Princeton: Princeton University Press, 1988): David Lampton, 'Chinese Politics: The Bargaining Treadmill', *Issues and Studies*, vol. 23 (March 1987), pp. 1–30; and Kenneth Lieberthal and David Lampton, eds, *Bureaucracy, Politics, and Decision Making in Post-Mao China* (Berkeley: University of California Press, 1992).

75 'The Party Draws up Blueprint for China's Future Market Economy', UPI, 14 November 1993.

76 Willy Wo-Lap Lam, 'Strange Case of the Missing Economic Czar with Nothing to Lose', *South China Morning Post*, 11 December 1993, p. 6.

77 He Pin, 'Difang zhuhou longhu dou' (Local dukes fight each other), *Zhongguo shibao zhoukan* (China Times Weekly), 7 November 1993, pp. 21–23.

78 John P. Burns, ed., *The Chinese Communist Party's Nomenklatura System* (Armonk, N.Y.: M.E. Sharpe, 1989). The election of candidates not previously approved by the centre does not appear to have put a dent in this control, since the election was in any case several steps removed from the popular vote.

79 Willy Wo-Lap Lam, 'Plenum's Push for Growth Masks a Power Scramble'. In tandem with the changes in civilian leaders, there has also been a series of reshuffles in the People's Liberation Army.

80 Willy Wo-Lap Lam, 'Strange Case of the Missing Economic Czar with Nothing to Lose'.

81 Wang Zhigang, *Zouxiang shichang jingji de Zhongguo* (China makes transition to a market economy) (Guangzhou: Guangdong l'uyou chubanshe, 1993), p. 135.

82 On Shanghai, see the chapter by Bruce Jacobs and Likiang Hong in this volume.

83 Willy Wo-Lap Lam, 'Strange Case of the Missing Economic Czar with Nothing to Lose', *South China Morning Post*, 11 December 1993, p. 6.

84 Chen Chien-ping, 'At the Third Plenary Session, Jiang Zemin Talked About Implementation of the Plenary Session's Decision, Urging Seizure of Favorable Opportunity to Speed Up, Deepen Reform', *Wen Wei Po*, 29 November 1993, p. 2, FBIS-CHI-93–228, 30 November 1993, p. 23.

85 Willy Wo-Lap Lam, 'Talks to Air Divisions Over Reform', *South China Morning Post*, 27 November 1993, p. 6.

86 Chen Chien-ping, 'At the Third Plenary Session, Jiang Zemin Talked About Implementation of the Plenary Session's Decision, Urging Seizure of Favorable Opportunity to Speed Up, Deepen Reform'.

87 Cf. David Lampton, 'A Plum for a Peach: Bargaining, Interest, and Bureaucratic Politics in China', in Kenneth Lieberthal and David Lampton, eds, *Bureaucracy, Politics, and Decision Making in Post-Mao China*, (Berkeley: University of California Press, 1992), pp. 33–58.

88 In actual implementation, some enterprises may have to pay more in taxes than they did while others less.

89 'Taxation Reform a Gradual Process', *China Daily*, 18 November 1993, p. 1.

90 Julia Leung, 'Minister Says Beijing, Provinces Have Reached Consensus on Adoption of Tax-Sharing System', *Asian Wall Street Journal Weekly*, 25 October 1993, p. 3.

91 'Report Shows Beijing Debating Whether to Slow a Hot Economy', *The Washington Post*, 2 December 1993.

92 'China Unveils Package of Productivity Reforms', *South China Morning Post*, Business Post, 11 December 1993, p. 1.

93 A researcher at the Commission for Restructuring the Economic System had this to say about the easing of credit prior to the Plenum: 'The period

immediately before a party plenum is a time for compromise . . . Rising debt, restrictions on how freely local officials could play the real-estate markets, credit limits – none of this helps when you're trying to get the provinces to pay more taxes and obey central policies.' Quoted in Carl Goldstein, 'Growth at Any Costs', *Far Eastern Economic Review*, 25 November 1993, p. 16.

94 'Inflation Darkens China's Growth', AP, 28 December 1993; Dan Biers, 'Chinese, Worried About New Taxes, Snapping Up Electronics', AP, 15 December 1993; Julia Leung and Joseph Kahn, 'Beijing Sets New Ceilings On Food Prices', *Dow Jones News*, 22 December 1993.

95 On tax evasion and tax compliance, see Frank Cowell, *Cheating the Government* (Cambridge, MA: The MIT Press, 1990); Richard Gordon Jr., 'Income Tax Compliance and Sanctions in Developing Countries: An Outline of Issues', *Bulletin for International Fiscal Documentation*, vol. 42 (1988), pp. 3–12; S. Richupan, 'Measuring Tax Evasion', *Finance and Development*, vol. 21, no. 4 (1984), pp. 38–40

4 Economic reform and the internal division of labour in China

Production, trade and marketing

Anjali Kumar

This chapter evaluates the extent to which the economic reforms undertaken over the period 1978 to 1993 have helped the development of a better regionally integrated economy. It first examines production structure to see whether there is any evidence of a shift away from the 'cellular structure' associated with the Maoist era, towards greater regional specialisation. Data indicate that China is still some distance from the structure of regional specialisation associated with developed economies. Building upon data provided by Chinese scholars, there is a suggestion that regional specialisation may have declined over time. The study next analyses available data on domestic trade flows, at the interprovincial level and shows indications of a relative decline, compared to the growth of domestic output, over the period 1985 to 1992. However the coverage of data used is not complete. The study estimates the extent to which the incomplete coverage of the data may affect the results. The estimates suggest that the direction if not the magnitude of the findings are likely to be robust, and the growth of domestic trade is not likely to have kept pace with output. In conclusion the study discusses the extent to which interpretations may be affected by specific factors.

THE SPATIAL DIMENSION OF CHINA'S ROUTE TO MARKET REFORM

China's commitment to the creation of a market economy has been the central plank of its programme of economic reform, and considerable progress towards this end has been achieved, since 1978, through the gradual withdrawal of the state from the allocation, pricing and distribution of goods. Between 1980 and 1992, the proportion of industrial goods allocated under the plan system had declined from 90 per cent to 12 per cent and there was a parallel reduction in the planned allocation of consumer goods. Radical progress was also achieved with price decontrol, in industrial products, transport services, grain and edible oils. China also opened up in terms of foreign trade and foreign investment from 1979. From 1985 to 1992, exports and imports grew at 17 per cent and 10 per cent per year, respectively, and the share of external trade in GDP rose from 10 to 39 per cent.[1] The state's role in industry declined, and the share of industrial output produced by state-owned units fell from 78 per cent in 1978 to 48 per cent in 1992. The overall retrenchment of the government from the economy is illustrated in the decline in the proportion of budgetary revenues in GNP, from 31.3 per cent in 1978 to 16.4 per cent in 1991.[2]

Developing the framework of a market economy in a large country like China requires not only the creation of markets, but the spatial integration of markets. The case for freer trade within a region rests upon a series of static and dynamic gains, to be achieved from production according to comparative advantage ('division of labour', in the Heckscher–Ohlin–Samuelson models of trade), increased competition (and consequently more product diversification), the benefits of scale economies,[3] and the diffusion of technical knowledge. Economic geographers point to the tendency for 'clusters' of production to develop at certain locations, and for growth in a given region to accelerate with a critical mass of enterprises.[4]

In the case of China, the limited degree of regional specialisation and the uniquely 'cellular' structure of the economy has received much comment.[5] Though geographically vast, attempts at achieving the local self-sufficiency emphasised in the Maoist era led to a duplication of industrial pattern by province. During this period, the inefficient location of industry was compounded by dispersal resulting from the 'Third Front' policy, of moving industrial enterprises towards the interior. Regional policies altered again, from the late 1970s, this time giving strong preferences to coastal areas for the location of industry. By late 1993, signs of change were apparent again, with the decision to open up the interior and extend the benefits given to coastal cities to locations in the hinterland and interior.[6]

A first question addressed in the present study is the extent to which the reforms undertaken over 1979 to 1993 encouraged the development of a more spatially efficient industrial structure. One essential ingredient for the facilitation of such structural change is the ability to move goods and factors between geographic locations. A second question examined, therefore, as a parallel to the first, is the extent to which there is evidence of spatial market integration, encouraging the freer mobility of goods and factors.

Some aspect of the reform process, such as the growth of private industry and trade would tend to increase internal exchange of goods and factors, due to the increased opportunities this represented for gains from trade. However other factors, inherent in the nature of the reform process, worked in the opposite direction, leading to regional tensions and conflicts which disrupted trade and factor flows. A key feature of the reform process was its decentralisation, and the withdrawal of the central government from certain functions. The system of central revenue collection, combined with redistributive centralised transfers was replaced by 'separate fiscal households', dividing public revenues and expenditures at each level. Local revenues were linked to prices and profits, as, under the system of property rights established with reform, all but the largest industrial enterprises belonged to local governments. A large part of local government revenues came from industrial profits. Each jurisdiction, therefore, wished to expand its industrial base, and keep industrial resources within its territory, by establishing its own factories. As a consequence, almost all groups of industry are represented in each province, and industrial plant is frequently undersized. Provincial and local authorities sometimes limited the entry of goods from other provinces to shelter small and relatively inefficient enterprises, invoking the 'infant industry' argument. In 1987, 80 factories in 21 provinces produced refrigerators, over 100 factories in 26 provinces produced televisions and 300 factories in 28 provinces could produce washing machines.

Second, in the case of interior provinces producing raw materials, provincial authorities had an appreciation of the adverse terms of trade they faced relative to coastal provinces producing final manufactures. In tandem with the regional policies favoring coastal cities, price controls which continued during the reform programme tended to favour manufacturing industry relative to producers of agricultural raw materials.[7] It was in the coastal areas that large processing industries were located. Authorities in interior provinces would tend to encourage the development of local processing industries, in an attempt to protect local value-added. Third, urban consumers of grain in large coastal cities also benefited from low controlled prices. Employment considerations, under circumstances in which labour mobility was severely constrained, also encouraged the establishment and protection of local industry. A lack of clarity in commercial laws permitted the consequent development of local protectionism. In addition, the export retention system led to a diversion of goods away from the domestic market and towards the export market. Since provinces were permitted to retain a part of export proceeds, with the overvalued exchange rate, as well as the differentials in retention rates across provinces, each province attempted to increase its holdings of the undervalued resource, foreign exchange, by diverting sales away from the domestic market.

There were real difficulties in mobility caused by the relatively low levels of investment, over this period, in developing an adequate transportation network. Growth in demand for freight services considerably outpaced the growth in supply, and in 1989 it was estimated that the demand for around 200 million tons of freight, or around 10 per cent of freight capacity, remained unsatisfied. China's rate of investment in transport has averaged around 1.3 per cent of GNP, while other developing nations' investments in transport ranged from 2 to 3.8 per cent of GNP.[8]

Finally, there is the issue of the interaction of domestic and external trade. Did an increase in the relative attractiveness and profitability of exports lead to a diversion of sales away from other provinces within the country? During the recent economic boom of 1992–93, the steep fall in imports has been attributed by some observers to the increased attractiveness of the internal market. In international trade theory, the economic case for regional free trade blocs raises the question of the extent to which such a bloc creates trade, or diverts trade away from areas outside the bloc.[9] In China, tolls, fees, barricades and other difficulties could reduce the relative attractiveness of domestic prices (if the tariff-equivalents of such barriers are estimated), except during periods when an overvalued exchange rate or a sharp rise in domestic prices could reverse this and increase the relative attractiveness of the domestic market.

This chapter first examines industrial structure and the degree of regional specialisation, relative to other large countries, and also over time, within China. Due to the relative paucity of attempts to estimate empirically shifts in industrial structure or internal trade, attention has been paid to assessing the extent to which such flows can be reliably measured.[10] It is shown below (pp. 103–9) that industrial structure has been relatively static, over the reform period, both in terms of sectoral composition and regional specialisation, and there may have been a tendency for regional specialisation to decline. China appears below its potential 'division of labour', compared to other large countries. Next, the chapter examines evidence on regional trade flows within China. Data presented here on interprovincial trade flows suggest that there may have been a relative decline in such trade flows over the period 1985 to 1992, compared to the rapid growth of output. However, the coverage of the data is not comprehensive since the principal source of data used is restricted to marketing through the state sector and rural cooperatives. Attempts at assessing the degree to which the data are representative are presented, by estimating the proportion of marketing which has been directed through such channels. The conclusions which can be inferred from available evidence are drawn together at the end.

INDUSTRIAL STRUCTURE: SECTORAL AND REGIONAL SPECIALISATION

Although there have been remarkable shifts in the ownership of industrial output over the reform period, there is evidence which suggests that the structure of industrial output over this period has remained relatively static. An analysis undertaken by one author, using a fifteen-branch classification of industry, suggests remarkable stability over time.[11] The share of light industries in output according to this measure was 33.3 per cent in 1980 and 32.8 per cent in 1990. More significant change had occurred earlier, between 1970 and 1980, when the share of this group rose from 25.5 per cent to 33.3 per cent in 1980.[12] It can also be shown that this is not due to offsetting changes in the composition of state and non-state output, or urban and rural output. The relative composition of each of these groups has also remained virtually unchanged. This is in spite of other considerable policy shifts which occurred over this decade, in terms of the move from plan to market allocation and pricing, ownership changes in industry, and external trade expansion.

There is also evidence to show that each major industrial group is located in virtually all provinces, and that firm size is also remarkably similar across provinces.[13] This structural similarity across provinces, in conjunction with a fairly static industrial structure over time, would suggest that China so far has not benefited from the opportunities for regional specialisation that its large internal market would permit. To assess the extent to which China may potentially gain from this, a comparison of China and other large regional markets was undertaken. The two comparators chosen are the European Community and the United States. The selection of the US is obvious, as another large, federal nation–state. The presence of 'manufacturing belts', and sometimes highly concentrated industries in a few specific towns, is notable. The choice of the EC is due to the fact that it is

Table 4.1 Comparison of average coefficients of structural difference:
China, USA and EC

	EC	USA	China
Structure measured by number of employees	0.333	0.262	0.197
Structure measured by output value	0.371	0.292	0.214
Structure measured by number of firms	0.333	0.162	0.157

Source: Appendix, World Bank (1993), Report No. 12291-CHA, Kumar (March, 1994)

increasingly approximating a single market, in the same sense as the US. Although the regions of the EC are individual countries, with huge differences between north and south, differences in size and also a high degree of linguistic and cultural diversity, there is evidence of relative regional specialisation.[14]

The analysis measures the difference in the shares of individual industries between each pair of regions within the three countries/ regions (i.e., for each pair of countries in the EC, and each group of provinces in China or states in the US), and then constructs an average of these differences for each of the three countries/regions considered. The higher the value of this measure, the greater the relative regional differences in industrial structure, and the higher the degree of local specialisation. Three different indices of industrial structure have been used: the shares of individual industries in output, employment and numbers of firms, in each region. A note on the methodology is provided in the Appendix.

Aggregated measures of difference, for each variable and for each of the three countries/regions selected, are presented in Table 4.1. Pairwise correlation coefficients between locations within a country, for the employment variable, are presented in Tables 4.2 to 4.4. The results show that regional differences in China are relatively low, suggesting that there is little industrial specialisation or regional industrial concentration. For example, in terms of shares in employment, the values for China, the US and the EC, respectively, are 0.2, 0.26, and 0.33, showing that the degree of differentiation is higher in both the EC and the US.[15]

A remarkably similar analysis of changes in China's structural differences over time has been undertaken by a Chinese scholar, who examines the changes in regional industrial structure over time, over ten provinces in China, measured in terms of employment shares.[16] These findings show that there has been an increase in regional 'similarity' over time (Table 4.5). Applying the same

Table 4.2 China: coefficients of structural difference of number of employees, 1991

	Region 1	Region 2	Region 3	Region 4	Region 5	Region 6	Region 7	Region 8	Region 9	Region 10	Region 11	Region 12
Region 1	0.000	0.161	0.145	0.088	0.106	0.138	0.298	0.106	0.187	0.235	0.105	0.232
Region 2		0.000	0.118	0.184	0.188	0.107	0.391	0.104	0.147	0.183	0.195	0.181
Region 3			0.000	0.200	0.218	0.141	0.364	0.124	0.126	0.229	0.165	0.205
Region 4				0.000	0.110	0.146	0.158	0.216	0.228	0.193	0.162	0.216
Region 5					0.000	0.144	0.306	0.155	0.238	0.222	0.153	0.235
Region 6						0.000	0.385	0.110	0.146	0.156	0.160	0.168
Region 7							0.000	0.351	0.372	0.425	0.285	0.365
Region 8								0.000	0.116	0.179	0.120	0.167
Region 9									0.000	0.191	0.181	0.171
Region 10										0.000	0.260	0.239
Region 11											0.000	0.219
Region 12												0.000

Note: The definitions of regions are as follows:
Region 1: Beijing, Tianjin, Hebei; Region 2: Shanxi, Inner Mongolia, Henan; Region 3: Liaoning, Jilin, Heilongjiang; Region 4: Shanghai, Zhejiang, Anhui, Jiangxi; Region 5: Jiangsu, Shandong; Region 6: Hubei, Hunan; Region 7: Guangdong, Fujian; Region 8: Sichuan; Region 9: Guizhou, Yunnan; Region 10: Tibet, Xinjiang, Qinghai; Region 11: Shaanxi, Gansu, Ningxia; Region 12: Guangxi, Hainan.
Source: calculated from data in China Industrial Statistical Yearbook, 1992

Table 4.3 United States: coefficients of structural difference of number of employees, 1987

	Region 1	Region 2	Region 3	Region 4	Region 5	Region 6	Region 7	Region 8	Region 9	Region 10	Region 11	Region 12
Region 1	0.000	0.176	0.164	0.171	0.302	0.263	0.225	0.378	0.261	0.270	0.322	0.157
Region 2		0.000	0.200	0.179	0.186	0.192	0.215	0.316	0.229	0.299	0.269	0.189
Region 3			0.000	0.131	0.310	0.285	0.177	0.404	0.251	0.269	0.296	0.144
Region 4				0.000	0.308	0.308	0.174	0.316	0.152	0.185	0.257	0.155
Region 5					0.000	0.208	0.277	0.421	0.306	0.413	0.275	0.276
Region 6						0.000	0.279	0.369	0.315	0.420	0.229	0.268
Region 7							0.000	0.308	0.258	0.248	0.304	0.149
Region 8								0.000	0.360	0.260	0.460	0.316
Region 9									0.000	0.249	0.209	0.222
Region 10										0.000	0.363	0.170
Region 11											0.000	0.305
Region 12												0.000

Note: The definitions of regions are as follows:
Region 1: Maine, New Hampshire, Vermont, Massachusetts, Rhode Island, Connecticut; Region 2: New York, New Jersey, Pennsylvania; Region 3: Ohio, Indiana, Illinois, Michigan, Wisconsin; Region 4: Minnesota, Iowa, Missouri, North Dakota, South Dakota, Nebraska, Kansas; Region 5: Delaware, Maryland, Virginia, West Virginia, North Carolina, South Carolina, Georgia; Region 6: Kentucky, Tennessee, Alabama, Mississippi; Region 7: Louisiana, Oklahoma; Region 8: Florida, Texas; Region 9: Montana, Idaho, Wyoming, Colorado; Region 10: New Mexico, Arizona, Utah, Nevada; Region 11: Washington, Oregon, Alaska, Hawaii; Region 12: California.
Source: calculated from data United States' Census of Manufactures for 1987 (Geographic Area Series), various issues

Table 4.4 European Community: coefficients of structural difference of number of employees, 1987

	Belgium	Denmark	France	Germany	Greece	Ireland	Italy	Luxembourg	Netherlands	Portugal	Spain	UK
Belgium	0.000	0.271	0.156	0.221	0.298	0.217	0.242	0.466	0.252	0.396	0.155	0.172
Denmark		0.000	0.212	0.274	0.327	0.211	0.400	0.561	0.217	0.423	0.198	0.204
France			0.000	0.183	0.327	0.232	0.255	0.551	0.231	0.402	0.137	0.064
Germany				0.000	0.463	0.349	0.204	0.500	0.270	0.538	0.297	0.185
Greece					0.000	0.277	0.436	0.649	0.409	0.217	0.232	0.326
Ireland						0.000	0.381	0.557	0.254	0.418	0.213	0.224
Italy							0.000	0.610	0.399	0.392	0.348	0.252
Luxembourg								0.000	0.491	0.791	0.550	0.570
Netherlands									0.000	0.490	0.309	0.225
Portugal										0.000	0.324	0.399
Spain											0.000	0.173
UK												0.000

Source: calculated from data in Industrial Statistical Yearbook (United Nations), 1991 and 1989

Table 4.5 China: structural difference by employment shares, 1980 and 1990

1990	Beijing	Tianjin	Shanghai	Jiangsu	Shandong	Henan	Hubei	Guangdong	Sichuan	Shaanxi
Beijing	0	31	39	43	50	51	39	51	36	38
Tianjin			21	32	41	39	43	50	38	36
Shanghai				37	49	49	43	58	49	40
Jiangsu					22	30	30	52	38	39
Shandong						26	25	47	32	42
Henan							31	58	25	30
Hubei								57	25	30
Guangdong									57	58
Sichuan										29
Totals		31	60	112	162	195	211	373	300	342

1980	Beijing	Tianjin	Shanghai	Jiangsu	Shandong	Henan	Hubei	Guangdong	Sichuan	Shaanxi
Beijing	0	90	97	127	134	106	78	94	61	76
Tianjin			45	63	60	72	70	81	69	71
Shanghai				69	82	90	79	113	0	70
Jiangsu					47	32	32	48	42	36
Shandong						17	23	42	31	34
Henan							32	49	28	29
Hubei								47	28	28
Guangdong									41	54
Sichuan										31
Totals		90	142	259	323	317	314	474	300	429

Source: Xiong Xianliang (1993) 'Interregional trade and international competitiveness: an analysis based on China's manufacturing industry' (Translation from Chinese). Economic Research (Jinghi Yanjiu), Vol. 8. pp. 71–75. (Data sources cited: 'China industrial economic statistics', 1991, and 'The data of the industrial survey of the People's Republic of China'.)

methodology to obtain an aggregate measure of 'difference' and expressing this on the same scale, regional 'difference' has gone down, between 1990 and 1980, from 0.59 to 0.26.

REGIONAL TRADE ANALYSIS

The above analysis suggests limited regional specialisation, and limited structural change over the reform period. This would be consistent with low factor mobility, and it is true that China has been slow in developing an integrated internal market for land, labour and capital. Even in the absence of factor mobility, China could still have made progress with product mobility. Markets for goods are likely to be less constrained by regulation than markets for factors, and there may have been benefits from interregional trade in goods even if regional specialisation in production was limited. The next issue examined, therefore, is the extent and direction of change in interregional trade over the reform period. To what extent did the shift in regional development policies of the reform years affect interregional trade, and what was the net effect on domestic trade, in view of the centripetal forces of decentralisation and protection of local industry?

There is considerable anecdotal evidence to suggest that internal trade flows have frequently been obstructed.[17] The best known examples are the 'export embargoes' or 'commodity wars', which occurred mainly over the years 1985 to 1988. Agroprocessing factories in coastal provinces suffered from capacity under-utilisation because of raw material shortages, although China was a highly competitive international supplier of both cotton and silk textiles. Raw materials from interior provinces were either diverted by regional governments towards local processors, or sold directly to overseas buyers. Embargoes or taxes were imposed on interregional exports. 'Wars' broke out between neighbouring provinces, with barricades and roadblocks, and sometimes local militia were called in to enforce them. The commodity wars also affected wool, tea and tobacco, but these faded by the end of the decade, with the decline in domestic demand, due to the recession and the diminution of the price differential between market and plan procurement. However, Hunan province put embargoes on its grain exports as late as 1990 and there was another episode in late 1993.[18] Liaoning Province declared in 1992 that it would not permit exports of fertilisers, except under the central plan, as it could not meet its own requirements.

Import restraints constituted a second form of internal trade restraint. Sichuan Province stated in 1993 that it had lifted government restrictions and checkpoints on trade, from the beginning of the 1990s.[19] But it still accords local suppliers preference in government procurement. Beijing, in 1992, restricted imports of hogs from Hebei. A province in the southwest decided to protect nineteen local products in 1989 and restricted the imports of these goods from other provinces. And an autonomous region in the west expressly prohibited the entry of 48 outside products. There are also numerous accounts of taxes, fees and fines collected by arbitrary 'inspection stations'. In Baihuting, suburban Fuzhou, vehicles carrying scrap iron were stopped and fines were demanded, with the threat that otherwise their goods would be confiscated for a token sum. A bamboo dealer in Sanming country in Zhejiang, who had bought 1,524 *yuan* worth of bamboo shoots to truck to Shanghai had paid a total of 546 *yuan en route*, for thirteen taxes and fees, by the time he had reached Tongxiang county in Zhejiang. With several hundred kilometers to go, and no knowledge of how many more inspection stations there would be, the dealer decided to sell his cargo in Tongxiang and return. Even in Guangdong Province, reputed to be free trade oriented, a series of checkposts, barriers, local blockades (including those set up by the Guangdong Province Administration of Industry and Commerce, or GPAIC, and the public security bureau) as well as numerous fees and fines, have been reported.[20]

China's concern over barriers to domestic trade and their consequences can be discerned from repeated official attempts to ban such constraints. In 1980, the State Council issued its Provisional Regulations relating to the Development and Protection of Socialist Competition, and again in 1982, it issued a Notice relating to the Prohibition of Blockades in the Sale of Industrial Products. In November 1990 (after the worst of the 'commodity wars' had ended) the State Council issued an order to remove all regional blockades to trade. In August 1993 an article banning restrictions on domestic trade was inserted in the 'anti-unfair competition' law.[21] Unlike the US, for example, China does not have any constitutional clauses which specifically prohibit constraints against interstate commerce.[22]

As other authors have pointed out, the form of domestic trade barriers have varied over time, and have been related to the periodic macro-economic cycles of China's economy. Thus export embargoes were the outcome of the excess demand of 1987 and 1988, and the shortage of raw material supplies relative to demand and processing capacity.[23] With the recession of 1989–90, export embargoes were replaced by import restraints, as interior provinces in particular attempted to protect themselves against the 'dumping' of goods from coastal areas. There are also indications that such barriers may have loosened up over the last few years. Both major manufacturers and township and village enterprises in Shanghai and Guangzhou have established countrywide marketing networks for some of their products. This is particularly true of certain manufactured consumer goods such as wrist-watches or radios, where firms from the south are now reported to be making inroads in the markets of northern provinces.

DOMESTIC TRADE: DATA FROM PROVINCIAL YEARBOOKS

To gauge the extent to which internal trade may have been affected by the combination of real and policy obstacles over the period since the mid-1980s, an analysis of available statistical data on trade was undertaken. Data on domestic trade are scarce, and alternative data sources were examined before the analysis below was undertaken. One source of data on internal trade is available in transport statistics. But these cover rail freight, for the most part, and are presented for goods which are still largely centrally distributed and are large users of the railway system. These consist mainly of grain (for consumer goods) and producer goods such as coal or timber. The coverage is clearly too limited to permit general conclusions to be drawn. Another possibility examined was regional input–output tables. But at present, provincial input–output tables are only available for a single year, 1987, which does not permit comparisons over time to be undertaken.[24] The principal data source used here therefore consists of data on imports, exports and retail sales collected and presented in the statistical yearbooks of each province. Information on imports and exports in these yearbooks is based on state-owned commercial units and rural cooperatives. The extent to which this may influence the findings is discussed below.

Data on imports and exports of individual provinces were collected and compared with data on aggregate retail sales and provincial GNP; that is, measures of domestic trade were compared with variables related to domestic output. The ratios of interprovincial imports and exports to total retail sales were then estimated, defining these ratios for each province as the sum of its interprovincial imports and exports, divided by retail sales or GNP, at that province. The results are summarised in Table 4.6.

Table 4.6 Domestic trade between provinces (1985–92)
(yuan million and per cent)

	1985	1988	1990	1991	1992
Total interprovincial imports	132205.6	141427.9	139696.8	167786.9	183601.7
Total interprovincial exports	95063.8	129850.8	129223.9	140445.2	151514.2
Total provincial retail sales	360923.6	524909.0	562113.4	589062.4	665978.0
Interprov. imports/interprov. retail sales (%)	36.6	26.9	24.9	28.5	27.6
Interprov. exports/interprov retail sales (%)	26.3	24.7	23.0	23.8	22.8
Total interprov. trade/retail sales (%)	63.0	51.7	47.8	52.3	50.3
Provincial GDP (all provinces) (yuan 100 m)	7194.9	11783.8	14269.4	16113.7	19853.2
Interprov. trade/total provincial GDP (%)	0.32	0.23	0.19	0.19	0.17

Note: Figures are of state-owned commercial units and rural cooperatives. 'Total' refers to all provinces for which data are available. In some cases data are not available for Guizhou or Tibet
Source: Data compiled from the China Statistical Yearbook and provincial yearbooks (various issues), by the State Statistical Bureau

A first finding is that in aggregate, for all provinces taken together, both domestic imports and domestic exports grew over time, in absolute terms. Disaggregated data on individual provinces show that imports increased between 1985 and 1992 in all provinces except the municipality of Tianjin.[25] Exports increased in all but four provinces (which included Shanghai and Tianjin). In the case of both exports and imports, there was a lull or reversal, over 1988 to 1990, when, in many provinces, interprovincial trade declined in absolute terms.

The annual average rates of growth of domestic interprovincial exports and imports, at 6.9 per cent and 4.8 per cent per year, were however slower than the rate of growth of total retail sales, and as a result, the share of domestic trade in retail sales (defined as {domestic imports+exports}/{domestic retail sales}) declined over time. The decline was pronounced between 1985 and 1990 (from 63 per cent to 48 per cent), with some marginal recovery since, to 50.3 per cent in 1992. Using a different denominator, provincial national income, a similar aggregate result is observed; domestic interprovincial trade did not grow as fast as total output.

These results are in marked contrast to external trade. Over the seven years, 1985 to 1992, international exports grew at 16.7 per cent per year, while imports grew by 9.7 per cent, on average, measured in dollar terms. Measured in domestic currency (for appropriate comparison with domestic trade), the rates are considerably higher, at 28 per cent and 20 per cent per year. These patterns would suggest a tendency for individual provinces to behave as independent countries, increasing their links with the external world, and in relative terms, reducing trade links with other provinces within the country.

There are some interesting differences between provinces in terms of domestic trade behaviour. Looking first at export ratios alone, on average for all provinces, domestic interprovincial exports as a percentage of retail sales declined from 36.6 per cent to 27.6 per cent over 1985 to 1992. However, in some provinces, these ratios stayed virtually constant (Hebei) or increased over time (Liaoning, Jiangsu, Zhejiang, Fujian, Jiangxi, Guangdong and Sichuan). With the exception of Sichuan, these are all relatively rapidly growing coastal provinces or their hinterlands. In terms of imports, Hebei, Jilin, Fujian, Jiangxi, Hubei, Guangdong and Guangxi were also able to raise domestic import ratios.[26] This suggests that more rapidly growing coastal areas may also be able to develop stronger trade links, in terms of domestic exports, with other interior areas. One significant implication is that 'trade diversion' does not appear to have occurred,

Table 4.7 China and other regional trading areas: interregional trade

	Interprovincial imports	Interprovincial exports	GDP/a	Interprovincial imports/GDP %	Interprovincial exports/GDP %	Total Interprovincial Trade/GDP %
China (1988) (Y 100 million)	1414.3	1298.5	11783.8	12.0	11.0	21.0
China (1990) (Y 100 million)	1397.0	1292.2	14269.5	9.8	9.1	18.9
EC (1989): (ECU million)	624.5	624.5	4406.9	14.2	14.2	28.3
FSU (1990): (Rouble million)						
Subtotal (Excluding Russia)	125752	95886	814602	15.4	11.8	27.2
Subtotal (all FSU countries)	182335	182335	2103179	8.7	8.7	17.3

Note: /a: the Chinese figures for the GDP column are GNP, by Chinese definitions
Sources: EC: Basic Statistics of the Community, 1990, 28th edition; FSU: Michalopoulos and Tarr (1992), China Statistical Yearbook and Provincial Statistical Yearbooks

as these areas simultaneously increased their domestic and external exports.

How does China compare, in terms of internal trade flows, with other countries? Comparisons are available for the former Soviet Union (FSU) and its individual republics, as well as for the European Community. Although these are not single countries today, the FSU was a single country in 1990, which is the year referred to here, and the EC is a common market area. The results are summarized in Table 4.7.[27] The data show that, in terms of ratios to GDP, internal trade in selected provinces in China, at 21 per cent in 1988, was lower than trade in the EC (28.3 per cent in 1989), and also lower than trade among the nations of the FSU, excluding Russia.[28] In 1990, internal trade ratios in China declined compared to 1988.

DOMESTIC TRADE AND INVESTMENT: THE CASS SURVEY

Another, secondary source of data on domestic trade as well as investment is available, through a survey undertaken by the Chinese Academy of Social Sciences (CASS). Data permitting a comparison of domestic trade and external trade at the level of individual provinces was collected by the CASS for five provinces, as part of a special investigation on internal trade undertaken for the World Bank in early 1993. Teams of persons were sent to each province and data were collected from 'provincial statistical bureaus and offices of cooperation'. The absolute values of provincial trade are higher in the CASS data, and the difference between the two series increases over time. Unlike the first source used above, the provincial statistical yearbooks compiled by the State Statistical Bureau, the CASS claims that its data are inclusive of urban and rural collective enterprises, while SSB data refer to state owned units and rural cooperatives. A relatively rapid growth in urban and rural collectives could then account for an increase in the spread between the two series. In terms of direction, the results of the two series are the same for all provinces, except for Guangdong. However, in this case, the CASS data use ratios to GDP rather than retail sales.[29]

Interprovincial and foreign trade ratios from the CASS study are presented in Table 4.8. The data echo the finding that domestic trade ratios are highly variable across provinces. Shanghai had been the most open, in terms of links with other provinces and until 1990, the ratio of external trade apparently exceeded domestic retail sales. However, the ratios in Shanghai more recently have dropped to

Table 4.8 Interprovincial and foreign trade ratios (1980–92) (per cent)/a

		1980	1985	1990	1991	1992
Guangdong	Interprov. trade	41.4	32.8	20.1	19.0	18.4
	Foreign trade	15.7	28.0	52.7	65.9	67.4
Shaanxi	Interprov. trade	66.4	56.1	45.6	47.5	45.1
	Foreign trade	0.3	3.3	15.0	21.3	12.2
Sichuan	Interprov. trade	46.3	33.4	39.9	42.8	42.3
	Foreign trade	7.9	5.2	12.0	14.7	19.2
Shanghai	Interprov. trade	221.6	125.1	79.9	77.4	—
	Foreign trade	76.8	83.0	100.7	106.5	111.7
Liaoning	Interprov. trade	50.0	35.3	44.8	48.1	45.2
	Foreign trade	49.6	69.6	65.5	70.8	—

Note: Interprovincial trade ratios are defined as domestic exports + domestic imports/ total retail sales for all provinces except Guangdong, where the denominator is provincial GDP
Source: CASS data

levels comparable to other provinces. These data also emphasise the finding that, unlike domestic trade ratios, external trade ratios have been rising rapidly, and this is true of all the provinces illustrated here, except Shaanxi. This too suggests that the relative attractiveness of the external and domestic markets favoured the former, and that trade has tended to develop more easily with the external world than with other provinces.

The CASS investigation also covers data on interprovincial investment. Data are available for six provinces, Guangdong, Shaanxi, Sichuan, Beijing, Shanghai and Liaoning, over the period 1985 to 1992 (Table 4.9). These six provinces represent a cross-section in terms of location, coastal as well as interior, from the north as well as the south, and from developed as well as backward regions.[30]

The first observation is that interprovincial investment as a proportion of total investment today is very low in most provinces. In five of the six provinces examined, the ratio in the most recent year is less than 3 per cent. The only exception is Shanghai, where interprovincial transfers account for almost a third of total investment. Second, in three of the six provinces, this ratio has declined over time (Guangdong, Shaanxi and Beijing). Sichuan has remained virtually constant and Liaoning has a small increase. Shanghai is the only province with a significant increase, which for the two years 1991–92 probably reflects inflows due to the Pudong investment zone. It also suggests that the declining internal trade ratio in Shanghai may be partially offset, in term of links with other provinces, by its increasing internal investment ratio. It is clear that the case of Shanghai is exceptional.

It is also notable that domestic investment flows from other provinces are less significant than external investment. Foreign investment as a proportion of total investment in recent years has been as high as 10–13 per cent in Shanghai, Liaoning and Beijing, and even higher in Guangdong (32 per cent). In all these provinces, there has been an increase in this ratio over time. In the interior provinces, however (Sichuan and Shaanxi), external investment has been stagnant or declining. The high and rising external investment in Shanghai suggests that this is not 'crowding out' domestic interprovincial investment flows; rather, both have been able to expand significantly at the same time. It must also be recalled that the increasing foreign investment ratio of Shanghai has coexisted with a high and rising foreign trade ratio.

There are also some limited data from the same source, though only for three provinces, on the outward investment of these provinces. It suggests that domestic outward investments increase when investment flows inward increase. Thus in Liaoning and Sichuan, inward investment has had a modest gain, or remained constant, over the period for which data are available, and outward investment has increased as well. In Shaanxi, there has been a general decline in inward investment as well as constant or falling outward investment in the most recent years. The inference is that provinces which are relatively more open tend to have both higher inflows as well as outflows.

INTERNAL TRADE AND MARKETING

Before drawing inferences from the above findings certain limitations of the data must be pointed out. The interprovincial data collected from the provincial yearbooks, which form the core of the analysis of the preceding section, are known to be restricted in coverage, to sales from retail outlets of state-owned units and rural cooperatives only. At present, as explained above, these data appear the best, if not the only, available sources for measuring internal trade flows. Nevertheless, given that the role of the private sector in the economy as a whole over this period is known to have been increasing, how serious is this omission? Although a precise measure of the coverage is not possible, an estimate of the degree of coverage is attempted here, through an analysis of the composition of retail sales by owner-

Table 4.9 Interprovincial and foreign investment in selected provinces

Province	1992	1991	1990	1989	1988	1985
Guangdong						
Total investment (RMB yuan billion	84.5	47.8	36.2	34.7	35.4	—
% Investment from other provinces	1.7%	2.3%	—	—	—	—
% Foreign investment	31.7%	28.8%	26.6%	25.9%	—	—
% Investment to other provinces	2.5%	—	—	—	—	—
Shaanxi						
Total investment (RMB yuan million)	15200	12493	10372	9518	9472	5799
% Investment from other provinces	2.4%	3.4%	3.7%	3.3%	3.7%	7.4%
% Foreign investment/a	2.2%	1.9%	2.2%	4.8%	3.7%	—
% Investment to other provinces	—	2.8%	2.9%	2.6%	3.2%	3.4%
Sichuan						
Total investment (RMB yuan million)	36390	28252	20390	21219	14488	8047
% Investment from other provinces	0.22%	0.25%	0.17%	0.07%	0.02%	0.01%
% Foreign investment/b	5.4%	—	1.5%	4.5%	5.2%	—
% Investment to other provinces	4.45%	4.78%	5.64%	2.83%	—	—

Beijing

Total investment/c (RMB yuan billion)	19.38	19.19	17.92	13.95	16.3	—
% Investment from other provinces	0.16%	0.14%	—	0.46%	0.44%	—
% Foreign investment	—	—	10.46%	12.87%	—	—

Shanghai

Total investment (RMB yuan billion)	32.5	25.8	22.7	21.5	24.5	11.7
% Investment from other provinces/d	32.9%	30.6%	—	28.4%	—	—
% Foreign investment/e	13.4%	3.6%	6.8%	7.4%	1.5%	0.5%

Liaoning

Total investment (RMB yuan billion)	—	31.8	26.29	24.32	26.13	—
% Investment from other provinces	—	2.48%	0.72%	0.70%	1.30%	—
% Foreign investment	—	—	13.23%	6.01%	—	—
% Investment to other provinces/f	—	0.75%	0.84%	0.41%	0.54%	—

Notes:
/a Shaanxi: There were only 18 foreign or foreign joint venture enterprises (1991)
/b Sichuan: The total for 1988 to 1992 was 6.6 billion RMB yuan. Data do not include investments below 0.3 million RMB.
/c Beijing: Total investment for 1992 is an estimate
/d Shanghai: In 4550 enterprises, including the Pudong Zone
/e Shanghai: Joint Venture investment statistics
/f Lioning: Figures for inward and outward investment in the context of 'horizontal integration'
Source: provincial yearbooks and CASS survey.

ship. These data are also compiled by the State Statistical Bureau (SSB) and published in the annual Yearbook of statistics.

A fundamental element of the movement towards the establishment of a market economy has been the decline in the role of the state in material allocation, as well as in pricing decision.[31] In 1980, 90 per cent of industrial goods, and 837 production materials were allocated under the plan system. By 1992, the proportion of industrial goods under the plan had declined to 12 per cent and the number of production materials in this category has been reduced to 19. Consumer goods whose planned allocation was administered by the Ministry of Commerce declined in number from 274 in 1978 to 14 in 1992. In 1978, 97 per cent of domestic retail goods and 93 per cent of farm produce was subject to fixed prices. By 1991 these ratios had fallen to 21 per cent and 22 per cent. Over 1992 and 1993, further radical progress was made with price decontrol, especially in heavy industrial products, transport services, grain and edible oils. It might therefore be expected that the role of the state in distribution would decline in the same fashion.

This conclusion is not supported by Table 4.10, which indicates that, although there has been a decline over time in the proportion of state-owned units in retail sales, most of this decline occurred in the period 1978 to 1985, when the share of the state in the ownership of retailing fell from over 53 per cent to around 40 per cent, in terms of the value of retail sales. Between 1985 and 1991, there is little perceptible change in this proportion. One reason for this finding may be that, although new distribution and retailing units have been established by the non-state sectors, their share in the total value of distribution remains small, because of their relatively small size. This is partly correct, but is not a sufficient explanation. As indicated in Table 4.11, individual and collective units have dominated distribution for years, in terms of numbers of units, on account of their small size. Thus in both 1985 and 1991, the share of the state sector in terms of numbers of units, was just over 5 per cent. But the increase over this period in individual and collective units, taken together, has been low. Although the 6.2 million individually owned units, which accounted for 75.6 per cent of domestic trade units in 1985, grew to 7.8 million, and 79.8 per cent of the total number of units by 1991, both the absolute number and proportional share of collective units declined (from 1.6 to 1.4 million units, and 19.1 to 14.7 per cent of the numbers of units). Looking at different provinces within China, the relative shares of state and non-state units are, on the whole, similar.

Table 4.10 Composition of total retail sales value by ownership (1960–91) (yuan 100 million and per cent)

Year	Total value of sales (Y 100m)	Retail sales by ownership				
		State-owned units %	Collective units %	Jointly owned units %	Individual units %	Sales of agricultural to non- agr. residents (%)
1965	67.03	53.0	43.2	0.0	1.9	1.9
1978	158.97	53.5	42.4	0.1	2.0	2.0
1985	430.5	40.4	37.2	0.3	15.4	6.8
1991	941.56	40.2	30.0	0.5	19.6	9.7

Source: China Statistical Yearbook, various issues

Table 4.11 Number and share of domestic trade units by ownership and region (1985–91)

	Total	State-owned units	Collective units	Individually owned units
1985				
Numbers of units	8250472	429424	1578953	6238600
Percentage	100.0	5.2	19.1	75.6
1991				
Numbers of units	9797708	534145	1443617	7817454
Percentage	100.0	5.5	14.7	79.8

Source: China Statistical Yearbook, 1986 and 1992

These findings indicate virtually no change in the state's share in the value of retail trade over 1985 to 1991, and a relatively constant state share in the total number of distribution units. It can also be shown that there was a steady absolute increase in the number of outlets under the Materials Circulation system, between 1985 and 1991. In terms of numbers, the outlets of the material supply system grew from 32,500 in 1985 to 51,200 in 1991; an annual average rate of growth of 7.9 per cent. There was also a large increase in the numbers of persons employed (over 300,000, or an increase of 5.5 per cent per year).[32] The growth of state-owned units in storage and transport (3.4 per cent per year) has also been faster than collectives or supply and marketing cooperatives for storage and transport (2.6 per cent and 0.2 per cent per year, respectively).[33]

The data above show that while the role of the state in allocation declined, it continued to play a large role in distribution, growing in absolute terms and perhaps increasing its share relative to the non-state sector. This finding is surprising in view of the overall sharp decline in the share of state owned enterprises in output value. It must be concluded that while the share of the state in productive enterprises has declined sharply, the state has not withdrawn from its dominant role in distribution.

How can the declining role of the state in allocation and price controls be reconciled with the maintenance of the state in distribution? One explanation is that, despite the steady presence and dominance of the state in distribution, there may have been a change in the orientation of state-owned units, towards more market-based functions and behaviour. In the past, state-owned shops were largely intended to focus on the sales of state-allocated goods. However, as the state withdrew from planned allocation, the facilities for distribution remained, and state-owned shops continued to serve as distribution centres, for enterprises wishing to sell their output on the free market. State enterprises within the Materials Supply system have made strong efforts to become more competitive and more market-oriented. This is supported by estimates which show that personnel employed at state-owned 'administrative units' grew relatively slowly, between 1985 and 1991, from 1.35 to 1.5 million, or 1.9 per cent per year.[34] At the same time, personnel at state-owned 'business units' grew at 4.8 per cent per year, and their numbers rose from 5 to 6.6 million. New forms of retail outlets appeared over this period, for example, outlets owned by the state but run by collectives, and outlets leased and run by individuals. By 1991, 522,000 persons were employed by such enterprises. The number of persons employed in jointly owned enterprises grew faster than the other categories (5.3 per cent per year in all, and 26 per cent per year for Sino-foreign joint ventures), though absolute numbers are still small (50,000 persons in all joint-venture distribution enterprises).

How do these data relate to the findings of the previous section on internal trade flows? Given that the coverage of the data on inter-provincial trade flows refer to retail trade, from state enterprises and rural cooperatives only, the preceding analysis of data on marketing can help determine (a) the share of these units in total retailing and (b) changes in this share, since 1985.

The share of state enterprises alone in total retailing (Table 4.10) was 40.4 per cent in 1985 and 40.2 per cent in 1991. Over the same period, the share of collectives declined from 37.2 per cent to 30 per cent, while the share of individual ownership increased in the same period (15.4 per cent to 19.6 per cent) and the share of agricultural sales to non-agricultural buyers also rose (from 6.8 per cent to 9.7 per cent). If the state owned enterprises and rural cooperatives of the interprovincial trade data include at least the state enterprises and some part of the collectives of the retail sales data, the maximum coverage of the internal trade data in 1985 was 77.2 per cent, and the maximum in 1991 was 70 per cent. The minimum in both years was just over 40 per cent. Moreover, there is little indication of a significant change in coverage over time. The actual coverage is likely to have been somewhere in between these limits.[35] If the coverage of internal trade data in the Provincial Yearbooks is somewhere between half and two-thirds of total retail sales, and if this coverage has not shifted markedly over the period investigated, it would be difficult to reverse the finding of the previous section, of a *relative* decline in domestic interprovincial trade, relative to output. Non-state trade would have to grow, not only faster than trade retailed through state marketing entities, but considerably *faster than non-state output*, to reverse this finding.

To summarise, although the data on internal trade given above indicate that there was a decline in the ratio of trade to output, this analysis shows that the primary data source used only applies to a part, and not to all, domestic retail trade. It is also true that statistical data on internal commerce are probably less reliable than data on primary or secondary production. Whether there was an overall decline in internal trade relative to domestic output depends on the behaviour of the part of domestic trade not captured by the published statistics. But only if non-state internal trade grew considerably faster than aggregate output, and from an adequately large base, would the findings above be reversed.

AN INTERPRETATION

To the extent that internal trade may indeed have grown slower than domestic output, what is the significance of this finding? As the introduction to this chapter explains, the implication is that China has not taken full advantage of the opportunity for regional 'division of labour' offered by the development of a market economy. Limited progress in this direction may itself have been a consequence of the pattern of economic reform adopted, and its embedded economic decisions, on the form of decentralisation, on the fiscal system, on relative prices, and on differential regional development. These were compounded by the dynamics of reform, particularly partial price deregulation and periodic macro-economic cycles, which together constituted a series of factors which engendered interregional economic tensions.

Qualifications to this result must be noted. First, some decline in the regional mobility of goods may be attributed to the decline in centralised allocation. At least a part of the centralised allocation may have been inefficient, in terms of spatial planning, and some goods were transported unnecessarily long distances. To this extent, the decline in trade need not reflect a decline in efficiency. Second, the relative decline in internal trade between provinces, compared to the growth in total retail trade, may also be due to the rapid growth of township and village enterprises, and a consequent increase in production as well as consumption within provincial frontiers.[36] Third, some of the decline (and it must be remembered that the decline was relative and not absolute) may have been the consequence of the relatively slow-growth of the transportation system, compared to overall economic growth.

It is possible that the worst of interregional trade restrictions occurred (in the form of export embargoes) during the 'boom' of 1987–88, and then in the slump which immediately followed (1989–90), due to the concomitant presence of other factors, such as partial price deregulation and large differentials in regional terms of trade. The data presented above show that the worst of the dips in interregional trade occurred between 1988 and 1990.

It also appears that the fiscal reforms introduced at the beginning of 1994, designed to gradually 'recentralise' a part of government revenues, together with the substantial progress in price decontrol, and the decision adopted at the Third Plenary session of the CCCP, in October 1993, to promote 'balanced' regional development, may help erode incentives to constrain regional trade. Additional work is desirable to see whether the pattern observed over this period can be corroborated, and whether it can be shown to alter in the 1990s.

NOTES

An earlier version of this paper was presented at the Workshop on East Asia: Politics, Economy and Society; Department of Political Science, University of Chicago. I am indebted to Professors Dorothy Solinger (University of California at Irvine), Karen Polenske (Massachusetts Institute of Technology), Thomas Rawski (University of Pittsburgh), Dali Yang (University of Chicago) and Nicholas Lardy (University of Washington at Seattle), as well as to many colleagues, notably Albert Keidel and Jun Ma for thoughtful comments. The findings, interpretations and conclusions expressed in this study are the result of research supported by the World Bank, but they are entirely my own and should not in any way be attributed to the above persons, to the World Bank, its affiliate organisations, or to members of its Board of Executive Directors or the countries they represent.

1 Measured as exports plus imports over GDP at (current) market prices.
2 World Bank (July 1993) and World Bank (November 1993).
3 Economic work relating plant size to cost efficiency, by industry, has calculated the 'MEPS' or minimum economic plant size by industry for a number of industries. Examples cited, in terms of minimum annual volumes of production, are 10,000 tons of soap, between 1 and 3 million tons for steel, 160,000 units for bicycles, 90,000 units for tractors, 200,000 tons for cement, 1 million units for automobiles, and 800,000 units a year for refrigerators. See HMSO 1975, as cited in Huang (1992) and Wu (1990).
4 Krugman (1991a, b and c) discusses the theory of 'cores' and its implications for industrial location. Murphy, Schleifer and Vishny

126 *Anjali Kumar*

(1989a and b) discuss the importance of scale economies, market size and market structure. Jacobs (1969), Romer (1986) and Porter (1989), as cited in Wang and Mody (1993), have offered explanations based on such theories to explain rapidly growing areas in China.

5 Commented on by Donnithorne (1972), and later by Lyons (1987), Huang (1992). Numerous Chinese scholars have written more recently about economic 'dukedoms' (Shen Liren and Dai Yuanchen, 1992), and 'block' economies (Wu Jianqi, 1993). Huang (1992) provides some empirical evidence.

6 Yang (1991) discusses the shifting emphasis of China's regional policy before and after the onset of reform.

7 Wu Jinglian and Zhao Renwei (1987), Wiemer (1992).

8 World Bank (1992). Report No. 10592-CHA.

9 Recent modifications and extensions of the classical theory of customs unions is available in de Melo, *et al.* (1992).

10 One measure of the regional integration of markets in China has been attempted by Byrd (1991) which suggests that, particularly for producer goods, integration is much lower than in corresponding markets in industrialised countries. Attempts to directly estimate trade flows have not been undertaken in this analysis.

11 Rawski (1993). One limitation on conclusions that can be drawn is that village level data are excluded.

12 It has been shown in more detail (Solinger, 1991) that the proportion of the gross value of industrial output in light industry rose noticeably in 1980 and 1981, suggesting that the early policy of 'readjustment' of 1979 to 1982 did affect industrial composition, albeit for a limited period.

13 World Bank (1993 November), W. Huang (1993) and Xiong Xianliang (1993). An analysis of the sectoral composition of state investment in fixed assets between 1986 and 1992 (Kumar 1994, February) also indicates remarkably little change in composition.

14 Most manufacturers are located in countries such as Britain and Germany, certain agricultural products are grown largely in Portugal or Spain, and Italy dominates the internal EC clothing industry.

15 Note that the absolute values of these numbers mean little; it is their relative size which is relevant, since the numbers could be 'normalised' to any corresponding numbers. Admittedly, the use of the EC and the US as comparators is not ideal, since these countries are at a more advanced level of industrialisation, and have not undergone the process of transition from a planned to market economy.

16 Xiong (1993). One drawback in his approach however is that a selection of ten provinces has been used, instead of all provinces in the country. The results could be sensitive to the regions selected. By contrast in the cross-sectional analysis undertaken here, all provinces in China are used (and all states, in the US), although these are grouped in 12 regions, to permit comparisons with the EC.

17 Forster (1991), Zhang, *et al.* (1991), Agarwala (1992), Findlay *et al.* (1992), Watson and Findlay (1992), Lyons (1992), Huang (1992), Feng (1993), *The Economist*, 26 June 1993. The Autumn 1993 volume of *Chinese Economic Studies* is a special issue on regional protectionism, with articles on the subject by several Chinese scholars.

18 These episodes were admittedly sporadic. It is reported that when grain rationing was lifted, grain began flowing from Hunan to Guangdong. *Baokan Wenzhai* (Periodicals Digest), 26 May 1992, p. 1.

19 Interviews conducted by the CASS in a survey (see below for more details).

20 See, particularly, Lyons (1992), and the CASS survey cited above. In June 1992, orders were issued to close checkposts and the GPAIC reduced the checkposts from 51 to 5. Guangdong complains that its neighbouring provinces of Jiangxi, Fujian and Guangxi have made no reciprocal attempts to reduce protection. (CASS survey reports.)

21 Discussed in Young and Ho (1993). Wedeman (1993) also points out that since 1979, both the State Council and the Central Committee had issued repeated orders to dismantle both vertical and horizontal impediments to trade. However, as Young and Ho (1993) also point out, the state's orders were never accorded the priority status of a self-contained law, but took the form of less formal circulars, or were included as minor elements of larger pieces of portmanteau legislation.

22 Article 6 of the US Constitution, the 'Interstate Commerce clause'.

23 Wedeman (1993) based on articles in *Chinese Economic Studies*, Fall 1993, by Feng Lianggang, Li Shihua, Li Youpeng, Li Zhengyi, Lin Wenyi, Sun Ziduo, Wu Jianqi and Xu Changming.

24 Another table is expected to be released by the authorities, perhaps as early as 1994. It has been indicated that this will probably not include provincial-level input–output tables. In the event that these do become available, comparisons of the flows in the two input–output tables would provide another source of data on interprovincial movements of goods, with possible subsectoral detail.

25 World Bank (1993). Report No 12291-CHA.

26 Import ratios also rose in some of the remote provinces; Sichuan, Yunnan and Shaanxi.

27 It must be added that international comparisons are notoriously difficult and that any interpretation of the data should take account of the possibility of a margin of error. The maximum difference in the ratios presented here, at 11 per cent, could be vulnerable to such error.

28 The trade to GDP ratio for Russia was much lower than for other FSU countries, at 11.1 per cent. On account of its large weight in the sample, this brings down the national aggregate markedly, if included.

29 Why the CASS data differ from the SSB data can be questioned, since the CASS teams too consulted local SSBs (as well as local branches of the CASS, Bureaus of Cooperation, the Ministries of Materials and Commerce, local Bureaus of Industry and Commerce, and other government agencies). While the similarity of the CASS and SSB numbers, as well as the gradually more rapid increase of the former, together with the explanation that the divergence is due to the wider coverage of CASS data, all help endorse their use, these data are used as a secondary and corroborative source of information here, rather than as a primary source.

30 The data were collected as part of a background study for this report, undertaken by the CASS. Data are collected from provincial authorities and Departments of Cooperation. Since the total investment in these provinces accounted for around 30 per cent of national investment,

128   *Anjali Kumar*

over the period, the sample should be reasonably representative of total investment. However, in a country of China's regional diversity, generalising from six provinces is still problematic and the results should be treated with caution.

31 The allocation of producer goods, until 1993, was undertaken through the Material Supply bureaus of the former Ministry of Materials and Equipment (MME). Consumer goods were distributed through the Ministry of Commerce (MOC), through large state-owned trading enterprises in cities, and through the network of All China Supply and Marketing Cooperatives in rural areas. This segmentation of responsibilities for internal marketing ceased in 1993, with the merger of these two ministries, to form a single new Ministry of Internal Trade (MIT).

32 In regional terms, increases appear smaller in relatively developed areas and larger in more backward areas. Thus, the growth of personnel in Beijing, Shanghai and Guangdong, in terms of personnel in the materials circulation system, was much lower than the national average (at 1.1 per cent, 0.4 per cent and 1.7 per cent per year on average).

33 World Bank (1993). Report No. 12291-CHA. Estimated from data in the *China Statistical Yearbook*, various issues.

34 World Bank (1993). Report No. 12291-CHA; Kumar (1994), March.

35 There is some evidence to suggest that definitions used by the State Statistical Bureau's data on the tertiary sector are also being revised. Data on the value of GNP originating in 'commerce', for 1991, as reported in the 1992 'Yearbook' (English version), have been revised upwards from Y 88.7 billion to Y 124.5 billion in the 1993 (Chinese version) Yearbook. There is a similar upward revision of Y 7 billion in the value of transportation and telecommunications. A part of these difference (around Y 9 billion) stem from reductions in the value of construction, under secondary industry (around Y 5 billion), but the rest is due to an upward revision in the estimated value of 1991 GNP.

36 A comparable analysis of intraprovincial trade, especially within some of the larger provinces, is desirable, but data are not available at present.

REFERENCES

Agarwala, R. (1992) *China: Reforming Intergovernmental Fiscal Relations*, World Bank Discussion Papers No. 178, China and Mongolia Department.

Byrd, W. (1991) *The Market Mechanism and Economic Reform*, M.E. Sharpe publications, New York and London

de Melo, J., Panagariya, A. and Rodrik, D. (1992) 'The New Regionalism: A Country Perspective,' *World Bank and CEPR conference on New Dimensions in Regional Integration*, Washington, DC, April.

Donnithorne, A. (1972) 'China's Cellular Economy: Some Trends since the Cultural Revolution', *China Quarterly*, No. 52, October–December, pp. 605–19.

Feng Lianggang (1993) 'On the "Wars" over the Purchase of Farm and Subsidiary Products', *Chinese Economic Studies*, Vol. 26, No. 5, pp. 87–94.

Forster, K. (1991) 'China's Tea War', Chinese Economy Research Unit, The University of Adelaide. mimeo.

Huang, Weixin (1992) *Economic Integration as a Development Device: The Case of the EC and China*, Nijmegen Studies in Development and Cultural Change, Vol. 9, Verlag Breitenbach, Saarbrücken and Fort Lauderdale.

Jacobs, J. (1968) *The Economy of Cities*, Vintage Books, New York.

Krugman, P. (1991a) 'Increasing Returns and Economic Geography', *Journal of Political Economy*, Vol. 99, No. 3, pp. 483–99.

——— (1991b) *Geography and Trade*, The MIT Press, Cambridge, Massachusetts, and London.

——— (1991c) 'History and Industrial Location: The Case of the Manufacturing Belt', *American Economic Review*, papers and proceedings, May, pp. 80–3.

Kumar, A. (1994) 'China: The Investment System and Public Investment Behavior', mimeo, World Bank.

——— (1994) 'China: Internal Trade, Output and Marketing', paper presented at the Workshop on East Asia: Politics, Economy and Society, Department of Political Science, University of Chicago.

Li Shihua (1993) 'Anatomy of Local Protectionism', *Chinese Economic Studies*, Vol. 26, No. 5, pp. 51–58.

Li Youpeng (1993) 'Current Regional Blockades and Suggested Solutions', *Chinese Economic Studies*, Vol. 26, No. 5, pp. 37–50.

Li Zhengyi (1993) 'In-Depth Exploration of the Question of Regional Blockades', *Chinese Economic Studies*, Vol. 26, No. 5, pp. 23–36.

Lin Wenyi (1993) 'On Local Protectionism in China's Market Development', *Chinese Economic Studies* Vol. 26, No. 5, pp. 59–78.

Lyons, T.P. (1987) *Economic Integration and Planning in Maoist China*, Columbia University Press, New York

——— (1992) 'Market-Oriented Reform in China: Cautionary Tales', Department of Economics, Cornell University, mimeo.

Michalopoulos, C. and Tarr, D. (1992) 'Trade and Payments Arrangements for the States of Former USSR', Studies of Economies in Transition Paper No. 2, World Bank, Washington D.C.

Murphy, K.M., Schleifer, A. and Vishney, R.W. (1989a) 'Income Distribution, Market Size and Industrialisation', *Quarterly Journal of Economics*, Vol. 104, pp. 537–564.

——— (1989b) 'Industrialisation and the Big Push', *Journal of Political Economy*, Vol. 97, pp. 1003–26.

Porter, M.E. (1990) *The Competitive Advantage of Nations*, Basic Books, New York.

Rawski, T.G. (1993) 'An Overview of Chinese Industry in the 1980s', Department of Economics, University of Pittsburgh, mimeo.

Romer, P.M. (1986) 'Increasing Returns and Long Run Growth', *Journal of Political Economy*, Vol. 94, pp. 1002–37.

Shen Liren and Dai Yuanchen (1992) 'Formation of Dukedom Economies and Their Causes and Defects', in *Chinese Economic Studies*, (ed.) Christine Wong and Dai Yuanchen, Vol. 25, Fall 1991–Summer 1992.

Solinger, D.J. (1991) *From Lathes to Looms: China's Industrial Policy in Comparative Perspective, 1979–1982*, Stanford University Press, California.

Sun Ziduo (1993) 'Causes of Trade Wars over Farm Products, Their Harmful Effects, and Suggested Solutions', *Chinese Economic Studies*, Vol. 26, No. 5, pp. 95–104.

Wang, Fang Yi and Mody, A. (1993) 'Industrial Growth in Coastal China: Economic Reforms and What Else?', mimeo, World Bank, Washington, DC.

Watson, A. and Findlay, C. (1992) 'The "Wool War" in China', in C. Findlay (ed.) *Challenges of Economic Reform and Industrial Growth: China's Wool War*, Allen and Unwin, Australia.

Wedeman, A.H. (1993) Editor's Introduction to *Chinese Economic Studies*, Vol. 26, No. 5, 1993 (special issue on regional protection).

Wiemer, C. (1992) 'Price Reform and Structural Change: Distributional Impediments to Allocative Gains' *Modern China*, Vol. 18, No. 2, pp. 171–196.

Wong, C. (1992) 'Fiscal Reform and Local Industrialization', *Modern China*, Vol. 18, No. 2, pp. 197–227.

World Bank (1992) *China's Railway Strategy*, Report No. 10592–CHA.

—— (1993) *China: Budgetary Policy and Intergovernmental Fiscal Relations*, Report No. 11094–CHA, 2 vols.

—— (1993) *China: Internal Market Development and Regulation*, Report No. 12291-CHA (green cover).

Wu, C. (1990) 'Enterprise Groups in China's Industry', *Asia Pacific Journal of Management*, Vol. 7, No. 2, pp. 123–36.

Wu, J. (1993) 'On the "Block Economy": Its Birth, Consequences and Cure', *Chinese Economic Studies*, Vol. 26, No. 5, pp. 9–23.

Wu Jinglian and Zhao Renwei (1987) 'The Dual Pricing System in China's Industry', *Journal of Comparative Economics*, Vol. 11, No. 3, pp. 295–308.

Xiong Xianliang (1993) 'Interregional Trade and International Competitiveness. An Analysis based on China's Manufacturing Industry', (translation from Chinese), *Economic Research (Jingji Yanjiu)*, Vol. 8, pp. 71–75.

Xu Changming (1993) 'On an Economic Policy Based on "Titled Regions"', *Chinese Economic Studies* Vol. 26, No. 5, pp. 79–86.

Yang, D.L. (1991) 'Reforms, Resources and Regional Cleavages: The Political Economy of Coast–Interior Relations in Mainland China', *Issues and Studies*, Vol. 27, No. 9.

Young, J.C. and Ho, H.H. (1993) 'China Moves Against Unfair Competition' *East Asian Executive Reports*, September, pp. 9–13.

Zhang Xiohe, Weiguo, L. Keliang, S. Findlay, C. and Watson, A. (1991) *The 'Wool War' and 'Cotton Chaos': Fibre Marketing in China*, Chinese Economic Research Unit, University of Adelaide, No. 91/14.

5 The many worlds of China's provinces

Foreign trade and diversification

Brantly Womack and Guangzhi Zhao

'Contemporary history no longer respects the isolation of China or any other country, by land or sea.'

Owen Lattimore, *Inner Asian Frontiers of China*, 1940

In the 1980s China became the world's fastest growing major economy, but the rate of economic growth is not the most novel feature of China's new economic direction. More impressive is that recent growth is a response to a decentralising tendency of Chinese economic policy, and as a result growth has produced an unprecedented diversification of economic activity. All provinces have benefited from the new policies, but they have thereby become less uniform. In conjunction with increasingly permissive policies concerning international economic activity and different degrees and directions of access to foreign markets on the part of provinces, the diversification of provincial involvement in international trade and in provincial patterns of trade is particularly marked.

Diversification and internationalisation are both widely viewed as desirable policy outcomes, and they are clearly related to a vast increase in China's material wealth. Permission to diversify has been a cornerstone of Deng Xiaoping's modernisation programme. At the household level the blessing was given for some to get rich first, and in the area of provincial trade the natural advantages of a place like Guangdong have been enhanced by preferential treatment by the centre.[1] Although the *avant garde* behaviour of Shenzhen Special Economic Zone has been an occasional bone of contention between conservatives and pragmatists since the early 1980s, in general the progress of advanced areas has been viewed as forging a path for the rest of the country. It could be argued that the progress produced by diversification and internationalisation has been an important contributing factor to the stability of the Chinese regime, even if the emerging civil society that they have encouraged also contributed to the ferment and eventual tragedy of Tiananmen.[2]

It is also clear, however, that the horn of plenty has some of the characteristics of Pandora's box. Growth has occurred with the permission of the centre, but not under its close supervision, and the direction of growth has been centrifugal. The centre could not regain the control it had just a decade ago without severe economic consequences; indeed, some worry that the centre is in danger of losing its general regulative capacity, and that the centrifugal effects of diversification might lead to national disorder.[3] Such concerns are heightened by the example of the Soviet Union. High rates of change and novel directions of growth inevitably raise questions about deeper consequences. In any case, even committed modernisers like Zhu Rongji have been forced to take strong regulatory action at the centre in order to slow the dizzying pace of growth and to control inflation.

By its nature diversity is hard to describe, and the big question of 'where is all this heading?' is too vast to be dealt with comprehensively. This article concentrates on one facet of these developments, namely, differences in the pattern and magnitude of international exports of China's provinces. The facet is an important one for three reasons. First, provinces are a traditional, stable and powerful level of government in China. Diversification at the provincial level is not only a natural first level of disaggregation, it is also one at which political articulation is possible. At the provincial level the contrast between real provincial discretion and political clout on the one hand and on the other their vulnerability to central interference might give rise to federalistic demands. In turn, diversification also poses internal problems for provincial governments in so far as they face rising demands from localities and citizens. Second, international trade is a major area of provincial diversity and one related to provincial wealth. The dimensions will be described below, but it is abundantly clear to foreign visitors that officials in every province consider foreign trade and investment as vital to modernisation. The third reason is fortunately more hypothetical: namely, if disunity develops in China, provincial differences based on disparities in international relations would undoubtedly play a role in the discord.

The first and most important task of this study is to produce a preliminary overview of the scale and diversity of the foreign trade relations of the various provinces. Because of the complexity of dealing with 30 different units in potential relationship with 160 countries, some basic limits of data have been adopted. The primary data base of this research is the 1990 provincial export data reported in the *Zhongguo Duiwai Jingji Maoyi Nianjian 1991* (Almanac of Chinese Foreign Economy and Trade 1991, hereafter *China Trade Almanac 1991*). The data collected concerns volume of exports, volume of exports to the top five destinations for each province, and rankings of destinations in terms of volume. The data is rather complete, with only two provinces (Sichuan and Tibet) lacking information on specific export destinations. Export data is used rather than import data because it is assumed to be more accurate for asserting a specific link between each province and a country of final destination.[4] However, the data does not report indirect trade, nor does it report unofficial trade, and these are serious limitations. Virtually all trade with Taiwan is reported as trade with Hong Kong, and a significant amount of Hong Kong trade is bound for other markets as well, including the United States. Unofficial trade is also a serious problem. For instance, Guangxi Province does not report trade with Vietnam in 1990, and yet unofficial Chinese esti- mates would place Vietnam second only to Hong Kong as a target for Guangxi exports. There was presumably an even greater volume of direct unofficial trade in 1990 between Fujian and Taiwan, and between Shandong and South Korea. In general, border trade is probably under-reported. Trend analysis is confined to the national level in this study because only recent provincial-level data on trade partners is available, and in any case the complexity of thirty-unit trends would be enormous.

The basic purpose of this research is to convey an overall sense of provincial diversification and its political implications, because the phenomenon is important and complex enough to require a general recasting of our image of China's political economy. A number of graphic techniques are used to facilitate a re-imagining of China's diversity of international relations in the 1990s, and the historical development of China's trade policy is presented in order to explain the context and novelty of current policies. The questions addressed are the following: How does provincial diversification and interna- tionalisation fit in with China's national political dynamics? What is the general scope and pattern of export diversification? What are the specific characteristics of coastal, inland and border provinces, and of their major partners? What are the political implications of provincial diversification?

The first section describes the development of national trade policy from 1949. It emphasises that the increase of Chinese trade in the 1980s occurred in a context of radically new policies that promoted economic differences among provinces. On the one hand, the general policies promoting market decentralisation and local initiative encouraged a new kind of localism, which we term market localism, to replace the traditional autarkic localism. On the other hand, the specific policies of internationalisation encouraged the inherent differences among provinces to unfold. First, overseas Chinese connections were encouraged, and then places with existing external advantages such as Guangdong and Fujian, and later the coastal provinces, were given special privileges. Even policies promoting more general economic internationalisation, such as those relating to foreign investment, in fact benefited the more developed trading centres more than the inland areas. Lastly, the vast improvement in China's relations with its neighbours in the 1980s has created very specific and localised trading opportunities for its border provinces.

The second section presents the diversity of provincial trading patterns. The patterns analysed include the relationship of provincial exports to provincial economic activity (which indicates how the significance of international openness differs among provinces), the five major export partners of each province (which details the specific trading 'world' of each province), and the index of trade dependence (which measures the concentration of trade with one or a few partners). The data are presented in tabular form, but, because the implications and geographical patterns are hard to grasp from columns of numbers, an attempt has been made to display the data in figures that convey an immediate, clear and accurate image of disparities. We then analyse three general categories of provinces: coastal, border and inland. Coastal provinces have what we term grand advantages of global access, which put them at the forefront of internationalisation and also make their trading patterns similar to national trading patterns. Border provinces have the petty advantage of convenient access to a specific neighbour. If the neighbour is Hong Kong, then the advantage is enormous; if it is Nepal, the advantage is less impressive. In any case, however, the trade of a border province is distorted toward its neighbours, and therefore its trading pattern differs considerably from the national pattern.

The third section on provincial trade dependence goes into more detail concerning the concentration of trade and the trading patterns of China's major trading partners. It is clear that provinces with both border and coastal characteristics (Guangdong is the outstanding example) have the highest volume of trade and also the highest trade dependence. Coastal provinces have high volumes of trade but low rates of dependence. Border provinces have unique trade orientations and are variable in amount of trade and dependence. Trade is relatively insignificant for inland provinces and in general they have low dependence. Looking at this pattern from the point of view of major trading partners, Hong Kong is one of the top five export targets for all provinces and is number one for twenty-three provinces. But its trade is spread unevenly, with the highest concentration in Guangdong and other southern provinces. Trade with Japan has a northern bias, though it is also well distributed. Trade with the United States and Europe fits the national trading pattern by being strongest on the coast. Other countries that are among the top five trading partners of one or more provinces tend to be concentrated in the border areas, because they are the exceptions to the national trading pattern.

The final section speculates on the political implications of provincial economic diversification. First, it is clear that the coastal provinces will be vitally interested in national trade policies. In general they would favour internationalisation, but it should be remembered that their economies are also the ones most exposed to external uncertainties. Border provinces would tend to be more focused in their international interests, and their interest in relations with a neighbour might well diverge from national policy. They are exposed to border difficulties as well as to trading opportunities. Inland provinces have less to gain from internationalisation, but they want the advantages enjoyed by provinces with better access. Secondly, all provinces have some characteristics in common, in that each will be pursuing its own advantages in interprovincial arenas but at home they will be managing similar conflicts based on market localism between localities and groups. Thirdly, all provinces have strong reasons to support the centre, and even stronger reasons not to confront and challenge the centre. Even though China is becoming more diverse domestically and in its international connections, we conclude that China is not about to fly apart.

NATION AND PROVINCE IN INTERNATIONAL TRADE

National trading patterns before 1980

As the controversial Chinese television documentary *River Elegy* (*He shang*) suggested, China has not been an ocean-oriented, international commercial culture, even though traditional domestic commerce was well-developed. The chaos of the first fifty years of this century in China did open the country to international contacts, but they were not of China's choosing and they were premised on conditions of vulnerability and backwardness. China was unevenly exposed to the advantages and disadvantages of international commercial contact, creating a broad contrast between coastal and hinterland areas. But even the most exposed areas were not modern, and the pattern of trade was dominated by the import of finished and luxury goods and the export of raw materials. Until 1890 opium was the primary import, and for most of the pre-1949 period the value of tobacco imports exceeded that of machinery imports.[5] China ran a chronic export deficit in its balance of trade, counterbalanced by remittances from overseas Chinese. In general, neither trade (amounting to 7 per cent of Gross Domestic Product in 1933) nor foreign investment transformed the Chinese economy; they led instead to a partial and uneven development.[6] Of course, considering the colonial transformation of other underdeveloped economies during this period, partial exposure had some advantages. New forms of opportunity went hand in hand with vulnerability in the non-Western world before 1949, a situation best illustrated in China by Japan's interest in Manchuria and later its occupation of the most developed areas of China in 1937–45.

Figure 5.1 illustrates the overall pattern of Chinese trade from 1949 to 1990. In terms of the total value of trade, the pattern is one of stagnation until the early 1970s, at which point the first of four sharp, multi-year increases occurred. The upper line charts trade as a percentage of Gross Social Product (GSP; *shehui zong chan zhi*; also translated as 'total output value'), and it makes clear that the general economic significance of trade declined in the 1960s, and returned to its earlier level only with the first rise in the early 1970s. The increasingly sharp rises in trade in the 1980s doubled its economic significance by the end of the decade.

The initial effect of the establishment of the People's Republic of China in 1949 was to sever the existing ties to the West, and to develop a new relationship with the Soviet Union based on state-to-state cooperation for development rather than on commercial, market-based trade. The scale of technological and trade dependence on the Soviet Union assumed in the Sino-Soviet Treaty of Friendship, Alliance and Mutual Assistance (signed on 14 February 1950) exceeded any previous bilateral dependence, and it might seem strange that a newly independent country, proud of having finally 'stood up' in the world, would assume such an apparently clientelistic posture.

Four factors modified dependence, two practical and two ideological. First, given the hostility of the West, and especially of the

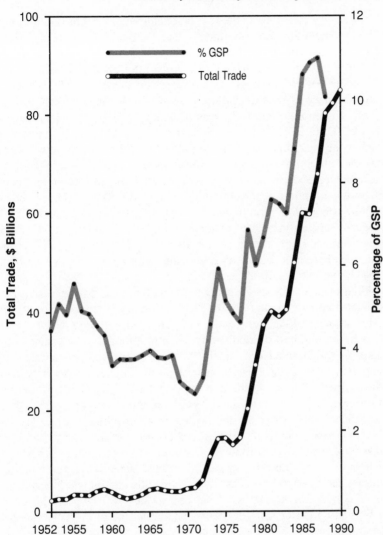

Figure 5.1 China's trade growth

United States, the Soviet Union was the only available major country with which China could pursue a modern economic relationship. Secondly, the economic aid provided by the Soviet Union concentrated on the establishment of a modern industrial base in China. In contrast to the previous period, it was not driven by Soviet commercial advantage, nor was it based on unequal treaties forced on the

Chinese. As plausible as the two practical factors might seem, in my opinion the following two ideological factors were more decisive. First, it was natural for China to learn from and be assisted by the Soviet Union because it was just embarking on the socialist road, while the Soviet Union was experienced and successful. China's rural revolutionary experience did not prepare it to build a national, urban-centred economy, and so it was a natural apprentice. Secondly, as Lowell Dittmer has argued, China's sense of its place in the world had to be recreated in 1949. Republican China and its allies were rejected, the old attitudes of the Chinese Empire were even less acceptable, and revolutionary success encouraged China to inject ideological optimism into finding a new world posture. The socialist camp provided a structured international peer group, and China became an enthusiastic member.[7] By 1957, however, China's achievement of transition to socialism and also its concerns about the socialist camp began an alienation from both the Soviet model and Soviet leadership.

Figure 5.2 describes the shift in China's trading partners from the Soviet-dominated pattern of the 1950s to the more diverse situation in later decades. Hong Kong is the most consistent trading partner, as it was in the first half of the twentieth century, though direct trade with Taiwan and South Korea in the 1990s will undoubtedly reduce its apparent trade share. Japan's trade share in the 1970s and 1980s is in the ballpark of its trade share in the 1920s and early 1930s, while the European share is less than it was in the interwar period. The American trade share of the 1980s is approaching earlier levels. Missing from the graph is the composition of non-major trading partners, which has shifted from Eastern Europe in the 1950s and 1960s to Asian countries in the 1970s and 1980s. If we combine the Soviet and Eastern European trade shares, the communist block share is 62 per cent in the 1950s, 21 per cent in the 1960s, 9 per cent in the 1970s and 3 per cent in the 1980s. The larger pie of the 1980s shows that while trade now has greater proportional significance, the distribution of trade has not returned to the lopsided distribution of the 1950s at the national level.

Even before the Soviet Union abruptly withdrew its assistance to China in July 1960, the Great Leap Forward provided an introverted model of modernisation in which the key resource was political mobilisation rather than importable inputs. The failure of the Great Leap Forward and the souring of relations with the Soviet Union led to a certain diversification of trade in the early 1960s, but primarily to meet pressing needs such as the shortage of grain. So, as the figures

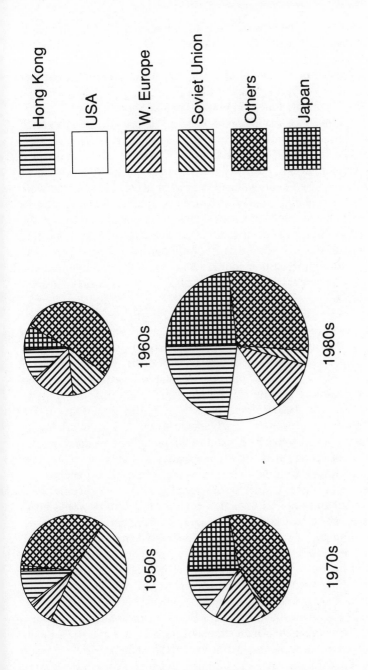

Figure 5.2 China's trading partners

illustrate, the significance of trade for China's modernisation plans actually declined in the 1960s. Moreover, even internal commerce declined after 1957 as the economy became exclusively state-owned and administered. A wave of trade expansion involving further diversification of partners and products occurred in the early and mid-1970s. This included important capital goods like chemical fertiliser plants, but the increase in trade activity merely returned foreign economic relations to the role in modernisation that they had enjoyed in the 1950s. Hua Guofeng's grandiose but short-lived development plans of 1977–78 were a more fleshed-out hybrid of Western inputs into state-planned central projects. These plans were similar to the role of Soviet aid in Chinese modernisation in the 1950s as well as to the attempts of various Eastern European countries in the 1970s, especially Poland, to jump-start modernisation by importing technological inputs from the West. Although Hua's plans began the growth in foreign trade that continued in the 1980s, the international economic policy that began to develop after 1979 was clearly different in concept.

The species of trade throughout the 1949–79 period was one of imports being directed by central perceptions of domestic shortfalls or modernisation needs, and of exports being arranged to cover the cost of imports. Even after the replacement of the Stalinist modern-isation model by a Maoist one, the derivative, centrally-controlled and non-market character of foreign trade retained the generic Stalinist pattern.[8] International trade was a firm monopoly of the centre, and not necessarily an advantage to the localities producing for export. Typically, the price paid to the producer was the domestic price, and any profit made on the international sale went to the state trading company. Even the state trading company was not necessarily trying to make a profit, since it was seeking to cover a specific trade deficit rather than to find as high a price as the market would bear. China's aversion to foreign debt might have encouraged exports to balance imports, but it probably also depressed the general level of trade. In any case, foreign commerce is peripheral and alien in a command economy and the tendency is to isolate its contact and influence. International trade was the small tail of a large dog, and exports were the tip of the tail.

Table 5.1 provides two general indicators of trade dependence: trade as percentage of Gross Social Product; and the Hirschman Index of trade dependence, an index of the skew of trade toward one or a few partners. The ratio of trade to general economic output is used as an indicator of the general openness of an economy, and the

Table 5.1 China's national trade dependence

	1951–55	1956–60	1961–65	1966–70	1971–75	1976–80	1981–85	1986–90
% GSP	4.71	4.26	3.73	3.41	4.5	5.9	8.36	10.22
Hirschman Dependence Index	54.88	48.98	27.77	30.92	31.87	33.93	39.29	37.02

higher the trade ratio the more the economy would be influenced by its trade performance.[9] The first row shows the doubling of the trade ratio in the 1980s, and therefore a corresponding increase in the potential influence of trade on the Chinese economy.

But the growing importance of trade does not by itself indicate a vulnerability to the trade policy of any particular country. If trade is evenly distributed among many partners, then general market conditions determine success or failure rather than the behaviour of any one partner. However, the more trade is concentrated with one or a few partners, the more trade is exposed to the decision making of dominant partners. The Hirschman Dependence Index is a measure of concentration of trade. If trade is exclusively with one country the Hirschman Index would be one hundred, if trade is spread evenly it approaches zero.[10] The formula is: $Index = \sqrt{a^{1^2} + a^{2^2} + a^{n^2} + p^2}$ where the a's are percentages of trade of major partners and p is the residual. The table documents the high level of trade dependence on the Soviet Union in the 1950s, and makes clear that, despite the greater significance of trade in the 1980s, the relationship is less concentrated. Considering that Hong Kong is the major trade partner in the late 1980s, the index would be reduced considerably with direct trade between China and Taiwan.

The concept of trade dependence is an important one in this paper, but clearly not in the sense of 'dependency' as it became popular in the 1970s. We can make use of James Caporaso's distinction between 'dependence' as external reliance on other actors, and 'dependency' as incorporation of less developed countries into the capitalist system and the structural distortions resulting therefrom.[11] As the preceding analysis suggests, China's economic structure before 1980 was the opposite of that implied by dependency (and indeed Caporaso refers to China and Albania as models of its opposite, namely, autarkic independence). The concept of trade dependence dates back to concerns about Germany's trade policies in Eastern Europe in the interwar period, and A.O. Hirschman's 1945 work *National Power and the Structure of Foreign Trade*, the source of the index, is the classic study. The index measures the degree of focus in the economy's exposure to trade partners, and since this varies over time in China and, as we shall see, by province, it is a useful analytic tool. A high score is intrinsically neither better nor worse than a low score, but a high score does imply that one or a few trade relationships are very important. At the national level, the present and foreseeable patterns of trade indicate a low and decreasing index of dependence. At the provincial level the situation is quite different, but the differences did not matter until not only the volume but more importantly the structure of foreign trade was transformed in the 1980s.

Clearly provincial trading patterns were not significant in the Stalinist economic framework. The level of foreign trade was low, its salience for local development was negligible, and production for foreign trade was indirect and assigned by the state. Indeed, places relying on comparative advantage experienced relative decline, especially in the 1960s and 1970s.[12] Given that there was no advantage to the producer to produce for export, it could be permitted and encouraged only by the central government's administrative decisions. Even though these decisions did not spread the obligation to produce for export evenly throughout China, the differentiation that occurred was at the behest of the command economy. Centrally-controlled trade was therefore less desirable to the localities and more transparent to the authorities than the market-oriented trade that sprang up in the 1980s.

The transformation of Chinese trade in the 1980s

Foreign trade not only grew along with the expansion of the economy in the 1980s, it was especially benefited by some of the general principles underlying Deng's reforms. Moreover, and central to our concerns here, the transformation in the approach to modernisation unleashed the economic initiative of lower levels of government. If the government had encouraged trade but had not changed its approach to modernisation, much of the diversification described in this paper would not have occurred. Therefore, in addition to the national trade patterns discussed above, the political environment of foreign trade policy must be considered. Three of these new principles of modernisation deserve special attention, namely, the shift from autarkic decentralisation to market decentralisation, the permit-

ting of private and local economic initiatives, and the encouragement
to internationalise.

From autarkic to market decentralisation

Decentralisation was an important aspect of the Maoist approach to
development, and it would a mistake to view the 1980 reforms as
simply a transition from a centralised Stalinist command economy to
a decentralised market. Not only did China lack the material pre-
requisites of a fully centralised command economy, but already in the
mid-1950s Mao had begun questioning the wisdom of a centre-
oriented development strategy. Decentralising measures were an
important part not only of the leftist economic interventions such
as the Great Leap Forward or the Learn from Dazhai campaigns, but
also of the more pragmatic policy phases that followed leftist failures.

Under Mao, decentralisation meant autarkic self-sufficiency.
Clearly an environment of shortage in basic goods invites such an
approach; self-sufficiency is the most complete form of economic
security. But Mao made this middle-peasant ideal into a cornerstone
of modernisation strategy. Every industrial enterprise should be
'small but complete', every county should develop its own manufacturing capacity for agricultural tools, every province should 'take
grain as the key link'. The resulting political economy has been
well described as cellular or honeycomb, since horizontal linkages
are minimised and even vertical linkages are reduced. The approach
encouraged localism, but not necessarily diversity, and certainly not
commercial diversity.

Under Deng Xiaoping and Zhao Ziyang decentralisation quietly
transformed its meaning, becoming market decentralisation in which
each area and unit produces to best advantage within an interdependent market network. By the 1980s the commercialisation of agriculture (percentage of output marketed rather than consumed) became an
official measure of modernity. The media now praised fruit-tree and
fish-pond millionaires, while earlier they had praised Mongolian
communes who with great hardship (and cost to their sheep production) had become self-sufficient in grain. What came to be called
socialist commodity production implied an abandonment of the
peasant ideal of guaranteed self-sufficiency. It permitted producers
to respond to market opportunities not only by investing their surplus,
but by reorienting their entire productive capacity, becoming at the
same time more profitable and more dependent on the market. Tea
villages and button towns reappeared.

The new decentralisation of the 1980s has encouraged a new variety of localism, one with profound implications for Chinese politics. The autarkic localism of cellular decentralisation was primarily concerned with shielding itself from central interference and oversight in order to survive and to pursue relatively modest private opportunities. Market localism has the potential to be more assertive and to be more ambitious in its pursuit of its own interests. Autarkic localism is merely defensive against intrusion, while the interdependence of the market inevitably involves localities in conflicts among themselves of both interests and ambitions. The suppliers of raw materials want to develop their own processing industries; the manufacturing centres want to secure their supplies and markets; the points of transit want to maximise their entrepot advantages. Moreover, the uncertainties and inconveniences created by inadequately controlled market localism give rise in turn to pressures for new dimensions of centralisation, or at least corporatism, in order to secure an orderly national market. Just as economic development has spread unevenly, so market localism makes different demands in different localities: sometimes for market expansion, sometimes for protectionist policies, sometimes for central support. Some of the political symptoms and consequences of market localism will be discussed in the third part of this chapter.

Increased private and local initiative

In theory, China could have pursued commodity modernisation through a more sophisticated central administrative structure, and indeed the central ministries grew and became more sophisticated in their controls in the 1980s. The various attempts at reforming the socialist economic mechanism in European communist countries, from Lieberman and Kosygin in the 1960s and the more ambitious Hungarian policies through Gorbachev's *perestroika*, had such projects. But China historically was less concerned about maintaining central administrative control in new campaigns, and in any case the mechanisms of central administrative control of the domestic economy were less developed.[13]

The encouragement of local initiative in the 1980s involved more than greater slippage in a socialist system, however. The ideological commitment to the elimination of differences between town and country and between mental and manual labour was condemned as ultra-egalitarianism, and everyone was encouraged to pursue individual profit and thereby to advance the common good. The general decriminalisation of material interest was even more important than the numerous new policies permitting local initiative, because it encouraged individuals and units to push at the edge of the permissible. As Ren Zhongyi, First Party Secretary of Guangdong Province in the early 1980s, put it: 'If something is not explicitly prohibited, then move ahead. If something is allowed, then use it to the hilt.'[14]

The quick success and popularity of rural decollectivisation in 1979–82 further encouraged looser reins at all levels of the economy, and different patterns of resources, opportunity and success led to increasing differentiation. The diversification related to foreign trade discussed in this chapter could only occur within the general diversification of society and economy. Otherwise, even if foreign trade had been considered essential to modernisation, its interface with the domestic economy would necessarily have remained under central administration and control. The policies that license and encourage local initiative in foreign trade derive from the general policy context of acknowledging material interest and encouraging initiative; they are unimaginable outside of that context. Foreign trade has merely added another dimension to a general pattern of diversification resulting from local and individual initiative.

International openness

Bold attempts to involve overseas Chinese, capitalist countries, firms and international economic organisations in China's modernization have been a vital part of Deng's reforms from the beginning. Clearly this has been the policy change that has most affected the scale of foreign trade in the 1980s and also its differentiated impact. Foreign trade increased its share of the national GNP from 6 per cent in 1978 to 10 per cent in 1990.[15] The tendency of foreign trade to diversify according to the natural advantages and access of different localities has been exaggerated by a policy pattern exemplified by the creation of the Special Economic Zones (SEZs) in 1980 and the permissions given to Guangdong and Fujian in 1979 to control some levels of foreign trade and to retain income from trade. These are policies that give special advantages of openness to regions and areas that already have better international access in order to encourage even more rapid development. Nevertheless, there have also been general encouragements to foreign trade in conjunction with China's efforts to work with the World Bank and to join the General Agreement on Tariffs and Trade (GATT). Lastly, toward the end of the 1980s border trade has been encouraged between inland provinces and neighbouring countries. Thus four elements of the general policy of international openness may be distinguished: first, openness toward ethnic Chinese; second, special policies toward areas with a trade advantage; third, general efforts to increase access to the world economy and to world economic organisations; and fourth, efforts to expand border trade.

Even before Deng Xiaoping took control in late 1978, policies toward overseas Chinese (primarily targeted at the Nanyang Chinese in Southeast Asia), Hong Kong and Taiwan were becoming more hospitable, and patriotic investment in the ancestral country was encouraged. In 1977 China adopted a more aggressive policy toward promoting the rights of overseas Chinese, reversing a pattern of neglect that had formed in the wake of the Indonesian troubles of 1965. It was intended to encourage a feeling of ethnic community and also investment in China. As luck would have it, the policy was announced just before Vietnam expropriated and expelled a large part of its ethnic Chinese population, and it contributed to the hostile confrontation between the two countries.[16] Restrictions on travel and gifts between Hong Kong and Guangdong were also eased, setting the stage for the special relationship between Hong Kong and Guangdong in the 1980s. Improvement of relations with Taiwan developed more slowly, but the policy of peaceful reunification suggested by the New Year's Message to Taiwan Compatriots in 1979 and developed into a nine-point programme by Ye Jianying in 1981 tended to remove Chinese barriers to indirect trade and investment from Taiwan, thereby increasing the pressure on Taiwan either to bear an increasing cost of enforcement or to moderate its policies.[17] Since Taiwan first relaxed its enforcement of controls of indirect contact and trade, then its policies on indirect trade, and only at the end of the 1980s began to modify controls on direct contact, Hong Kong has been a major conduit and beneficiary of Taiwanese interest in the mainland.

The opening to 'greater China' was not only the first component of international openness, it still plays a central role in external trade and investment, as indicated by Hong Kong's trade share in the 1980s. Indeed, although Hong Kong's trade share will undoubtedly diminish as Taiwan begins direct trade, the share of ethnic Chinese may well increase in the 1990s. Since such trade is grounded in kinship ties, its local impact in China is unevenly distributed. The export trade share of Hong Kong ranges from 8 per cent in Liaoning to 82 per cent in Guangdong. It might be speculated that, given the ethnic and locational specificity of ethnic contacts, such trade and investment would tend to intensify in given locations rather than distribute itself more evenly in pursuit of further locational advantages.

The second aspect of international openness, special treatment to advantaged areas, is closely related to the first. Just as the overseas Chinese were a special part of the international market (and had been so throughout the twentieth century), their places of origin, especially Guangdong and Fujian, were singled out for permissive treatment. Special treatment of Guangdong began in 1979, symbolised by the creation of the SEZs in Shenzhen, Zhuhai, Shantou and Xiamen in 1980.[18] However, unlike the involvement of the overseas Chinese, the permissive policies did have a tendency to spread when they had proven themselves successful. In 1987 special permissiveness was extended to all coastal provinces and since 1989 Shanghai's Pudong development has been the largest focal point of government encouragement. Meanwhile, the rest of the country is attempting to move through the door opened by Guangdong. For example, Hebei Province has announced the establishment of four major economic zones, and it is estimated that there are more than two thousand special zones of various sorts, most at the township level, taking more than 2.4 million hectares out of agricultural production.[19] As permissiveness broadened, it also deepened, allowing rural cooperative enterprises to become involved directly in international trade. In sum, the overall pattern of the spread of permissive policies from advantaged areas has contributed to the rapid growth of these areas, but it has also tended to exacerbate the different rates of development between internationally advantaged and disadvantaged areas. However, permissive policies have tended to expand, so privileges granted to the advanced can be viewed by the envious remainder as the thin edge of a wedge of more general policy reform.

A third frontier of international openness that has directly affected national trade policy was China's responsiveness to the expectations and demands of international economic organisations and of major trading partners. Integration into the world economy has required the development of legal structures and statistics, encouraged movement toward currency convertibility, and has reintroduced large-scale, foreign-funded projects into China for the first time since the 1950s. From the formulation of China's first Joint Venture Law in July 1979 to the decisions in 1992 to publish all tariff rates, rules and regulations, the attempt to involve global investors, traders and economic institutions in modernisation has been a potent force in regularising access and information concerning China's external and internal economic activities. Pressures for global integration have increased general access to foreign markets, as well as foreign access to China, and these pressures continue with China's attempt to enter GATT. Such global openness has uneven effects on foreign and domestic participants because it treats equally those with unequal endowments, but it is an improvement over the previous two categories of openness because it does not give special treatment to the already advantaged.

The last and most neglected aspect of international openness has been the improvement of relations between China and its neighbours and the great increase in overland border trade. In 1978, China had strained or hostile relations along much of its border. The Soviet Union, Mongolia, Afghanistan, India, Burma, Laos, Vietnam – all were sufficiently alienated that mutual trade was minimised. By contrast, relations with every neighbouring country (including some new countries, in the case of the Soviet Union) have improved in the late 1980s, and trade is playing an increasingly important role in the relationship. Moreover, with the relaxation of central control, border provinces are eager to promote trade and cross-border cooperation since it provides an international outlet to these provinces, which are generally inland areas without direct access to a global market. Unfortunately for the purposes of this chapter, border trade is often informal and not well controlled or reported. For instance, in 1990 Guangxi's trade with Vietnam was estimated to be $150 million, making Vietnam Guangxi's major trading partner after Hong Kong, but in national and provincial statistics for that year no trade between the two is reported. Even without the diplomatic problems that existed between Vietnam and China, border trade will tend to be underreported because of the ease of smuggling. Despite such problems the provincial data presented below allow a distinction between inland, neighbouring and coastal trading patterns. Border trade with a neighbouring country is a rather restricted advantage compared to the grand advantage of coastal access to world markets, and one task of this chapter will be to differentiate between what we will call petty and grand advantages in international trade.

The general argument of this section has been that not only has the volume of international trade expanded enormously and its role in national development has been enhanced, but, more importantly for our purposes, the role of the provinces has been transformed by the new policy context of modernisation. The emphasis on commodity trade has allowed market specialisation at every level, replacing the Maoist ideal of self-sufficiency. The new permissiveness toward material incentives has produced a benign attitude toward local initiatives and has encouraged trade by allowing profit retention. Lastly, the four dimensions of international openness – namely, encouragement of overseas Chinese connections; special permissiveness to regions with special endowments; openness to global markets and economic institutions; and border trade – have both encouraged a rapid growth in local involvement in foreign trade and have insured that the impact of trade would differ widely between provinces. In a word, China moved from a policy minimising a relatively uniform and centrally controlled foreign trade to one that encouraged diverse agents to pursue trade according to their endowments. The results of this policy of diversification are the subject of the next section.

THE DIVERSITY OF PROVINCIAL TRADING PATTERNS

It is inevitable that Chinese provinces enjoy a high degree of practical autonomy despite the unitary structure of the national party-state. In most cases they are ancient political units, they administer populations that average 35 million and range above 100 million, and their personnel is fairly stable. As a result, even though the factors influencing trade diversification discussed above affect China down to the village level, the provincial level is a prominent and significant unit of analysis.

In the 1980s, the practical autonomy of the provinces combined with the different advantages of each province to produce significant diversification in many aspects of development, including foreign exports. As a result, the context of provincial autonomy has changed. Vis-à-vis the centre, each province presents a more individuated set of resources and problems than in the past, and each has a greater stake in further central permissiveness, at least in those policy areas that have favoured or might favour that particular province. It is clear that provinces now have more clout against the centre than they did ten years ago, and it can be anticipated that this clout will increase in the event of succession crises in Beijing. Vis-à-vis one another, the interests of the provinces are more divergent, more interdependent, and therefore more likely to conflict, as the concept of market localism discussed above would suggest.

The purpose of this section is to describe provincial diversity of export patterns in order to sketch the range of provincial differences on this important dimension. We will first present the general data, and then discuss their patterns and implications.

Table 5.2 contains the basic provincial export data upon which

Table 5.2 Provincial trading partners 1990 ($ million)

Province	% in na ex	% in GSP	USA	Hong Kong	Japan	W. Germ	Singapore	USSR	N. Korea	EEC	Burma	Saudi Arabia	Sri Lanka	Thailand
Beijing	2.75	6.51	164.28	289.06	185.12	82.36		44.24						
Tianjin	3.72	10.31	227.46	351.63	244.93	101.23		62.55						
Hebei	3.62	5.26	120.00	341.00	701.00									
Shanxi	0.95	2.99	22.55	147.74	136.74	19.50		14.81						
Inner-Mongolia	0.68	3.24	12.74	52.34	59.41			98.53		24.69*				
Liaoning	11.66	12.53	1,052.00	471.00	2,255.00		499.00							
Jilin	1.57	4.49	19.74	215.23	180.64		21.06							
Heilongjiang	2.26	4.24		175.09	172.09			160.86						
Shanghai	11.07	13.48	745.33	1,029.61	759.08	229.76	182.11	358.95	76.30					
Jiangsu	6.14	4.07	385.44	653.63	587.91			110.74		463.12				
Zhejiang	4.70	5.57	226.63	659.83	345.19	137.20		94.94						
Anhui	1.36	2.74	51.00	177.00	115.00			94.00		80.00				
Fujian	4.66	12.57	268.00	1,057.00	286.00	105.00	56.00							
Jiangxi	1.17	3.65		208.86	52.50	30.34	27.24	40.32						
Shandong	7.28	5.81	260.00	590.00	920.00			207.00		400.00				
Henan	1.81	2.44	49.46	305.37	96.30			77.68		107.49				

Hubei	2.23	3.38	61.18	478.20	92.56	34.14		83.83
Hunan	1.68	3.12	71.55	558.03	68.47	36.69		38.77
Guangdong	21.99	18.32	403.00	8,709.00	288.00		140.00	41.48
Guangxi	1.52	5.32	61.20	382.41	55.33	24.35		8.35	6.80
Hainan	0.98	15.78		351.80	32.50		9.90	
Sichuan	2.32	2.62						
Guizhou	0.32	1.79	18.94	43.35	32.09	8.98		
Yunnan	1.17	4.84	22.12	96.28	68.45		142.73		19.12
Tibet	0.03	2.07						
Shaanxi	0.96	3.24	27.39	140.12	68.92	13.05			11.13
Gansu	0.39	1.95	14.12	54.82	38.31		29.09	
Qinghai	0.14	3.16	9.01	34.48		3.84		6.46
Ningxia	0.16	3.43	25.66	8.74				4.24
Xinjiang	0.70	4.07	13.14	57.68	106.05	13.34		72.81

Note: The data for this table are mainly from two sources. The provincial GSP is excerpted from the Chinese Statistics Yearbook 1991. The original data are in Renminbi. They are converted into US dollars using the exchange rate of 1990. The rest of the data are expected from the *Almanac of Chinese Foreign Economy and Trade 1991*. West Germany is listed separately because it is one of the largest trading partners. Other West European countries are listed under the heading EEC. * stands for export to Great Britain. The export partners data are missing for Sichuan and Tibet.

much of the analysis of this chapter is based. The first data column, percentage of national exports, gives the share of each province in national exports, and directly reflects differences in trade volume. The second data column, exports as a percentage of provincial GSP, indicates the significance of each province's export activity as a percentage of its general economic activity. The country columns indicate amount of exports of each province with their top five trading partners. The provinces differ in their reporting of European trade, some reporting countries separately and some simply as the European Community. For most purposes the data is combined in our statistics. It is important to remember that the data here can be expected to under-report border trade, especially with Vietnam, and that trade with Hong Kong includes trade with Taiwan, South Korea and many other end destinations. It should also be noted that the trade statistics used here do not include the full value of goods involved in export processing, but only the value added in the processing. This method understates Guangdong's gross imports and exports.[20] The aggregate provincial trade for 1990 is $48.01 billion, while the reported national figure in $52.07 billion. The difference appears to consist of direct trade by national ministries.

The data of Table 5.2 and of Table 5.3 below are perhaps more accessible in their general import in Figures 5.3 and 5.4. Figure 5.3 gives a rough idea of the national significance of the exports of various provinces, as well as the shares of the major national trading partners in the trade of each province. Figure 5.4 give a picture of the relative importance of trade to the economies of each province by setting the size of the pie according to the ratio of exports to provincial production (GSP). The shares of major national trading partners in Figure 5.4 have been adjusted to account for the large amount of indirect trade passing through Hong Kong. Unfortunately it is impossible to make an accurate adjustment because no data are available that would break down Hong Kong's indirect trade by province of origin. So we have taken Hong Kong's overall amounts of re-exports, excluding re-exports to China, and have added Hong Kong's imports from China in order to construct a set of factors of Hong Kong trade which have been used to adjust the shares of the US, Hong Kong, Japan, West Europe and residuals for all provinces.[21] This method undoubtedly understates Guangdong's exports to Hong Kong because many of Guangdong's exports are daily necessities consumed in the colony, but in comparison with Figure 5.3, it indicates in general the importance of Hong Kong as a final trade destination. It should be recalled that Taiwan and South Korea cannot

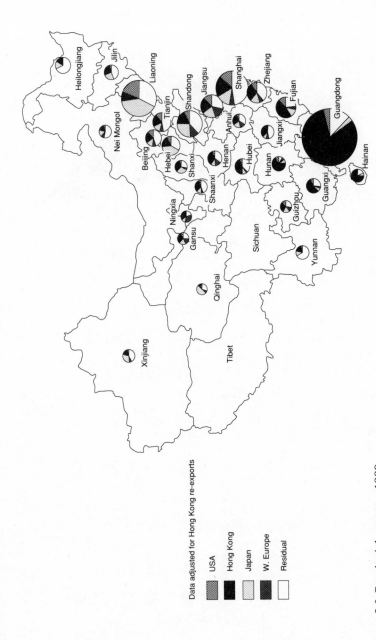

Figure 5.3 Provincial exports, 1990
Source: Computed from China Trade Almanac, 1991

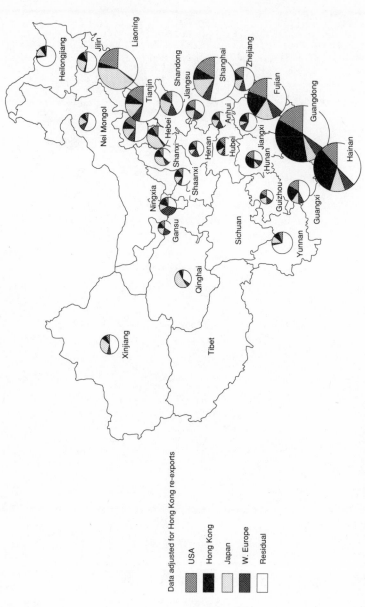

Data adjusted for Hong Kong re-exports

USA

Hong Kong

Japan

W. Europe

Residual

Figure 5.4 Export share, provincial GSP, 1990

be displayed because we do not have provincial-level trade data for them. Part of their trade is unofficial and therefore 'off the map', and the official part inflates the Hong Kong share in Figure 5.3 and the residual in Figure 5.4.

In theory, a province could have pies of quite different sizes if its GSP were very much larger or smaller than the national average. The clearest case of this is Hainan Island, whose trade volume is not particularly high but whose GSP is quite low. As a result, Hainan's trade is very important to Hainan itself, but not to the national total, and its pie is small in Figure 5.3 and large in Figure 5.4. But the general similarity of the sizes of the provincial pies in the two figures indicates that the provinces for whom trade is important (those with the big pies in Figure 5.4) are usually those who are major exporters (those with the big pies in Figure 5.3).

The most striking aspect of the size of the figures is the great differences between the coastal and inland provinces. For most of the inland provinces trade is still peripheral to their economic development. Export in most inland provinces only accounts for around 1 per cent of the national total, and as low as 2–3 per cent of their GSP (the data is presented in Table 5.2). All top ten provinces in exports in 1990 are from the coastal region. About 22 per cent of the total national export was conducted by Guangdong, the leading province in trade. Liaoning and Shanghai account for 11 per cent respectively. The share of export in provincial GSP of all the coastal provinces, except Jiangsu, also rank the highest in comparison with inland provinces, ranging from 18.32 per cent in Guangdong to 5.26 per cent in Hebei. Even if the exports of certain coastal provinces, such as Fujian and Hainan, are less important nationally, they prove to be essential in provincial economic development – exports are 12.57 per cent in Fujian's GSP and 15.78 per cent in Hainan, second only to Guangdong. All in all, for coastal provinces, trade has become central for economic growth, as indicated by the export share of provincial GSP, and these provinces are the primary participants and beneficiaries of the national policy of international openness.

The trading patterns of the various provinces and their partners will be analysed in greater detail below, but some general observations can be made on the basis of the two figures. First, Hong Kong's trade share as final destination (Figure 5.4) is about half of China's total exports to Hong Kong (Figure 5.3).[22] Hong Kong remains a significant export destination in its own right, but beyond southeast China its share is exceeded by the other major trading partners. And the residual, which includes Taiwan and South

Korea, has become quite large. In some places, for instance Fujian and Shanghai, Hong Kong's share may be exceeded by trade with Taiwan; in Shandong its share might be smaller than South Korea. But it should be recalled that re-exports are not simply transshipments through the port of Hong Kong. Re-exports involve goods that are bought abroad and then sold abroad, and this can involve significant commercial functions. China in general and Guangdong in particular depends on the commercial expertise of Hong Kong as well as on its consumption.

Secondly, the residual is large because the graphic technique limits the number of 'slices' in the pies. Some components of the residuals for each province cannot be known for certain; for instance, re-export destinations such as Taiwan and South Korea. But the major destination for Hong Kong re-exports (excluding re-exports to China) was the United States; Taiwan and South Korea were only 24 per cent and 14 per cent, respectively, of the US figure in 1990. In some cases, especially in border provinces, major trading partners of particular provinces are only minor trading partners at the national level. Data on the top five export targets of each province will be presented and analysed below.

Thirdly, there are regional patterns of trade, the most obvious being Hong Kong's prominence for Southeast China. There is a less obvious weighting of Japanese trade toward the Northeast, while US and European trade is heaviest on the coast. If we include patterns among minor partners, it is clear that border provinces trade heavily with neighbouring countries. These regional patterns are highlighted more clearly in Figure 5.5.

Although the present analysis cannot venture below the provincial level, the diversifying effects of trade are present at each level of society. The importance of trade to coastal provinces has permeated even the rural areas which used to be the most cellular and autarkic. The rural town and village enterprises are noteworthy examples. They abandoned the old 'self-production and self-consumption' economic model and incorporated themselves into the export-oriented economy. Exports from rural town and village enterprises increased rapidly from about 4 billion dollars in 1985 to more than 12 billion dollars in 1991, constituting more than 20 per cent of total national exports.[23] These export-oriented town and village enterprises are mostly located in the coastal provinces.[24]

Not surprisingly, the greatest intraprovincial regional differences occur in the leading provinces. Guangdong Province has led the national average in GNP and per capita GNP growth by at least three percentage points since 1979, but the Pearl River Delta, the most active area of Guangdong, between Guangzhou and Hong Kong, has led Guangdong by two to four percentage points. In 1990 Guangdong's per capita Gross Domestic Product was 1.5 times the national average, the Pearl River Delta was 1.8 times Guangdong, and Shenzhen Special Economic Zone, the richest part of the Pearl River Delta, was 1.9 times the Delta's average.[25]

The patterns of provincial trade differ between three broad groups of coastal, inland and border provinces. Clearly, coastal provinces are the export leaders in terms of volume and per cent of GSP. But a simple distinction between coastal and inland provinces would miss the distinctive pattern of border provinces. These categories are additive rather than exclusive: a coastal/border province overlays the characteristics of each category. If we rank the provinces according to their export share in GSP, we see that almost all the border/inland provinces have a higher proportion than the other inland provinces (see Table 5.3). Tibet is the exception, but its relatively low export activity can be explained by the physical extremes of its own geography and of its mountain border with India and Nepal. Conversely, if we compare the border/coastal provinces with the coastal provinces, the high volume of trade is shared, but the former show the trade skew characteristic of border provinces.

Border trade existed before the late 1980s, but was small in scale and often discouraged at that time. Starting from the late 1980s, it has become much more lively – more so even than the official data would indicate, since there is much smuggling, gift exchange and informal trade. For example, Heilongjiang's border trade with the Soviet Union has increased 30 times since it started in 1987. Exports to the Soviet Union made up 33 per cent of the total export of Heilongjiang in 1990. The 19 border towns and counties, which used to be among the poorest even in Heilongjiang, have greatly prospered as a result. The GSP of these towns and counties increases at an average rate of 11 per cent annually.[26] They also start to set up 'Border Economic Cooperation Zones' which will no doubt further integrate the economic development of both sides.[27] Border trade in Heilongjiang is but one example. For Xinjiang, the growth rate of total exports in 1989 was 20.8 per cent, but the exports to the former Soviet Union increased by 142.38 per cent. Border trade of Inner Mongolia with the former Soviet Union increased by 28.01 per cent and with Mongolia by 59.62 per cent in 1990. Burma and Nepal are never important in terms of trade nationally, but they are among the top five trading partners to Yunnan and Tibet respectively. In fact,

Table 5.3 Provincial exports by region

Province	Share in natl. exports %	Share in GSP %	Top 5 not in natl.	Top 5 in natl.	Location
Guangdong	21.99	18.32	2	3	c,b
Liaoning	11.66	12.53	1	3	c,b
Shanghai	11.07	13.48	1	4	c
Shandong	7.28	5.81	1	4	c
Jiangsu	6.14	4.07	0	5	c
Zhejiang	4.70	5.57	0	5	c
Fujian	4.66	12.57	1	4	c
Tianjin	3.72	10.31	0	5	c
Hebei	3.62	5.26	0	3	c
Beijing	2.75	6.51	0	5	c
Sichuan	2.32	2.62	0	5	i
Heilongjiang	2.26	4.24	1	3	i,b
Hubei	2.23	3.38	0	5	i
Henan	1.81	2.44	0	5	i
Hunan	1.68	3.12	0	5	i
Jilin	1.57	4.49	1	4	i,b
Guangxi	1.52	5.32	2	3	c,b
Anhui	1.36	2.74	0	5	i
Yunnan	1.17	4.84	1	4	i,b
Jiangxi	1.17	3.65	1	4	i
Hainan	0.98	15.78	3	2	c
Shaanxi	0.96	3.24	0	5	i
Shanxi	0.95	2.99	0	5	i
Xinjiang	0.70	4.07	0	5	i,b
Inner-Mongol	0.68	3.24	0	5	i,b
Gansu	0.39	1.95	0	4	i
Guizhou	0.32	1.79	0	4	i
Ningxia	0.16	3.43	0	3	i
Qinghai	0.14	3.16	1	3	i
Tibet	0.03	2.07	3	2	i,b

Source: *Zhongguo Duiwai Jingji Maoyi Tongji Nianjian 1991 (Almanac of Chinese Foreign Economy and Trade 1991); Zhongguo Tongji Nianjian 1991 (China Statistical Yearbook 1991)*
Note: In the last column of the table, c = 'coastal provinces', b = 'border provinces', i = 'inland provinces'. The differentiation of coastal and inland provinces is determined by the criteria set up by the Chinese State Statistic Bureau in an article named 'Economic Growth in Different Areas' in *Beijing Review*, Vol. 29, No. 49, 8 December, 1986, p 21.

advantage' of coastal trade. Since this is a permanent, geographic advantage, it implies a longer history of international interaction, a more developed commercial and communications infrastructure, and greater familiarity with world markets. Since access to practically every world market is improved by being on the coast, the coastal trading pattern tends to be more diverse, and it reflects global factor advantages. Because their specific location vis-à-vis certain partners is not a factor, trade patterns of coastal provinces tend to be similar to national trading patterns. Moreover, for all of the preceding reasons, coastal provinces tend to act as conduits for the products of inland provinces. Since significant transportation costs are still involved, and smuggling into major ports is risky, the trade tends to be more formal and to be reported in official statistics.

By contrast, the trade advantage of a border province lies in the fact that, assuming normal relations, the communications and transportation costs with a specific foreign partner or partners approaches zero, what we call the 'petty advantage' of border trade. This is also a permanent, geographic advantage, although its historical and infrastructural implications have been obscured by China's hostile relations with many of its neighbours until the last few years. In principle, however, a border province could develop unique contacts and expertise concerning its neighbour. Unlike the coastal provinces, the petty advantage can involve cross-border ethnic and familial ties. In the case of Guangdong and Fujian, the ties are with Han Chinese; in the other cases there exist ethnic minorities that straddle the border.[28] The transportation advantage of a border province is monopolistic at the border and significant for the entire bordering country. It should be noted, however, that border provinces often have poor communications with the rest of China, and it might be more convenient for some other provinces to use coastal avenues to reach a neighbouring country. For instance, it might well be easier to ship goods from Shanghai or Guangdong to Ho Chi Minh City than to transport them overland to Guangxi and then down the length of Vietnam. Distance and 'economic distance' can be different, especially with technological changes in transportation and communication.

The most important difference between the petty advantage of a border province and the grand advantage of a coastal province is that the petty advantage is linked to a specific neighbour. The factor advantages of trade do not necessarily reflect world patterns, and therefore border trade is less likely to be affected by the world economy. If a neighbour is poor, then the border province might serve as a source for manufactured goods or even investment. Again, if the neighbour is poor, there is simply not much potential for trade. The Yunnanese sometimes describe their border trade as '*jiaohua maoyi*', trade among beggars. However, even a poor neighbour expands the market available to local producers and thereby increases economies of scale. Cross-border shopping can be alert to

The most important difference between the petty advantage of a border province and the grand advantage of a coastal province is that the petty advantage is linked to a specific neighbour. The factor advantages of trade do not necessarily reflect world patterns, and therefore border trade is less likely to be affected by the world economy. If a neighbour is poor, then the border province might serve as a source for manufactured goods or even investment. Again, if the neighbour is poor, there is simply not much potential for trade. The Yunnanese sometimes describe their border trade as '*jiaohua maoyi*', trade among beggars. However, even a poor neighbour expands the market available to local producers and thereby increases economies of scale. Cross-border shopping can be alert to the smallest and most temporary comparative prices. A border provides numerous opportunities for informal trade and for smuggling, and therefore official statistics are likely to under-report border trade.

The trading pattern of a border province is distorted toward its neighbour, and therefore it tends to be quite different from the general national pattern. A change in China's policy toward a neighbour has its greatest effects on bordering provinces, since they might change from being on the military's front line to being first in line for trade in the space of a few years. The fact that Chinese diplomacy is managed in terms of national interest as viewed from Beijing means that the interests of border province are different in both scale and content from national policy making.

The relationship between Guangdong and Hong Kong is a unique combination of grand and petty advantages, because its neighbour is a global entrepot and a major investor in Guangdong. Since most of Guangdong's external trade is investment-related, the availability of Hong Kong capital has been the main engine of its export expansion. Indeed, geographical closeness is not the major dimension of Guangdong's border advantage with Hong Kong; other provinces are not so far away. The ethnic link, reinforced through investment and encouraged by national, provincial and local policies, has been more important.

Fujian's relationship with Taiwan is also developing into a petty advantage of such scale that it embarrasses our terminology. Its success is not well represented in our data because Taiwan investment and trade has expanded only recently. The ethnic link between Taiwan and Fujian is not as strong as that between Guangdong and Hong Kong, and the Taiwan Straight is not as convenient as a land border. Both of these factors reduce the 'border effect' for Fujian of improving relations with Taiwan. An analogous relationship has developed between Shandong and South Korea. South Korea has concentrated half of its China investments in Shandong, reflecting and magnifying trade links.[29] It is important to note that in discussing border provinces each case tends to be unique because the petty advantage is specific. It is a matter of local convenience rather than (or sometimes in addition to) global access.

Geographic location is not the sole reason for the differences in trade development in each province.[30] China is a country where human factors are no less important than natural factors. Moreover, geography is inextricably intertwined with other societal factors, and, as China's earlier policies have demonstrated, it can only display the advantages described above in a favourable political environment. But it is clear that grand and petty advantages with respect to trade are significant and non-transferable, and they contribute to the diversification of China's provinces in the 1980s and beyond.

PROVINCIAL TRADE DEPENDENCE

Trade dependence at the provincial level must be differentiated from national trade dependence in order to avoid misleading inferences. The major difference is that trade policy is made at the national level, and therefore the primary dependence of provincial trade (if one cares to take such a provincial point of view) is on national trade policy. Similarly, the trading partner is usually dealing with China as a unit in determining its policies, and so trade with a particular province is likely to be aggregated with all other provinces as a factor in determining policy, and then weighed with other political factors that lie completely beyond the province.

If one thoroughly analyses a province using national categories, then provincial trade with other provinces should be included along with international trade. The data are not available for such a study, but if they were available they would undoubtedly balance some of the dependencies described below. For instance, Guangdong would not look so dependent on Hong Kong if its trade with other provinces were factored in, and Henan would not appear so autarkic if inter-provincial trade were included. Guangdong is certainly the most extreme case of external orientation, and yet it is estimated that one-third of its production is oriented toward the rest of China, one-third is consumed within the province, and one-third is exported.[31] Other provinces, especially Hunan, supply 20–30 per cent of Guangdong's food.[32] Guangdong's interprovincial trade reinforces its image as an outward-oriented province, but the outward orientation is bi-directional, towards the rest of China as well as towards Hong Kong.

Even with these reservations in mind, the trade dependence detailed in Table 5.4 is still significant. The economy of a province with a high volume of trade and a high dependence index is vulnerable to fluctuations in trade with one partner; the economy of a

Table 5.4 Provincial export dependence 1990

Province	In national export %	Dependence rate	Location	First partner
Guangdong	18.32	82.66	c,b	HK
Hainan	15.78	75.09	c	HK
Guangxi	5.32	54.41	c,b	HK
Qinghai	3.16	54.14	i	Japan
Fujian	12.57	50.92	c	HK
Hunan	3.12	47.33	i	HK
Liaoning	12.53	47.25	c,b	Japan
Hubei	3.38	47.12	i	HK
Hebei	5.26	46.75	c	HK
Shanxi	2.99	45.05	i	HK
Jilin	4.49	43.59	i,b	HK
Ningxia	3.43	42.91	i	HK
Heilongjiang	4.24	41.89	i,b	USSR
Henan	2.44	41.37	i	HK
Gansu	1.95	41.34	i	HK
Jiangxi	3.65	40.88	i	HK
Inner-Mongolia	3.24	40.49	i,b	USSR
Anhui	2.74	39.28	i	HK
Guizhou	1.79	39.26	i	HK
Xinjiang	4.07	38.94	i,b	Japan
Jiangsu	4.07	37.00	c	HK
Zhejiang	5.57	36.34	c	HK
Shandong	5.81	36.02	c	Japan
Shaanxi	3.24	35.52	i	HK
Yunnan	4.84	34.45	i,b	Burma
Beijing	6.51	30.85	c	HK
Shanghai	13.48	29.81	c	HK
Tianjin	10.31	29.36	c	HK
Tibet	2.07	N/A	i,b	HK
Sichuan	2.62	N/A	i	HK

Note: The data for geographic location comes from *Beijing Review* vol. 29, No. 49, 8 December 1986. Other data comes from the *Almanac of Chinese Foreign Economy and Trade 1991*. For Hirschman's Index of trade dependence, see note 8.
i = inland provinces, c = coastal province, b = bordering province. 1990 National dependence rate 41.68

province with less trade and less dependence is more buffered. Secondly, the table makes clear that there are significant differences in the direction of provincial trade dependence as well as in level of dependence. In general, four patterns of trade dependence can be distinguished.

First, coastal/border provinces not only rely heavily on foreign trade for their overall economic development, but also tend to have a higher trade dependence rate on their neighbouring countries. They enjoy both the petty advantages of border provinces and grand advantages of coastal provinces. Trade in these provinces constitutes a high proportion in their GSP, and the trade dependence rate of these provinces also ranks at the top. For example, the dependence rate of Guangdong on Hong Kong is 82.66 per cent. The close proximity of Hainan and Fujian with Hong Kong and Taiwan puts them into the category of coastal/border provinces too. Both of them have a high dependence rate on Hong Kong, with Hainan 75.09 per cent and Fujian 50.92 per cent. Since most trade with Taiwan goes through Hong Kong, it is incorporated into the trade with Hong Kong.

The availability of Hong Kong's service industries has allowed Guangdong to depend on Hong Kong for the handling of its trade rather than to develop service industries appropriate to its level of trade. Guangdong's tertiary industry in 1989 was 34 per cent of its gross domestic product, a considerable increase from 25 per cent in 1980 but still lower than India or Pakistan. The national share of tertiary industry in GDP in 1990 was only 27 per cent, placing China in second-to-last place in the World Bank ranking, the last place being Uganda.[33] One could say that the high level of re-export trade through Hong Kong is evidence of a dependence of China on Hong Kong for tertiary commercial services.[34]

Second, coastal provinces that are not also border provinces have the least export dependence. They have more diverse trading relations with a greater variety of countries. This is true of provinces like Jiangsu, Zhejiang, Shandong and Shanghai. The trade dependence as well as trade partner patterns of these coastal provinces more or less follow the national patterns.

Third, the trade dependence rate of inland/border provinces seem to vary as suggested by Table 5.4, ranging from 43.59 per cent of Jilin to 34.45 per cent of Yunnan. However, what is unique with these provinces is that, rather than following the national pattern, they tend to have a high trade dependence on their own neighbouring countries. For example, Burma has never been an important trading partner at the national level, but it is the largest partner for Yunnan.

Trade dependence of border provinces is influenced by the level of development of the border provinces and their neighbouring countries. Even though a commodity composition study is not done in this paper, it seems clear that provinces that have a strong economic infrastructure or that are neighboured by an affluent foreign country or region tend to have a high trade proportion in GSP and a high dependence rate. For example, an important reason for Guangdong to become the leading trading province in China is that it borders Hong Kong, which not only provides an export market, but also capital investment. On the other hand, provinces which are relatively less advanced economically and bordered by poor foreign countries or regions tend to have a relatively low trade share in GSP and a low dependence rate. For instance, Yunnan, which is bordered by Burma, has the lowest dependence index of the border provinces. In such situations it can be expected that there will be a small investment outflow from the border provinces to their poorer foreign neighbours rather than incoming capital investment.

Fourth, inland provinces do not have the petty advantages in developing foreign trade discussed above, nor do they have the grand advantages of international openness. Similar to inland/border provinces, the dependence rate of these provinces varies greatly from province to province, but it should be recalled that a high dependence rate is not as significant when the level of trade is low. Unlike inland/ border provinces, their number-one trading partners basically follow the national pattern.

Table 5.5 makes clear that Hong Kong is an indispensable partner to all the provinces, not only to those provinces which are geographically close to it. Hong Kong is among the five major export partners for all provinces. It is the largest export partner for 23 provinces, and the second largest for 4 provinces. China is also Hong Kong's dominant partner, because China is not only the market for its import and export, it is also the market for re-export.[35] Hong Kong is an impressive manufacturer and consumer for its size, but its role as an entrepot and as supplier of trade services is essential to its trade role with China. Of course, its role as a re-exporter will diminish as South Korea and Taiwan develop direct trade links. Indeed, since the normalisation of relations with South Korea in 1992, 70 per cent of trade with China is now direct, and Hong Kong has slipped a notch among South Korea's trading partners.[36]

Figure 5.5 is intended to contrast the overall patterns of provincial exports between the four panels rather than to display detailed information about each province. The first panel of Figure 5.5

Table 5.5 Major provincial export partners 1990

Province	HK	Japan	USA	W. Germany	USSR	EEC	Singapore	Unique partners
Beijing	1	2	3	4	5			
Tianjin	1	2	3	4	5			
Hebei	1	2	3	4	5			
Shanxi	1	2	3	4	5			
Inner-Mongol	3	2	5		1	4		
Liaoning	4	1	2					
Jilin	1	2	5		3		4	
Heilongjiang	2	3			1			4[1]
Shanghai	1	2	3	4			5	
Jiangsu	1	2	4		5	3		
Zhejiang	1	2	3	4	5			
Anhui	1	2	5		3	4		
Fujian	1	2	3	4			5	
Jiangxi	1	2		4	3		5	
Shandong	2	1	5			3	4	
Henan	1	2	4		3			
Hubei	1	2	4	5	3			
Hunan	1	3	2	5	4			
Guangdong	1	3	2				4	
Guangxi	1	3	2	5				4[2]
Hainan	1	2		5				3[3], 4[4]
Sichuan	1	2	5	3	4			
Guizhou	1	2	3	4		5		
Yunnan	2	3	4		5			1[5]
Tibet	1	2						
Shaanxi	1	2	3	4	5			
Gansu	1	2	4			3		
Qinghai	2	1			3	5	4	
Ningxia	1	3			4	3		
Xinjiang	3	1	5	4	2			

Note: Under the column of 'Unique partners': (1) North Korea; (2) Saudi Arabia; (3) Sri Lanka; (4) Thailand; (5) Burma
Source: *The Almanac of Chinese Foreign Economy and Trade 1991*

displays the southern bias of exports to Hong Kong. While Hong Kong is the dominant trade partner of all but the most remote provinces, with Shandong and Yunnan as the closest exceptions, it is also clear that Hong Kong's relationship to Guangdong Province is unique among China's external relations in terms of its focus and intensity. It would be surprising if the relationship remained as strong as it is at present through the 1990s, because it undoubtedly is a result of the immaturity of Guangdong's direct relations with the global economy as well as the natural geographical advantages of the relationship. The absolute value of Guangdong's Hong Kong trade will undoubtedly increase, but diversification in Guangdong, espe-

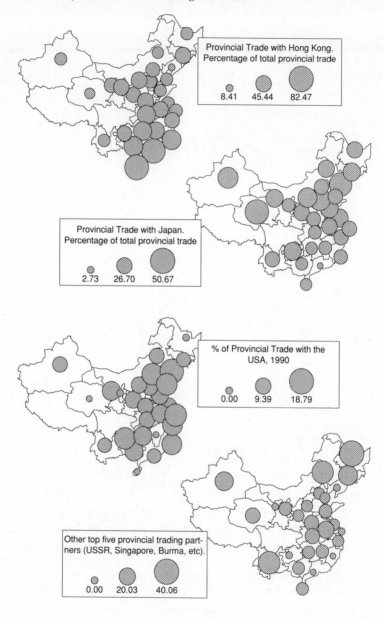

Figure 5.5 Patterns of provincial exports

cially after the establishment of direct trade with Taiwan, will probably increase, and therefore lessen dependence. Nevertheless, even at
half the current level of dependence the economic fates of Hong
Kong and Guangdong would remain closely and inextricably tied.

Japan is the second-ranked trading partner, both nationally and by
number of provinces. Its trade share has expanded steadily since the
1950s, and it has more than kept pace with the trade explosion of the
1980s. The second panel of Figure 5.5 illustrates a northern bias in
Japan's provincial trade shares. It is unusually significant not only for
close provinces such as Shandong, Hebei and Liaoning, but also for
northern border and inland provinces such as Xinjiang, Qinghai and
Shanxi. Two factors that may influence Japan's northern reach are
that, as distant as Japan is, it is still the closest industrial economy to
these regions, and, given the small volumes of trade, a large purchase
of a single major export can affect export share. In any case, it is clear
that geography affects exports to Japan, but Japan has a large
presence throughout China's international economy.

The current dispersion and volume of exports to the United States
and Western Europe are roughly similar. However, it should be
remembered from Figure 5.2 that Europe has been a much steadier
trade partner for China than has the United States, and the uncertainties since 1989 in American trade policy toward China suggest that
the volatility in the relationship has not yet disappeared. The third
panel of Figure 5.5 shows a relatively even pattern of exports to the
United States, and a noticeably larger share with Shanghai and the
coastal provinces.

The fourth panel of Figure 5.5 provides a collective illustration of
the proclivity of border provinces to trade with their neighbours and
their resulting deviance from the national pattern of trade shares.
The distinctive trading pattern of the border/inland provinces can be
expected to increase rapidly in the 1990s because of its late start in
the 1980s, though it certainly does not have the explosive potential
of the border/coastal provinces. Nepal can hardly be Tibet's Hong
Kong, nor will Tibet be Nepal's Guangdong. Nevertheless, the
transformation of China's borders from zones of isolation to
zones of commerce is already transforming life in these areas and
building new external relations. Moreover, the possibility of entrepot
trade over inland borders is not insignificant, especially for Xinjiang
(through Kazakhstan) and Yunnan and Guangxi through Vietnam.

Off the maps, and rapidly increasing their trade since 1990, are
Taiwan and South Korea. Taiwan's imports from the mainland have
increased 27-fold from 1979 to 1992, with an annual growth rate of

27 per cent, while exports have grown 223-fold, or 58 per cent annually.[37] Both countries have been exporting more to China than they have been importing, and in 1993 exports are growing rapidly while imports are stagnant. In terms of total trade, Taiwan and South Korea were China's fourth and fifth largest trading partners in 1992.[38] Although the export rankings are less impressive, most of Korean and Taiwan investment in China is in export-oriented industry. In 1988 Taiwan's investment was primarily in Fujian Province, but since then it has been shifting towards Guangdong.[39]

THE POLITICAL IMPLICATIONS OF ECONOMIC DIVERSIFICATION

The tea-leaves of provincial diversification are no more decisive about China's political future than the analysis of any number of other major trends, from succession politics to the structural problems of communist regimes. Nevertheless, the diversity of economic situation described above can lead to some plausible hypotheses about perceived economic interests, and while these in turn may not determine who the political actors of the future will be, they might suggest what international interests the leaders at the provincial level might have in mind. We will begin with differences between border, inland and coastal provinces, and then consider generic characteristics of provincial politics of diversity. Lastly we will address the relationships of provinces to the centre.

Looking first at the differentiation between border and inland provinces, it is clear that trade is not an overwhelming interest for either, but it is significantly more important for border provinces. In general, it would seem that inland provinces would have less at stake in international openness, but it must be remembered that the stake of border provinces is quite specific and quite divergent from the national pattern. Thus, a border province like Xinjiang might have much in common with inland provinces on global trade issues. The political leadership of border provinces is likely to become quite involved with the neighbouring country, and it would be likely to favour better relations in its own area, though a bordering province would also be the location of the most acute difficulties in a specific relationship, be they territorial disputes, smuggling, drugs, or ethnic unrest.[40] Inland provinces are less constrained. They might struggle to promote their own international access, or feel free to indulge in heartland nationalism.

Border provinces differ from coastal provinces in the specificity of their international openness. Coastal provinces have the grand advantages of access to the global market, and therefore they are more prosperous, trade is more important for them, and the general environment and structure of trade is a more vital concern. Moreover, the trade pattern of coastal provinces more closely resembles the national pattern, so their concern would focus on the general policy trend. Coastal provinces, and especially cities like Shanghai and Tianjin, would be more concerned about interprovincial barriers to trade. They might therefore have a common interest with the global market in transparency of the national domestic market, although their local economies would be the most exposed to pressures as well as to opportunities. Border provinces have an intense interest in trade with countries of relatively minor national importance, and therefore they might be indifferent to globalisation of trade, but protective and shielding of their own special arrangements. Provinces that are both coastal and border, like Guangdong and Fujian, might be expected to share both characteristics, and be at once intensely interested in specific international relations (with Hong Kong and Taiwan, respectively) and also committed to general policies of openness.

The major difference in internationalisation is between coastal and inland provinces. Clearly coastal provinces have a much more vital interest in the external economy. They would presumably be interested in defending and pushing forward their trading privileges, while the inland provinces would demand the extension of coastal advantages to themselves. This is not necessarily a zero-sum game, but the conflict between inland and coastal provinces over the international marketing of scarce resources can become hostile. The coast has the advantages of money and the national structure of the economy, and the inland areas the advantages of possession and the needs of basic production. These inherent disparities are compounded by national pricing and taxation policies that in the 1980s have been much heavier on the inland provinces. Such conflicts have led to 'wool wars' and 'tobacco wars' between provinces in the 1980s, in which the inland province prohibits the shipment of a specific product.[41] In the late 1980s the conflict advanced to a higher level of sophistication, in which provinces (including coastal provinces) attempted to reserve their local markets for locally produced goods by banning 'imports' from other provinces. But it should be emphasised that such conflicts are premised on the existence of a national market and are therefore expressions of market localism rather than autarkic localism. For instance, Hunan prohibited the sale of rice to Guangdong at one point because it argued that Guangdong should pay more. This action caused the price of Hunan rice to tumble, and as a result the ban was lifted. In a more 'modern' case of market protection, Beijing Municipality forbade the installation of Shunde water heaters from Guangdong in order to protect the local product. Not to be deterred, Shunde began an advertising campaign for its water heaters on Beijing television, and the resulting consumer pressure forced a policy change.[42]

Despite the general interest of coastal areas in global trade, it should be noted that specific problems of openness will be felt there first, leading perhaps to protectionist tendencies against global forces, anti-foreign problems and outbursts, and so forth. Moreover, the familiar societal institutions of the party-state will tend to be weakest in the areas of greatest international exposure and economic development, perhaps encouraging local political as well as economic entrepreneurship.

If we take a more general view of provincial diversity, generic similarities of provincial situations become apparent. First, market localism, the attempt to secure private advantage in an increasingly interdependent and unrestricted context, will condition the general political environment. While this does not necessarily imply a war of all against all, it does imply a connection-building, deal-making, haggling and shielding of all with and against all, and at every level of society. The level of potentially conflictual commotion can rise even if open confrontation is minimised. Like bicyclists and motorists on a crowded road, each can assert their interest and advantage without looking the other in the eye. The provinces themselves will be in the roles of exasperated regulators within their boundaries and at the same time of participants in the national scramble. The provinces are, after all, centres in the eyes of their localities just as they are localities in the eyes of the centre.

Secondly, the provinces will all have to cope with the relative decline of the salience and resources of public institutions. They will have more to do with relatively less fiscal strength, and therefore the effective capacity of the province to provide expected levels of service may well decline. For instance, as economic activity pushes up inflation and life-style expectations, provinces find it increasingly difficult to pay their teachers. Thus the provincial governments of even the most prosperous provinces are likely to have their hands full with their basic governmental responsibilities.

As long as China remains prosperous and growing, it is hard to imagine a serious level of interprovincial hostility resulting from provincial diversification. While the rate of growth in the coastal provinces exceeds that of the inland provinces, all provinces have benefited enormously from Deng Xiaoping's policies. In contrast to development experience in much of the world, the rich are getting richer but the poor are getting richer also, though not necessarily as fast. To take an extreme example, the agricultural production per capita of the minority areas of Guizhou Province was 25.7 per cent of the national average and 52.4 per cent of the provincial average in 1985; by 1988 it had sunk to 17.3 per cent of the national average and 41.2 per cent of the provincial figure. On the other hand, agricultural productivity did increase, GSP increased at 7 per cent per year from 1985-89, and the number of desperately poor people decreased by half.[43] Thus, the poorest regions of one of China's poorest provinces have benefited from reform, and their implicit demands are for more aid from the centre rather than for a reversal of policy direction.

Since the apparent source of wealth is the external connection rather than interprovincial exploitation, the contest is between the haves and the want-to-haves, a competition which sometimes involves conflict, but is basically more of a race than a battle. It is possible to imagine different levels of enthusiasm and commitment to international openness among the provinces, but it is not currently to the detriment of any of them, and it is not likely to become so in the foreseeable future. It is perhaps indicative of a common denominator of provincial interest in diversification that a plan put forward by Li Peng in September 1990 to reform fiscal relations between centre and provinces was defeated by provincial opposition led by Governor Ye Xuanping of Guangdong.[44] Another difficulty to consider is the possibility of exclusivist or separatist tendencies in the rich coastal provinces. In our opinion it is unlikely for several reasons that a coastal province or provinces would challenge the centre or attempt to establish autonomy. First, outside of Tibet and Xinjiang, there is no tradition of ethno-nationalism that could legitimise separatist tendencies. The chaos of the first half of the twentieth century is a negative memory both for China as a whole and for each of its parts. Secondly, control over military power in China is concentrated at the centre, and this is not likely to change in the foreseeable future.[45] In any confrontation, therefore, the centre holds trump. Thirdly, the nationwide participation in political demonstrations related to the Tiananmen events of May and June 1989 indicated the general importance of the national political arena, the political leadership of Beijing even in unofficial and confrontational politics, and the absence of popular local agendas demanding more autonomy from the centre.[46] Of course changes could occur, but in the meantime the fate of European post-communist regimes has demonstrated the pitfalls of separatism.

We can conclude, then, that even serious tensions between centre and provinces are not likely to eventuate in confrontation or separatism. We can go further and emphasise the basic common interests between centre and provinces. First and most obviously, the centre is responsible for the modernisation policies that have led to the current prosperity and to provincial diversification. The depth of the central leadership's commitment to modernisation and openness can be seen in the steadiness of policy after Tiananmen and the reaffirmation of commitment at the Fourteenth National Party Congress at the end of 1992. Difficulties in international openness are more likely to be bilateral (for instance, with the United States over Most Favored Nation status) rather than general policy reversals. In times of crisis at the centre, it would be clear to all contenders for power that the measure most likely to win support and to diffuse opposition would be a guarantee of continuity in economic modernisation and international openness. Any more progressive central regime would almost certainly remain committed to openness as a matter of principle, while even a more repressive regime might well try to allay international and domestic concerns by reaffirming economic openness.

Second, the provinces need the national ordering provided by the centre. It has become particularly obvious in 1993 that unrestrained investment and growth can lead to an overheating of the economy, and that the centre must intervene and regulate. Zhu Rongji's current attempt to reconstruct the centre as an effective regulator of the national economy may inconvenience the current plans of provinces, but it would be difficult to claim that it is not in their long-term interest. Provincial interest in an effective centre goes beyond controlling inflation. The provincial political and economic structures are modelled on the centre, and any fundamental attack on central institutions would imply a critique of provincial institutions. Relations with other provinces and with foreign countries are regulated by the centre, and no province is in a position to provide these services for itself. Therefore, while provinces might pursue measures that would give them more autonomy from the centre in various areas, a province that threatened to disrupt the central order might well be seen as a threat by other provinces.

The last and most basic common interest between even the most diversified province and the centre is that the internal market of China is essential to prosperity. This is true for Hong Kong as well as for the PRC, and it is rapidly becoming a factor for Taiwan. To be separated from China would mean to cut oneself off from the one-fifth of the world's population that one identifies with ethnically and politically, and that is the major source for trade and resources. To damage the unity of China would put at risk the context of provincial prosperity. At a time when China's neighbours and the rest of the world feel the gravity of the China market, it is difficult to imagine a part breaking free of the surface. And while market localism might be more aggressive and contentious than autarkic localism, commercial development implies a spreading network of interdependence. This chapter has described the variety of international interdependence that developed in the 1980s, but these new external orientations are premised on internal unity, they are not centrifugal forces. Great uncertainties remain for China's politics in the 1990s, but the lines differentiating the many worlds of China's provinces probably do not mark fractal patterns.

Although this positive prognostication is not intentionally optimistic, it should be noted that research is usually biased toward rational action by participants and toward the continuation of perceived trends. Events at Tiananmen in 1989 are caution enough that things can happen that no one intends or desires. As long as central succession is uncertain and there is no definition of provincial autonomy, it is impossible to preclude vicious circles leading to national disruption. But diversification, including the dimension of international diversification discussed in this chapter, does not by any means make this possibility either inevitable or desirable.

NOTES

The authors would like to thank the Miller Center of the University of Virginia for its research support, and the University Service Center of Chinese University of Hong Kong and the University of Binghampton for hosting seminar presentations. Thomas Rawski, Yun-Wing Sun and Herman Schwartz provided helpful comments on earlier drafts.

1 See Ezra Vogel, *One Step Ahead in China: Guangdong Under Reform* (Cambridge: Harvard University Press, 1989).
2 The emergence of the term *shimin* (civilians, cityfolk) during the demonstrations and the participation of the *getihu* (individual entrepreneurs) in the 1989 demonstrations are particularly striking signs of the political consequences of societal changes. See Jonathan Unger, ed., *The Pro-Democracy Demonstrations in China: Reports from the Provinces* (Armonk: M.E. Sharpe, 1991).
3 Chen Yuan, the son of Chen Yun, has been a spokesperson for these concerns. See He Pin, Gao Xin, 'Chen Yuan–Taizi dang touhao zhongzi xuan shou', *Minzhu Zhongguo*, no. 8 (February, 1992), pp. 25–32.

4 Further research will be concerned with the differences of export and import patterns, which are considerable.

5 See Albert Feuerwerker, 'Economic Trends, 1912–1949', in John K. Fairbank, ed., *The Cambridge History of China*, volume 12 (Cambridge: Cambridge University Press, 1983), pp. 28–127, esp. pp. 120–127.

6 *Ibid.*, p. 126.

7 Lowell Dittmer, 'China's Search for its Place in the World', in Brantly Womack, ed., *Contemporary Chinese Politics in Historical Perspective* (Cambridge: Cambridge University Press, 1991), pp. 209–61. Its other, unstructured peer group was the third world.

8 For a general treatment see Franklyn Holzman, 'Foreign Trade Behavior in Centrally Planned Economies', in Henry Rosovsky, ed., *Industrialization in Two Systems* (New York: John Wiley, 1966). Nicholas Lardy applies this model to China in the second chapter of *Foreign Trade and Economic Reform in China, 1978–1990* (Cambridge: Cambridge University Press, 1992), and John Kamm gives a more existential account of pre-reform trade practice in Guangdong in his chapter, 'Reforming Foreign Trade', in Ezra Vogel, *One Step Ahead*, pp. 338–94.

9 Ordinarily the ratio of trade to GNP is used as an indicator, but, as Lardy details, cross-national comparisons of China's trade ratio are quite problematic in any case. It happens, however, that the ratio of trade to GSP corresponds quite closely to his preferred estimates of the GNP trade ratio, which would be 5.8 per cent in 1978 and 9.4 per cent in 1988. See Lardy, *Foreign Trade*, Appendix B, pp. 150–55 for a full discussion.

10 See A.O. Hirschman, *National Power and the Structure of Foreign Trade* (Berkeley: University of California Press, 1980, original 1945) for the development of the index, especially Part Two, pp. 85–162. To illustrate the formula: If all trade were with one country, the equation would be: $\text{Index} = \sqrt{100^2 + 0^2 + 0^2 + 0^2} = 100.$ If trade were spread evenly among one hundred partners, it would be $\text{Index} = \sqrt{100(1^2)} = 10.$ As Hirschman points out in his original formulation (p. 99), the index measures the departure from equal shares of trade, not dependence on one partner. Sometimes the Hirschman Index is given on a scale of one to zero, but we have retained Hirschman's original scale. To convert, divide by 100 (i.e. add a dot in front).

11 James Caporaso, 'Dependence, Dependency and Power in the Global System: A Structural and Behavioral Analysis', *International Organisation*, 32: 1 (Winter, 1978), pp. 13–45.

12 A good illustration would be the sugar cane regions of Fujian Province, which were artificially impoverished in the 1960s and 70s because policies stressed local grain self-sufficiency. With such controls eased and then lifted, sugar production tripled between 1976 and 1981. See Nicholas Lardy, 'State Intervention and Peasant Opportunities', in William Parish, ed., *Chinese Rural Development: The Great Transformation* (Armonk: M.E. Sharpe, 1985), pp. 46–49. According to Thomas Lyons, 'of the 11 chronic-poverty counties [in Fujian] of 1977–79, one is traditionally the largest fruit producer, two are leading sugar producers, one is the largest tea producer, one is the largest tobacco producer, and three are among the leading producers of seafoods.' Lyons, *China's War on Poverty: A Case Study of Fujian Province, 1985–1990* (Hong Kong

Institute of Asia–Pacific Studies, Chinese University of Hong Kong, 1992), p. 27.

13 Alexander Eckstein, *China's Economic Revolution* (New York: Cambridge University Press, 1977). As discussed above, however, the management and role of foreign trade adhered closely to the Stalinist model.

14 Quoted in Vogel, *One Step Ahead*, p. 81.

15 See Lardy, *Foreign Trade*, Appendix B, pp. 150–155.

16 Chang Pao-min, *Beijing, Hanoi and the Overseas Chinese* (Berkeley: Center for Chinese Studies, 1982).

17 See 'Message to Compatriots on Taiwan', *Beijing Review*, 1979, no. 1 (5 January), pp. 16–17; 'Chairman Ye's Elaborations of Policy Concerning Return of Taiwan to the Motherland and Peaceful Reunification', *Beijing Review*, 1981, no. 40 (5 October), pp. 10–11.

18 The policy changes toward Guangdong are described in Vogel, *One Step Ahead*.

19 For Hebei see *Dow Jones International*, 9 March, 1993; for overall zone development see Associated Press, 10 February, 1993.

20 See Pak-Wai Liu, Yun-Wing Sun, R. Yue-Chim Wong and Pui-King Lau, *China's Economic Reform and Development Strategy of Pearl River Delta* (Hong Kong: Nanyang Commercial Bank, 1992), pp. 28–31. The statistics used are based on the MOFERT (Ministry of Foreign Economic Relations and Trade) method, the alternative is the Customs method, which is closer to international usage. Using the Customs method, Guangdong's exports would be 30 per cent of national exports in 1990.

21 The Hong Kong data is from *Hong Kong 1993* (Hong Kong, Government Information Services, 1993), p. 430. We have not attempted in Figure 5.4 to separate Taiwan or South Korea from the residual because we lack provincial-level data, but national data is presented in this analysis.

22 Two assumptions of this estimate should be noted. First, our choice of the MOFERT method of calculating exports, discussed above, reduces the apparent role of Guangdong and of Hong Kong. Secondly, our calculations assume that Hong Kong's re-exports to destinations other than China originate in China. Given the pattern of Hong Kong's re-exports this is a plausible assumption. See *Hong Kong 1993*, p. 430.

23 See David Zweig 'Internationalizing China's Countryside: The Political Economy of Exports from Rural Industry', *China Quarterly* No. 128 (December 1991), p. 718. Nicholas R. Lardy 'Chinese Foreign Trade', *China Quarterly*, No. 131 (September 1992) p. 710.

24 Zweig, 'Internationalizing China's Countryside'.

25 Calculated from Pak-Wai Liu, *China's Economic Reform*, pp. 1–3.

26 All the figures concerning trade increase and border trade come from *Zhongguo Duiwai Jingji Maoyi Nianjian (Almanac of Chinese Foreign Economy and Trade)*.

27 Li, Chunlei 'Dakai guomen, bian bu zai qiong' (Opening the Doors, the Border Will No Longer Be Poor), *Liaowang Zhoukan (Outlook Weekly)*, No. 22, 1 June, 1992.

28 The Nung minority on the Vietnam–Guangxi border had the monopoly on border trade until the 1990s, and it is still common for the border porters to be Nung.

176   *Brantly Womack and Guangzhi Zhao*

29 Xinhua News Agency, 22 February 1993.
30 See Lardy, pp. 711–714, for a very interesting discussion of Guangdong's advantages over Shanghai in coping with the remaining administrative limits on market access and in dealing with interprovincial supply problems.
31 Information supplied by Dr. Yung-Wing Sun of Chinese University of Hong Kong.
32 Pak-Wai Liu *et al.*, *China's Economic Reform*, p. 19.
33 Pak-Wai Liu *et al.*, *China's Economic Reform*, pp. 56–57.
34 Of course, trade with Taiwan and South Korea had to go through intermediaries for political reasons.
35 See Michele Ledic, 'Hong Kong and China: Economic Interdependence' in *China in the Nineties: Crisis Management and Beyond*, David S.G. Goodman and Gerald Segal, eds, Oxford: Clarendon Press, 1991, pp. 201–8.
36 *China Daily*, 21 August 1993.
37 Ricky Tung, 'Economic Interaction Between Taiwan and South China's Fukien and Kwangtung Provinces', *Issues and Studies*, 29: 7 (July 1993), p. 33.
38 The largest trading partners were Hong Kong, the United States and Japan, in that order. Xinhua News Agency 22 February 1993.
39 Ricky Tung, 'Economic Interaction', pp. 29–30.
40 A good example of border province activism would be the grand plans for Mekong development of Wu Guanglan, Party Secretary of Yunnan Province. See *Far Eastern Economic Review*, 16 September 1993, pp. 68–70.
41 There is an excellent analysis of these conflicts in Chen Dongshen and Wei Houkai, 'Some Reflections on Interregional Trade Friction', in *Gaige*, no. 2 (20 March 1989), pp. 79–83. Available in JPRS-CAR-89-077, 24 July 1989, pp. 5–9.
42 Pak-Wai Liu *et al.*, *China's Economic Reform*, p. 21. At last report, Beijing still charges a higher installation fee for Shunde water heaters. See also *Far Eastern Economic Review*, 18 October 1990, p. 89.
43 Li Renshan, 'Guizhou shaoshu minzu zizhi difang jingji shehui fazhan qingkuang cunzai wenti yu jinhoufazhan di jianyi'. (Current problems in the economic and societal developmental situation in Guizhou's autonomous minority localities). In Guizhou sheng shaoshu minzu jingji yanjiu hui, ed, *Guizhou sheng shaoshu minzu jingji yanjiu* [Economic research concerning the national minorities of Guizhou Province] (Guiyang: Guizhou minzu chubanshe, 1991), pp. 1–9. Thomas Lyons describes a similar situation in Fujian, and analyses the effectiveness of a national anti-poverty campaign, in *China's War on Poverty*, but Guizhou is an even more impoverished area.
44 See *Far Eastern Economic Review*, 4 April 1991, p. 26.
45 See Ellis Joffe, 'Regionalism in China: The Role of the PLA', paper presented at the conference *Security Dimensions of Chinese Regionalism*, Hong Kong, June 1993.
46 See Unger, *The Pro-Democracy Demonstrations*.

6 Guangdong

Greater Hong Kong and the new regionalist future

David S.G. Goodman and Feng Chongyi

In 1979 Guangdong Province was the tenth largest aggregate economy in the People's Republic of China and its population had the fifteenth highest GNP per capita. By 1992 its population – some 65.25 million permanent residents – was still only the fifth highest in terms of GNP per capita, but from almost every other perspective it could claim to have become the wealthiest provincial-level unit, having just surpassed both Jiangsu and Shandong in late 1992 as the largest aggregate economy.[1] Where the PRC economy grew 8.4 per cent per annum during 1979–91, that of Guangdong increased at a rate of 12.0 per cent per annum, as measured by national income. Relative growth differentials were particularly marked during 1988–92 when China's total domestic production value rose by 14 per cent per annum, but Guangdong's grew by 22 per cent per annum.

However, Guangdong is less important for its wealth or the rapid rate of growth it has achieved during the 1980s and into the 1990s than for the manner of those achievements. Guangdong's relatively rapid rise to be Number One provincial-level economy has resulted from a high level of economic integration between the province, or more accurately the Pearl River Delta, and Hong Kong. Pressures for Hong Kong to restructure its economy during the late 1980s combined with the PRC's change in policy direction to lead to the creation of Greater Hong Kong. A substantial proportion of Hong Kong's industrial base transferred across the border during 1990–92, so that now some three million people in Guangdong are employed in Hong Kong-sourced enterprises.

The emergence of Greater Hong Kong has not only led to Guangdong's dramatic rise in wealth, it has also provided the essential boost to the development of China's economic growth generally. At the same time it has the potential to present a major challenge to the future of the PRC in a number of ways. Within China the growth of a prosperous South may be socially disruptive as well as politically divisive. Guangdong has acted as a beacon for a substantial migratory population, and its success story has been a cause of resentment as well as a model for emulation to other provinces. Decentralisation of central authority to Guangdong has been a necessary part of economic development since 1978, and provincial autonomy has clearly increased. Although Hong Kong is to be incorporated into the PRC in 1997, at present an international boundary divides the two parts of Greater Hong Kong. While internal pressures may be pushing Guangdong away from the PRC's political centre in some ways, external pressures are pulling it towards centres of economic activity, not only in Hong Kong but also in the Asia–Pacific region.

Guangdong's rise to wealth and status, its traditions of independence, its regional identity, its distance from Beijing and now its apparent greater political proximity to Hong Kong – even before 1997 – have all led a variety of commentators to suggest the potential for the province's future political separation from the PRC if not a general political disintegration. The growth of Greater Hong Kong certainly presents the PRC with a series of political ambiguities, not least in its desire to develop the region's economic potential whilst maintaining its own political control of the region. However, separation and disintegration are less likely items for China's political agenda than the mediation of potential conflict between Beijing and Guangzhou, and amongst Guangdong and other provinces: the management of ambiguity rather than its immediate resolution.[2]

GUANGDONG IN TIME AND SPACE

Since the establishment of the PRC, Guangdong Province has continued to act in its customary role as China's major gateway to the outside world. The Canton Trade Fairs (until the 1980s) and then the establishment, with the reform era, of Special Economic Zones (SEZ) in Shenzhen and Zhuhai, followed by Shantou, have provided a strong sense of historical continuity. There is even a sense in which Guangdong is, as it was historically, recognised as China's gateway not least because northerners regard its inhabitants as 'southern barbarians' and therefore either more dispensable or already corrupted by foreign barbarians. In fact, most of the population is related to Han Chinese who migrated south, with only 0.59 per cent distributed amongst 52 minority nationalities, almost exclusively along the provincial borders, or on Hainan Island, established as a separate province in 1988 but previously an integral part of Guangdong.

The province's apparent homogeneity is offset by Guangdong's inherent social diversity. The different parts of Guangdong regard themselves very much as distinct and even separate communities such that social relationships, including marriage, rarely cross communal boundaries. The lack of homogeneity is demonstrated clearly through Guangdong's intense linguistic diversity. Cantonese, the language of central and western Guangdong dating back to at least the Song Dynasty, is the dominant language. However, Cantonese itself has many dialects, some of which are barely communicable to other speakers of Cantonese. In addition, many in northern Guangdong are Hakka-speakers; in the Chaozhou region of eastern Guangdong a variety of Hokkien is spoken; as is the language of Leizhou in southern Guangdong. Moreover, these differences have political consequences, and right down to the present Guangdong's politics have frequently been determined by relations amongst factions based on Canton, Chaozhou, different parts of the Pearl River Delta and the Hakka.

This internal political diversity influences interpretation of Guangdong's tradition of regionalism and autarchy, which is born largely out of its distance from the various northern capitals rather than any local movements for political separation. Provincial histories often take pride in the fifteen or so independent governments or *de facto* regimes established in Guangdong since the province's incorporation into the Empire in 214 BC. However, almost all of these represented alternative national governments, rather than movements for an independent Guangdong. The notable exception is the attempt by warlord Chen Jitang to establish a localist political identity during the late 1920s and first half of the 1930s, but even that was essentially a function of relations between Chen and Chiang Kaishek.[3]

Guangdong's reputation for regionalism remained even after 1949, but largely because of tensions between local communists and the national Long March leadership generation. During the Sino-Japanese War and the Civil War, Guangdong and Hainan had sustained communist movements not only independent of the main Chinese Communist Party organisation in North China, but also to some extent abandoned by the rest of the communist movement. In 1949 the new CCP government was understandably cautious about the establishment of communist rule in Guangdong, and the province was not 'liberated' until after the formal establishment of the PRC elsewhere. Natives of Guangdong, such as Ye Jianying and Fang Fang, were

originally returned to the province to provide leadership alongside
Feng Baiju and Gu Dashun who had remained active in Hainan and
the East River base areas throughout the 1930s and 1940s. This policy
changed in 1952 with the rectification of the Guangdong CCP through
the agency of the Southbound Work Team sent from Beijing under
Tao Zhu, which removed local cadres and replaced them with
'northerners'. In 1957 resentment led to an armed uprising in Lingao
County, Hainan, by some 361 former guerrilla veterans displaced by
outsiders; and in turn that resulted in the final removal from the
Guangdong leadership of almost all remaining pre-1949 local CCP
leaders.

Guangdong's traditions are thus those of diversity and individualism
rather than of a strong regional identity and a drive for separatism,
and these in part help explain the sustained migration of people
from the province throughout Southeast Asia, Australia and North
America. However, most maintain strong links with their home town
or village. Throughout the twentieth century the wealth of these
Overseas Chinese has been important to Guangdong Province, with
remittances to relatives and support for the infrastructural development of home towns. For the most part these activities have not been
politically oriented, though during the 1911 Revolution and the Sino-
Japanese War they contributed substantially to public activities. In
1979, a peak year, some $518 million was remitted to relatives; and
since 1979 some $1 billion has been donated to build schools,
universities, libraries, hospitals, roads, bridges, factories and other
facilities. For example, Shantou University, Jiaying University and
Wuyu University have all been established with such support. Overseas Chinese have invested millions of dollars back in their native
places – it is estimated that some 80 per cent of foreign-funded
enterprises in Guangdong are from these sources – pioneering industrial development in Guangdong and providing both capital and
technology for modernisation.

POLITICS IN GUANGDONG

The 1980s were clearly an important period of transition for Guangdong
Province, politically as well as economically. The structures of government changed frequently between 1983 and 1988 to keep pace with
changes wrought by economic growth, though there has been relative
stability since 1989. In 1988, the current provincial boundaries were set
when Hainan Island was separated and established as a province and
Special Economic Zone.

Rapid change in Guangdong Province has largely resulted from the 'Special Policy' proposed by the Guangdong CCP in June 1979 and adopted by national government and the CCP centrally the following month. The policy provided for Guangdong to be given greater ability to respond to its own needs in agriculture, industry, transport, commerce, education, culture, technology and public health. The province was given more autonomy to manage its own foreign trade, including the determination of prices for export goods and the establishment of organisations in Hong Kong and Macao for trade promotion and information gathering. New fiscal independence came in the form of a fixed tax payment – negotiated for five years – instead of a certain percentage of revenue sent to central government. In addition the province was granted increased investment decision-making powers, use of foreign currency, and the establishment of an independent provincial investment company that could deal directly with overseas business and financial institutions. The province gained the ability to determine the distribution and supply of materials and resources within Guangdong; increased leeway to set certain prices and to allow market determination for certain other prices; greater flexibility to determine wages, including raising salaries and bonuses above national guidelines; and the authority to establish 'experimental export districts', the first of which was the Shenzhen SEZ.[4]

The results have been quite remarkable, with the near total restructuring of Guangdong's rural and urban economies in a relatively short time. Equally important has been the institutionalisation of greater autonomy. When central government attempted a higher degree of control over finance, foreign currency, planning and other economic activities of all the provinces between 1988 and 1991, Guangdong managed to minimise the negative effects. Indeed, during the second half of 1989 Guangdong explicitly declared a policy of 'business as usual', not least to reassure those in the private and individual sectors and its foreign investors.

In the period from 1949 to the early 1980s, Guangdong's leaders were also key national figures. Ye Jianying, Tao Zhu and Zhao Ziyang all held various senior provincial positions before the Cultural Revolution; as did Yang Shangkun in the late 1970s. However, in the reform era Guangdong has seemed to be under the leadership of nationally less outstanding figures. Its leaders have been more prominent in Guangdong than nationally: Ren Zhongyi, First CCP Secretary in Guangdong from 1980 to 1985, and recognised as '*the* great provincial enterpreneur of the reform period';[5]

Liang Lingguang, Governor of Guangdong from 1983 to 1985; and Ye Xuanping, Governor of Guangdong from 1985 to 1991, and son of Ye Jianying. Interestingly, among the current (1993) twenty-six leading officials of the Guangdong provincial government (the Governor and and six Vice-governors, the Chairman and eight Vice-chairmen of the Standing Committee of Guangdong Provincial People's Congress; the Chairman and nine Vice-chairmen of Guangdong Provincial People's Political Consultant Conference), nineteen are natives of Guangdong, a much higher proportion than would have earlier been the case.

Before the current reform era, Guangdong had some reputation as a crucible of democratic and liberal politics. The Taiping Rebellion, Kang Youwei, Liang Qichao and Sun Yatsen all had Guangdong origins, and in the mid-1920s the attempt to reunite the country under the cooperative leadership of the CCP and the Nationalist Party (KMT) was based on Guangzhou. That reputation did not disappear completely after 1949. Most spectacularly, in November 1974 three Cantonese collaborated as Li Yizhe to write the Guangzhou wall-poster, 'On socialist democracy and the legal system', which provided a detailed critique of the absence of and need for democratic and legal forms. However, thereafter Guangdong surrendered almost any role as a promoter of liberalising politics. It is not surprising that there was little popular support for Li Yizhe during the mid-1970s, but from 1976 on, when public support was often much in evidence elsewhere in China, there were few resonances in Guangdong. During the Tiananmen Incident of 5 April 1976 Guangzhou was extremely calm. At the turn of 1986–7 when students elsewhere demonstrated for free elections there were no demonstrations in Guangzhou. In 1989, while other citizens rallied to support student demonstrators in Beijing by turning out themselves and by contributing food and services, in Guangzhou the students demonstrated but private business people raised the prices of food and drink on sale to the students, and the workers complained that the students had stopped them from getting to work on time and had jeopardised their bonuses.

THE GUANGDONG ECONOMY IN REFORM

The impact of reform and the 'special policy' of June 1979 on the Guangdong economy show dramatically in the relative growth rates of the provincial and national economies before and after the start of the reform era. The average growth rate for GDP in Guangdong Province during 1953–78 was 5.1 per cent per annum, 1 per cent lower than the average national rate of growth, but 12.6 per cent per annum during 1979–91, 3 per cent higher than the national average. By 1992 Guangdong Province had a permanent population of some 65.25 million people. Its GDP in that year was 221.8 billion *yuan* RMB, an increase of 19.5 per cent over the previous year; with per capita GDP at 3440 *yuan*, 68 per cent higher than the national average.

Gross growth statistics mask the fundamental changes that have taken place in Guangdong's economic structure. There has been a massive decline in the agricultural labour force; considerable growth in exports; and last but by no means least, an explosion of light industry. Before reform, almost three-quarters of the labour force comprised agricultural labourers. Now the figure is much less than half on official figures, with the real figure much lower since part-time workers in village and township enterprises, of whom there are many in Guangdong, are classified as agricultural labourers. By 1992 agricultural output accounted for little more than 20 per cent of GDP. From almost nothing exports have grown to be worth more than $18 billion, and about 65 per cent of provincial GDP. The development of light rather than heavy industry has always characterised the economy in Guangdong. By 1991 that imbalance had grown further with light industry producing almost 70 per cent of total industrial output value.

Foreign investment and the development of the new collective sector, based on town and village enterprises, are the keys to understanding many of these changes. Guangdong is the provincial-level unit with by far the largest foreign investment as well as the largest export earnings. Direct foreign investment in Guangdong from 1979 to 1989 amounted to $5.11 billion and indirect foreign investment to $1.44 billion. These were 33 per cent and 48 per cent respectively of the national totals for the same period. In 1992 the province received $4.86 billion in foreign capital which was roughly a quarter of the national total; one-third of all investment in Guangdong came from abroad. There are more than 21,000 foreign-funded or joint venture enterprises, accounting for nearly half of all such enterprises in China. In 1992 foreign-funded and joint enterprises in Guangdong provided more than one third of the provincial industrial output value (the national average is about 4 per cent).

Guangdong has been China's largest export earning provincial-level unit since 1986. From 1979 to 1992 export earnings increased on an average of 20 per cent per annum. In 1979 the provincial total export value was under a billion dollars. By 1992 it had risen to more than \$18 billion, and accounted for one quarter of the national total export value. One-third of goods produced in Guangdong are sold on the international market, though, as will be discussed later, Guangdong's foreign trade like its economy in general is dominated by the relationship with Hong Kong and the latter's role in East Asia.

The collective sector was deliberately developed in the early 1980s in Guangdong as an alternative strategy to reforming the state sector and state-run enterprises. According to Lin Ruo, the political problems were too great, both within the province and in relations with Beijing. Instead, the provincial leadership determined to develop various forms of collective enterprises through extra-budgetary means.[6] By 1992 collective enterprises had become responsible for over 40 per cent of Guangdong's industrial output and more than a quarter of the province's export earnings. In contrast, by 1992 the state sector produced well under 40 per cent of provincial industrial output; the national average was about 53 per cent.

In general a large part of the collective sector comprises town and village enterprises either started by local governments, or essentially established as joint ventures between local governments and private entrepreneurs. In comparison to the collective sector elsewhere, practice in Guangdong – often referred to as the 'Pearl River Delta Model' – has from the start involved the widespread establishment of both foreign partnerships and share-holding companies, and has consequently been more export-oriented and has more closely involved private enterprises and entrepreneurs.

Guangdong has the largest private and individual sectors of the economy of any provincial-level unit. By 1992 it had the largest number of both individual and private sector industrial and commercial enterprises, which were the largest employers, with the largest volume of retail sales, and the largest amount of tax paid. More than 2.4 million people or about 4 per cent of the population are employed in Guangdong's individual and private sectors. Some 7 per cent of the province's total output value is derived from these sectors; as are more than 2.5 billion *yuan* RMB paid in taxes, which account for one-tenth of the national total paid by all individual and private sector enterprises.

A further major feature of Guangdong's spectacular economic growth has been the SEZs, approved as experimental export districts (and only later renamed Special Economic Zones) under the special policy of 1979. Shenzhen, next to Hong Kong; Zhuhai, next to Macao; and Shantou, across the Taiwan Straits from Taiwan in the north of the province, were established during 1979–81. Despite the political goals of the CCP leadership in Beijing, the success of the SEZs has come as islands of capitalist practice within the PRC. Shenzhen – the most successful as well as the most famous – has expanded from an original area of 327.5 square kilometers and a population of some 71,400 into a modern metropolis. In 1992 it annexed Baoan County to become an SEZ with a land area of over 2,000 square kilometers, and a population in excess of a million.

Shenzhen is proud of its role as 'a socialist Hong Kong' and the attention it has received within the PRC. Many central government ministries, almost all provincial-level units and municipalities, and thousands of enterprises from all over China have established their offices, branches or 'domestic link' ventures in Shenzhen, for business, information or enjoyment. Literally thousands of officials, children of high officials, managers, engineers, college graduates, workers and young villagers from all over China have swarmed to Shenzhen. Moreover, large numbers of senior cadres from central and provincial governments have visited Shenzhen on inspection tours or to study its methods and practices, and only Chen Yun of the CCP's senior leadership has not visited.

GUANGDONG IN CHINA

As might be expected, given such rapid change in so relatively short a time, strains have been placed on Guangdong's relations with both Beijing *qua* centre of politics, and other provincial-level units. However, the resultant relationships and power complexes – economic as well as political – are by no means simple, not least because the modernising state is simultaneously changing shape. Indeed, in the excitement of describing Guangdong's development, it is easy to overlook the essential initial central ingredients to the success story, particularly in terms of financial incentives and budgetary arrangements. Guangdong's development since 1978 owes much to the province's location and past, but it also has resulted from its interaction with central government. There are tensions with Beijing and other provinces, but these are more often than not creative tensions that lead to new ideas and policies. Moreover, though there may be resentment and an attempt to rein Guangdong in to some extent, it is also clear that Guangdong has been by no means the most advantaged province of the reform era in every regard.

The starting point for Guangdong's period of spectacular growth was the decision by Beijing to permit the province to take advantage of its special position and to seek investment, technical and technological assistance outside the PRC. The advantage to Beijing was simple, at least at first: Guangdong could develop without the financial burden being borne from central funds, and indeed funds that would otherwise have been used in Guangdong could be distributed elsewhere. In cash terms alone the policy has proved to be remarkably successful. By 1991 only 3 per cent of the province's total capital investment was derived from Beijing-supplied funds.

At the same time, as part of the June 1979 special policy on the province's development, Beijing and Guangdong reached a revenue-sharing arrangement that was both a radical departure from earlier practices and, though it has been a success in many ways, has also proved a cause of some resentment. Beginning in 1980 it was agreed that Guangdong would remit only a small and fixed amount of its revenues for five years to central government given the low level of Beijing's expected investment and expenditure in the province. In effect this was a financial contract between the PRC and Guangdong Province: Guangdong guaranteed to supply Beijing with a certain amount of revenue, and had full use of any surplus it could generate.

The low level of remittances to central government agreed between Beijing and Guangdong has been a source of friction between both Guangdong and Beijing, and Guangdong and other provinces, not least since, with rapid economic growth, Guangdong was soon remitting only a very small proportion of its revenues to Beijing. Whereas in 1978 it passed on 31 per cent to Beijing, by 1984 Guangdong was remitting only 3 per cent of its total revenue. In contrast at the provincial-level in 1984 Shanghai and Zhejiang (which had admittedly larger economies) remitted 81 per cent and 38 per cent respectively of their revenues, and Hubei (even with a smaller economy) contributed 25 per cent of its revenues.[7]

Demands on Beijing and the central exchequer have caused central government to reconsider its original agreement with Guangdong, which it now considers to have been overgenerous toward the province. Other provincial-level units, notably those dominated by older patterns of heavy industrial development or more dependent on central funds – it is rumoured that Shanghai, Liaoning and Shanxi have been particularly vocal – have seemed somewhat resentful of Guangdong's relative rise in economic wealth and supportive of attempts to extract more from that province in tax and other revenues.

In 1982 and 1986 Guangdong was pressured into 'lending' money to Beijing, in the full knowledge that the loan was unlikely ever to be repaid. In 1979 Guangdong had only bought some 817 million *yuan*

RMB's worth of bonds. By 1991 the province had spent 7 billion *yuan* RMB in the purchase of bonds or the making of loans. In 1988 the contract arrangements between Guangdong and Beijing were readjusted. Instead of a fixed amount contracted for five years, there would be a progressive increase of 9 per cent per annum in the revenues remitted by the province to the centre. At about the start of 1991 Beijing even considered unilaterally abandoning the financial contract and reverting to a system where Guangdong would remit a certain percentage of its revenue to central government.

As the discussions on revenue-sharing arrangements between Guangdong and Beijing during 1988–91 bear witness, there is often a general feeling on the part of some provinces and their leaders that Guangdong is 'exploiting the interior'. Some provinces have retaliated by charging or demanding higher prices for goods sold to Guangdong, particularly grain and raw materials in short supply in the province. One extreme example is the 'rice war' which appears to have developed with Hunan Province during 1990 and 1991. Through the 1980s Guangdong's development had been such that its rural economy no longer produced sufficient staple crops, particularly rice. Provincial planners argued from a perspective of economic rationalism that it made more sense for the province to buy its grains from elsewhere and to concentrate on its comparative advantages in cash crops and light industrial development. The province tried to buy rice from Hunan, but that province refused to supply Guangdong at market price, arguing that because Guangdong had economic advantages unavailable to Hunan the former should be prepared to pay above market prices. Guangdong provincial authorities retaliated by trying to circumvent the Hunan government, offering higher prices direct to the local producers and arranging its own transport. Hunan attempted to stop Guangdong's grain lorries entering the province and at one stage the military was involved as conflict escalated.[8]

On the other hand the tensions and potential for confrontation are balanced by interdependence and cooperation. Guangdong and its leadership not only remain an integral part of the communist party state, but its senior leaders are still clearly subject to the nomenklatura of the CCP's Central Committee. For all their strongly committed Guangdong regionalism, they remain national politicians. In the final analysis, as would be expected for social as well as political reasons, their allegiances are to the national CCP. Thus there was not even a personal revolt in early 1991 when the former reforming Governor, Ye Xuanping, was posted to Beijing despite having explicitly and publicly stated that he preferred to stay in his post in Guangdong.

Although they may be envious of its success, leaders of other provincial-level units readily acknowledge Guangdong's achievements and regard it as a source of experience, technology and manufactures. According to Governor Zhu Senlin, the rest of the country currently consumes about one-third of all Guangdong's manufactures and produce,[9] and visitors stream in from all over China. For its part, Guangdong relies to some considerable extent on other provinces for fuel supplies, raw materials (cotton and steel in particular) grain, machinery, personnel and markets. Guangdong has to maintain good relations with them both to support the development of the national market and to ensure its supplies of capital goods, raw materials and energy. In 1989, Guangdong derived only 20 per cent of its supplies of capital goods, raw materials or energy from arrangements governed by the national plan; a figure which dropped below 10 per cent in the cities and counties of the Pearl River Delta.[10]

In any case it seems likely that Guangdong's position as Number One will be challenged in the near future. Following Deng Xiaoping's inspection tour to the province in early 1992 other provincial-level units have been vying with each other to follow Guangdong's experience in both export-oriented production and the introduction of market reforms. Guangdong's special policy of June 1979 is now being surpassed in scale and extent by new arrangements, of which that for Shanghai's Pudong District is probably the most famous. Around China a series of new economic regions are emerging, each based on the integration of several provincial economies both domestically and internationally. Many of these new economic regions – the Lower Yangtze cities of the Shanghai hinterland in Zhejiang and southern Jiangsu are obvious examples – have a greater potential for rapid economic growth and a stronger industrial base than Guangdong. This new pattern of economic regionalisation, based on reciprocal trade as well as geographical proximities and cultural affinities, clearly challenges Guangdong's share of the national market. At the meeting of the Eighth National People's Congress in March 1993 Guangdong was already being somewhat sidelined, with Shanghai, Jiangsu and Shandong receiving more attention.

Though Guangdong has become a model for emulation as far as economic development is concerned, cultural and educational achievements have lagged well behind national norms. One indicator of this difference is that since 1982 average personal expenditure on cultural purposes only accounted for about 3–5 per cent of individual living expenses in Guangdong per annum, whereas in the country as a whole it has averaged 4–9 per cent.[11] As during the era of the Republic of China, since 1949 – when Beijing and Shanghai have remained the national centres of intellectual life – very little philosophy, science or art has been published in Guangdong, or even written by natives or inhabitants of the province. Very few novels or collections of poems written in or about Guangdong have received national prizes or recognition during the reform era.

The pass mark in examinations for entrance to institutions of higher education required in Guangdong is lower than the national average, and lower even than many of the economically less developed provinces, such as Jiangxi or Fujian. According to the 1990 census, for every 100,000 people in Guangdong there were only 1,338 graduates from higher education; the national average was 1,422 per 100,000. One result is that Guangdong has had to import experts and technicians from other parts of China: some 79,000 came to the province between 1983 and 1990.[12]

On the other hand, Guangdong is clearly a trend-setter in various different aspects of popular culture. Guangdong's food culture is both famous and emulated, particularly the eating of all kinds of animals. In addition, less traditional pursuits, such as popular songs, jazz music, restaurant concerts, ballroom dancing, discotheques and karaoke, were all established first in Guangdong before spreading to other parts of the country, at least in the period since 1949. However, new fashions have not completely replaced old traditions, even though audience numbers for local opera performances have declined. There has been a revival of interest in folk religions and practices made possible by economic development.

Guangdong as a whole, and not just the SEZs, has also acted as a magnet attracting people from all over the PRC. During 1949–52 some 20,000 northerners followed the CCP forces into Guangdong. According to official statistics, by 1990 an additional 9.3 million people had moved into Guangdong for work during the 1980s. This authorised importation of labour exists alongside the influx of large numbers of people 'blindly looking for work', as many as two to three thousand a day at Chinese New Year.

GUANGDONG AND HONG KONG: ECONOMIC INTEGRATION

Even a rapid glance at Guangdong's trade and investment statistics reveals the importance of Hong Kong to the province's economic development. On 1992 figures, some 80 per cent of Guangdong's exports go to, and 70 per cent of its imports come from Hong Kong. Hong Kong is overwhelmingly Guangdong's largest source of direct foreign investment, accounting for over three-quarters of the total since the mid-1980s. Moreover, substantial amounts are involved. Taiwan invests more in Guangdong than in Fujian where it effectively sources about 70 per cent of industrial output. This investment represents 25 per cent of Taiwan's investment in the PRC. Yet Taiwan's investment in Guangdong only accounts for 6 per cent of provincial foreign investment. Japan, which is the third largest investor in Guangdong only supplies 4 per cent of provincial foreign investment.

In effect, since the late 1980s a single area of economic activity has come into being. The degree of interpenetration is such that there is now only limited value in describing the activities of Guangdong and Hong Kong separately. Greater Hong Kong is a growing area of economic integration that originated in the economic interaction between Hong Kong and the Pearl River Delta area. Moreover, this area has been a magnet for the attraction of economic activity in East Asia, as Hong Kong's entrepot role for trade and investment in China has expanded almost beyond recognition.

Geography has been perhaps the single most important factor in Guangdong's economic integration with Hong Kong across the land bridge between the two. During 1990–92 much of Hong Kong's industrial capacity transferred its operations across the border to Guangdong. By 1992 some three million people were employed in Hong Kong's economic enterprises, now physically located in Guangdong. However, by the late 1980s such a transformation was not an obvious development. Integration has seen an economic partnership between the provincial economy of a partially reforming centrally planned economy and one of the most vigorous free market economic environments. Economic integration has resulted largely from individual economic enterprises making judgements about their own development. The only exception would be the provision of infrastructure by the governments of Guangdong and the SEZs, but these were intended to encourage Guangdong's economic development generally and not exclusively in relation to Hong Kong.

The driving force in economic integration until recently has been competitive market forces and the search for short-term profits. However, during the early 1990s a number of Hong Kong companies together with a number of different groups of PRC academics have started discussing the possibilities for more formal integration. One stimulus to such discussions is the sure knowledge of Hong Kong's incorporation into the PRC in 1997. Though Hong Kong is guaranteed a separate existence for a further fifty years within the PRC, 1997 represents the opportunity for even more formal integration than has already been agreed from a number of perspectives, military and political as well as economic.

The degree of economic integration between Hong Kong and Guangdong is, as already indicated, most readily observable in the scale and type of trade and investment flows between the two. However, it is also observable, if less accurately quantifiable in the widespread use of the Hong Kong currency in Guangdong – where it is estimated that in excess of 30 per cent of Hong Kong notes now circulate – and the relatively free flow of commercial and technical information between Hong Kong and Guangdong, particularly through the coverage of radio and television.

Hong Kong has always been an important trading partner for Guangdong. In 1980 about 48 per cent of Guangdong's total exports went to Hong Kong. By 1992 this figure had increased to 84 per cent and Guangdong sourced 72 per cent of its imports from Hong Kong. Hong Kong's trade dependence on Guangdong, and indeed on the PRC, has been considerably less. Hong Kong took about 47 per cent of the PRC's exports in 1989, of which about 80 per cent were then re-exported. 38 per cent of the PRC's imports were sourced from Hong Kong and about 70 per cent had been Hong Kong re-exports. In 1990, Guangdong was responsible for 24 per cent of Hong Kong's exports to China and over 28 per cent of its imports. In 1985, Guangdong had a deficit in its trade with Hong Kong equivalent to 3 per cent of its total provincial trade turnover. By 1990 that had grown to a surplus of 92 per cent.

Hong Kong has had an increasing role as an intermediary in handling the PRC's trade. Little information is available on re-exports as part of the trade flow between Guangdong and Hong Kong. However, in 1990 42 per cent of Guangdong's exports came from compensation trade and foreign participant firms, most of which are Hong Kong-based. It therefore seems reasonable to assume that Hong Kong plays a significant role in Guangdong's foreign trade intermediation. Indeed, Hong Kong's role would appear to be quite complex, since it also has major direct investments in Guangdong's exporting and outward-processing industries.

Direct foreign investment from Hong Kong into Guangdong also confirms the extent of economic integration. In 1991 Hong Kong provided 63 per cent of realised and 73 per cent of contracted direct foreign investment in Guangdong. Moreover Hong Kong-sourced foreign direct investment in Guangdong has a much higher ratio of utilisation to contracted value (some 80 per cent) than the average for all investing countries in Guangdong during 1985–9. These investments are usually concentrated in quick-return, low technology, assembly and manufacturing production and have been the basis for Guangdong's rapid growth in exports and GDP.

In turn there can be little doubt that the growth of Guangdong has assisted Hong Kong industry to remain internationally competitive essentially by vertically integrating the production process. Certainly all the evidence from Hong Kong entrepreneurs is that they have welcomed relocation with open arms. The advantages in Guangdong are the supply and cost of labour, which is plentiful and cheap, the low costs and plentiful supply of land, and the ease of access. Not only are the sites for new enterprises close at hand and reached easily, but there are no language barriers. Many of the Hong Kong entrepreneurs come from Guangdong, and not only speak the same language, but have close family ties.[13] This means that companies can both hire local labour, and even local management, and yet remain essentially family firms. It is not uncommon to find Hong Kong entrepreneurs with an established home on both sides of the border; using family members from Hong Kong in Guangdong; or employing family members in Guangdong. In any case, the sense of familiarity with native place in Guangdong is often a starting point for the development of a specific economic activity.

GUANGDONG AND HONG KONG: CULTURAL INTERPENETRATION

The influence of families, the importance of shared language and the availability of commercial information on both sides of the border all point to the cultural as well as the economic integration of Guangdong and Hong Kong. It is undoubtedly the case that Guangdong is well-served by officially controlled and sanctioned media. However, the emergence of Greater Hong Kong is as much a social and cultural phenomenon as it is economic, and that too is largely through processes out of the hands of the party-state.

Guangdong is well-served by radio and television stations, newspapers and journals, many of which are well-known for promoting new ideas, and providing a window on the styles and fashions of Hong Kong, Macao and the rest of the world. However, a far larger boost to the emergence of Greater Hong Kong comes from other media and modes of interaction between Hong Kong and Guangdong. Guangdong Provincial Commercial Radio was founded in March 1991, and plays an important role in providing specialised information services to enterprises. Computer networks and electronic mail are extensively used for the dissemination of information publicly. The inhabitants of Guangdong have better quality and more radios, television sets, record players and videos than those in other provinces. This equipment allows those in Guangdong easy access to music, programmes and material from Hong Kong.

Language is of course an important dimension of the ease of access for those in Guangdong to Hong Kong's cultural activities. Cantonese is the dominant language in Hong Kong as it is in Guangdong. Until relatively recently, the standard Cantonese, even in Hong Kong, was that spoken in Guangzhou. Interestingly, increased economic integration and the development of Greater Hong Kong has led to the Hong Kong version, characterised by its neologisms and technologically-aware derivitives, becoming the standard. Actors in plays broadcast on one of Guangdong Provincial Television's Cantonese Service channels may now speak in Hong Kong rather than Guangzhou accents even when the action may be set in Guangzhou itself.

A common language between Guangdong and Hong Kong has meant that books, magazines and journals, as well as television and radio programmes, and popular songs produced in either Hong Kong or Guangdong may be fully appreciated in the other. Indeed, the relative technological sophistication of people in Guangdong is put effectively to work in obtaining, distributing and disseminating material from Hong Kong. For the most part the flow of communications and information is from Hong Kong to Guangdong, but there is also a reverse flow, particularly in television programmes. The impact of the Hong Kong mass media, vivid television programmes in particular, has so concerned Guangdong authorities that they have several times attempted to curb the use of the extra antennae that must be fitted to Guangdong television aerials to permit reception of Hong Kong television broadcasts.

With reform and the greater openness to the outside world, there has been an exponential increase in both the movement of people between Hong Kong and Guangdong, and the circulation of Hong Kong publications. Since the late 1980s an average of ten million border crossings between Guangdong and Hong Kong have been made every year, by land, sea and air. Every day four trains with fourteen carriages depart from each side of the border in Guangzhou and Hong Kong, for a 59-minute journey to the other terminal. Ferries of various kinds link Hong Kong to all nearby cities and towns in Guangdong. Several flights each day take less than an hour and hundreds of customers between Guangzhou and Hong Kong.

Though it is relatively easy to quantify the increased interaction between Guangdong and Hong Kong, it is somewhat harder to assess its impact on the values or consciousness of either society. It is generally fashionable to highlight the increase in prostitution and gambling in Guangdong, and to ignore the evolution of less sensational features such as more sophisticated consumerism, the drive for better health care, or the development of independent personalities and the use of individual initiative. One development which, given the almost general lack of interest in environmental protection measures elsewhere in the PRC would seem to result directly from the impact of integration with Hong Kong, is the adoption of regulations and procedures for an Environmental Protection Agency in Guangdong.[14]

All the same it is clear that there are less desirable aspects of cultural and economic integration which have increased considerably. Crime may have grown simply because of modernisation and its dislocations, rather than because of increased integration. However, it is certainly the case that cross-border crime and smuggling have grown phenomenally during the early 1990s.

The incidence of smuggling into Guangdong has increased with reform, and most particularly since 1989. In that year, Guangdong's security authorities solved 4,100 cases, arrested 5,100 smugglers, and seized goods worth 400 million *yuan* RMB. However, it seems likely that this accounted for only a small part of the total. The smugglers include not only those who smuggle full-time for a living but also many local policemen and soldiers. There is a flourishing trade in both goods and people, and the smugglers use increasingly advanced vehicles for transportation. For example, in early autumn 1992, 140 boats used for smuggling were captured in the sea off Jiazi. They included ex-service gunboats, torpedo boats, escort vessels and submarine chasers. A favourite concern of the smugglers is the luxury car market. Cars stolen in Hong Kong are transported on a variety of craft to Guangdong. It is even possible to order a specific car through various dealers in Guangdong which will then be stolen off the streets of Hong Kong – and in some cases even the USA – and then exported to Guangdong.

Drug trafficking in Guangdong is a grimmer problem. Despite vigorous efforts waged by Guangdong police to eradicate drug trafficking and drug addiction, they continue to grow and flourish in the province. According to one report, in the years 1979 to 1982 only three to five drug addiction cases were uncovered every year. From 1983 to 1986 the number of drug trafficking and addiction cases handled each year increased from 40 to 60. After 1987 the number of people involved in drug trafficking offences and drug use amounted to more than a hundred cases a year. In 1990, the number of cases rose further to more than 1,000 each year. 816 persons engaged in drug trafficking and or subject to an addiction were arrested in Guangzhou alone in that year. In the decade to 1991, more than 1,000 major drug trafficking cases were uncovered in Guangdong, 2,500 drug traffickers were arrested, and nearly 400 kilograms of heroin and 1,400 kilograms of opium and other drugs were confiscated.[15] Several drug criminals were imprisoned or even sentenced to death. However, the stern penalties have not served to stop the illegal trade in drugs. From July 1991 to January 1993 the province cracked down on 1,452 drug cases and arrested 2,163 drug traffickers, among whom 51 were sentenced to death. As is the case elsewhere there has also been a significant rise in drug-related offences, including robbery and illegal arms trades.

GUANGDONG IN EAST ASIA: STRATEGIC AND SECURITY CONSIDERATIONS

Guangdong's position in East Asia has become almost as important to its current and future development as its relationship with Hong Kong, and has the potential to grow in significance. In the light of the closer relationship between Guangdong and Hong Kong that has already emerged, the removal of the international border between them seems likely to be little more than a symbolic political act, at least in the short term. However, Hong Kong's intermediary role between East Asia and China may well change as a result of its incorporation into the PRC. In any case, Guangdong's relations with the countries of East and Southeast Asia have already started to increase for reasons largely unrelated to Hong Kong's future development.

Although the proportion is currently incalculable, it is known that a substantial proportion of East Asian, and indeed external foreign trade and investment generally, with Guangdong is routed through Hong Kong, and appears in official data as sourced from Hong Kong. In the post-1997 future external traders and investors may increasingly prefer to do business directly. To some extent that trend has already started to emerge. Though direct trade and investment between Guangdong on the one hand and Japan, Thailand and South Korea on the other has increased steadily during the 1990s, direct economic relations with both Taiwan and Singapore have grown dramatically. Half of all Taiwan's direct foreign investment now goes to Guangdong; and during 1993 Singapore has become a major investor in the establishment of Guangdong enterprises.

One important stimulus to these developments was the PRC's enforced policy change after June 1989, when the Western or at least industrialised countries felt shocked into a change of stance or style in their relationships. Beijing dramatically turned its international attention closer to home and the establishment or improvement of relations in East and Southeast Asia. Within a remarkably short period of time, diplomatic relations with Thailand, Malaysia, Singapore, Indonesia and South Korea were either formally created for the first time since 1949 or raised to the highest levels. These improved diplomatic relations certainly facilitated economic relations, usually driven by overseas Chinese, many of whom, particularly in Thailand, Kuala Lumpur, Singapore and Indonesia, are Cantonese.

Guangdong, or at least the Guangdong Provincial Government for its part, has not been slow to see the importance of East and Southeast Asia to its future economic development. The current provincial five-year plan signals the province's intention to engage in off-shore processing to take advantage not so much at this stage of cheap labour (though that too is a possibility) as of materials unavailable or in short supply in Guangdong. One obvious area for development which has been rumoured for some time is the iron and steel industry, at a very low level of production in Guangdong. Though lacking adequate capital investment and possibly also the requisite technology, Vietnam does have the appropriate iron ore and coal deposits. Current planning in Guangdong also appreciates the wider applications of international divisions of labour: that Guangdong and other parts of the region might cooperate to provide goods to yet a third part of the region. For example, Australian wool might then be processed in Malaysia for the textile industry in Guangdong to produce clothes for sale in Japan.

These strategic perspectives on East Asia are also of military concern. The province's economic and social integration with Hong Kong as well as political arrangements in and after 1997, the potential for social unrest in both Guangdong and Hong Kong as a result of economic modernisation, the importance of the economic development of China's southern coast, and the wider context of relations with Vietnam and Taiwan and throughout the South China Seas have meant that Guangdong is a major focus of People's Liberation Army (PLA) activity. The Guangzhou Military Region has (as its name implies) its headquarters in Guangdong though with security responsibilities for coastal Guangxi and Hainan, the interior provinces of Hunan and Hubei, as well as Guangdong. One of the Military Region's two group armies (the 42nd) has its headquarters in Guangdong; and units of the PLA Air Force (PLAAF) are based there. The South China Fleet of the PLA Navy (PLAN) has its headquarters at Zhanjiang, and bases throughout the province, including Yulin where a marine force is stationed.

The specific features of Guangdong's economic development are an essential part of the assessment of the province's security environment, and thus a major determinant of PLA troop deployment in the province.[16] Hong Kong and Taiwan are high on the agenda for all PLA forces in Guangdong, as are Vietnam and the Spratly Islands. The latter are of less interest to PLA land forces, but certainly have influenced the development and location of both PLAAF and PLAN units in the province. The 42nd group army are likely to be the first PLA troops to be involved in Hong Kong, and appear to have been assigned that role for 1997 and beyond.

The PLAN South China Naval Command is based at Zhanjiang in Guangdong. The South China Fleet has about one-third of all the PLAN's ships with at least one aviation division, including a heavy bomber regiment, assuming patrol duties in the South China Sea. The PLAN South China Naval Command is not, however, limited to Zhanjiang, for there are important bases in Guangzhou and Yulin. Moreover, it would appear that future planning provides for the expansion of the South China Fleet with the development of a blue water navy, and consequently to its potential naval power in East and Southeast Asia. This goal is indicated by preparations for the development of an aircraft carrier force. In 1985, the then head of the PLAN, Liu Huaqing (a member of the Standing Committee of the Political Bureau of the CCP since late 1992), established a pilot warship captain's course, linked to the command of an aircraft carrier, at Guangzhou Naval Academy.[17]

GREATER HONG KONG AND THE REGIONALIST FUTURE

At first sight the emergence of Greater Hong Kong seems to confirm those arguments that suggest the PRC is headed for political disintegration. Changes in and wrought by central government have given Guangdong greater autonomy in its own affairs. The outside world, and particularly the markets of Hong Kong, have redirected Guangdong's attention and shaped its perspectives on planning and development. However, Greater Hong Kong is not a regionalism of separatism, but results rather from a series of more complicated processes, including both domestic and international factors.

Rather than seeking to separate itself from the PRC, the foundation of Greater Hong Kong's strength is precisely that it brings together different parts of the Chinese world to their mutual benefit. The overseas Chinese in the countries of East and Southeast Asia – some 25 million people (excluding Hong Kong and Taiwan from this calculation) – and particularly Cantonese whose families originated in Guangdong, have been at the forefront of trade and investment from abroad.

However, Greater Hong Kong is a magnet that attracts people within the PRC as much as it proves attractive to investors and business people in East and Southeast Asia. In addition to the inward migration of labour there has also been the internal inward flow of capital. Investors from elsewhere in the PRC, individual as well as corporate, have been increasingly involved in Guangdong's development. Moreover, the further economic growth of Guangdong depends not only on the province's access to other PRC markets but also on the lack of economic barriers to that interaction.

The economic and social interpenetration of Guangdong and Hong Kong continues to evolve despite its historical roots and its rapid recent development. The dynamic nature of this relationship is emphasised clearly from a geographic perspective. The whole of Guangdong has not yet been transformed as a result of its relationship with Hong Kong. The first area to be influenced centred on the sixteen cities and counties at the heart of the Pearl River Delta – often called the 'Small Delta'. Rapidly, however, the area of economic interaction has expanded to encompass a much larger area – the Large Delta – the thirty-one cities and counties centred on Guangzhou, Shenzhen and Zhuhai, and including Foshan and the 'four small tigers' of Shunde, Nanhai, Zhongshan and Dongguan. In effect, Greater Hong Kong is an expanding area of economic activity generated around the Guangzhou–Hong Kong axis.

Despite the successes of regional economic integration to date, there remain few pressures to place such regionalism on a more formal basis or to establish political institutions. One reason is the complexity and sensitivity of politics affecting Greater Hong Kong: those involved in Guangdong, Beijing and Hong Kong are likely to have fundamentally different agendas for its development. Despite the advantages gained so far from cooperation, Guangdong has a tendency to be resentful of its role as the provider of cheap labour; Beijing is mindful of its decreased ability to control Guangdong now, let alone problems it may face in Hong Kong after 1997; and Hong Kong business people are not only concerned about the post-1997 political environment, they also have worries about economic over-dependence on Guangdong.

For the most part proposals to establish regional economic institutions have come from either academics in China, or officials in Guangdong. These have ranged from suggestions of a Chinese East Asian Economies Free Trade Area encompassing Guangdong, Fujian, Taiwan, Hong Kong and Macao, to more narrowly focused vehicles for cooperation. A most recent example was the initiative by Wang Zuo, Director of the Guangdong Government Office for Economic Reform, who proposed the establishment of a 'Larger Hong Kong Open Economic Ring' which would bring together Shenzhen, Zhuhai and Daya Bay, as well as Hong Kong and Macao, would jointly issue Hong Kong currency and practise Hong Kong free port import-export customs controls and procedures.[18]

The complexity of its political environment and the reluctance to develop regional political institutions emphasises the extent to which the strength of Greater Hong Kong has resulted from different boundaries for political and economic activity. Those in Greater Hong Kong, and Guangdong more generally, do not seek an independent formal political existence, not least because economic growth has resulted from cooperation between different comparative advantages, created largely by political history, in a relatively free, open and expanding market.

The apparent contradiction between economic and political factors that results is even attractive to (and consequently supported by) those outside the immediate vicinity of Greater Hong Kong, particularly in the PRC. For example, investors in the PRC may choose to invest in enterprises in that country through Hong Kong rather than directly, because of Hong Kong's regulatory framework and the guarantees this provides compared to investment procedures within the PRC. It is generally accepted that PRC investment through Hong Kong into the PRC is a larger source of investment than provided from the USA and Japan. Brokers in Hong Kong estimate that something like $30 billion is now invested in the PRC by investors in the PRC through institutions in Hong Kong.

Political geography suggests that the lack of synchrony between economic and political boundaries is both dysfunctional and an inherently unstable situation. However, this is to ignore the deliberate, purposive and extremely useful political ambiguity that equates China with the PRC, thereby lessening tensions across political borders. Of far greater interest than separatism is the question of whether the processes of regionalism that have created Greater Hong Kong are unique to relations between and about Guangdong and Hong Kong, or may be repeated elsewhere in the PRC.

NOTES

1 Unless otherwise indicated, all figures and statistics are official data from *Zhongguo tongji nianjian* and associated publications. The other richer provincial-level units per capita GNP in 1992 were (in order) Shanghai, Beijing, Tianjin and Liaoning. See *Zhongguo tongji zhaigao 1992*, p. 7.
2 For details see David S.G. Goodman 'Provinces confronting the state?', in Kuan and Broisseau (eds), *The China Review 1992*, The Chinese University Press, Hong Kong, 1992.
3 John Fitzgerald 'Increased Disunity: The Politics and Finance of Guangdong Separatism, 1926–1936' in *Modern Asian Studies* Vol. 24, No. 4 (1990), p. 745.
4 Guangdong CCP Provincial Committee, 'The Chinese Communist Party, Guangdong Province, Announcement on Giving Full Play to Favourable Conditions, Expanding Foreign Trade, and Accelerating Economic Development', in Ezra Vogel, *One Step Ahead in China: Guangdong under Reform*, Harvard University Press, 1989, pp. 85–86.
5 Ezra Vogel, *One Step Ahead in China: Guangdong Under Reform*, Harvard University Press, 1989, p. 314.
6 Lin Ruo, 'Retrospect of Reform and the Opening Up in Guangdong', in Lin Ruo and others (eds), *Gaige kaifeng zai Guangdong* [Reform and the Openness in Guangdong], Guangdong Gaodeng Jiaoyu Chubanshe, 1992, p. 18.
7 P. Ferdinand, 'The Economic and Financial Dimension', in D.S.G. Goodman (ed), *China's Regional Development*, London, Routledge, 1989, p. 45.
8 Chao Chien-min, *'T'iao-t'iao* vs. *k'ua-k'uai*: A perennial dispute between the central and local governments in Mainland China', in *Issues and Studies*, August 1991, p. 31.
9 Zhu Senlin, 'The Development of the Guangdong Economy has been Accelerated by Opening Up to the Outside World', *Nanfang Ribao*, 20 January 1993.
10 Zhang Zizheng and Shi Zupei (ed), *Gaige kaifang zhong de Guangdong jingji* [The Guangdong Economy in Reform and Openness], Guangzhou, Zhongshan Daxue chubanshe, 1992, p. 207.
11 Yuan Peishu, 'Guangdong wenhua xiaofei de tedian he qushi' ['Special Features and Trends of Consumption on Culture in Guangdong'], in *Yangcheng Wanbao*, 2 December 1992.
12 Li Zuoming 'Dui Guangdong rencai gongzuo de huigu he sikao'

['Review and Analysis of Personnel Work in Guangdong'], in *Xueshu yanjiu*, No. 3, 1991.

13 Details of various surveys of Hong Kong entrepreneurs and their attitudes to investment in Guangdong are contained in Industry and Research Division, Federation of Hong Kong Industries, *Hong Kong's Offshore Investment*, 1990.

14 C.W. Lo, 'Law and Administration in Deng's China: Legalization of the Administration of Environmental Protection', in *Review of Central and East European Law*, No. 5, 1992, p. 453.

15 *BBC Summary of World Broadcasts*, FE 1180, B2–5, 18 September 1991.

16 This discussion of the PLA in Guangdong draws on D.S.G. Goodman, 'The PLA and Regionalism: Guangdong Province', in *The Pacific Review*, Vol. 7, No. 1.

17 You Ji and You Xu, 'In Search of Blue Water Power: The PLA Navy's Maritime Strategy in the 1990s', in *The Pacific Review*, Vol. 4, No. 2, p. 137.

18 'Guangdong Official Discusses "Larger Hong Kong Economic Ring"', in *BBC Summary of World Broadcasts*, FE-1622, B2–4, 25 February 1993.

7 Regionalism in Fujian

Simon Long

On the face of it, Fujian ought to offer an interesting case study in the centrifugal pressures facing the Chinese polity. Starved of central government investment for three decades because of its location as the front-line in any potential conflict with Taiwan, Fujian is still suffering, indirectly, from Beijing's policies. It is Beijing's refusal to renounce the eventual use of force in the reunification of Taiwan that is cited by Taiwan as the reason for the failure to open the 'three links', of air, sea and mail links.

The absence of those links is the biggest single comparative disadvantage Fujian faces in its race to catch up economically with its neighbour Guangdong. Meanwhile, across the Taiwan Straits, is a population as many as 85 per cent of whom are descended from residents of Fujian Province. Many speak the same language, and still know where their family villages and graves are situated. Hundreds of thousands have visited since Taiwan liberalised contacts in 1987. Several hundred have opened businesses in Fujian. Many more are deterred by the absence of direct links.

In July 1993 Beijing tried to slow down Fujian's late spurt of growth – imposing a brief credit squeeze and investment restrictions because of national 'overheating' that few Fujian officials recognised as a problem in their region. Several dozen 'development zones' were closed, and, even after central government shifted its emphasis in late 1993 from restraint to growth, it still tried to slow down the 'blind investment' which was fuelling the boom in the south.

In sum, Fujian would seem to serve its own perceived interests by pursuing links with 'Greater China' independently of Beijing. There are a few, tentative signs that this is happening. But there is virtually no evidence for the existence of a 'Fujian nationalist', or 'Greater Taiwan' movement in Fujian.

Before examining the economic forces that may or may not be

propelling Fujian away from Beijing and towards a more autonomous provincialism or 'regionalism', this chapter will first sketch the unusual military history of the province, and current military organisation there. The military history is essential to an understanding of Fujian's comparative poverty, as compared to some other coastal provinces. And the organisation of the military will be an important factor in any attempt to formalise a rift of any sort with the central authorities.

THE STRATEGIC MOTIVES BEHIND FUJIAN'S 'BACKWARDNESS'

'In the past, relations between Fujian and Taiwan were poor', said the Deputy Mayor of Fuzhou in September 1993, 'so the nation invested little in Fujian.'[1] The implicit complaint is a constant refrain in Fujian officials' efforts to explain their province's 'backwardness'. Whatever the justice of the accusation, the perception of comparative poverty is a topic of particular sensitivity at the moment. Of the thousands of Chinese boat people who risked their life-savings and personal safety in hazardous illegal emigration attempts in 1992 and 1993, most have come from Fujian Province. They have spoken plausibly on arrival of dire poverty in the Fujian countryside. Fujian officials deny these stories, saying that it is simply the lure of high wages, especially in the United States, that tempts relatively well-off Chinese farmers into these missions. It is even claimed that some employ migrants from other parts of China – notably Sichuan – to work their farms. Whatever the truth, even the official statistics reveal the interior of Fujian as a poor region, a result in part of the province's strategic location.

Viewed in the starkest terms, the coastline of Fujian Province is the informal ceasefire line in China's Civil War. The Beijing government would like the world to see that line as an internal division as arbitrary as the border between the two Koreas, or as the 17th parallel Demilitarised Zone that once cut Vietnam in half. Whereas Taiwan, by lifting, in 1991, the 'temporary provisions' in force during the 'communist rebellion' has, in effect, declared the civil war over, Beijing has never renounced the goal of national reunification, nor its perceived right to use force to achieve that end. Almost every major 'state of the nation' speech at government and party functions includes in its peroration a reaffirmation of the commitment to reunifying Taiwan, which was stated in a 'white paper' published in August 1993.[2]

Hence the PRC's military disposition in Fujian has always been dominated by the potential for conflict across the Taiwan Strait. Since 1978–79, however, Fujian has also been the front line in a very different kind of war – for the hearts, minds and pockets of 'Taiwan compatriots'. If Taiwan were to be enticed peacefully into the embrace of Beijing's sovereignty, its close geographic, historic, cultural, linguistic and religious ties with Fujian Province would be amongst the most important baits. And if the process of political unification were to be fostered by expanding economic interdependence, Fujian would be the nexus of commercial interchange.

Balancing these diametrically opposed perceptions of Fujian's role has given the province a unique position in the interplay between national security, regional autonomy and central authority. The primacy of the goal of 'national reunification' implies a far greater degree of central government and military power in Fujian than anywhere else in China. But the importance of Fujian's links with Taiwan, and (given the absence of direct communications) hence with Guangdong and Hong Kong as well, implies the opposite – a centrifugal tendency towards provincial autonomy, or towards 'Greater China', or 'Greater Hong Kong', rather than 'Greater Beijing'. The potential for tension implicit in these conflicting tendencies has to date been minimised by an attempt to keep the two processes – of military preparedness and economic integration – as separate as possible.

It is commonly said on both sides of the Taiwan Strait that 'Taiwan has always been part of China'. It is just as true to say it was long 'part of Fujian'. Following the Qing dynasty's defeat in 1683 of Koxinga and his Ming loyalists, Taiwan became, in 1684, a prefecture of Fujian Province. It was not until 1887, under the 'self-strengthening' period of Governor Liu Mingquan, that Taiwan's status was upgraded, and it became the twentieth province of Qing China. It was as a province that Taiwan reverted to China after the period of Japanese colonialism from 1895–1945.

In April 1950, Hainan fell to the communists, with 125,000 KMT troops evacuated to Taiwan. In May, a further 125,000 were evacuated from the Zhoushan islands, about 120 kilometers east of Shanghai. By June preparations in Fujian for an invasion of Taiwan were in full swing. Between 150,000 and 300,000 assault forces were massed in Fujian. New airfields were built, with 400 aircraft deployed and an armada of invasion barges and sequestered junks and sampans. In February, General Su Yu, addressing the Third Field Army, assigned to attack the offshore islands and Taiwan, acknowledged that, militarily, the 'liberation' of the big islands, especially Taiwan, 'is an extremely big problem and will involve the biggest campaign in the history of modern Chinese warfare'.[3] But the capture of Hainan had encouraged the communists to believe that Taiwan, too, could be taken without undue difficulty, despite its greater distance from the mainland, and despite its being the last redoubt of the KMT armies.

All of this changed, however, with the outbreak of the Korean War on 25 June 1950. Two days later, President Truman announced that US forces would go to the aid of South Korea under United Nations auspices, and that the Seventh Fleet would go into the Taiwan Strait to deter a communist invasion of Taiwan. Already, some communist troops, from Lin Biao's Fourth Field Army, were being redeployed from southern China to the northeast.[4]

Beijing thus felt 'cheated' of Taiwan, and for the next decade, Fujian remained an area of high military tension. The fear of a 'second front' in the US-led 'war against communism' in Korea dominated Chinese military perceptions of Taiwan for the period of the Korean War, and in a modified form throughout the 1950s. As the US stepped up supplies of arms to Taiwan, troop deployments in Fujian became more defensive in nature. This did not, however, prevent Beijing from provoking the two 'off-shore islands' crises of 1954 and 1958 by stepping up its bombardments of Quemoy and Matsu just off the Fujian coast.

After the defusing of the 1958 crisis, however, there was a twenty-year military stalemate. Despite bellicose statements from Beijing, full-scale invasion never seemed feasible or imminent. And despite hopes in Taiwan that internal chaos in China, especially during the famine following the Great Leap Forward in the early 1960s, and later during the Cultural Revolution, would facilitate a KMT restoration, the posture on both sides was fundamentally defensive.

The whole picture was transformed again by Deng Xiaoping's triumph over the 'Maoists' in China in 1978. The formation of an informal alliance with the US against the Soviet Union, had already implied a commitment to 'peaceful reunification' with Taiwan. So too, did the new philosophy of the primacy of economic development, requiring a rapid expansion of foreign trade and the use of foreign capital and technology, with a particular emphasis on the resources of the overseas Chinese community. The ramifications of the dramatic changes in the world for China's Taiwan policy were formalised in September 1981, with Marshal Ye Jianying's 'nine principles' on reunification with Taiwan.[5] The second of the two contradictory strains of policy towards Fujian outlined above came to the fore – its role as an economic and patriotic lure to 'Taiwan compatriots'.

However, from the security point of view, Fujian has remained a special case. The fear of a US-backed invasion from Taiwan may have long receded. But Beijing, as noted, has never renounced what it sees as its right to reunify Taiwan militarily in certain circumstances. The precise definition of those circumstances has shifted. They include a declaration of independence by Taiwan; serious civil disturbance there; a military alliance between Taiwan and China's enemies; the development by Taiwan of nuclear weaponry; the adoption, by any country, of a 'two China policy' to an extent that threatens the stability of the Taiwan Strait, or the security of the Chinese mainland; the frustration of efforts at peaceful reunification.[6]

Of these, the most commonly cited are the first – a declaration of independence by Taiwan – and the last – the general warning that Beijing will not wait forever. Beijing constantly repeats the implicit threat to use force, especially when it sees evidence of any strengthening of the independence movement in Taiwan. A report by Taiwan's Government Information Office on 5 December 1991 claimed that the threat to use force had been made 17 times since March, including a speech by President Yang Shangkun in which he warned 'those who play with fire . . . will be burned to ashes'.[7]

In 1993, it was noteworthy that Chinese police vessels in January and February opened fire on at least three occasions in international waters between Taiwan and Japan. Although China said the incidents arose from 'misunderstandings' following anti-smuggling patrols,[8] they followed what was perceived in Beijing as a setback for pro-reunification politicians in the KMT in a government reshuffle. The attacks served as a reminder that there is a threatened military option for Beijing short of full-scale invasion – a naval blockade.[9] Taiwan's ability to strengthen its naval power through the acquisition of submarines and anti-submarine helicopters[10] has doubtless been one factor in China's recent investment in upgrading its own navy. Chinese submarine commanders reportedly continue to practise blockading manoeuvres,[11] although it is debatable whether China's naval capacity is sufficient to make a blockade feasible against an increasingly well-equipped Taiwan. In August 1993, at the same time as the Kuomintang was holding its Fourteenth National Congress in Taipei, unusually large-scale military manoeuvres were undertaken in Guangdong. In Taiwan, some analysts read this as an oblique warning to the KMT not to go too far in abandoning its traditional 'one China' stance.[12]

The implications for military strategy in Fujian of this policy are twofold. Firstly, a military establishment has to be maintained in which the ability to implement the threatened use of force appears at least a possibility. Secondly, any moves by the regional military towards greater independence from central authority are likely to be stamped on especially rapidly.

CURRENT MILITARY ORGANISATION IN FUJIAN[13]

Fujian is now part of the Nanjing Military Region, of which the Fujian MR marks the southeastern boundary. The Nanjing MR is an amalgamation of the older Fuzhou and Lower Yangtze, or Nanjing, Military regions. The region incorporates the Jiangsu, Zhejiang, Anhui and Jiangxi military regions and the Shanghai garrison command. The Nanjing MR is the base for three group armies: the 12th, in Northern Jiangsu; the First, near Shanghai; and the 31st, in Fujian itself. The Nanjing MR has two armoured divisions, eleven infantry, one artillery and one air defence division. This makes it smaller only than the Beijing Military Region, in the north and the Jinan Military Region in central China. The naval tasks of the Nanjing Military Region are undertaken by the East Sea Fleet, headquartered at Shanghai, with bases at Wusong, Dinghai, Hangzhou and Fuzhou. It is responsible for the coastal area south from Lianyungang in the north, to Dongshan in southern Fujian, covering seven coastal defence districts. The International Institute for Strategic Studies estimates it has at its disposal two submarine squadrons, two escort, one mine warfare and one amphibious squadron, about 270 patrol and coastal combat craft, and one marine cadre division.[14] The 31st Group Army is headquartered at Xiamen, just opposite Taiwan.

As elsewhere in China, frequent rotation of senior military officers both at the level of the Military Region in Nanjing, and at the Fujian provincial level, has helped prevent the growth of strong local links among military leaders. There is no strong evidence of resistance to central authority among the regional military leadership. However, as in the case of the Guangzhou Military Region, there has been speculation based on the region's failure to send troops to take part in the initial martial law operations in Beijing – that is prior to 22 May 1989 – that there may have been resistance to the use of the PLA against the civilian population. In the case of the army in Fujian, there clearly was some reluctance. On 22 May – that is, just three days after the imposition of martial law – the Nanjing Military Regional Command issued a statement of support. Individual military districts and group armies in the region began issuing statements the same day. But, according to Fujian radio, the statement of support for martial law from the party committee of the 31st Group Army was only forthcoming after 'several days of earnest study'. The 31st was one of the very few Group Armies not represented in the suppression of the democracy movement in Beijing.[15]

However, one should not make too much of this hint of fractiousness. Firstly, there were good strategic reasons for not bringing the 31st to Beijing. Quite apart from the logistical problem of its distance from the capital, there was probably also a residual fear of some sort of provocation or intervention from Taiwan if there were a nationwide uprising. Certainly there were protests in Xiamen and Fuzhou, as across the country, and to weaken the defence of the province may have appeared strategic folly. Secondly, any problems in the command structure were presumably dealt with in a major reshuffle in 1990. Typically, two officers in key positions – Nanjing Military Region Commander Gu Hui, and 31st Group Army Commander Liu Lunxian – both took up their posts in that reshuffle. Neither has deep roots in the region, and if the reshuffle was an effort to root out any incipient military fiefdoms, they were presumably appointed for their reliability.

If there are serious problems in the military in Fujian, they seem more likely to relate to the pervasive corruption in the Chinese army as a whole revealed in July 1993, when the army's most senior leaders were quoted in the official media bemoaning 'a growing tide of corruption, money worshipping and hedonism'.[16] Hints of problems in Fujian itself can be read into remarks by Defence Minister Chi Haotian when he visited the province in April 1993. Ostensibly there to confer an honorary title on the 'Eighth Company of Gulangyu' (an island off Xiamen), General Chi made a point of warning soldiers against 'the temptations of wealth and high position . . . money worship, individualism, and other erroneous ideas'.[17]

FUJIAN'S ECONOMY: GREATER HONG KONG? OR GREATER BEIJING?

In the absence of a breakdown of the central administration, a precondition for regionalism in Fujian taking on a military and political nature would appear to be a distinct economic base, whose interests were threatened by central control from Beijing. If Fujian is allowed to pursue relatively independent economic policies unfettered by Beijing, and those policies are reaping benefits, there would seem to be little reason to risk confrontation with Beijing – 'If it ain't broke, why fix it?'. Moreover, the frequent warnings from the centre that 'without the strong leadership of the Communist party, new turmoil and wars would arise and the nation would be split' do carry weight. There are advantages to provincial leaders in a system of government where the Communist Party, even if it wields less and less real power, at least cements China together, providing a relatively peaceful environment for economic growth.

Nevertheless, the transformation of Fujian's economy in recent years has given it a unique character. Like many other mainland provinces, it has also shown signs of a strong provincial, and sub-provincial protectionist tendency. In December 1990, for example, at the nadir of that year's slump in retail sales and industrial output, *People's Daily*, in one of many reports about the rise of local protectionism, reported the story of a truck loaded with five tons of grapes which passed through one hundred road blocks *en route* from Shandong to Fujian.[18] However, there is little evidence that economic pressures are leading Fujian's political leaders to seek any formal increase in autonomy, either at the provincial level, or in conjunction with those other parts of the region with which Fujian's economic interests have become so closely enmeshed.

Fujian, along with Guangdong, is often seen nowadays as the third leg of the 'south China' growth triangle whose other components are Taiwan and Hong Kong. The provincial economies have already been diverging from many mainland provinces in a variety of ways: the levels of growth achieved, the emphasis on exports, the dependence on foreign investment, and the ownership structure of industry. Their geographic proximity and linguistic and cultural affinity to Hong Kong and Taiwan have made them the natural focus of the PRC's efforts to enhance economic cooperation with 'Greater China'. Hence, it was in these two provinces that China's first four 'Special Economic Zones' – Shenzhen, Zhuhai, Shantou and Xiamen – were established in 1980.

Of the two mainland provinces, Fujian has been very much the poor relation, and still is, even in comparison with coastal provinces to the north, but especially compared with Guangdong. Partly, this is simply a function of size. Fujian's population at the end of 1991 was officially estimated at less than half that of Guangdong (30.79 million, as against 64.39 million). Moreover, Fujian's development is constrained by geography – a relatively thin strip of arable land along the coast gives way to inhospitable mountain terrain in the interior. But Fujian residents also, as we have seen, complain that they started from a very low economic base, blamed on several decades of under-investment in the province by the central authorities. It is true that there was a reluctance to locate nationally important industries in an area which for some of the period has been seen as potentially vulnerable to foreign invasion. Under the 'third front strategy' only some medium-sized industrial enterprises were established in the inland mountainous regions.[19] For similar reasons, Fujian's infrastructure is still less developed. Power, transportation and communications constitute serious bottlenecks.[20]

Although it remains a relatively small economic power in its own right, Fujian has done well out of the reform era. Its rates of growth in every sector of economic activity have been faster than the national average. In 1978, per capita GNP in Fujian was less than three-quarters of the national average – at RMB 273. By 1991, Fujian was, by this measure, above average for the country as a whole – with per capita GNP of RMB 1,811.7, 105.7 per cent of the national average. The province had seen extraordinarily rapid rates of growth of industrial output, and in foreign trade, especially in imports.

The figures in Table 7.1 predate Fujian's 'spurt' for growth in 1992–93. After Deng Xiaoping's southern tour in early 1992, the province began to be far more successful in attracting foreign investment. Its share of total disbursed foreign investment in China grew from 4.1 per cent in 1990 to 7.6 per cent in 1992. The proportion reached a remarkable 16.5 per cent, or $5.46 billion in 1993, a year in which provincial officials said $11.2 billion of foreign investment had been committed, 10.2 per cent of the national total, and more than had

Table 7.1 Comparative average annual growth rates, 1978–91[21]

	National growth per cent	Fujian growth per cent
Population	1.4	1.7
Labour force	2.9	3.3
GNP	8.8	10.5(a)
Per capita GNP	7.2	8.8(a)
National income	5.5	6.7(a)
Total industrial output	15.5	19.4
Total agricultural output	15.2	16.6
Total investment in fixed assets	18.6	22.1
Retail sales	15.0	16.5
Exports	16.7	23.7
Imports	14.2	54.8

Note: (a) real average annual growth rate

Table 7.2 Foreign investment in Fujian[22]

Implemented foreign investment	1990	1991	1992	1993
US $ million	426.8	570.9	1,465.6	5,460.0
% of national total	4.1	4.9	7.6	16.5

been committed in all the preceding 14 years of the reform programme.[23] The amount continued to be tiny compared with the money flowing into Guangdong, but the ratio of foreign investment in Guangdong to that in Fujian lowered from 4.7:1 in 1990, to 3.2:1 in 1992.

The momentum was maintained in 1993. In the first seven months of the year, 2,998 new foreign investment contracts were approved in Fujian (an increase of 141 per cent over the same period in 1992), involving $7.2 billion (an increase of 263 per cent). Disbursed investment of $1,579 million had already exceeded the figure for the whole of 1992, and represented a 109 per cent increase over the first seven months of that year. Foreign investment played an important role in spectacular economic growth for the period – provincial GNP up 25.7 per cent in real terms, industrial output 36.6 per cent, and exports up 38.9 per cent.[24]

In figures published for the whole country for the first half of 1993, Fujian was reported to rank first among all China's provinces for the average size of investment project, with an average investment of $2.3 million. It ranked behind Guangdong, Jiangsu and Shandong, however, in terms of contracted foreign investment.[25] Provincial officials themselves, however, claimed that by the end of July, Fujian was second only to Guangdong in terms of foreign investment actually disbursed that year.[26]

The sharp improvement in Fujian's performance in attracting investment can be attributed to the increase in interest from Taiwan. Because of the legal restrictions they face, and the accompanying logistical problems, Taiwan investors have lagged far behind those in Hong Kong in realising projects in China. However, Taiwan investment in the mainland increased 212 per cent in 1991, and 223 per cent in 1992, according to Chinese figures, and Taiwan's share of total foreign investment in China has grown from 6.4 per cent in 1990, to 9.5 per cent in 1992, and 18.2 per cent in 1993, according to Chinese figures. Taiwan's figures are always considerably lower than those produced on the mainland. In part this is because of under-

212 *Simon Long*

Table 7.3 Taiwan and Hong Kong's share in direct foreign investment in China[27]

	1990	1991	1992
Taiwan disbursed investment in China, $ million	222.4	471.9	1,050.5
% of total disbursed foreign investment in China	6.4	10.7	9.5
Hong Kong	2,431.7	2,486.0	7,507.1
% of total	54.9	57.0	68.2

reporting by Taiwan businesses; in part it reflects the uncertain domicile of the Hong Kong companies commonly used as vehicles for Taiwan investment in China; in part, too, it perhaps reflects overestimates by Chinese officials keen to advertise their region's success in attracting external and foreign capital (although, as noted below, there is probably 'miscounting' – as Hong Kong – as well as over-counting). According to Taiwan's Investment Commission, it had approved 1,262 new Taiwanese investment projects worth $1.14 billion in China in 1993, as well as 8,067 old projects worth $2.02 billion that were only recorded after more stringent reporting procedures were introduced in Taiwan in 1992.[28] The Commission noted that the most popular destination for this 'official' investment was not Fujian, but Shanghai.

It is noteworthy that even despite the boom in Taiwan investment in the mainland in 1992, its share of total foreign direct investment actually fell. But, despite the reservations about the figures expressed above, they probably still significantly understate the amount of Taiwan investment. Many Taiwan businesses invest capital in the mainland indirectly, through Hong Kong. This is to accord with Taiwan's restrictions – although many do invest directly, without informing the Taiwan authorities. Up to $5 million can be taken out of Taiwan each year by individuals without authorisation. Nevertheless, it seems certain that Taiwan capital is also a factor behind the phenomenal growth in 'Hong Kong' investment in the mainland.

While Fujian, as we have seen, has achieved impressive rates of growth in the reform period, it has until recently not been as successful as elsewhere in engendering spectacular industrialisation based on foreign-invested export industries. In part this is a consequence of the lack of direct links with its most obvious source of investment capital – Taiwan. This has meant that it is impossible to view Fujian's own progress through the 'open door' in isolation from the much broader process of regional economic integration, of which Hong Kong is the hub as the most important entrepot for the re-export business, the most important source of capital and the business centre, and to which Guangdong is much the more important mainland contributor.

Taken together, Fujian and Guangdong attracted more than half of contracted foreign investment in China from 1983–91 – $20.3 billion, or 40.7 per cent of the total, in Guangdong, but less than a quarter of that – $4.9 billion – or 9.9 per cent of the national total in Fujian. In third place among China's provinces and municipalities was Shanghai, with $3.5 billion, or 7.0 per cent.[29] In 1990, 78.4 per cent ($2.1 billion) of contracted foreign investment in Guangdong came from Hong Kong, and 9.6 per cent ($257.3 million) from Taiwan.[30]

Of Taiwan's revealed investment in the mainland, as at 30 April 1991, 15.2 per cent, or $191.5 million went to Fujian, and 25 per cent ($315.9 million) to Guangdong.[31] In this sense, Fujian had failed in one of the tasks it has set itself – to become the main focus for Taiwan's economic integration with the mainland economy.

Comparative figures for the boom period that followed that date are not available. However, Fujian officials are now confident that they are finally reaping the dividends of several years of intensive efforts in investing in facilities for Taiwan investors. In September 1993, officials in Xiamen claimed to have the largest concentration of Taiwan capital anywhere in China.[32] And, in Fuzhou, the Deputy Mayor claimed that in the January to July period, the city (which incorporates the 'Mawei' Special Investment Zone, aimed, like Xiamen's 'Jimei' district, primarily at Taiwan investors) had attracted 168 Taiwan investors, with a total investment of $240 million, increases of 200 per cent and 280 per cent respectively over the same period in 1992.[33] One result of the investment boom has been the steady increase in the proportional importance of Fujian Province in the national economy as a whole. But Fujian still accounts for less than 3 per cent of total national income.

Table 7.4 Fujian, provincial share of national income[34]

	Current prices, %
1987	2.2
1988	2.4
1989	2.6
1990	2.6
1991	2.8

Table 7.5 Fujian, industrial output[35]

	1990	1991	% growth	% national total 1990	% national total 1991
RMB billion, 1990 prices	42.8	50.9	18.3	1.7	1.8

Note: National growth rate of GVIO (Gross Value of Industrial Output) = 14.2 per cent

Table 7.6 Chinese exports by selected province, municipality and Special Economic Zone, January–June 1993[36]

	US $ million	% of total
Total	37,149	100
Guangdong Province	15,386	41.4
(Shenzhen SEZ)	(5,841)	(14.8)
Shanghai	2,347	6.3
Liaoning Province	2,308	6.2
(Dalian)	(1,967)	(5.3)
Fujian Province	2,099	5.7
(Xiamen)	(909)	(2.4)
(Fuzhou)	(710)	(1.9)
Jiangsu Province	1,851	5.0
Shandong	1,713	4.6
Zhejiang	1,615	4.3

This growth has in turn been led by foreign investment, for export. That Fujian is still, even after the new spurt of growth launched by Deng Xiaoping in early 1992, a comparatively insignificant player in this nation-wide drive, can be seen from trade figures for the first half of 1993. Fujian's exports were barely more than a third of those from the Shenzhen Economic Zone alone.

To a greater extent than elsewhere in China, growth in Fujian has been led by foreign investment and private-sector investment. One effect is that, like Guangdong, Fujian is now very different in its economic structures from other parts of China, although in 1991, more than half of Fujian's industrial output still came from the state sector.

Table 7.7 Structure of industrial production in Fujian by ownership, compared to national total, 1991[37]

	% shares Fujian	% shares PRC
State-owned	51.4	63.8
Collective	19.1	29.5
Private and other	29.5	6.7

The proportion of industrial production from the 'private and others' sector is probably in fact even higher than these figures suggest, because of the numbers of private industries registered as 'collectives' for political reasons. In Fuzhou, 40 per cent of industrial output is contributed by the foreign-owned sector.[38]

The structural differences in Fujian's economy are not in themselves necessarily a force for regionalism. China is now a patchwork of provincial economies, all at a different stage of the transition from dominance by state ownership to a quasi-market system. Fujian is making that transition faster than most – partly because of the relatively undeveloped state of the non-state sector in the early 1980s, and partly because it has various advantages for foreign investors.

Indeed, to a certain extent, foreign capital helps integrate Fujian with the economy of the interior of China through its requirement for labour. As noted, in 1993, Fujian officials claimed significant numbers of migrant farmers were working fields in Fujian, whose leaseholders were seeking more lucrative employment in foreign-owned joint ventures, or even taking to the seas to emigrate. No figures are available for the proportion of migrant labour employed in Fujian. Visits to factories suggest that in Xiamen, a local labour shortage has attracted migrants, whereas in Fuzhou, most factory workers were local to the province.

In addition, some of the spurt in foreign investment in 1992–93 was attracted not by the traditional lures of cheap land and bountiful labour. Rather, it was drawn by what was perceived to be an opening up of the market in China itself, accompanied, of course, by the very rapid rise in affluence in some parts of China. Most foreign enterprises continued to use Fujian as a base for assembling of manufacturing products that were then sold abroad. Most joint venture licences still required that 80 per cent of output at least be exported. But more and more investors – the Taiwan-invested Golden Key Motorcycle Company in Fuzhou, for example – were building factories to sell exclusively into China. Assuming continuing growth and further opening of the Chinese economy, this is a trend likely to continue.

So, while Fujian may, in economic terms be rushing into 'Greater China' or 'Greater Hong Kong', that process does not in itself entail rupture with 'lesser China'. In some respects, it actually enhances Fujian's economic integration with China. To the extent, for example, that the domestic market continues to increase in importance for Fujian's enterprises, the provincial authorities will presumably be keener to resist any resurgence of local protectionism.

FUJIAN AND CENTRAL ECONOMIC POLICY

As in the case of other rapidly growing coastal provinces, there is evidence to suggest that provincial and municipal level officials in Fujian have been at odds with central government over its efforts to moderate growth rates. Economic policy in the PRC during the 'austerity period' of late 1988 to early 1992, might be summarised as the history of failed attempts by the centre to recoup powers devolved to the provinces. Provincial investment, spending and growth thwarted the centre's attempts to damp down industrial growth in the processing industries in order to remedy the perceived structural imbalances that led to the boom–bust cycles of the 1980s.

In 1991, Prime Minister Li Peng had to throw in the towel to the provinces, in the face of the reformist onslaught led by Deng Xiaoping. In his report to the National People's Congress, he endorsed the idea that 'regions having the appropriate conditions should go faster wherever possible'.[39] In July the government revised its economic growth targets from Mr Li's conservative 6 per cent[40] up to 9 or 10 per cent for 1992, to be maintained for the rest of the decade.[41] Taken together, the two pronouncements seemed to give Fujian greater official latitude than ever before to pursue its hell-for-leather race for growth. In reality, a national out-turn in real GDP growth of 13.2 per cent was achieved, accelerating even further to an estimated 13.5 per cent in 1993. Consistently, China as a whole, and provinces like Fujian in particular, have out-performed the central goverment's growth targets. This is both cause and effect in the process of ceding ever greater economic policy freedom to the provinces.

Fujian has taken advantage of the new latitude, as we have seen, to step up its efforts to woo foreign, especially Taiwan, investors with the construction of improved port facilities at Xiamen and Fuzhou, and with the opening of dozens of 'development zones'. Some of these were approved by the central government,[42] but others were illegal. Hence, Fujian was a target for a central government campaign to close down unauthorised zones in July–September 1993.

That campaign was part of a new period of 'semi-austerity' to cool down what was acknowledged to be a dangerously overheated economy. Its particular targets were irresponsible bank lending, and a related 'bubble' that had inflated the property market – from both of which Fujian had suffered particularly acutely. In September, the provincial governor stressed how serious some of these problems had become.[43]

On the other hand, officials interviewed in September 1993 in Xiamen and Fuzhou in effect denied that overheating had been a problem in their cities. They argued that since their rapid growth had been led, on the demand side, by increases in exports and foreign investment, they should be allowed to continue to grow at the rates achieved in the first half of the year (around 25 per cent real GNP growth). However, businesses there reported that 'semi-austerity' was having a very damaging impact on production, primarily through an acute shortage of bank credit.[44] Officials implied that, at the provincial level, central directives would be flouted in so far as was possible. Central government efforts to impose the new policies would have to rely on macro-economic levers still in Beijing's control – such as a broad degree of control over the money supply and bank credit.

Another threat to the provincial government came in the form of Beijing's intention, announced in December 1993, to increase its share of total national tax revenue from 38 per cent in 1992 to 60 per cent, over a period of several years. Fujian does not perceive itself as rich, and has in the past enjoyed favourable tax-sharing arrangements with Beijing (based on an annual negotiation of, in effect, a lump-sum transfer of revenues), leaving the benefits of increased revenue derived from unexpectedly rapid growth with the provincial-, and in some cases, lower-level governments. The pill was sweetened by the imprecise time-frame in which the reform was to be implemented, and by a restructuring of the whole tax system which may have the impact of increasing the total tax take.

The implementation of the reform is likely to lead to new sources of economic tension between Fuzhou and Beijing. There is, too, likely to be a prolonged conflict between Fujian's desire for economic growth at as rapid a rate as possible, and Beijing's concern with stability. Fast growth, unevenly spread, is inflationary – it creates shortages of raw materials and tightens bottlenecks. Since 1992, growth has been led, on the demand side, by huge increases in investment, funded by commensurate increases in credit and the money supply. Inflation is feared as a dangerous source of potential social unrest.

There will be an almost structural tension between Fujian, which still has many opportunities for rapid growth, and central policy, which will want to moderate growth nationally to a level where price rises and other destabilising social effects can be contained. As noted, Fujian officials, in discussing the problem look first to the area for which they are responsible. Inflationary pressures could be sustained more than elsewhere, they argued, because of the above average rises in personal incomes. That their policies might be having impacts elsewhere in the Chinese economy as a whole did not appear to impinge greatly on their thinking.

ECONOMIC AND CULTURAL PRESSURES FOR REGIONALISM

Hence there is an economic basis – albeit somewhat tenuous – for regionalism in Fujian. However, as suggested above, the centrifugal pressures produced by rapid growth rates, may be mitigated by the increased dependence on other parts of the Chinese economy that the growth also causes. The more 'Greater China' grows, the more its continued success will rely on developing markets within its constituent parts, and within 'lesser China', rather than continuing to rely on the developed world, and in particular the United States. Meanwhile development of China's infrastructure should facilitate integration within China, giving the North and the West an enhanced role in supplying Fujian with its requirements of energy, raw materials, and labour.

However, there is another potential for anti-Beijing feeling – the involvement of Taiwanese tourists and business-people in the province. This presents two potential regionalist pressures: that directed at a quasi-Fujianese unity; and the growth of Chinese East Asia.

As part of the bid to entice Taiwan investors, Taiwan officials habitually stress the close cultural, linguistic and social affinities between Fujian and Taiwan. Kong Chang-cai of the Xiamen Taiwan Affairs office says 'after Taiwan people have landed at the airport and heard people speaking southern Fujian dialect – just like their own language – and checked in at a hotel where the dishes served are just like in Taiwan, they feel as if they've come home'.[45]

It is true that the language known in Taiwan as 'Taiwanese' is spoken in southern Fujian as 'southern Fujianese', or 'Minnanhua'. And in some senses, the opening of Fujian has led to a kind of Taiwanese cultural invasion of the province. Taiwan television is widely watched where it can be received; Taiwan pop music is very popular; and many people in Fujian have first hand experience of 'the Taiwan experience' through their workplace, or through family visits. As elsewhere in China, people are convinced that their relatives in Taiwan have fared far better materially and, in a sense, spiritually, than have those left behind.

Hence, in a time of disintegrating central control, it is possible that an appeal to unify with Taiwan at the expense of the rest of China might have a constituency in Fujian.

As previously mentioned, provincial- and lower-level authorities in Fujian are already building for the opening of the 'three links' with Taiwan. At present, the main obstacles to this are perceived to lie on the Taiwan side of the Strait, and so the issue is not a particular focus for anti-Beijing resentment. However, it is probably safe to assume that, given the huge economic potential for Fujian of the opening of direct links with Taiwan, provincial leaders would like to see the central government adopt a more conciliatory posture. In March 1993, for example, Fujian Governor Jia Qinglin boasted that the 'mini three links' – of direct exchanges with the Taiwan controlled off-shore islands of Quemoy and Matsu – had already opened. He went on to say that he would welcome provincial-level talks with the Taiwan authorities at governor level, but prefaced this with a pointed remark that 'contacts . . . are up to the central authorities to decide'.[46]

Meanwhile, Fujian's unofficial and even illegal links with Taiwan are proliferating.[47] It was the growth of cross-Strait crime that in part inspired the foundation in 1990 of Taiwan's 'Straits Exchange Foundation' that has since engaged in a series of dialogues with a Chinese counterpart organisation. Taiwan wanted the mainland's help in clamping down on smuggling, piracy and illegal emigration from Fujian to Taiwan. The concern became all the greater when smuggling began to encompass firearms, narcotics and products of endangered species such as rhinoceroses and tigers, for which the Chinese medicine industry in Taiwan had a huge appetite. An unprecedented spate of hijackings of Chinese civil airliners in 1993 provided a further spur. No fewer than ten airliners, almost all *en route* to or from airfields in Fujian were hijacked to Taiwan.

Meanwhile, Taiwan had relaxed its ban on mainland labour to allow some fishing vessels to employ sailors from Fujian. The lure of the higher living standards in Taiwan continued to make itself felt in a steady exodus of illegal emigrants. In early 1994, there were more than 2,000 still in Taiwan awaiting repatriation to Fujian.

So there are reasons for Fujian to differ with Beijing over Taiwan policy. Whereas the nuisance factor – crime, smuggling and hijacking – appears to be seen in Beijing as a useful bait for drawing Taiwan into political talks, it is likely to be felt more acutely in Fujian. Meanwhile, the increased contact is building a favourable popular image in Fujian of the affluence of life in Taiwan.

CONCLUSION

The unique economic situation of Fujian inevitably entails a degree of political autonomy as well. Concern at this phenomenon as early as 1991 was perhaps indicated by the transfer of Fujian's governor Wang Zhaoguo to the Taiwan Affairs Office in Beijing. There is a parallel to the move the same year of Guangdong's governor Ye Xuanping to the Chinese People's political Consultative Committee. It is interesting, however, that both men were assigned to 'united front' posts, where their experience in dealing with forces outside the CCP might be turned to advantage.

However, as I have argued above, Fujian has been a prime beneficiary of the reform policies, even if it has not had the success in attracting the levels of foreign investment it had hoped for. This might change if direct communication and trade links with Taiwan were opened. In Taiwan itself, one argument against liberalising economic contact with the mainland too quickly is that it helps the formation of a political constituency in Taiwan for Beijing interests. In Fujian, too, there are, as I have suggested, the germs of a similar contradiction between central government policy and local trading interests.

These considerations notwithstanding, Beijing has consistently called for the opening of direct links, and it is only if Fujian begins to see the obstacle as lying not so much in Taiwan's refusal, as in Beijing's unwillingness to relinquish the threat of military invasion that Fujian would find itself at odds with central government on this key issue affecting future development.

Despite the harping on the provincial links with Fujian, increased contact has also, to a certain extent, heightened a sense of distinctness. Several generations of separate development has made Taiwan a very different place to the mainland, even to Fujian, the ancestral home for 80–85 per cent of the population. It should also be borne in mind that Fujian itself is not a cultural or linguistic whole. Whereas Taiwanese and Xiamen residents talk 'Taiwanese' to each other, northern Fujian residents converse not just with Taiwan visitors, but with the southern Fujianese in standard Chinese.

For the time being, moreover, the absence of direct links with Taiwan means that any centrifugal pressures brought about by the opening to the outside world are diffused, into a broader regional context. But both politically and militarily, that regional context has no – even inchoate – administrative or organisational structures upon which a drive for autonomy or independence might be founded. Politically, Fujian – as well, of course, as Taiwan and Hong Kong and other mainland provinces – is a separate entity. They are equivalent, as provinces of the People's Republic.

Although, as we have seen, there was a hint of rebelliousness in the ranks of the Fujian military in 1989, the high command since then has had ample opportunity to revamp the military leadership in the military to ensure that those now in charge are fundamentally loyal to the regional command in Nanjing, and beyond that to the central Military Commissions in Beijing. As pointed out earlier, this is all the more likely to be true of Fujian because of its strategic importance to the Taiwan question. So, rather than being a factor militating towards greater provincial autonomy in Fujian, the military appears to be a force lending implicit weight to those in the province in favour of continued national Chinese cohesion. This is not to rule out the possibility of some form of Fujian nationalism becoming an important factor in local politics in the future. Rather, it is to suggest that a growth of regionalism is likely to be provoked first by a disintegration of central authority, rather than to be in itself a significant contributor to that process of disintegration.

NOTES

1 Interview with the author, Fuzhou, 3 Sept 1993.
2 Xinhua News Agency, 31 Aug 1993. 'The Taiwan Question and the Reunification of China'. Printed in *Summary of World Broadcasts, Part Three* (SWB), 2 Sept 1993, FE/1783, S 1/1.
3 *People's China*, Vol. 1, No. 10, 16 May 1950. Quoted in Allen Whiting, 'China Crosses the Yalu', Rand Corporation, 1960.
4 *Ibid.*, p. 45.
5 Reprinted in F. Gilbert Chan, 'China's Reunification and the Taiwan Question', Asian Research Service, Hong Kong, 1984.
6 Simon Long, 'Taiwan: China's Last Frontier', Macmillan 1991.

7 SWB, 10 Dec 1991, FE/1251 A 3/3. The threat was also repeated in the August 1993 'White Paper' (see note 2)

8 Julian Baum, 'Signal Guns', *Far Eastern Economic Review* (FEER), 18 February 1993.

9 See Paul H.B. Godwin, 'The Use of Military against Taiwan: Potential PRC Scenarios', in *If China Crosses the Taiwan Strait: The International Response'*, ed. Parris H. Chang and Martin L. Lasater, University Press of America, 1993.

10 Julian Baum, 'Prepare to Surface', FEER, 4 February 1993.

11 Tai Ming-cheung, 'Lacking Depth', FEER, 4 February 1993.

12 Tai Ming Cheung and Nayan Chanda, 'Exercising Cution' FEER, 2 September 1993. On Taiwan officials' interpretations, see authors interview with Foreign Minister Ch'ien Fu, 17 August 1993.

13 This section relies heavily on information contained in Michael D. Swaine, 'The Military and Political Succession in China', Rand Corporation, Santa Monica, California, 1992.

14 'The Military Balance 1992–1993', The International Institute for Strategic Studies, London, 1992.

15 Timothy Brook, 'Quelling the People: The Military Suppression of the Beijing Democracy Movement', Oxford University Press, 1992.

16 See Renmin Ribao, 21 July 1993. Quoted in Simon Long, 'Chinese Top Brass Deplore Army Graft', *Guardian*, 30 July 1993.

17 SWB, 24 May, 1993, FE/1696, B2/8.

18 Renmin Ribao editorial, 8 February 1990, apparently in response to the decision by the then Communist Party of the Soviet Union to relinquish its constitutional guarantee of the 'leading role'.

19 Hideo Ohashi, 'The economic development of Fujian province', in *China Newsletter*, Nov–Dec 1992.

20 See, for example, 'Fujian Governor speaks on problems facing province', SWB, 16 Sept. 1993, FE/1795 G/7.

21 Derived from 'Zhonguo Tongji Nianjian, 1991', 'Fujian Tonji Nianjian, 1990', and Hideo Ohashi, *op cit.*

22 Derived from *China Statistical Yearbook, 1992*, and 'Foreign Investment in China, 1992', *China Newsletter*, JETRO, July–Aug 1993.

23 *China Economic News*, 1994, No. 4.

24 Xinhua News Agency, 28 Aug 1993. In SWB, 15 Sept. 1993, FEW/0299 WG/2.

25 Xinhua News Agency, 24 Aug 1993. In SWB, 1 Sept. 1993, FE/WO297 A/2.

26 See note 24.

27 See note 25.

28 Taiwan Investment Commission, Reuters report, 12 Jan 1994.

29 MOFERT statistics, from *Business China*, 13 July 1992.

30 'Post 1997 Economic Integration in Southern China', Asia Research Centre, Murdoch University, Western Australia, 1992, ('Post–1997'), p. 86, quoting *Hong Kong Economic Journal*, 2 Nov 1991.

31 'Post-1997', p. 123.

32 Author's interview with Kong Changcai, Deputy Director, Xiamen Taiwan Affairs Office, 1 Sept 1993.

33 See note 1.

34 Derived from *China Statistical Yearbook*, 1988, 1989, 1990, 1991 and 1992, 1993 and Guangdong and Fujian provincial statistical communiqués for 1991.
35 *China Statistical Yearbook*, 1993
36 *China's Customs Statistics*, Series Number 46, 1993, p. 6.
37 Derived from Statistical Communiqué of the State Statistical Bureau of the PRC on the 1991 National Economic and Social Development (28 February 1992), and 'Industrial Production Figures of 29 Provinces and Municipalities in the Year 1991', *China Economic News Supplement*, 1992, No. 4, 1 June 1992.
38 See note 1.
39 Li Peng Work Report to National People's Congress, 20 March 1991. In SWB, FE/1347, 7 April 1991, C2/5 (cf. his speech in 1990).
40 Government Spokesman Yuan Mu, press conference, Beijing, 16 July 1992.
41 Quoted by *China Daily*, 25 June 1992.
42 'Fujian swings doors wider to the outside world', *China Economic News*, 5 April 1993.
43 See note 20.
44 Authors' interviews Aug 30–Sept 4, in Xiamen and Fuzhou, with, *inter alia*, He Lifeng, Deputy Mayor, Xiamen; Chen Der Chu, Tsann Kuen (China) Enterprise Co. Ltd; Weng Chengshou, Xiamen University, Taiwan Research Institute; Yang Biying, Vice Director, Fuzhou Planning Commission.
45 See note 32.
46 'Fujian Governor on contacts with Taiwan', SWB 1 April 1993, FE/1652 C1/4.
47 There is an excellent account of the growth of these contacts in Ralph N. Clough, 'Reaching Across the Taiwan Strait: People to People Diplomacy', Westview, 1993.

8 Shanghai and the Lower Yangzi Valley

J. Bruce Jacobs and Lijian Hong[1]

Shanghai now entirely has the conditions [to develop] a bit more quickly. In the areas of talented personnel, technology and administration, Shanghai has obvious superiority, which radiates over a wide area. Looking backwards, my one major mistake was not to include Shanghai when we set up the four special economic zones. Otherwise, the situation of reform and opening to the outside in the Yangzi River Delta, the entire Yangzi River Valley and even the entire nation would be different.

Deng Xiaoping[2]

Make Shanghai an outward-oriented, multi-functional, modernised international city.

Jiang Zemin[3]

Shanghai has a unique position in China. It is by far China's wealthiest area and has extensive human resources. Yet, as Deng Xiaoping stated during his inspection tour of the South, Shanghai has not been able to take full advantage of its wealth and human resources. After outlining its comparative wealth, this chapter examines Shanghai's relationship to the centre and how this has inhibited Shanghai's development in the post-Mao period. We then consider recent changes in the centre's policies towards Shanghai and Shanghai's responses. Finally it considers whether Shanghai has manifested any tendencies towards regionalism either within China or internationally.

SHANGHAI'S WEALTH

Shanghai, with a per capita income of RMB *yuan* 5,204 is far and away China's wealthiest provincial-level unit, greatly exceeding Beijing (RMB *yuan* 3,718), Tianjin (RMB *yuan* 3,139), Liaoning (RMB *yuan* 2,186), Guangdong (RMB *yuan* 2,159) and Zhejiang

Table 8.1 Per capita income of Shanghai, Hangzhou, Guangzhou, Dalian and Shenzhen, 1991 (RMB *yuan*)

	Whole municipality	Urban areas
Shanghai	5,414	6,114
Hangzhou	2,999	5,404
Guangzhou	4,536	5,928
Dalian	3,104	4,841
Shenzhen	17,744	22,085

Source: Calculated from *Zhongguo chengshi tongji nianjian 1992* [Urban statistical yearbook of China 1992] (Beijing: Zhongguo tongji chubanshe, 1992), pp. 50, 52, 57, 105, 107, 112, 116, 118, 123

(RMB *yuan* 2,045).[4] It is also clearly China's most productive provincial-level unit with a per capita product of RMB *yuan* 6,406 compared to Beijing (RMB *yuan* 5,125), Tianjin (RMB *yuan* 3,761), Guangdong (RMB *yuan* 2,785), Liaoning (RMB *yuan* 2,697), Zhejiang (RMB *yuan* 2,350) and Jiangsu (RMB *yuan* 2,153).[5]

Yet, when we compare Shanghai to other urban areas rather than to provincial-level units, Shanghai loses some of its apparent advantage. Guangzhou does not trail too far behind and Shenzhen appears much more wealthy (Table 8.1).

It should be noted that a Shenzhen source gives much lower 1990 per capita income figures for Shenzhen: RMB *yuan* 4,785 for Shenzhen Municipality and RMB *yuan* 6,963 for the Special Economic Zone.[6]

The Shanghai economy is primarily industrial, though the service sector is becoming increasingly important. In 1991 the primary sector accounted for only 3.89 per cent of product, by far the lowest proportion among China's provincial-level units.[7] The secondary sector accounted for 64.28 per cent of Shanghai's product, the largest proportion in China.[8] The tertiary sector accounts for 31.83 per cent of Shanghai's product. This is considerably less than the 39.67 per cent of Beijing, where the central government accounts for an important part of the service sector, and less than Tianjin (35.30 per cent) as well as three of China's poorest provincial-level units.[9]

The relative importance of the secondary and tertiary sectors provides a broad overview of changes in Shanghai's economic development strategies. Prior to 1956, the tertiary sector grew at a faster rate than the secondary sector. However, owing to the acceleration of industrial production, the secondary sector occupied an ever-increasing proportion of Shanghai's product. 'Shanghai's economic

Table 8.2 Structure of the Shanghai economy by sector (per cent)

	Primary sector	Secondary sector	Tertiary sector
1952	5.9	52.4	41.7
1957	3.9	58.7	37.4
1970	4.7	77.1	18.2
1978	4.0	77.4	18.6
1980	3.2	75.7	21.1
1985	4.2	69.8	26.0
1990	4.4	64.8	30.8
1991	3.9	64.3	31.8

Source: Shanghai tongji nianjian 1992 [Shanghai Statistical Yearbook 1992]; edited by Shanghai shi tongji ju (Shanghai: Zhongguo tongji chubanshe, 1992), p. 33

development was decided by the secondary sector.'[10] In 1980, the growth rate of the tertiary sector began to exceed that of the secondary sector, 'but in total production, the secondary sector still remains decisive and definitely no basic change has occurred.'[11] Yet, perhaps this evaluation by a senior Shanghai municipal economist is too pessimistic. The December 1984 'Shanghai Municipality Economic Strategy' emphasised development of the tertiary sector to serve the entire nation. At that time the tertiary sector accounted for 21.9 per cent of Shanghai's product.[12] As Table 8.2 shows, Shanghai had met the 'Strategy' document's goal of having the tertiary sector account for 30 per cent of product by 1990, but the original goal of 50–60 per cent of product by the year 2000 has been revised downward.[13] According to Mayor Huang Ju, Shanghai seeks to have the tertiary sector account for 45 per cent of GNP in the year 2000 and 60 per cent in 2010.[14]

SHANGHAI'S CRUCIAL IMPORTANCE TO THE CENTRE

Why did Deng Xiaoping commit his 'major mistake' and fail to include Shanghai when planning the special economic zones?[15] At the heart of the question is Shanghai's crucial importance for central government revenues. Prior to the economic reforms, Shanghai provided one-fifth to one-fourth of central government revenue according to Shanghai economists.[16] (Shanghai has 1.1 per cent of China's population and 0.1 per cent of its area.[17]) Thus, when beginning reforms in the late 1970s, the centre could not afford to take risks with Shanghai and such other major contributors to central revenue as

Jiangsu. Rather it experimented in Guangdong, which provided the centre with less than 1 per cent of its funds. The importance of Shanghai to central revenues was revealed during the Cultural Revolution when, despite the importance of the 'Gang of Four' in Shanghai, production in Shanghai was protected and the city remained relatively calm and one of the few places in China where goods were available.

China's arcane fiscal system, to quote senior Chinese economists in Beijing and the provinces, remains 'secret', 'unfair', 'defective' and 'unable to satisfy requirements'.[18] Basically, each provincial-level unit negotiates a minimum or base amount to be paid to the central government annually. Two systems prevail. Guangdong arranged to keep the full surplus over and above its base amount. Shanghai and Jiangsu had to pay a fixed proportion of their fiscal revenues above the base amount to the centre. While historical circumstances play a role in determining the base amount each province must pay, the system is extraordinarily arbitrary and secret. Thus the base amount as well as any percentages above the base amount paid to the centre depend upon historical background, the negotiating skills of the provincial representatives and any *guanxi* ('particularistic ties') which the provincial officials may have with the centre. To the best of our knowledge, no source provides details of contracts between the centre and each of the provincial-level units. Thus, our knowledge of the base amount and of the proportion above the base amount which any province must pay the centre remains anecdotal and problematic. Informants disagree, for example, about whether Shanghai's latest arrangements enable it to pay the base amount only or whether it must pay a proportion of revenues above the base amount. (One informant noted, however, that Shanghai's revenues would not exceed the base amount because any surplus funds would be left in the subordinate districts rather than placed in municipality funds!) With these caveats in mind, we demonstrate the crucial importance of Shanghai to central revenues.

On the basis of informants, it is clear Shanghai pays the highest base amount to the central government (Table 8.3).

Taxes are by far the largest source of government revenues. In 1986 taxes accounted for 92.5 per cent of revenue while income from enterprises only contributed 1.9 per cent of total government revenues.[19] These government revenues are divided into two categories: central and local. Central revenues, which in 1991 accounted for 38.76 per cent of total revenues,[20] appear to come primarily from centrally-owned enterprises. These funds come from localities, but do

Table 8.3 Base amounts contributed by provincial-level units to the central government (RMB *yuan* million)

Province	Base Amount*
Shanghai	10,300–16,500
Jiangsu	7,000–10,000
Zhejiang	3,000–4,000
Sichuan	1,000
Guangdong	800–1,300
Fujian	100

Note: * Range of estimates given in interviews.

not belong to the localities. In 1991, Shanghai provided RMB *yuan* 14,913 million in central revenue to the central government, 10.65 per cent of the total central government revenues of RMB *yuan* 139,700 million.[21] However, this is only a small portion of the central fiscal income emanating from Shanghai.

Shanghai also gives a large proportion of its local revenues to the centre. In 1991 Shanghai had local revenues of RMB *yuan* 16,509 million, ranking second among provincial-level units only to Guangdong, which had local revenues of RMB *yuan* 17,735 million.[22] However, Shanghai ranked only sixteenth in local expenditure, spending only RMB *yuan* 7,742 million compared to Guangdong, which ranked first in expenditure, spending RMB *yuan* 18,248 million.[23] In local revenues, Shanghai had a 'surplus' (revenue income less expenditure) of RMB *yuan* 8,767 million, which went to the central government. Thus, over half (53.10 per cent) of Shanghai's *local* revenue went to the central government. No other provincial-level unit made such contributions out of local revenues (see Table 8.4).

In an attempt to calculate Shanghai's total contribution to central revenues, we have calculated Shanghai's total fiscal revenues (central and local) and subtracted Shanghai's local expenditures. This suggests Shanghai now contributes about 17 per cent of total central revenues. Recently, Mayor Huang Ju appeared to validate this statistical method by disclosing that Shanghai delivered RMB *yuan* 27,000 million in tax revenues to the centre in 1992,[24] a figure comparable to our calculated figure of RMB *yuan* 24,343 million in 1991 (Table 8.5). The statistics suggest that Shanghai contributed much larger proportions in the early 1980s (Table 8.5).

People from Guangdong justify Guangdong's disproportionately low contribution to central revenues by arguing that Guangdong

Table 8.4 'Surplus' as percentage of local revenue, 1991 [(Local revenue – local expenditures) / local revenue × 100]

Province	' Surplus' (%)
Shanghai	53.10
Zhejiang	22.04
Tianjin	18.28
Jiangsu	11.93
Beijing	11.74
Liaoning	6.19
Shandong	0.71

Source: Calculated from *Jiangsu zai quanguo de[,] shixian zai Jiangsu de diwei (1991)* [The Position of Jiangsu in the Nation and of municipalities and counties in Jiangsu (1991)] ([Nanjing]: Jiangsu sheng tongji ju, 1993), pp. 23–4

Table 8.5 Estimated contribution of Shanghai to central revenue, 1981–91

	Central revenue (RMB yuan million)	Shanghai contribution to centre (RMB yuan million)	Shanghai contribution (%)
1981	22,470	18,546	82.54
1982	25,850	18,001	69.64
1983	37,200	18,195	48.91
1984	52,450	18,547	35.36
1985	70,790	21,779	30.77
1986	91,670	19,864	21.67
1987	90,580	18,751	20.70
1988	104,550	19,581	18.73
1989	110,550	22,394	20.26
1990	136,790	20,910	15.29
1991	139,970	24,343	17.39

Sources: Calculated from *Shanghai tongji nianjian 1992* [Shanghai statistical yearbook 1992]; edited by Shanghai shi tongji ju (Shanghai: Zhongguo tongji chubanshe, 1992), p. 53; and *Zhongguo tongji nianjian 1992* [Statistical yearbook of China 1992] (Beijing: Zhongguo tongji chubanshe, 1992), p. 227

has received very little centrally funded investment in contrast to Shanghai, the recipient of considerable central investment. While this argument may have validity when comparing Shanghai and Guangdong, Shanghai clearly has contributed much more to the centre than it has received via central investment. During 1950–83, basic construction investment in Shanghai totalled RMB *yuan* 35,011 million. Of this, the centre invested 42.33 per cent or RMB *yuan*

14,781 million in central units located in Shanghai.[25] Thus, the total accumulated central investment in Shanghai over twenty-four years was less than the Shanghai fiscal contribution to the centre in the final year alone (see Table 8.5).

Other analyses validate this conclusion. Under Mao, according to Lardy, the centre invested only 5.6 per cent of Shanghai revenues in Shanghai during 1953–57, a figure that declined to 1.9 per cent in 1958.[26] Shanghai continued to contribute much more to the centre than it received in investment from 1949 to 1975. Furthermore, Shanghai contributed more than a half million skilled workers to other provinces by the early 1970s.[27]

While statistical sources do not provide information on central investment by province, Chinese statistics do suggest Shanghai clearly continues to receive a disproportionately small amount of the fixed capital investments made in state-owned units in comparison to Shanghai's fiscal contributions in the post-Mao period as well. Shanghai received 6.44 per cent of fixed capital investment in state enterprises during 1981–85 and 6.78 per cent in 1986–90. However, these figures declined to 5.73 per cent in 1991 and 5.37 per cent in 1992.[28] Of course, Shanghai does receive a disproportionately high percentage of fixed capital investment on a per capita basis.

THE EVOLUTION OF SHANGHAI'S DEVELOPMENT POLICIES

The crucial importance of Shanghai to central government revenues persuaded the centre to sacrifice Shanghai when it began the post-Mao reforms. The centre had little experience with reforms and feared a disaster. Because Guangdong and Shenzhen made few contributions to central revenues and because of their propinquity to Hong Kong, the centre decided Guangdong and Shenzhen were more suitable for experiments. Shanghai basically remained in the 'planned economy'. With few funds available for local use, Shanghai's growth remained relatively slow and its infrastructure remained backward.

Despite this, Shanghai scholars led the way in considering 'Regional Economic Development Strategy'. On 26 February 1981, a bi-monthly seminar on 'Questions of Economic and Social Development Strategy' met in Beijing for the first time. (It continued to meet regularly until March 1989.) In 1982, Shanghai scholars launched their own monthly seminar to discuss 'Regional Economic Development Strategy', a model which Liaoning and other places soon followed. The Shanghai Party Committee and Shanghai Municipal Government considered this work important.[29]

In 1984, the Shanghai Municipal Party Committee and the Shanghai Municipal Government formally organised the study of 'Shanghai Economic Development Strategy'. In September 1984, the State Council sent an Investigation and Research Group to Shanghai under the leadership of Ma Hong. This Group assisted Shanghai in preparing a document and invited many scholars and specialists from Shanghai as well as the whole of China to participate. The State Council Investigation and Research Group and the Shanghai Municipal Party Committee submitted an 'An Outline of the Report Concerning Shanghai Economic Development Strategy' which the State Council approved in February 1985.[30]

The State Council's approval of the Strategy document marginally increased the funds available to Shanghai. During 1950–83, Shanghai retained only 13.2 per cent of its funds while the centre took 86.8 per cent. The Strategy document allocated Shanghai 23.2 per cent of its funds leaving the centre with 76.8 per cent.[31] This was an improvement, but Shanghai still suffered from poor housing and transport.

Furthermore, the centre's treatment of Shanghai made it fall behind its competitors. According to a Shanghai official responsible for planning reform,

At present, Shanghai faces both domestic and overseas challenges. Internationally, such countries and regions of the Asian region as Singapore, Malaysia, Thailand, Taiwan and South Korea have succeeded Japan in relatively quickly realising social and economic leaps. From a domestic perspective, such places as Guangzhou, Shenzhen, Zhuhai and Shantou in the South, relying on the geographical superiority of neighbouring Hong Kong and Macao *and special policy,* have become the gateway for economic interchange between the mainland and Hong Kong and have made relatively great strides in opening to the outside. In such neighbouring areas as Jiangsu and Zhejiang, the cooperative economy is comparatively important. Their enterprise management mechanisms are relatively vital and their local economy and foreign trade have developed relatively quickly making them powerful competitors of Shanghai. In the North, Dalian, Tianjin and Qingdao have begun establishing large-scale economic and technology development zones. The progress of reform in places like Shenyang and Harbin has gained attention. From south to north, these places in the areas of reform, opening and development have all raised a challenge to Shanghai. [emphasis added][32]

In 1988 the centre, following representations from Shanghai leaders, agreed to allow Shanghai to move to the financial responsibility system. Shanghai agreed to provide RMB *yuan* 10,500 million to the Centre annually. This gave Shanghai an additional RMB *yuan* 1,400 million per year. While helpful, this was not a huge amount considering that it would only fund one kilometre of an underground rail transit system. The contract between the central government and Shanghai provided for no changes over a five-year period. Thus, the central government and Shanghai will negotiate in 1993 for the arrangements which will begin in 1994.

Despite the agreement between Shanghai and the central government for no change over five years, in 1992 the central government asked for a RMB *yuan* 400 million 'contribution'. Shanghai's 'contribution' was less than Guangdong's RMB *yuan* 1,000 million 'contribution', but Shanghai pays much higher amounts to the centre. The central government also 'borrows' funds from the provinces to cover its deficits. The central government 'borrows' these funds in face-to-face talks with provincial officials. Although the central government promises to repay the debts when it obtains more funds, the provincial authorities clearly realise the funds will not be returned. They dare not, however, reject the centre's requests. In early 1993, Mayor Huang Ju revealed that Shanghai forwards about 80 per cent of its tax revenues to the centre.[33] This is less than the 86.8 per cent Shanghai gave the centre in 1950–83, but still only provided Shanghai with an extra RMB *yuan* 2,229 million in 1992.[34] Furthermore, Mayor Huang Ju expects the situation to continue unchanged for the next few years.[35]

Of course, localities are not totally helpless in dealing with the centre. Localities use one technique called 'Fishing Projects', in which a locality proposes a project which appears both desirable and inexpensive, thus inducing the centre to invest. Costs then escalate and the Centre puts in more funds in order to not waste the earlier investment. The first investment 'gets the hook in'.

The key policy changes for Shanghai occurred in 1990 and especially in 1992. Shanghai had been sacrificed at the beginning of the reform programme. The South had benefited greatly, but the country as a whole did not. Shenzhen and even Guangdong could not make all of China prosperous. To make the whole country prosperous required

China's economic powerhouse, its 'Dragon Head' – Shanghai – to be prosperous.

As a result of its remaining in the 'planned economy' and ensuring the centre its revenues, Shanghai had poor roads, communications, housing and environment as well as a relatively slow growth rate. Shanghai lacked an underground rapid transit system, unlike Beijing which had two lines and Tianjin which had one line. Because Shanghai had given so much of its income to the centre, it had accumulated 'debts' to its population which, according to a senior Shanghai economist, totalled RMB *yuan* 40–50,000 million. This sum would be required to fix public transport, roads, the port and housing, which averaged only some six square metres per person even including the spacious housing in rural areas. Unlike Guangdong, which had control over its local revenues, Shanghai had to go 'cap in hand' to the centre for major investment funds, a process that inevitably slowed Shanghai's growth.

Why is Shanghai so important to China? First, as noted above, Shanghai is China's wealthiest area and a key industrial centre. Second, unlike Shenzhen, it has sufficient size to be a true 'Dragon Head'. Third, Shenzhen cannot become a major financial centre because it can never become distant from Hong Kong. Fourth, Shanghai's geographical location gives its proximity to both the north and south coasts as well as the Yangzi River Valley. No other Chinese city has such an advantageous geographical position. Fifth, Shanghai has China's most numerous and talented human resources in the fields of science and technology, economics and finance, and management, as well as excellent and numerous quality workers.

All of these factors led to the decisions in 1990 and especially in 1992 to promote Shanghai and its Pudong region east of the Huangpu River. (The centre of Shanghai is in Puxi, that is 'west of the Huangpu River'.) Following decisions of the Party Centre and the State Council, on 18 April 1990 Premier Li Peng announced Pudong would be developed and opened to the outside. 'The development of Pudong and the opening of Pudong to the outside is a matter having important strategic significance for Shanghai and for the entire nation.'[36] Twelve days later, on 30 April 1990, Mayor Zhu Rongji announced ten preferential policies for the development of Pudong. These policies included such incentives as tax holidays and relief, encouragement for the establishment of service industries, a free-trade zone and land use for periods of from fifty to seventy years.[37]

However, Shanghai economists unanimously agree that Pudong

development really began only in 1992 following Deng Xiaoping's inspection tour of the South. At this time two important things happened. First, Pudong obtained five more 'preferential policies' which Mayor Huang Ju announced on 10 March 1992. These new policies gave Shanghai Municipality more authority to make decisions regarding investment approval, allowed Shanghai to issue stocks and securities and permitted trading in Shanghai of stocks issued in other Chinese localities. They also authorised foreign department stores and supermarkets in Pudong, China's largest free-trade zone in Pudong, and the operation of foreign banks, finance companies and insurance companies in Shanghai. The purpose of these measures was to make certain Pudong 'has new impetus and vitality as a key area within China for reform and opening to the outside during the next decade.'[38]

Second, tax rates for enterprises in Shanghai were lowered. Previously Shanghai enterprises had paid income tax rates of 55 per cent. With the addition of many other taxes such as an energy tax and an education tax, enterprises retained only 15–18 per cent of income and some retained only 8–9 per cent of income. The Shanghai Cigarette Company, according to a leading Shanghai economist, paid as much tax as the whole of Guangzhou Municipality![39] In 1992, however, the enterprise income tax was lowered to 33 per cent, thus allowing enterprises to keep an additional 22 per cent of income. This greatly increased the capital available in Shanghai.

Shanghai people emphasise the importance of the centre 'giving' Shanghai a 'policy' – the preferential policies of 1990 and 1992. Without a policy, Shanghai could not develop. With a 'policy', Shanghai can use its various capabilities to progress and develop. This very widespread belief suggests Chinese have reified the concept of 'policy' into something very concrete. In fact, a recent Shanghai publication states this explicitly, 'policy is wealth'.[40]

The centre now actively supports Shanghai because it believes a robust 'Dragon Head' will lead to a healthier dragon. The centre has funded two major suspension bridges over the Huangpu River connecting Puxi and Pudong. (A Shanghai joke states that Zhu Rongji built bridges when he was in Shanghai.) The new policies have brought considerably more capital, both domestic and foreign, into Shanghai. Shanghai has much new construction. The Park Hotel, a pre-liberation twenty-four-storey building, remained Shanghai's tallest building well into the 1980s. Now it is a 'little brother'. People say that at any one time roads are being dug in 6,000 different places. Other funds come through real-estate development. Shanghai lacks sufficient funds to build new housing so the municipality leases land, which is very expensive, to foreign and domestic investors who develop the land while the municipality uses the funds to build new housing in suburban areas. This process also brings in large amounts of capital to Shanghai. Thus, according to Shanghai economists, capital is more readily available in Shanghai than elsewhere.

But 'policy' stability clearly concerns many people in Shanghai. On 11 May 1993, during a visit to Pudong, Party General Secretary and State President Jiang Zemin felt it necessary to say, 'The centre's policy to develop and open Pudong is firm and unvarying. It will not change'.[41] During a visit of 13–14 May 1993, CCP Political Bureau Standing Committee Member and Vice-Premier Zhu Rongji quoted Jiang Zemin's words and called them an 'important statement'.[42] Shanghai people hope the current attempts to use 'macro-control' to cool the economy will not affect Shanghai's ability to obtain investment funds. Pudong has just begun developing and must be allowed to continue. Loans, as one senior Shanghai economist explained, are like grain rations in the past. Then one required money, but a person also required a ration coupon to obtain grain. Now, people may have funds, but they still need permission to obtain loans. Shanghai requires the policy stability which Jiang Zemin and Zhu Rongji have promised.

THE PUDONG NEW DISTRICT AND THE DIRECTION OF SHANGHAI'S DEVELOPMENT

In an effort to develop the Pudong area rapidly and efficiently, Shanghai Municipality has established a new 'small government' for the area. Parts of three urban districts and two counties were combined into the Pudong New District (*Pudong xinqu,* sometimes translated as Pudong New Area) on 1 January 1993. A vice-mayor, Zhao Qizheng, heads the Pudong New District, which has a higher administrative status than other Shanghai districts. The Pudong New District Administration Committee 'is the leading and policy-making organ with full powers and responsibility for development, construction and social administration within the scope of the New District.' The Administration Committee has ten functional bureaus and offices.[43] The Pudong New District has a population of 1,380,000 and an area of 518 square kilometres.[44] Thus, it has 10.7 per cent of Shanghai's population[45] and 8.2 per cent of Shanghai Municipality's area. But Pudong New District is much larger when compared to urban Shanghai, being 69.1 per cent of urban Shanghai's size and having 1.84 times the area of Shanghai's central districts.[46] Pudong New District is about five-sixths the size of Singapore.

Pudong's advantage is its large, relatively empty area located directly opposite Shanghai's commercial centre, the Bund. With the new communications links including the two new suspension bridges, three tunnels (one still limited to military use) as well as the planned inner and outer ring roads, transport from Shanghai's commercial centre west of the Huangpu River (Puxi) to Pudong will be extremely convenient.

The Pudong New District will have six special zones. Work on four, all foreign-trade related, has begun. The Lujiazui Finance and Trade Zone, located just opposite the Bund, emphasises the development of such service industries as finance, trade, commerce, real estate, information and consultancy. The Waigaoqiao Free Trade Zone, located twenty kilometres from the Shanghai city centre in the northeast section of Pudong New District at the mouth of the Yangzi River, will have a bonded storage area, an export processing zone and a trade management centre. The Jinqiao Export Processing Zone, located in the centre of Pudong New District, will produce high-technology products in relatively large-scale operations. The Jinqiao Export Processing Zone will also have a 'high-class' residential area as well as many green spaces. The Zhangjiang High-Tech Park, located in the central southern part of Pudong New District, will use Shanghai's strengths in science and technology to develop such key areas as electronics and information technology, space science and aerospace technology, life sciences and technology, materials science and technology and environment science and technology. The development of each of these zones requires substantial infrastructure development.[47] The authorities hope to use integrated planning with good housing, trees and green areas, and space for parking cars.

Change is occurring rapidly in Pudong. People talk of 'Pudong speed', a take-off of the term 'Shenzhen speed', to describe the rapid construction as well as the speed with which the government should approve projects. In the words of an official Pudong New District publication, 'The Shanghai Municipal Government has submitted the short-term objective for the development of Pudong in the next three years of realising a change each year and a major change after three years.'[48] Yet, major problems do exist. The quality of the new construction in Pudong appears quite ordinary, even by Chinese standards. Furthermore, the standards of service seem low. During a mid-1993 visit to the Pudong New District Office, service at the counter was languid. That evening, the Orient TV news reported that the Pudong petrol station had angered many motorists and taxi drivers by refusing to accept coupons and demanding cash. And the Shanghai telephone system and service seem far behind the standards in Nanjing and Beijing.

The development of Pudong cannot be separated from the development of Shanghai as a whole. Pudong relies on Shanghai's talented workforce for labour and personnel and thus hopefully will reduce Shanghai's unemployment rate. (Pudong's labour force lacks the skills of Puxi's labour force.) Although officially only 2 per cent, Shanghai has a real unemployment rate substantially higher as many of its state enterprises are considerably over-staffed. Pudong may thus increase the efficiency of Shanghai's industry. Pudong may also help relieve the population pressure in Puxi as more and more people move to Pudong. (Some university-based consultants in Pudong stated the initial motive for developing Pudong was to relieve Puxi population pressure.) The relationship between Pudong and Puxi is mutually beneficial: Pudong depends upon Puxi's skills and knowledge while Puxi, being adjacent to Pudong, benefits from the 'policy' given to Pudong.[49]

Pudong also forms an integral part of Shanghai's current development strategy. This strategy requires structural adjustment. The tertiary sector now has priority while the secondary sector requires 'positive readjustment' and the primary sector 'stabilisation'.[50] Since Shanghai will not be allowed to increase its industry substantially and since its relatively few exports cannot sustain an international port,[51] Shanghai needs to develop its service industries and provide such services as information, transport, warehousing, introduction, exhibitions, insurance and legal services to customers from other parts of China and overseas. For example, foreign businessmen now need to travel widely over China to several provinces. Shanghai could provide services for other provinces and enable foreign businessmen to come to Shanghai alone. In such a way, Shanghai could reach the goal, which the centre has assigned, of becoming 'three centres', i.e. an international trade, economic and financial centre. Yet, at present, the formulas are abstract, preliminary and crude. Much work is necessary before the formulas can be refined into detailed blueprints.

SHANGHAI'S LINKS TO THE CENTRE

Why did the centre change its policies towards Shanghai, giving tax relief in 1988 and preferential policies in 1990 and 1992? Chinese analysts focus on three reasons why the centre invests in or assists particular localities. First, a locality may need investment. Second, particular localities may have advantages for particular projects. The Ministry of Metallurgy finally placed the Baoshan Steel Factory in Shanghai rather than in Zhejiang because Shanghai has talented technical personnel and high-quality workers.

Finally, observers emphasise the particularistic ties (*guanxi*)[52] which local leaders have with the centre. Shandong has received considerable investment because Shandong people have considerable decision-making power in several central-level ministries which control huge investments in the areas of transport and resources (e.g. the Ministry of Petroleum).

Like Shanghai, Jiangsu Province has long been a key source of central revenues, but, unlike Shanghai, Jiangsu still suffers from heavy central taxation and relatively slow growth as it has not obtained tax relief and other preferential policies since 1988. Jiangsu observers tend to emphasise the importance of Shanghai's *guanxi* with the centre. They note that both Jiang Zemin and Zhu Rongji went to the centre from Shanghai, bringing lots of Shanghai cadres with them. Qiao Shi also worked in the Shanghai underground, giving three of seven members of the Political Bureau Standing Committee substantial connections with Shanghai. Furthermore, each year Deng Xiaoping and many other central leaders spend the Chinese New Year in Shanghai. At minimum, these Jiangsu observers say, this demonstrates that Deng and other central leaders have an interest in Shanghai and consider it important.

Shanghai observers disagree with this Jiangsu analysis. They note that Deng and other central leaders came to Shanghai for the Chinese New Year celebrations well before the policy changes. Furthermore, they note that Chen Yun is a Shanghai native, but he did not give Shanghai any particular assistance. The key changes, they argue, occurred in 1992 after Deng's important speech following his inspection tour of the South. Jiang and Zhu had already been in Beijing for some time. Furthermore, Shanghai analysts believe Jiang Zemin and Zhu Rongji have central rather than Shanghai perspectives now that they have central responsibilities. Of course, it is easier for Shanghai leaders to get past gatekeepers and transmit their messages to the centre, but the key, according to these analysts, is still Shanghai's importance to the national economy rather than Shanghai's *guanxi* with the centre.

As noted above, Shanghai received some preferential policies in 1990, though the key changes occurred in 1992. According to

Shanghai analysts, Shanghai received some policy relief in 1990 because Shanghai was peaceful during the April–June 1989 period which led to the Beijing and other massacres on 4 June 1989. Zhu Rongji, according to many Shanghai people, was the hero. He reputedly made two statements about the period which have received little publicity elsewhere in China, but which Shanghai residents cherish. First, Zhu promised that the military would not enter Shanghai. Second, he declared that history would evaluate the events (and that there was no need to debate them now.)

SHANGHAI: A REGIONAL CENTRE?

The centre has given Shanghai an explicit regional leadership role. In his report to the Fourteenth National Party Congress, Jiang Zemin said:

> We must take the development and opening of Pudong in Shanghai as the dragon head, advance another step to open cities on the banks of the Yangzi River and establish Shanghai as an international economic, financial and trading centre as soon as possible, in order to induce a new economic leap in the Yangzi River Delta and the entire Yangzi River Valley.[53]

Can Shanghai become a regional centre as well as an international centre? This section argues that the Shanghai region remains limited to areas in Jiangsu and Zhejiang which are both geographically close and have linguistic and historical ties to Shanghai. Here it is argued that a Shanghai-induced economic leap along the length of the Yangzi River Valley remains problematic. (Shanghai's potential participation in international regionalism is discussed in the next section.)

In the post-Mao decentralisation process, local authorities have gained new powers, including the ability to establish horizontal economic cooperation between provinces without reference to the centre. Analysts in Beijing argue a trend of direct deals between provinces has developed. However, the experience of the Shanghai Economic Region during the 1980s raises considerable doubts about the ability of provincial-level units to overcome their strong administrative power in order to work together.

In December 1982, the State Council established a 'Shanghai Economic District Planning Office' under the leadership of Shanghai Mayor Wang Daohan. Originally the Shanghai Economic Region encompassed ten municipalities (incorporating fifty-seven counties), including Shanghai and areas in Jiangsu and Zhejiang provinces near Shanghai. In December 1984, the State Council enlarged the Shanghai Economic Region to include all of Jiangsu and Zhejiang as well as Jiangxi and Anhui. In 1986 Fujian also joined the Shanghai Economic Region.[54] (Shandong applied to join, but was not accepted.) In some ways the Shanghai Economic Region harked back to the old East China Great Administrative Region of the early 1950s. However, the Shanghai Economic Region lacked the administrative clout of the old East China Great Administrative Region. If the Shanghai Economic Region had been a State Council organ with delegated authority rather than simply an office, it would have had considerable power. But it lacked both administrative power and funds. Later, the office was transferred to the State Economic Commission.

The Shanghai Economic Region could only try to consult and coordinate. Its primary successes were in the areas of transportation and communication, which function better if coordinated over a large area. For example, the Shanghai Economic Region had success in managing aspects of Lake Tai. It prepared plans for railways, highways and motorways. But the Shanghai Economic Region did not prove successful in various industrial sectors where it attempted to develop industries according to comparative advantage and avoid duplication. In this area the local governments proved too powerful and the Shanghai Economic Region could not prevent duplication. When Wang Daohan retired as Mayor of Shanghai, the Shanghai Economic Region had even less power. Ultimately, it was abolished in the late 1980s. Economic Regions were also set up in Manchuria and North China. Like the Shanghai Economic Region, the Northeast and North China Economic Regions approximated the Great Administrative Regions of the 1950s. These two Economic Regions have also been abolished.

The lesson of these Economic Regions is that the administrative power of the provincial-level governments is very great. Lacking administrative power, the Economic Regions, even with some moral support from the centre, could not accomplish much on the basis of 'consultation' and 'compromise'. The provincial-level units still retain their administrative powers; thus it remains unlikely that Shanghai will be able to lead a multi-province regional grouping. Imperial China divided the core of the Lower Yangzi region into three provinces (Jiangsu, Zhejiang and Anhui) in order to split the 'region's powerful gentry . . . into competing elites' focused on different administrative systems.[55] Furthermore, each of these three provinces had territory in other regions with parts of Jiangsu and Anhui in the North China region and parts of Zhejiang in the South-east Coast region.[56] A century later, this administrative division of natural economic regions has become a much stronger force in inhibiting regional integration.

In considering supra-provincial regions, it is useful to examine the relationships between Shanghai and its two neighbouring provinces, Jiangsu and Zhejiang, both of which would need to be included in any Shanghai-led multi-province region. Shanghai and Jiangsu basically have a competitive relationship. Like Shanghai, Jiangsu is a key source of central revenues and has been forced to retain its 'planned economy'. Unlike Shanghai, Jiangsu has failed to obtain the preferential policies given to Shanghai in 1990 and 1992. With the exception of the growth in Southern Jiangsu led by the 'township enterprises', Jiangsu has developed relatively slowly, especially when compared to Guangdong. This has led to resentment on the part of Jiangsu.

Jiangsu has China's highest industrial product and competes with Shanghai in many areas including textiles and machinery for supplies and markets. In order to assist the Jiangsu economy, Jiangsu tends to engage in 'local protectionism' Jiangsu residents, for example, tend to brush their teeth with Jiangsu rather than Shanghai toothpaste. Thus, Shanghai and Jiangsu have an uneasy, competitive relationship.

Shanghai's relationship with Zhejiang is much closer. Zhejiang is much smaller than Jiangsu and its economy tends to complement rather than compete with Shanghai's. Zhejiang supplies raw materials for Shanghai's textile industry. When rationing existed, Shanghai accepted Zhejiang cloth ration coupons, thus consolidating its sources of supply. Zhejiang supplies a substantial portion of Shanghai's building materials and construction teams, providing expertise to overcome Shanghai's lack of bedrock. While much of the Jiangsu economy has remained 'planned', Zhejiang has moved much more rapidly towards a 'market' economy.

Although a multi-provincial Shanghai-led economic region including the whole of Jiangsu and Zhejiang remains unlikely, considerable economic integration has occurred in what is loosely referred to as the Yangzi River Delta. Since the Yangzi River Delta is an informal geographical term which does not reflect any formal governmental organ, the definition of the region remains ambiguous. In Jiangsu it certainly includes the areas of Suzhou, Wuxi and Changzhou municipalities on the southern bank of the Yangzi River. A few people include Zhenjiang (though we do not), but it definitely does not include Nanjing. Some people limit the region to the southern bank of the Yangzi River, but other include Nantong Municipality on the north bank. In Zhejiang, the Yangzi River Delta encompasses the Shanghai–Hangzhou corridor including Jiashan, Jiaxing and Hangzhou. Some say it also includes Huzhou on the southern shore of Lake Tai, but most exclude Shaoxing and Ningbo from the Yangzi River Delta region.

Professor G. William Skinner's preliminary study of the Lower Yangzi Macroregional System in 1982 confirms the above analysis. The 'inner core' of the macroregion includes Shanghai, Suzhou, Wuxi and Changzhou, the very areas most economically integrated with Shanghai. In Jiangsu the 'outer core' includes Nantong, Yangzhou and parts of Yancheng and Huaiyin as well as Zhenjiang and Nanjing. In Zhejiang the 'outer core' includes Jiashan, Jiaxing, Huzhou, Hangzhou, Shaoxing, Ningbo and Zhoushan. Other areas in Jiangsu, Zhejiang and Anhui belong to either the 'near periphery' or the 'far periphery'. In the period since 1982, some areas of the 'outer core' may have developed and become economically more integrated with Shanghai, but Skinner's meticulous methodology basically confirms the observations in the preceding paragraph.

The links between Shanghai and Southern Jiangsu, Skinner's 'inner core', are especially important. The languages of the whole southern bank of the Yangzi River from Shanghai to Danyang (between Changzhou and Zhenjiang) belong to the Wu (Shanghai) group. West of Danyang, including Zhenjiang and Nanjing, the population speaks Mandarin. This language affinity helps bind the Shanghai and Southern Jiangsu areas together, and assists four types of flows or transfers – personnel, technology, information and finance – which enhance the economic integration between Shanghai and Southern Jiangsu.

The personnel flows have been particularly important. During the 1950s and the Cultural Revolution, many Shanghai cadres were forced to leave Shanghai in order to raise the capacity of the 'interior' as well as to break up the capacity of a 'bourgeois' Shanghai, which the centre did not trust. Many Shanghai cadres were sent to Southern Jiangsu, while others, who had been sent further and were not allowed to return to Shanghai owing to Shanghai's tight population controls, later settled in Southern Jiangsu and Nantong where they were near Shanghai and could speak the local dialect and eat familiar food. Suzhou, Wuxi, Changzhou and Nantong are called the Four Great Guardians, the imposing warriors in Buddhist temples; similarly the four municipalities help and support Shanghai. The sent-down Shanghai cadres established many of the successful township enterprises in Southern Jiangsu and they have helped establish economic links between their enterprises and Shanghai. Such links include supply, marketing and contracting out.

The four types of flows can be intimately linked. Personnel flows can also bring technology, information and financial flows. 'Sunday Engineers', who work for Shanghai state enterprises during the week and consult for Southern Jiangsu township enterprises on Sundays, bring technology and information.

While evidence suggests a Shanghai Economic Ring or Circle, based on Shanghai, the Southern Jiangsu cities of Suzhou, Wuxi and Changzhou and the Shanghai–Hangzhou corridor in Zhejiang is developing into an integrated regional economy, the development of an integrated regional economy based on the entire Yangzi River Valley appears problematic. There are several impediments to integration of the Yangzi River Valley as a whole, including lack of human resources, poor transportation, weak infrastructure, a shortage of capital as well as provincial and local 'administrative power'. Local protectionism is strong in centres along the Yangzi River Valley. Efficient and integrated use of resources would make up-river areas suppliers of primary products for industrialised Shanghai. Such integration might raise the standard of living in Shanghai, but up-river areas fear they would gain little and thus resist such integration. Up-river centres themselves hope to be the foci of more integrated areas. Wuhan would like to be the centre of an integrated Hubei economy and Chongqing of an integrated economy in southeastern Sichuan. If closer centres such as Nanjing, not to mention smaller centres such as Wuhu in eastern Anhui and Jiujiang in eastern Jiangxi, have yet to become part of the Shanghai Economic Ring, what is the likelihood of Wuhan and Chongqing becoming closely integrated with Shanghai?

The lofty notion of 'Shanghai as the dragon head inducing a new economic leap in . . . the entire Yangzi River Valley' has its allure,[57] but interviews reveal the Chinese have yet to work out methods to implement the integration of Shanghai with the Yangzi River Valley. In fact, according to senior Shanghai economists, China has no experience of having a large centre carry along a periphery, though the experience of Hong Kong in inducing growth in the Guangzhou Delta as well as in such places as Shanghai and North China may provide some guidance. The economists feel integration between Shanghai and the interior requires both sides to have a mutual interest. For example, if Shanghai can assist inland areas to market and export their products and help them obtain better prices, this would benefit both the inland areas and Shanghai. Such developments will require Shanghai to develop its service industries.

SHANGHAI AS A POTENTIAL INTERNATIONAL REGIONAL CENTRE

A number of major growth centres in China appear to have become integrated with particular areas external to the People's Republic of China. A huge proportion of Guangdong's foreign investment and foreign trade is related to Hong Kong (see Table 8.10), while a significant proportion of foreign investment in Fujian appears to come from Taiwan. Similarly, until recently, Japanese investment has played an important role in Dalian. At the end of 1990, Japanese investment in Dalian totalled $551 million, the largest amount from any single source and about one-third of the foreign investment.[58] Japan remained the largest foreign investor in Dalian until the Spring of 1993, when Hong Kong investment surpassed Japanese investment.[59] Japan dominated Dalian's foreign trade in 1991 (see Table 8.10). To examine whether Shanghai has any particular ties with a place external to the PRC, we first consider foreign investment and then trade flows.

Foreign investment

Shanghai seems different in not being tied to any particular place external to the PRC. First of all, Shanghai has received relatively small amounts of foreign investment. In 1991, Shanghai ranked only fifth among provincial-level units and had less than 13 per cent as much foreign investment as Guangdong (Table 8.6).

Table 8.6 Actual utilised foreign investment (end of 1991)

Province	Amount (US$ million)
Guangdong	2,583.75
Liaoning	645.18
Fujian	570.49
Shandong	373.08
Shanghai	330.25

Source: *Jiangsu zai quanguo de[,] shixian zai Jiangsu de diwei (1991)* [The Position of Jiangsu in the Nation and of municipalities and counties in Jiangsu (1991)] ([Nanjing]: Jiangsu sheng tongji ju, 1993), p. 23

Table 8.7 Major sources of foreign investment in Shanghai (end of 1991)

Source	Amount (US$ million)	Per cent of total
Hong Kong	400.45	25.74
Japan	325.29	20.91
US	236.76	15.22
Germany	75.67	4.86

Source: *Shanghai tongji nianjian 1992* [Shanghai Statistical Yearbook 1992]; edited by Shanghai shi tongji ju (Shanghai: Zhongguo tongji chubanshe, 1992), p. 358. Percentages calculated by authors

Furthermore, no particular country dominated Shanghai investment (Table 8.7).

Any analysis of foreign investment patterns requires caution. When the field research for this chapter was conducted, the 1991 statistics were the latest available. However, in 1992 foreigners invested $58,000 million in China, an amount equal to the accumulated total for the previous thirteen years. In the first half of 1993, foreign investment again totalled $58,000 million.[60] Similar proportionate increases have occurred in Shanghai. In 1992 Shanghai's utilised foreign investment totalled $3,357 million, an amount equal to the accumulated total of the previous twelve years.[61] As of mid-1993, Hong Kong accounted for just over half (50.4 per cent) of agreed (and not actually utilised) foreign investment.[62] However, in 1992 the number of foreign countries and regions investing in Shanghai increased from 38 to 46.[63] As 'Hong Kong investment' frequently originates elsewhere, these statistics continue to suggest no particular country dominates Shanghai investment.

Figures are available for foreign investment in Pudong until the end of 1992. These suggest a preponderance of Hong Kong investment, though this may result from the ability of Hong Kong entrepreneurs to move quickly following the opening of Pudong (Table 8.8).

Table 8.8 Major sources of foreign investment in Pudong (end of 1992)

Source	Amount (US$ million)	Per cent of total
Hong Kong	943	61.2
US	140	9.1
Japan	113	7.3
UK	56	3.6

Source: *Shanghai shi Pudong xinqu shouce* [Shanghai Pudong New Area Handbook] (Shanghai: Shanghai yuandong chubanshe, 1993), p. 5

Table 8.9 Shanghai trade flows, 1991

	Exports (per cent)	Imports (per cent)
Hong Kong	18.79	24.97
Japan	15.94	18.96
US	14.13	14.73
Germany	5.79	20.77

Source: *Zhongguo duiwai jingji maoyi nianjian 1992* [Yearbook of China's Foreign Economic Trade 1992] (Beijing: Zhongguo shehui chubanshe, 1992), p. 270

Trade flows

Trade flows provide a second variable to evaluate whether a locality has particular ties with a place external to the PRC. In 1991 Shanghai's trade was fairly evenly balanced between a variety of partners with no particular country dominating (Table 8.9).

According to a recent Shanghai analysis, from 1980 to 1991 Hong Kong led Shanghai's imports and exports, accounting for between 17 per cent and 22 per cent of trade. Despite an 11.4 per cent increase in trade between Shanghai and Hong Kong in 1992, Japan replaced Hong Kong as Shanghai's leading trade partner in 1992.[64] This reinforces the analysis that no single partner dominates Shanghai's trade.

For comparison, we have found a useful source which provides similar details for China's thirty mainland provinces, the fourteen municipalities with special planning powers, the fourteen open coastal cities and the five Special Economic Zones.[65] In an effort to detect Chinese localities having special relationships with places external to the PRC, Table 8.10 lists all such cases where one place accounts for at least one-third of either exports or imports.

Clearly, the trade of many localities in China is dominated by one trading partner. Shanghai has a relatively wide spread of foreign trading partners as well as sources of foreign investment. Thus, unlike Guangdong, Fujian and many other areas of China, Shanghai does not appear to be part of any particular international 'economic ring'.

CONCLUSION

Unlike Guangdong, Shanghai does not appear to have a strong sense of 'localism'. There may be several reasons for this difference. First, Shanghai has a considerably more cosmopolitan tradition than

Table 8.10 Chinese localities having substantial foreign trade with one partner (1991)

Locality	Country	Exports (%)	Imports (%)
Tianjin	Japan	(21.04)	34.19
Hebei	Hong Kong	(19.36)	38.03
Shanxi	Hong Kong	(23.07)	34.03
Inner Mongolia	former USSR	33.81	52.57
Liaoning	Japan	37.68	42.58
Dalian	Japan	50.15	65.76
Jilin	Hong Kong	37.65	(12.77)
Changchun	Hong Kong	39.15	(11.23)
Changchun	USA	(2.92)	49.90
Heilongjiang	former USSR	33.51	66.65
Harbin	former USSR	n.a.	58.85
Nanjing	Hong Kong	(30.53)	39.09
Nantong	Hong Kong	35.04	(21.82)
Nantong	Japan	(32.93)	42.58
Zhejiang	Hong Kong	(29.86)	36.84
Ningbo	Hong Kong	35.62	(24.80)
Wenzhou	Hong Kong	(32.90)	51.90
Fujian	Hong Kong	44.50	52.63
Jiangxi	Hong Kong	39.78	67.1
Yantai	Hong Kong	43.85	n.a.
Henan	USA	<7.91	44.79
Hubei	Hong Kong	50.20	50.89
Wuhan	Hong Kong	53.29	53.90
Hunan	Hong Kong	49.28	43.10
Guangdong	Hong Kong	83.06	73.21
Guangzhou	Hong Kong	88.83	53.33
Shenzhen	Hong Kong	87.10	72.33
Zhuhai	Hong Kong	76.74	71.57
Shantou	Hong Kong	61.6	93.54
Zhanjiang	Hong Kong	83.64	92.49
Guangxi	Hong Kong	54.65	44.50
Hainan	Hong Kong	69.05	64.35
Sichuan	Hong Kong	37.94	33.60
Chengdu	Hong Kong	48.84	(12.7)
Chengdu	Japan	(4.48)	49.96
Chongqing	Hong Kong	37.16	n.a.
Guizhou	Hong Kong	(31.17)	48.09
Yunnan	Burma	(30.32)	35.43
Tibet	Japan	n.a.	53.49
Shaanxi	Japan	(12.22)	51.75
Xi'an	Japan	(3.41)	39.67
Gansu	Hong Kong	40.95	73.23
Qinghai	Hong Kong	(24.3)	64.28
Xinjiang	former USSR	(16.1)	54.0

Source: *Zhongguo duiwai jingji maoyi nianjian 1992* [Yearbook of China's Foreign Economic Trade 1992] (Beijing: Zhongguo shehui chubanshe, 1992), pp. 239–360
Note: In cases where one place accounts for less than one-third of either exports or imports the precise figure is given in brackets.

Guangdong. In many ways, Shanghai is a creation of the foreign imperial powers which had considerable influence through the establishment of educational institutions and their imperial governments within Shanghai. Second, Shanghai lacks a long history and thus lacks a long history as a separate identity. Third, Shanghai is the source of many internal Chinese immigrants from Northern Jiangsu, Zhejiang and other places. This internal heterogeneity works against feelings of 'localism'. Fourth, historically and at present, the lower Yangzi River Valley has been a much more integral and integrated part of the Chinese Empire than Guangdong. Lower Yangzi Valley scholars dominated the imperial Chinese polity and today people with considerable Shanghai background also play important roles in Beijing.

Field research in Shanghai does not suggest Shanghai people wish to separate from China. Rather, they wish Beijing would show more concern for Shanghai's problems. Shanghai people have considerable confidence in their own abilities. They are confident they can be successful provided Beijing gives them a good 'policy' with which to work.

Despite its wealth and new 'policy', Shanghai still faces many problems. The poor infrastructure and housing lowers the living standard of many residents. Furthermore, the remnants of the 'planned' economy still create many problems. Many state enterprises remain feather-bedded and inefficient. Industrial restructuring remains a priority.

NOTES

1 The authors gratefully acknowledge grants from the Australian Research Council and support from the Asia Research Centre, Murdoch University enabled the preparation of this paper. The authors also express their appreciation to Professor G. William Skinner and Mr Zhu Xingqing for their valuable comments on an earlier version and for providing relevant sources. The many insights of numerous colleagues and friends in Shanghai, Nanjing, Beijing, Manchuria and Shenzhen have proven very helpful.

2 'Zai Wuhan, Shenzhen, Zhuhai, Shanghai dengdide tanhua yaodian' ['Important points of talks in Wuhan, Shenzhen, Zhuhai, Shanghai and other places', in *Deng Xiaoping wenxuan*, Vol. III, 1993, Beijing: Renmin chubanshe, p. 376.

3 Calligraphy of General-Secretary Jiang Zemin dated 10 May 1990, in *Shanghai Pudong xinqu touzi hauanjing yu fazhan gianjing* [Investment Environment and Development Prospects for the Pudong New District, Shanghai] (Shanghai: Shangai Pudong xinqu guanli weiyuanhui bangongshi, [1993]), frontispiece; and in *Shanghai shi Pudong xinqu*

shouce [Shanghai Pudong New Area Handbook] (Shanghai: Shanghai yuandong chubanshe, 1993), frontispiece.

4 The per capita incomes of the remaining provincial-level units range from Jiangsu (RMB yuan 1,836) to Guizhou (RMB yuan 728). The nation-wide average per capita income is RMB yuan 1,401. *Jiangsu zai quanguo de[,] shixian zai Jiangsu de diwei (1991)* [The Position of Jiangsu in the Nation and of municipalities and counties in Jiangsu (1991)] ([Nanjing]: Jiangsu sheng tongji ju, 1993), p. 6.

5 The per capita products of the remaining provincial-level units range from Heilongjiang (RMB yuan 2,056) to Guizhou (RMB yuan 879). The nation-wide average per capita product is RMB yuan 1,725. *Ibid.*, p. 4.

6 *Shenzhen jingji tegu nianjian 1992* [Shenzhen Special Economic Zone Yearbook] (Guangzhou: Guangdong renmin chubanshe, [1992]), p. 729.

7 Calculated from *Jiangsu zai, op. cit.*, pp. 2–3. The primary sector accounts for over 8 per cent of product in Beijing and Tianjin, and for 27.2 per cent nationally.

8 Calculated from *ibid.*, pp. 2–3. Industrial product accounts for over 50 per cent of total product in seven other provincial-level units: Heilongjiang (56.26 per cent), Tianjin (56.03 per cent), Liaoning (54.98 per cent), Shanxi (54.75 per cent), Jiangsu (54.23 per cent), Beijing (52.18 per cent) and Zhejiang (50.09 per cent). Nationally, the secondary sector accounts for 45.86 per cent of China's total product.

9 Calculated from *ibid.* Nationally, the tertiary sector accounts for 26.94 per cent of China's total product. The tertiary sector is substantial in the following poorer provincial-level units: Tibet (35.57 per cent), Qinghai (34.14 per cent) and Ningxia (32.23 per cent).

10 Wu Weiyang, '1992 nian Shanghai jingji zhanwang' [Shanghai Economic Forecast for 1992], in *1992 nian Zhongguo jingji zhanwang* [China Economic Forecasts for 1992] (Beijing: Guojia xinxi Zhongxin, 1992), p. 218.

11 *Ibid.*, p. 219.

12 'Shanghai shi jingji fazhan zhanlüe' ['Shanghai Municipality Economic Strategy'], in *Zhongguo diqu jingji shehui fazhan zhanlüe xuanpian* [Selected Articles on China's Regional Economic and Social Development Strategy]; edited by Yu Guangyuan (Beijing: Zhongguo caizheng jingji chubanshe, 1990), p. 1344. The full 'Strategy' Document, prepared by the Shanghai Municipal Government (*Shanghai shi renmin zhengfu*) and the State Council's Investigation and Research Committee for the Reform and Revitalisation of Shanghai (*Guowuyuan gaizao zhenxing Shanghai diaoyan zu*), appears on pp. 11–19. The 'Strategy' document specifically lists the following service industries: commerce, finance, insurance, trusts, transportation, communication, science and technology, education, culture, journalism, travel industry, public utilities, real estate, service, medical, accountancy, law, information and consulting. Note that official Shanghai statistics give a somewhat higher figure than the 'Strategy' document, stating that the tertiary sector accounted for 25.1 per cent of product in 1984, see *Shanghai tongji nianjian 1992* [Shanghai Statistical Yearbook 1992]; edited by Shanghai shi tongji ju (Shanghai: Zhongguo tongji chubanshe, 1992), p. 33.

13 'Shanghai shi jingji fazhan zhanlüe', *op cit.*, p. 14.

250   *J. Bruce Jacobs and Lijian Hong*

14 *Xianggang jingji ribao* [Hong Kong Economic Daily], 28 December 1992, p. 32.
15 See quotation at beginning of this paper.
16 Shanghai contributed 17.6 per cent of central expenditure in 1953–1957 and 33.2 per cent in 1958 according to Nicholas R. Lardy, *Economic Growth and Distribution in China* (Cambridge: Cambridge University Press, 1978), p. 135.
17 *Shanghai tongji nianjian 1992, op. cit.*, p. 26.
18 For a useful introduction see Michel Oksenberg and James Tong, 'The Evolution of Central–Provincial Fiscal Relations in China, 1971–1984: The Formal System', *China Quarterly*, No. 125 (March 1991), pp. 1–32. See also Lardy, *op cit.*, for the pre-reform system and James Tong, 'Fiscal Reform, Elite Turnover and Central–Provincial Relations in Post-Mao China', *The Australian Journal of Chinese Affairs*, No. 22 (July 1989), pp. 1–28; Christine P.W. Wong, 'Central–Local Relations in an Era of Fiscal Decline: The Paradox of Fiscal Decentralization in Post-Mao China', *The China Quarterly*, No. 128 (December 1991), pp. 691–715; and Christine P.W. Wong, 'Fiscal Reform and Local Industrialization: The Problematic Sequencing of Reform in Post-Mao China', *Modern China*, Vol. 18, No. 2 (April 1992), pp. 197–227.
19 *Zhongguo tongji nianjian 1987* [Statistical Yearbook of China 1987] (Beijing: Zhongguo tongji chubanshe, 1987), p. 618.
20 Calculated from *Zhongguo tongji nianjian 1992* [Statistical Yearbook of China 1992] (Beijing: Zhongguo tongji chubanshe, 1992), p. 227.
21 Calculated from *ibid.* and *Shanghai tongji nianjian 1992, op. cit.*, p. 53.
22 *Jiangsu zai, op. cit.*, p. 23.
23 *Ibid.*, p. 24.
24 *Jiefang ribao* [Liberation Daily] (Shanghai), 17 March 1993, p. 5.
25 Xu Riqing, Du Yanshuang and Zhao Kaitai, 'Wanshan Shanghai shi difang caizheng de yanjiu' [A Study on Perfecting Shanghai Municipality's Local Finances], in *Shanghai jingji fazhan zhanlüe yanjiu* [Research on Shanghai's Economic Development Strategy]; edited by Chen Minwen (Shanghai: Shanghai renmin chubanshe, 1985), p. 243.
26 Lardy, *op cit.*, pp. 134–35.
27 *Ibid.*, pp. 163–64.
28 Calculated from *Shanghai tongji nianjian 1992, op. cit.*, pp. 279–80 and *Zhongguo tongji zhaiyao 1993* [A Statistical Survey of China 1993] (Beijing: Zhongguo tongji chubanshe, 1993), pp. 20, 22.
29 Yu Guangyuan, 'Xu' [Preface], in *Zhongguo diqu jingji shehui fazhan zhanlüe xuanpian, op. cit.*, pp. 5–6.
30 Zhang Guangsheng and Zhuo Fumin, 'Shi zhengfu jingji guanli zhineng de zhuanbian' [Changes in the Municipal Government's Economic Management Functions], in *Shanghai jingji tizhi gaige shinian* [The 10 Years of Economic System Reform in Shanghai] (Shanghai: Shanghai renmin chubanshe, 1989), pp. 49–56.
31 Xu Riqing *et al.. op. cit.* pp. 243, 247 and interview.
32 Chen Yu, 'Shanghai jingji tizhi gaige de chubu gouxiang' [Preliminary Conceptions on Economic Structural Reform in Shanghai], in *Shanghai jingji tizhi gaige shinian, op. cit.*, p. 23.
33 *Jiefang ribao*, 17 March 1993, p. 5.

34 Calculated from *ibid.*

35 *Ibid.*

36 Text in *Pudong xingu youhui zhengce yu caozuo chengxu* [The Preferential Policies and Operation Procedures of the Pudong New District] (Shanghai: Shanghai shi renmin zhengfu Pudong kaifa bangongshi [and] Shanghai shi renshi ju Pudong xinqu banshiqu, 1992), p. 3.

37 'Shanghai Pudong kaifa shi xiang youhui zhengce' [Ten Preferential Policies for the Development of Pudong, Shanghai], in *Shanghai Pudong xinqu zhengce faqui quizhang 1990.9–1992.6* [Policies, Regulations and Rules for the Pudong New District, Shanghai, September 1990–June 1992] (Shanghai: Shanghai shi Pudong xinqu guanli weiyuanhui bangongshi, 1992), pp. 1–2. The text of these ten policies also appears in *Pudong xinqu youhui zhengce yu caozuo chengxu, op. cit.*, p. 30, where it states the State Council has approved the ten preferential policies.

38 '1992 nian Zhongyang dui Shanghai Pudong xinqu xin zengjia de zhengce youhui he peitao zijin zushi' [New Additional Policies Preferences and Accompany Financial Measures of the Centre for Pudong New District, Shanghai in 1992], in *Shanghai Pudong xinqu zhengce fagui quizhang 1990.9–1992.6, op. cit.*, pp. 3–5 and *Pudong xinqu youhui zhengce yu caozuo chengxu, op. cit.*, p. 31.

39 Attempts to check this statement suggest it has some validity. In 1991 the profits and taxes of the Shanghai cigarette industry, i.e. the Shanghai Cigarette Company, totalled RMB yuan 1,581 million, see *Shanghai tongji nianjian 1992, op. cit.*, p. 157. (See *ibid.*, p. 155 for statement that the cigarette industry has only one 'unit' [*danwei*].) In 1991 Guangzhou Municipality had local revenues of RMB yuan 4,848.92 million and expenditures of RMB yuan 3,070.96 million, leaving a budget 'surplus' of RMB yuan 1,777.96 million, an amount roughly similar to the profits and taxes of the Shanghai Cigarette Company, see *Zhongguo chengshi tongji nianjian 1992* [Urban Statistical Yearbook of China 1992] (Beijing: Zhongguo tongji chubanshe, 1992), p. 581. In 1991, the Shanghai Cigarette Company ranked ninth among China's industrial enterprises in terms of total profits and taxes, behind only Daqing Petroleum, four steel companies, two other cigarette companies and a petro-chemical company, *Zhongguo gongye jingji tongji nianjian 1992* [Industry and Economics Statistical Yearbook of China 1992] (Beijing: Zhongguo tongji chubanshe, 1992), p. 421.

40 Xia Keqiang, 'Xu' [Preface], in *Pudong xingu youhui zhengce yu caozuo chengxu, op. cit.*, p. v.

41 'Jiang Zemin tan Pudong kaifa' [Jiang Zemin discusses Pudong development], *Pudong kaifa* [Pudong Development], No. 6 (June 1993), p. 4.

42 'Zhu Rongji shicha Pudong shi yaoqiu . . . ' [During an Inspection Visit to Pudong, Zhu Rongji requests . . .], in *ibid.*, p. 5.

43 *Shanghai Pudong xingu guanli jigou jianjie* [An Introduction to Administrative Organs of the Pudong New District, Shanghai] (Shanghai: Shanghai Pudong xinqu shangwu zixun fuwu zhongxin, 1993), p. 1. Information on the ten bureaus and offices appear in *ibid.*, pp. 2–11.

44 *Shanghai Pudong xingu touzi huanjing yu fazhan qianjing, op. cit.*, p. 1.

45 *1992 nian Shanghai Pudong xinqu tongji nianbao* [1992 Statistical

Yearbook of Pudong New District, Shanghai] (Shanghai: Shanghai kexue jishu chubanshe, 1992), p. 9.

46 Area comparisons calculated from *Shanghai tongji nianjian 1992, op. cit.*, p. 13.

47 From several interviews and a variety of Pudong New District Publications including *Shanghai Pudong xinqu touzi huanjing yu fazhan gianjing, op cit.*, pp. 11–20.

48 *Ibid.*, p. 9.

49 This paragraph relies on the analyses of several Shanghai social scientists.

50 Interview with key Shanghai economic official.

51 In 1991, Shanghai exported $5,740 million worth of goods, less than 8 per cent of China's total exports of $71,910 million. *Zhongguo tongji nianjian 1992, op. cit., p. 627, and Shanghai tongji nianjian 1992, op cit.*, pp. 347–48. By value, 16.1 per cent of China's imports and 14.1 per cent of China's exports passed through Shanghai, *ibid.*, p. 347.

52 J. Bruce Jacobs, 'A Preliminary Model of Particularistic Ties in Chinese Political Alliances: *Kan-ch'ing* and *Kuan-hsi* in a Rural Taiwanese Township', *China Quarterly*, No. 78 (June 1979), pp. 237–273.

53 Jiang Zemin, Report to the 14th CCP Congress (12 October 1992), *Renmin ribao*, 21 October 1992, p. 2.

54 Wang Daohan 'Xu' [Preface], in *Changjiang sanjiaozhou diqu chanye jiegou he buju* [Industrial Structure and Distribution in the Yangzi River Delta Region] (Beijing: Zhongguo jihua chubanshe, 1991), p. v. and *Zhongguo jingji nianjian 1986* [Economic Yearbook of China 1986] (Beijing: Jingji guanli chubanshe, 1986), VII–204.

55 G. William Skinner, 'Cities and the Hierarchy of Local Systems', in *The City in Late Imperial China*; edited by G. William Skinner (Stanford: Stanford University Press, 1977), pp. 342–43

56 G, William Skinner, 'Regional Urbanization in Nineteenth-Century China, in *ibid.*, pp. 214–15.

57 Jiang Zemin, see quote at beginning of this section.

58 *Dalian touzi zhinan* [Guide to Investment in Dalian] (Dalian: Dalian shi duiwai jingji maoyi weiyuanhui, [1991]), pp. 7–8, 47–48.

59 Interview in Dalian, August, 1993. Hong Kong investment now totals $1,100 million compared to Japanese investment of $900 million. Japanese investment is still much greater than US investment ($270 million), which ranks third. Taiwan ($170 million) and the Republic of Korea ($100 million) rank fourth and fifth.

60 Speech by Professor Sun Weiyan, President of University of International Business and Economics, Melbourne, Australia, 1 October 1993.

61 *Renmin ribao (haiwai ban)*, 30 August 1993, p. 2; *Jiefang ribao*, 17 March 1993, p. 1.

62 *Wenhui bao* (Shanghai), 4 August 1993, p. 1.

63 *Renmin ribao (haiwai ban)*, 30 August 1993, p. 2.

64 *Wenhui bao* (Shanghai), 4 August 1993, p. 1.

65 *Zhongguo duiwai jingji maoyi nianjian 1992* [Yearbook of China's Foreign Economic Trade 1992] (Beijing: Zhongguo shehui chubanshe, 1992), pp. 239–360.

9 North China and Russia

Michael B. Yahuda

No consideration of the international significance of Chinese region-alism and of its future direction can be complete without taking into account Manchuria[1] and Inner Mongolia. They have a history of being separated from the Chinese heartland. Indeed it was only with the establishment of the People's Republic that the region became integrated with China proper. In the early years it then became the pathfinder for the revolution. Land reform and the estab-lishment of the institutions of the command economy took place in Manchuria first which then became the model for their development throughout the country. But the new era brought on by the reforms since 1978 has hit this area hard. Having been at the vanguard of the development of the Chinese command economy, the region has been outpaced by the more market-oriented coastal provinces in the south.

China's north, as one of the major centres of heavy industry and mining, may be said to have become the Chinese equivalent of 'the rust belt'. In the fifteen years since the economic reforms and the policies of openness were adopted in 1978, this region has been continually outpaced by the southerly coastal provinces. The latter have prospered from the tremendous growth of the non-state sector allied to close association with Hong Kong and Taiwan, while the north has been held back by its traditional industries and the problems of its northern neighbour. In some respects this may suggest a reawakening of the traditional geographical divide between a more conservative, bureaucratic north oriented to inner Asia and the more commercially minded, less officially controlled south with a maritime orientation. Whatever truth there may be in this suggestion must be tempered by the realisation that the leadership in the north is very much committed to following the path of reform and openness too.

There is also a sense in which China's north may be said to envision its relations with other parts of the country in terms of

interdependence. Indeed this is how the advocates of regional development in Beijing have depicted its larger advantages. With the
exception of coastal Liaoning Province, the north would be expected
to provide primarily industrial primary goods and other heavy industrial products.[2] One of the arguments heard in northern, as in western
China is that the terms of domestic trade have been set unfairly and
that they can be altered.[3] The goal of the north would seem to be to
alter the terms of engagement so that instead of the regions breaking
away from Beijing a new arrangement based on more equitable
relations between the regions would be reached with Beijing acting
as the broker or arbitrator. From this perspective the provinces of
northern China would seek to bargain a better deal for themselves,
and it would be of interest to explore the extent to which the north
could seek to use its external links to improve its bargaining position.

Northern China has also been seen as an area of potential international economic significance in the development of what was called
in China in 1988, 'the Great Northeast Asian Economic Circle'.[4] That
envisaged the northern Chinese region as playing a pivotal role in
cultivating an economic nexus incorporating the Russian Far East,
Japan, the two Koreas and the Mongolian Republic. Although five
years later that still seems a distant objective, economic and social
relations between Russia and China's north have deepened, and it is
important to examine these as part of a broader analysis as to where
this region fits into the pattern of Chinese regionalism as a whole.

Facing Russia and the Mongolian Republic, China's north is of
obvious importance in terms of national security. China's defence
analysts still warn of the possible dangers posed by Russia's remaining forces in the region. Moreover, China's own defence forces in the
region cannot relax as long as North Korea's future is so uncertain.[5]
Since these matters of high strategy and politics remain the domain of
Beijing, rather than of the region of northern China, and the focus
here is upon the significance of the region, the discussion here will
centre on the politics of the economic relations.

This chapter will first seek to provide a political and economic
profile of the north China region. It will then consider the relationship
with Russia, before proceeding to discuss the significance of northern
China within the broader context of regionalism in China as a whole.
The chapter will conclude with an assessment of the extent to which
aspects of north China's international regional relations may have
affected its relations with Beijing and Beijing's relations with
Moscow.

THE POLITICAL–ECONOMIC SIGNIFICANCE OF NORTH CHINA

North China embraces the three provinces of Manchuria (or the North-East), Heilongjiang, Jilin and Liaoning together with the Autonomous Region of Inner Mongolia (ARIM). It is not normally regarded as a coherent region, since Manchuria is usually treated as a separate entity in its own right. But this part of China to the north of the Great Wall can be regarded as a region. Traditionally Manchuria was outside the core eighteen provinces and it has been open to Chinese migration only since the middle of the 19th century. In part the Manchu decision to allow Chinese to settle in their home-land was occasioned by the strategic imperative to resist Russian encroachments on the vast empty plains after the territorial conces-sions in the 1858 and 1860 treaties brought the Russian border to the Amur (Heilongjiang) and Ussuri (Ussuli) Rivers. But the area soon came under the dominant influence of first the Russians and then the Japanese. After the collapse of the Qing in 1911, Manchuria was ruled by the warlord Zhang Zuolin before Japan invaded in 1931 and set up the puppet state of Manchukuo. After the defeat of Japan in 1945 it was occupied by the Soviet Union for about a year and then it became the main battleground where the Chinese civil war was won and lost. It has also been one of the invasion routes into the Chinese heartland, as was demonstrated by the Manchus, the Japanese and finally by the Communist armies themselves. After the nation-wide communist victory, Manchuria continued to be at the fulcrum of Chinese strategic concerns, first, as the vulnerable rearguard for the Korean War and, later, as the flashpoint for the brief border battles with the Soviet Union. But Inner Mongolia too has been an area of strategic significance. There was the possibility during the period of Chinese weakness before 1949 that it might join up with the Mon-golian Republic whose independence was guaranteed by Moscow. And from 1966 until Soviet troop withdrawals from the Mongolian Republic in 1989/90 it was in the strategic front line. Moreover Mongolia, like Manchuria, was populated by Han Chinese settlers only from the late 19th century onwards.

However, the reason for treating northern China as a coherent region centres on questions of political economy and the interna-tional economic links with Russia. In the era of economic reform and the open door regionalism within, China has acquired an external orientation. At both central and local instigation different parts of China have sought to take advantage of their geographical locations to enhance their regional economic development by increasing their association with the economies of adjacent countries. As early as 1985, officials and academics in Heilongjiang (with the blessings of the then Ministry of Foreign Economic Relations and Trade) tried to interest their Japanese counterparts in the idea of an integrated approach to the economic development of Northeast Asia collaborating with the Russian Far East.[6] Although they did not succeed in the first instance, their idea has remained as a tantalising goal. Meanwhile, all four provinces have continuously deepened and extended their economic and social relations with Russia, despite the political upheavals that have taken place, so that, as we shall see, a considerable proportion of China's trade with Russia involves them, and that trade has become significant for the provincial economies.

Northern China played the most prominent part as the focus for the development of the Soviet-style heavy industry in the course of the First Five-year Plan (1953–57), when huge state-owned enterprises were built. The vast open plains of Manchuria also provided the opportunity to establish state farms which could not be so easily set up in the densely populated arable lands of traditional China. Both Manchuria and ARIM became in effect the model of China's orthodox Communist political economy. Manchuria in particular possessed the character of an advanced and favoured region. Its first leader in the period of the People's Republic, Gao Gang, was purged in 1954 amid accusations of having tried to establish an 'independent kingdom' there. However, the charge appeared to refer to his alleged attempt to appoint his own followers to key positions and not to an attempt to pursue an independent line in the region. As we have seen Manchuria was a trailblazer for national policies. Although he had his separate link with Stalin, there is no evidence to suggest that the Soviet leader affected the running of Manchuria or that there was a Soviet factor in his downfall. Gao Gang was purged for conspiring to promote himself as second only to Mao.[7] In Mao's later years the famous Da Qing oilfield was extolled as a Maoist model of self reliance. Mao's nephew, the leftist Mao Yuanxin, had tried to use Liaoning Province as a bastion in the radical's struggle with the reformers. Indeed to this day Liaoning still ranks as one of the richest of China's provinces in terms of the value of its total output.

But Manchuria and ARIM have not done well in the course of China's 'second revolution' of marketisation. In the fifteen years of reform Manchuria has gone from being the beneficiary of China's command economy with privileged grants of cost-free investment, priority access to supplies and a favourable pricing mechanism to becoming one of the principal losers in the reforming more market-oriented economy. Even the relatively wealthy Liaoning Province, which has benefited in the reform era from its coastal location, has been described by its governor, Yue Qifeng, as being in a poor position. In March 1993 he told the National People's Congress, 'The province's economic position in the country is gradually moving to the back row.' He went on to explain what he identified as 'the so-called "north-east situation"' as having arisen because of 'a long period of influence by the planned economy, a situation of lagging behind in ideological understanding; having outmoded equipment and facilities; lacking competitive power in industrial production; having slow economic development, low economic efficiency and decreasing revenue income.' He went on to explain that, although the 'north-east situation' was gradually being eliminated, it would take 'a relatively long period' for it to be thoroughly eliminated.[8]

The astonishing growth of the Chinese economy since 1978 has been led by the non-state sector of small-scale collective and private enterprise. As a result the interior provinces of ARIM, Heilongjiang and Jilin have not only witnessed their economic growth rates continuously outstripped by the likes of the southern coastal provinces of Jiangsu and Guangdong by the factor of two or three every year, but they have also sensed that the price mechanism has been deliberately tilted against them as they have been among the principal suppliers of heavily subsidised energy and industrial raw materials to the light industrial producers of the south. Indeed the secretary of the Party Committee of Heilongjiang Province openly complained to the NPC in March 1993 that 'the deficits incurred by raw material products delivered to other localities under mandatory plans have been aggravated increasingly'[9] It should be noted that the leaders of all these provinces were committed to radical reform and had well-formulated schemes to change the situation. Nevertheless, it is instructive that, despite being perhaps better situated than their former Soviet counterparts, these centres of communist economies dominated by state-owned enterprises were still being held back after fifteen years of reform by factors that would not seem unfamiliar in the former Soviet Union.

Liaoning is the key province of Manchuria as it was in the Japanese days. Since the mid-1980s its position has been enhanced still further by the central authorities, who designated it as one of the country's privileged coastal provinces. It was particularly favoured in terms of investment in the first three decades after 1949, but even now it accounts for 6 per cent of all Chinese investment (with 3.4 per cent of the population), 80 per cent of it state-owned. In 1986 Liaoning had 7 per cent of China's major plants (the same as Shanghai) and in 1992 it still ranked as China's fourth largest province by GNP per capita after Shanghai, Beijing and Tianjin. But other figures tell a different story, as might be expected from a centre of traditional communist industry. Productivity is below the national average. For example, in 1989 figures output per worker in thousand *yuan* for Liaoning was 15.3 (the national average 16.6); output per unit of capital 117 *yuan* (the national average 140); and output per unit of energy 1647 *yuan* (the national average 2891). As a favoured province of the central government, it is not surprising that Liaoning enjoys the largest provincial share of foreign *government* loans in China – mainly in large-scale construction projects.[10] There is some evidence that the province is beginning to show positive results for its reform efforts. By the end of 1993 the industrial structure had been readjusted so that the output ratio of primary products to finished products stood at 6:4, as compared with the original 8:2. At the same time 50 per cent of Liaoning's products for exports are finished products, whereas in the past 85 per cent were raw materials.[11] Nevertheless, as we have seen, the provincial leaders still feel that the province is still losing ground relative to those further south.

If Liaoning may be said to be still holding its own in some respects while falling behind in others because of the well-known problems of state owned-industries, the relative positions of ARIM, Heilongjiang and Jilin have declined. Not only are their productivity figures marginally worse than those of Liaoning, their rates of growth have been below the national average since 1979 and their significance in the national economy has fallen. Changchun in Jilin used to be China's largest producer of motor vehicles. In 1981 its output of 60,000 vehicles accounted for 34 per cent of national production; but its 1989 output of 84,000 accounted for only 14 per cent. Meanwhile, coastal Liaoning had improved its position by increasing its percentage of the national total from 3 per cent to 8 per cent.[12] Although Heilongjiang at the behest of the central authorities had increased its output of both coal and oil, methods of exploitation had not improved and the famous Daqing oilfield was almost exhausted with only 3–5 years production left.[13]

Heilongjiang officials have long complained that their production served the needs of the central government rather than those of the local community. Moreover, they claimed that it was unfair and unjust that the prices of their products were kept artificially too low, so as to provide cheap energy and other key resources that in effect amounted to subsidising the southern and coastal producers of consumer goods. Under these conditions their productivity would always look bad and they were being asked to compete on unfavourable terms. As we have seen, five years later they were still making the same point. On the other hand, they recognised that the only way out for them was to engage more deeply in the reform process. They claimed to be actively considering pilot projects for reforming the state-owned sector and to be encouraging the collective and private sectors. The officials were satisfied with the progress achieved in agriculture, where the reforms had resulted in more efficient use of cultivation under plastic (of great importance in the harsh climate) that had led to yields improved by over 20 per cent. The lower ratio of people to land is thought to hold out the potential for the production of significant quantities of surplus food as the application of scientific methods becomes more widespread. But this is still being held back by adverse factors, such as irrational pricing, poor supplies, insufficient numbers of trained personnel, organisational problems, etc. Nevertheless official figures for 1992 and 1993 show grain output to have reached record highs.[14]

As for ARIM, despite a claimed drop in the number of loss-making 'budgetary industrial enterprises' in 1992, one third were announced as operating at a loss, one third were breaking even and only a third were said to be profitable – which seems to be the standard formulation used on such occasions.[15] Meanwhile, Heilongjiang, like many of the officially designated inland provinces, is confronted with the more deeply set structural problem of continually falling behind the growth rates of the favoured and better situated coastal provinces, especially in the south. Compare, for example, the growth rate of its GDP in 1992 of 6 per cent, 'the highest . . . in the past four years' (i.e. half the national average) with that of 19.5 per cent for Guangdong Province.[16]

These disparities have led not to separatist demands, but to calls for greater fairness in the terms of economic exchanges and burden-sharing within the Chinese economy as a whole. The inland provinces of Manchuria demanded and obtained similar treatment for their cities and river ports as apply in the coastal provinces. They demand and frequently obtain continued subsidies to sustain the old state-owned enterprises as they are supposedly being transformed. Meanwhile, the relationship between coastal Liaoning and the two inland Manchurian provinces is a complex mixture of divergence and interdependence that has led to different comparative advantages and to different relations with the centre.

Although Manchuria is home to a large number of diverse ethnic groups, many of them, being the descendants of the semi-nomadic groups who used to inhabit the region, are not collectively large in number. They account for less than five per cent of a total Manchurian population of more than 101 million. Moreover, they have been subject to a process of assimilation. For example, the once proud Manchus are virtually indistinguishable from the Han as their language is no longer spoken and as their way of life has disappeared. The one exception is the 2 million strong Korean nationality, with 1.2 million living in the Yanbian Autonomous County in Jilin. As relations have improved with South Korea since the mid-1980s, they have been able to resume ties and they have been very active in developing economic relations of both the formal and informal varieties. In this sense they are seen by the provincial authorities as being very much an asset.

Inner Mongolia is in a different category. The original inhabitants, the Mongolians, now number over 3 million. But they are a minority in their own region, as they are outnumbered by a Han Chinese population of nearly 18 million. After their having suffered greatly during the Cultural Revolution, the onset of the reforms ameliorated their conditions and have also facilitated the exchange of family visits across the border with the Mongolian Republic. Since the mid-1980s there have been signs of burgeoning Mongolian nationalism within ARIM. Because of the restrictions on access to information it is difficult to gauge the depth and prevalence of such sentiments, let alone such discontent as they may have spawned. But there are continuing reports of incidents, and there is no doubt that the Chinese authorities take a very serious view of the situation. In April 1992 the official news agency responded to reports of 'violent riots' by denying that an independence movement was gaining momentum in the region. Thus implicitly conceding that such a movement existed.[17] The prospects for Inner Mongolian independence seem very poor. The Han outnumber the Mongolians by at least a factor of 6:1 and they control the security apparatus, the People's Armed Police and the Military. These have acted ruthlessly in the past, especially to non-Han people, and there is no reason to believe that they would not do so again. The existence of the Mongolian Republic may be seen as a source of inspiration and support for the Inner Mongolians, but it should also be recognised that the Republic has its own reasons to prefer an accommodation with the Chinese state. If it is to succeed in developing its economy, Mongolia needs to have good working relations with its giant neighbour. Moreover, people in the Republic are very much aware of nationalist sentiments in China that seek to reabsorb their country as the former Province of Outer Mongolia. Accordingly, they have been careful to avoid what could be construed as provocative acts. Perhaps one of the reasons why the Chinese authorities have encouraged cross-border trade is to give the Mongolian Republic every incentive to cooperate.

NORTH CHINA'S RELATIONS WITH RUSSIA

It is more than eight years since officials and others within Heilongjiang first depicted the vision of what they called a 'Great Northeast Asian Economic Circle', embracing Japan, the two Koreas, the Russian Far East and Mongolia, with northern China at the hub. So far there are few signs of its emergence. In part, realisation of this vision has been held back by political difficulties. The instabilities that led to the collapse of the Soviet Union are still attendant upon its successor, the Russian Federation, and they continue to be an obstacle to the evolution of close economic relations. They have delayed the process of reform on the Russian side and kept the two economies at two different and not easily compatible stages of institutional development. Moreover, Moscow appears to fear that an influx of Chinese labour into the Russian Far East could have undesirable demographic consequences for the sparsely populated region. In addition, the stalemate in Russo-Japanese relations blocks Japanese participation in such a bold regional scheme. The closed hardline posture of the North Korean regime and the impasse in improving its relations with the South also militate against the development of northeast Asia as a so-called 'Natural Economic Territory' (NET).[18]

There are, however, economic factors that would continue to hold back the development of the area as a NET even if the political problems were to ease. The weak infrastructure of the region could only be overcome by investments of enormous proportions involving many billions of dollars just to bring the transportation systems up to necessary levels. At the same time there would have to be a major transformation in the character of the indigenous institutions and the managerial and technical capacities of management and associated personnel. The difficulties in transforming a region that has been substantively enmeshed in the operations of a command economy to one that can be attuned to the operations of a market economy should not be underestimated. In fact some of these problems are evident in the United Nations Development Programme (UNDP) sponsored Tumen River Delta project. Little has happened in the two years since the six governments of Japan, China, Russia, North and South Korea and Mongolia agreed to develop jointly the lower reaches of the river delta. The political barriers, bureaucratic obstacles and, above all, the forbiddingly vast investments that would be required to modernise the port and develop appropriate transportation have militated against substantive development. The disadvantage of investing in infrastructure is that the financial returns would be long-term and diffused, while at the same time the economic environment is far less attractive to commercial investment than what is available elsewhere.

Coastal Liaoning, however, is in a different situation. It is one of the key points of access for developing economic relations with South Korea and Japan. Development is most rapid in the coastal zone stretching from the Dalian area southwards into neighbouring Hebei. The province is already looking forward to transforming the port into the 'Hong Kong of northern China' – a centre of trade, finance, tourism and information.[19] As we have seen, Liaoning has been able to attract foreign investment for infrastructural development. It is a leading export outlet ranking only just below Shanghai.[20] Perhaps more than the other three provinces, Liaoning is better positioned both to transform its state-owned sector and to attract foreign-related business. But by virtue of its location, its orientation is necessarily less towards Russia.

Bilateral economic relations with Russia, however, have not fared badly. If some of the more ambitious forecasts of the potential significance of Sino-Russian trade for their respective economies have failed to materialise, the actual growth and development of that trade has been solid and important for the border regions and for Chinese defence industries.[21] Having maintained a value of about $4 billion since 1989 (which included all the 15 republics of the former Soviet Union), trade with Russia jumped to $5.86 billion in 1992 and was officially expected to reach nearly $7 billion in 1993. While a long way behind the value of China's trade with Hong Kong, Japan or the USA, the Russian trade is not far behind that of say Taiwan, South Korea and Singapore. But it is significantly different in quality, in that the others are important sources of investment, technology transfers and managerial knowhow, while the Russian trade is important primarily as providing a market for consumer goods of perhaps secondary quality, and as a supplier to particular sectors such as China's military industries and as a provider of raw and processed industrial materials. For example, 44 per cent of

Russian exports valued collectively at $3.35 billion consisted of chemical fertilisers and chemical raw materials.[22]

Perhaps the most surprising element of the Russian trade was that nearly half of it was taken up with border trade that reached $2.7 billion. Chinese exports accounted for $1.45 billion. Moreover in the first three months of 1993 total bilateral border trade was valued at $900 million, over half the total trade value during the same period in 1992.[23] Indeed the significance of the trade with Russia for northern China was made clearer by the Russian consul in Shenyang when he pointed out that 70 per cent of the total for China as a whole was carried out with the three Manchurian provinces alone.[24] Meanwhile the Statistical Bureau of ARIM claimed that its trade with the CIS and Mongolia 'went beyond the simple barter trade and developed towards overall cooperation in the economy, technology and trade . . . In 1992, the regional total volume of import and export was US$940 million, up 56.7 per cent from the previous year'. The amount of barter trade was put at $430 million, more than double the 1991 figure.[25]

The Russian factor has clearly acquired significance in the economy of northern China. It accounts for a third of the region's trade.[26] It is of particular importance in Heilongjiang, where the local economy has benefited from the opening of the border area to economic relations with the northern neighbour and from the up-grading of communication and transportation facilities. Thus trade companies have the right to deal directly in the Russian market, and Harbin has become a major trading centre for the border trade. Four cities bordering the Russian Far East have been given the same status and incentives as the Shenzhen SEZ. More than 250 Sino-Russian joint ventures in light industry, market vegetables, service industries, timber processing, etc., now operate on both sides of the border. More than 20,000 Chinese workers are employed across the border. Heilongjiang has been visited by Russian senior trade officials and by military delegations. The settlement of the border (while leaving on one side the unresolved contention over Bear Island at the confluence of the Ussuri and Amur (or Heilongjiang) Rivers) has still further eased trading conditions.

However, the significance of the Russian factor can be exaggerated. The fact that the economic relationship is bilateral only limits its actual and potential growth in the immediate future to what the Russian Far East can bear. With a total population of only 15 million and requiring vast investment in infrastructure developments and lacking both a culture and an institutional framework that are geared to a market type economy, the Russian Far East does not present a suitable partner in itself for transforming northern China. It can provide a useful supplement and it can contribute to invigorating the adjacent border counties, but it can neither provide a substantive market in itself for Chinese goods, nor can its supplies of basic commodities such as timber and cement (needed though they may be) in themselves provide a basis for economic lift-off.

In fact the Russian factor may be of deeper significance for the broader Chinese economy. This is particularly true of the defence sector of the economy where the Chinese have not only purchased advanced weapons, such as the two squadrons of the SU-27, but they are known to be employing key personnel from the former Soviet military industrial complex. These are assisting Chinese defence establishments to overcome many of their technological short-comings across the entire spectrum of modern weaponry from sub-marine engines to missiles and nuclear warheads. In the longer term Russia as a whole could be a major market for Chinese consumer products, especially once the country begins its long-awaited recovery. Even in its present depressed state, Chinese goods are available on the markets of Russia's major cities. China is already an important market for Russian raw materials and industrial supplies, but again, once Russia and its Far East are better organised, the potential of the Chinese market would be very great indeed.

NORTH CHINA AND CHINESE REGIONALISM

One of the arguments for proposing that regionalism is growing in significance stems from the perception that at different points on China's periphery so-called natural economic territories (NETs) are emerging that involve regions of China with adjacent neighbouring territory. The example most usually cited is that of Hong Kong, Taiwan and southern China (or more precisely distinct parts of it, namely Guangdong and Fujian). This is sometimes referred to as 'Greater China' or as the 'Great South China Economic Circle'. Earlier in this chapter doubt was cast on the feasibility of developing a 'Great Northeast Asia Economic Circle'. In particular attention was drawn to the difficulties in overcoming the political problems in Russo-Japanese relations and in those of the two Koreas; and of the difficulties in raising the huge amounts of investment in developing the necessary infrastructure. This was especially evident in the problems experienced in seeking to get off the ground the Tumen River Delta project as sponsored by the UNDP, despite the high-minded enthusiasm expressed by the six participating governments.[27] The problems of raising thousands of millions of dollars that are required simply to prepare the necessary infrastructure for a deep-water port and its various handling facilities, allied to a proper transport and communications back-up, have apparently proved too daunting, especially when compounded by the numbing effects of the North Korean bureaucracy even when it does not mean to be obstructive.

For the period 1985–93 the authorities of the Manchurian provinces and of Heilongjiang in particular have looked forward to the opening of fully-fledged economic relations with Russia or its Soviet predecessor. So far the results have not met expectations. Border trade has developed initially on a barter basis and then in part on the basis of hard currency, but, despite apparently impressive percentage figures of growth, the actual impact has been local rather than regional. As we have seen, there are deep-seated reasons to suspect that, as long as the economic relations are confined to bilateral Sino-Russian arrangements, the potential will remain limited. Only once the other countries of Northeast Asia can be drawn into a multilateral framework will the prospects improve substantially.

Regionalism in North China, however, has developed in a more complex way than might be suggested by the concept of the NET. It involves utilising a plurality of links involving both the centre in Beijing, adjoining provinces and as many foreign outlets as possible. To give but one telling example: Heilongjiang industrial managers refused to accept Russian machine tools, despite being assured that these were more advanced than what they had and that they were the most easily applicable to their state-owned enterprises, whose technology was of an earlier generation of the same kind of technology. The managers regarded the Russian machinery as outdated and, since they had to market their products elsewhere in China and even abroad, they preferred to obtain the more advanced technological machinery available from elsewhere in the Asia–Pacific region.[28] Accordingly, Heilongjiang has made special efforts to appeal to traders and investors from Japan, South Korea, the USA, Thailand, Singapore and Australia, as well as Hong Kong and even Taiwan – with some success.[29] Indeed, just as the economic nexus of 'Greater China' has benefited from the ties of kinship and geography that link Chinese outside the mainland with those inside, so the ethnic ties between Koreans in Manchuria (notably the 1.2 million in Yanbian Autonomous County of Jilin) and South Korea have led to all kinds of economic enterprise.

Hence the most likely development of a NET in the immediate

future centres on northern China itself. It would involve using the comparative advantages of the coastal province with those of the inland ones. The latter would attract a degree of interest because of their access to Russia and Mongolia. Meanwhile, as the cost of land and labour should rise in Liaoning so manufacturing might be shifted inland. The difficulty remains, however, in the continued predominance in all four provinces of the state-owned enterprises. As we have seen, these are millstones which hold back the advance of these provinces. But since they reflect national rather than local priorities and since their costs are driven by national rather than by local or market criteria, their operations are still heavily subsidised by Beijing. The provinces are therefore drawn into a complex web of bargaining involving the three levels of region, centre (i.e. Beijing) and international.

CONCLUSION

Since this chapter has argued that north Chinese regionalism does not involve separatism or even what some have called 'economic warlordism', it will conclude by addressing some of the larger questions that arise from its depiction of the region as interdependent rather than independent. Two questions in particular will be considered: Where does the north China region fit into to the more general pattern of Sino-Russian relations? And, has its regional identity and bargaining strength facilitated its emergence as a semi-independent factor in a triangular or perhaps quadrilateral relationship involving itself, Beijing, Moscow and the Russian Far East?

The scope of Sino-Russian relations is both deep and broad, as it involves some of the most important foreign and domestic interests of both countries. From the perspective of Beijing the birth of Russia out of the collapse of the Soviet Union affected its own legitimacy at home and was a major factor in inducing Deng Xiaoping to revitalise the pursuit of rapid economic growth as a way of meeting the expectations of the Chinese people for better living standards. Beijing is also keen to utilise Russia as a counterweight to what it perceives as the American attempt to impose its hegemony throughout the world. That gives a sharper dimension to Chinese arms purchases from Russia and to the use of Russian experts in China's own military industrial complex. From the perspective of the Russian government the relationship with China is important in stabilising potentially disruptive border regions, providing an opening to the Asia–Pacific region and cultivating economic relations of potentially great significance. But President Yeltsin's main priority is to develop still better relations with the West for both economic and political reasons. That may not be true for his opponents, but the Chinese government has punctiliously followed diplomatic norms in dealing with the established government in Moscow rather than in flirting with the oppositionists. Given the greatness of the issues involved, Beijing has kept tight control over the political and strategic dimensions of the relationship.

There is as yet no sign that northern China has been an independent factor at these exalted levels. Indeed the region lacks the channels through which to exercise influence, even if that were thought desirable. Unlike some of the more reform-minded provinces, none of the leaders from the north sits on the Politburo, let alone its Standing Committee. The last leader of national significance was the military figure of a somewhat leftist reputation, Li Desheng, who was withdrawn to Beijing by Deng Xiaoping in 1985 after twelve years of command of the Shenyang Military Region (SMR). Since then the SMR has enjoyed the reputation of being relatively conservative in outlook and totally loyal to Beijing. It has few links with the local civilian authorities (except at lower levels). Moreover, the border guards belong to the People's Armed Police and are also directly under the command of Beijing rather than of any local authority.[30]

There are, however, indications of a growing network of relations between northern China and the Russian Far East Maritime Region that is in fact independent of either Moscow or Beijing. Indeed both capitals welcome such relations.[31] There is considerable cross-border traffic of people and goods, some of it of a not entirely welcome kind, such as drugs and smuggling. But this too has had its beneficial side, as it has led to closer cooperation between the local and national security forces of both sides.[32] However, alleged violations of Chinese maritime rights by Russian fishing and other vessels have led to a number of them being detained by the Chinese navy and thereby taken matters beyond the local purview to that of national governments. But in handling the problem the Chinese were mindful of local as well as national interests.[33] There is clearly no conflict of interest involving the national capitals in the improvement of relations between the two border regions.

These cross-border relations may be seen as strengthening the bargaining powers of these border provinces with Beijing. Central leaders have sought to reassure those provinces that they would not be badly affected by the current austerity measures.[34] In any case as major centres for China's ailing state-owned enterprises, their interests are well-embedded in the remaining institutional centres of the command economy in Beijing. So that, although the provincial leaders see themselves as reformers, their provincial interests enjoy the sympathy of some of the more conservative leaders in Beijing.

Despite there being a close correspondence between the interests of the Chinese northern and the Russian Far-Eastern regions on the one hand, and those of Beijing and Moscow on the other, there are no signs as yet of the regionalisation of foreign economic relations being used by any of the four parties as a basis for pressurising any of the others. However, the potential for that to happen clearly exists.

Northern China shares with the other border and coastal regions an interest in opening out still more to the adjacent states, but, unlike some of the others, it has an abiding interest in seeing the centre in Beijing retain substantive regulatory powers over the economy – at least until the problems of the state-owned enterprises have been overcome. Perhaps the concept that best explains the regionalism of northern China is interdependence, rather than autonomy, or still less economic warlordism. In addition to cultivating relations across the state border and requiring of Beijing to provide subsidies and to exercise a regulatory role, northern China needs continual economic intercourse with the other regions of China, not only through provincial and other local bureaucracies, but also between enterprises and markets. Accordingly, the situation of northern China challenges Beijing in at least two ways. Firstly, it requires of it that it should play an effective role as the political and economic centre of the country – not by reverting to old-style commandism, but by transforming itself into a strong quasi-federal authority able to regulate the market economy and the bargaining between regions. Secondly, it requires of it the capacity to adapt its relations with neighbouring states – in this case Russia – to take into account the semi-autonomous character of their regional economic association.

NOTES

1 This paper draws heavily on the authors's 'The PLA and Regionalism in Manchuria', prepared for the IISS and CAPS conference on Security Dimensions of Chinese Regionalism held in Hong Kong 25–27 June 1993.
2 See Dali L. Yang 'China Adjusts to the World Economy: The Political Economy of China's Coastal Development Strategy' (*Pacific Affairs*, Spring 1991) pp. 42–64; and Fuh-Wen Tzeng, 'The Political Economy of China's Coastal Development Strategy' (*Asian Survey*, March 1991) pp. 270–84.

3 Gaye Christoffersen, 'Xinjiang and the Great Islamic Circle: The Impact of Transnational Forces on Chinese Regional Economic Planning' (*The China Quarterly*, No. 133, March 1993) pp. 146–50.
4 Christofferson, *op. cit.*, p. 131
5 For a view of the potential danger posed by the nearly 700,000 Russian forces and a fleet of 500 ships, both said to be increasingly modernised see Zhu Chun, 'A Discussion About the Situation and Security Problems in the Asia-Pacific Region', *International Strategic Studies* (Beijing, No. 1, 1993) p. 20. The North Korean situation is too delicate to be discussed in public by the Chinese, however there can be little doubt about their concern.
6 For a perhaps over-optimistic outline of what was proposed see Gaye Christoffersen, 'Economic Reforms in Northeast China' (*Asian Survey*, December 1988) pp. 1245–63.
7 For detailed analysis see, Frederick C. Tiewes, *Politics at Mao's Court* (White Plains, N.Y.: M.E. Sharpe, 1979) ch. 5.
8 BBC *Summary of World Broadcasts Part 3, The Far East*, (henceforth, *SWB*) 20 March 1993, *FE/1642 C1/8* and *SWB* 29 March 1993, *FE/1649 C1/4*.
9 *SWB* 20 March 1993, *FE/1642 C1/8*.
10 Much of this paragraph too is drawn from *ibid.* pp. 172–73.
11 *Xinhua* report, 19 January 1994, *SWB FEW/0318 WG/9*.
12 *Ibid.*, p. 127.
13 According to Governor Shao Qihui in *Ming Pao*, 30 March, 1993 (in BBC *Summary of World Broadcasts-SWB*-FE/1654).
14 See economic results of the first three quarters of 1993 for Heilongjiang, ARIM in *SWB* 1 December 1993 *FE/WO310 G/1*.
15 *SWB*, 26 May 1993, *FE/WO283 A/2*
16 Heilongjiang Statistical Communique in *SWB*, FE/WO277, C1/8.
17 *SWB FE/1346*.
18 This suggestive but imprecise term seems to have first been coined by Robert A. Scalapino to desribe the burgeoning relations between Hong Kong, southern China and Taiwan once the political barriers between them had weakened.
19 Xinhua, 9 December 1993, in *SWB FEW/0312 WG/11*.
20 See Table 7.6 in Simon Long, 'Regionalism in Fujian' in this volume.
21 For an unduly high forecast see, for example, Nicholas R. Lardy, *China Enters the International Economy*.
22 *SWB*, 16 June 1993, *FE/WO286 A/8*, quoting Xinhua News Agency of 9 June 1993.
23 *Ibid.*
24 Xinhua, 13 February 1993, in *SWB*, 24 February 1993, *FE/WO270 A/6*.
25 See the 'Inner Mongolia Statistical Communiqué' of 18 February 1993, in *SWB FE/WO275 C1/11*.
26 Computed from the trade figures of their respective provincial statistical communiqués issued in 1993.
27 For an example of Beijing's enthusiasm see, 'Tumen River Delta: Far East's Future Rotterdam', in *Beijing Review*, April 20–26 1992, pp. 5–6.
28 Author's interviews in Harbin, March 1988.

29 'Heilongjiang Opens Door Wider', in *Beijing Review*, September 21–27 1992, p. 31.
30 For further discussion of these points see Swaine, *The Military and Political Succession*, *op. cit.*; and my 'The PLA and Regionalism in Manchuria' *op. cit.*
31 See, for example, Vice Premier Zou Jiahua's encouragement to the border areas of ARIM to develop what he called 'an export-orientated economy . . . a major advantage of the border areas'. Xinhua, 19 March 1993, in *SWB FE/1643 C1/9*. For its part, Moscow has attached sufficient importance to Heilongjiang Province as to send Deputy Prime Minister Aleksandr Shokhin to visit one of its small border towns. *SWB*, 20 April 1993, *FE/1667 A1/2*.
32 See accounts by Russian sources in *SWB*, 7 July 1993, *FE/1734 A1/4*. On 18 and 19 March 1993 a high-level Russian military delegation from the adjacent border region visited military and civilian leaders of Heilongjiang and agreed on further measures to strengthen links, *SWB FE/1644 A1/2*.
33 See comment by an unnamed Chinese official on 'unpleasant incidents involving Russian vessels', *Xinhua*, 16 July 1993, in *SWB FE/1744 A1/3*.
34 See the remarks of Vice-Premier Zou in note 26.

10 Xinjiang
Relations with China and abroad

Peter Ferdinand

The purpose of this chapter is to look at the relations between Central Asia (i.e. chiefly the republics of the former Soviet Union) and China's Northwest. It will chiefly focus upon the autonomous region of Xinjiang and the impact of its developing relations with the outside world upon the cohesion of China, and also upon China's foreign policy.

It will first consider the historical legacy of Xinjiang's relations with the outside world. It will then look at Xinjiang's development strategies of the 1980s, and the impact which these have had upon relations with Beijing. Finally it will consider the implications which these will have for the PRC's foreign policy.

THE GEOGRAPHICAL AND HISTORICAL LEGACY

Xinjiang occupies one-sixth of the total area of China today, but it has only 1.2 per cent of the population. The larger area of Central Asia, including the republics of the Former Soviet Union (FSU) is considerably larger than that of Western Europe, but with only a tenth of the population. Not only is the territory of Xinjiang extremely large, it is both rugged and diverse. The consequence is that the peoples living there have evolved fundamentally different ways of life to cope with this. The main differences were between the wandering pastoral nomads of the north, predominantly Kazakhs, and the more settled inhabitants of the oases, predominantly the Uighurs.

In addition to these divisions there were also those between ethnic groups and between tribes. A majority of the people come from Turkic-speaking groups such as Kazakhs and Uighurs, but the distances are so immense that primary loyalties were to kinship groups and tribes rather than to nationalities as such. This has meant that their societies were both far-flung and vulnerable to outside manipulation.

Xinjiang is part of the enormous borderlands to the north and west, which were a constant source of anxiety to Chinese emperors because of the danger that a mighty, ruthless, hostile army might suddenly emerge and cause havoc in China proper. Thus, although Xinjiang was never regarded as part of the Chinese heartland, it was the object of sustained attention as a front line of defence. Xinjiang was seen as the door to Mongolia, and Mongolia was seen (at least in more recent centuries) as the door to the capital in Beijing. According to Lattimore writing in the 1930s, effective control of Central Asia by the Chinese has been estimated as lasting only about 425 out of 2000 years, with present Chinese rule there the fifth major period.[1]

If Xinjiang was regarded as an area of front-line defence by imperial China, it was also a source of repeated trouble. Controlling the region was an enormously complicated and expensive task. China's relationship with it fluctuated dramatically. Sometimes China was able to dominate it. Sometimes control had to be abandoned because of the cost.

In 1760 China appeared at the height of its power in Inner Asia, with much of Central Asia isolated and dependent upon it. By 1860 the Qing system there had crumbled. Russian influence had penetrated into the region, Russian merchants competed with Chinese ones, and there were riots, followed by full-scale rebellions. Furthermore, Islam served as a potent rallying cry. The government attempted to grant limited autonomy to local rulers and to devise equitable tax and military obligations. These were, however, undermined by the actions of Chinese merchants and officials, who violated agreements and relations with the non-Chinese. There were a series of these rebellions in the first half of the nineteenth century. They culminated in a large Muslim rebellion in the 1860s in the Ili region led by Yaqub Beg, who set up an East Turkestan government. It was finally defeated in 1878. Some estimates have suggested that up to half the population of Xinjiang died as a result of the fighting, or the famines and diseases unleashed by the rebellion.[2]

Xinjiang was formally incorporated into the Chinese Empire in 1884, yet rebellions continued. In the first half of the twentieth century, however, its relationship with the rest of China was relatively weak, even antagonistic. Between 1911 and 1949 it was effectively outside the control of the national government, although it remained, just, within the Chinese orbit, being ruled by a number of independent-minded Chinese. There were several armed uprisings, and between 1933 and 1942 it was ruled by a warlord, Sheng Shicai, with Soviet support. The national disintegration into which China sank during this period meant that it offered few economic opportunities to Xinjiang. This was exacerbated by the enormous distances which had to be travelled for trade with China. Meanwhile, the Soviet Union in this period began to offer significant opportunities for Xinjiang, and the newly-constructed Turkmenistan–Siberia railway offered a more rapid link with both the Far East and Europe. Kashgar, to the west, was only twelve days from Soviet rail contact, but 2,500 miles from a similar point in China. In addition the Soviet leadership was attracted to Xinjiang not only by its mineral and other resources (it was the Soviet Union which first began oil production there), but also to pre-empt possible Japanese infiltration into the region. Thus Soviet troops were periodically stationed in Xinjiang, and it was also a valuable supply route for Soviet equipment which was being sent to aid the Nationalist Chinese. In 1944 another independent Kazakh and Uighur East Turkestan Republic was established, which controlled the northwestern Ili region until 1946.

> It is difficult to depict adequately the degree of savagery and the intensity of fighting which periodically swept over the province . . . From 1911 to 1942 no Sinkiang [sic] administration completed its rule without the death of the governor or of an immediate member of his household. In the field, fame went to the warrior, not on the basis of strategy, but on the basis of cruelty against his foe.[3]

Then, towards the end of the Civil war in China, the Ili region was captured by forces under the command of General Wang Zhen, and he and the first party secretary, Wang Enmao, were to rule over it for most of the following forty years.

ETHNIC COMPOSITION OF THE POPULATION

The population of Xinjiang at the time of Liberation was dominated by local minorities, chiefly Uighur and Kazakh. Only 8 per cent of the population at that time were Han Chinese. Since then there has been a steady influx of Han Chinese into the region. Firstly there were the remnants of the Nationalist armies which surrendered there to the Red Army, and were forced to settle down to life there in farming, industry or construction. These were organised by the Production and Construction Corps (PCC). Currently their staff and their families number about 2 million people. They have reclaimed land, run state farms, built factories, highways and railways. They operate largely autonomously and produce about half of the region's cotton, a quarter of its grain, and account for about 20 per cent of local GNP.[4] Secondly there were skilled technical and administrative personnel who were drafted there, especially during the 1950s, to assist in the development of the region. Already by 1957 the Han Chinese share of the population had roughly tripled to 23 per cent.[5] Then thirdly there were the young people drafted to the distant countryside after the end of the Cultural Revolution. Fourthly there were former members of the PLA who served there and who remained on completion of their military service. Fifthly. there were former inmates of prison camps in Central Asia who stayed on after their release, not least because (at least until the later 1980s) they could be prevented from returning to their homes further east. Lastly the economic reforms of the 1980s have attracted some Chinese eager to make money.

By 1975 the proportion of Han Chinese in Xinjiang had risen to 38 per cent of the total and it has stayed roughly at that figure since (see Table 10.1).

This influx of Han Chinese into Xinjiang might be expected to intensify frictions with the native population. This tendency has been aggravated by three further facts. The first has been the stationing of large numbers of PLA troops in the region to serve as a defensive line against possible attack from the Soviet Union. The second has been the use of Xinjiang for the testing of atomic and nuclear weapons, which has had the effect of irradiating parts of the region. The third was the Cultural Revolution. Although the latter was not directed specifically against minorities, it was nevertheless the case that all manifestations of the 'four olds'[6] were savagely repressed, and the chief agents carrying out these attacks tended to be Han Chinese Red Guards. There was active discrimination against minority languages, customs and religion. In Xinjiang the Red Guards wrought especial havoc, destroying mosques and religious works. Muslims were forced to raise pigs, and Muslim candidate members of the CCP were obliged to eat pork.

The consequence was that in the early 1980s, as the regime attempted to make amends for its earlier handling of minority relations there, there were various legacies which proved difficult to overcome. However much the leadership might proclaim their desire to turn over a new page in their relations with the region, it was difficult for the local population to take this simply at face value. There were a number of simmering grievances which, in the more relaxed atmosphere of the early 1980s, came into the open. For

Table 10.1 Inhabitants of Xinjiang by nationality (1990)

	Total	Growth 1982–90	Muslims	Non-Muslims	Nomads
Uighur	7,194,675	20.2%	x		
Han Chinese	5,695,626	7.8%		x	
Kazakh	1,106,989	22.6%	x		x
Hui	681,527	19.4%	x		
Kirghiz	139,781	23.7%	x		x
Mongols	137,740	17.2%		x	x
Dongxiang	56,464	40%	x		
Tajiks	33,512	26.5%	x		
Sibe	33,082	20.9%		x	
Manchus	18,403	101.4%		x	
Uzbeks	14,456	16.3%	x		
Russians	8,082	203.6%		x	
Daurs	5,398	23.6%		x	
Tatars	4,821	17.4%	x		
Tibetans	2,158	8.4%		x	
Total	15.16 million	15.9%	9.2 million	5.9 million	1 million

Source: Thomas Hoppe, 'Die chinesische Position in Ost-Turkestan/Xinjiang', CHINA aktuell, June 1992, p. 360

example, there were occasional demonstrations by minorities against Han Chinese, even attacks on them. Students demonstrated against having to share dormitories with Han Chinese. There were public protests in Urumqi and even in Beijing by students from Xinjiang about the nuclear test site at Lop Nor. According to a speech by former provincial leader Wang Enmao in June 1988, 'there are still people who oppose the Hans and want them to return to the interior . . . who say those who oppose Hans are heroes and those who unify with Hans are traitors . . . who say "we minority nationalities are still the slaves of others." '[7]

Even though Wang claimed that these were only the views of a few people 'hiding in dark corners', the problem was serious enough to worry and divide the leadership in Beijing. There were at that time clear disagreements in the leadership over how the issues should be handled. Some, such as Hu Yaobang, were prepared for more conciliatory policies. He advocated more genuine consideration for local needs, and the phased withdrawal of Han Chinese officials. Others wanted to take a much tougher line. A hard-line Han official was quoted as saying:

> You give them autonomy and they will only turn round and create an East Turkestan. Hu Yaobang also wants to withdraw Han cadres to the interior. That would be surrendering Xinjiang to the Soviet Union and Turkey. Only a traitor would do such a thing. To stabilise Xinjiang we must send hard-liners like Wang Zhen.[8]

Nevertheless ethnic and religious unrest has continued, if sporadically. The last serious outbreak was in 1990 in Baren county, south of Kashgar, when around 50 local people were thought to have been killed by security forces (the official account claimed 22 deaths, including seven policemen). This followed protests against newly imposed restrictions on religious activities. Then in 1992 there were a number of terrorist bombs in Urumqi, one of which was planted on a bus, killing several people. Another bomb exploded in a government building in Kashgar in June 1993, killing three people. And in autumn 1992, as in 1989, there were a serious of demonstrations in a number of provinces with Muslim communities, including Xinjiang, over magazine articles regarded as offensive to Muslims.

SECURITY RELATIONS WITH CENTRAL ASIA

China's traditional reason for concern over Xinjiang, namely the fear of invaders emerging from the deserts and the steppes, clearly no longer applies. Yet the Sino-Soviet frontier remained a source of concern. In the immediate years after Liberation, the PRC could only gradually reduce Soviet influence. Chinese currency did not begin to replace local and Soviet currencies until November 1951. 'Many of Xinjiang's minority people considered Soviet control preferable to that of the Chinese, and thought of the Soviet government as a potential liberator.'[9] Then the Sino-Soviet dispute kept Xinjiang on the front line of possible confrontation. For example, between 1972 and 1977 the Soviet Union took 2,800 square kilometres from China.[10] More seriously, Soviet and Chinese nuclear testing sites, as well as nuclear bases, faced each other across the Xinjiang–Kazakhstan border. This ensured that the security of the autonomous region remained a prominent concern of Beijing.

It might be expected, therefore, that the collapse of the Soviet Union would lead to improved security relations with Central Asia. Yet a permanent improvement has not been made. The chief reason is that there is now a renewed sense of fluidity about the politics, both domestic and international of the region, which would make premature any assumption about long-term stability. The borders of states in the whole arc of territory to Xinjiang's north and west are all in various ways either contested or contestable. This stretches from Kazakhstan, through the rest of the Central Asian states of the FSU, through to Afghanistan and Kashmir. All of these states have nationalities whose traditional homeland straddles current frontiers. Although in the FSU at least the current leaders still agree that any attempt to change frontiers by force would court disaster, since it could provoke military confrontation, civil war has already come to Tajikistan, and now it has flowed over to merge with the civil war in Afghanistan. There have already been bloody clashes in the Fergana valley in Uzbekistan. Some leaders, such as Presidents Karimov of Uzbekistan and Nazarbaev of Kazakhstan, are vying for influence as they attempt to raise the profile of their states vis-à-vis others in Central Asia. There is an increasing self-confidence in the region which rejects the old relationship of elder brother and younger brother with Russia and China. And the ongoing dispute over Kashmir to the southwest is a reminder of how long such issues may persist.

In addition, other countries nearby have discovered new interests, and possibly goals, for their foreign policies in the region. Turkey and Iran in particular have expanded their activities. It may be premature to assume that this will lead to security disputes, but from the Chinese point of view the possibility of increased Turkish involvement in the region is unwelcome, since various 'East Turkestan' organisations are based there. The most prominent of these is the Eastern Turkestan Foundation, which was established in 1978 by the acknowledged leader of emigré Uighurs, Isa Yusuf Alptekin. Although run by people who left Xinjiang around 1949, it has attracted more recent Uighur emigrés. More worrying for China is the fact that the Turkish government has taken up the cause of Turks, or people of Turkic background, abroad. It has established a ministry to pursue their interests. Former President Ozal and former Prime Minister Demirel both talked of a Turkic homeland stretching from the Balkans to the Great Wall of China (i.e. well to the east of Xinjiang) and were attacked by the *People's Daily*.[11] The World Turkic Conference of March 1993 denounced 'Chinese atrocities' in Eastern Turkestan and urged a dialogue with the Chinese authorities to prevent the destruction of the Turkic peoples there.

If it was simply a matter of Xinjiang alone, the situation is one which Beijing ought to be able to control. The population of Central Asia is quite small, and the various nationalities are quite divided amongst themselves. The leaderships of the republics in the FSU have a great many worries without wishing to antagonise their largest and most powerful neighbour. It is true that in Kazakhstan a non-violent Kazakh nationalist party is allowed to exist, and the chief plank of its programme is reunification with the Kazakh nation in Xinjiang. And Uighur Liberation Committees have been set up in Kazakhstan, Kirghizstan and Tajikistan, together with an International Uighur Union for Uighurs living throughout the CIS. Yet the leaders of the Central Asian republics have enough problems at home without taking on China. Even the retention of nuclear weapons by Kazakhstan was undertaken with an eye to deterring possible Chinese incursions into the region.

Nevertheless, the security situation from the Chinese point of view is unsatisfactory. There have been the demonstrations mentioned above, and these were followed by inspection tours by senior PRC leaders, even including Qiao Shi. Yet in August 1993 Xinjiang party secretary Song Hanliang addressed a meeting in Kashi Prefecture at which he declared that national separatism still poses a major threat to Xinjiang's stability.[12]

Fundamentally, however, the uncertainty is caused by the wider sense of political fluidity throughout Central Asia. Whatever China may do at home, it cannot control what happens beyond its borders, especially now there is much greater contact between the peoples of

Xinjiang and their kin across the frontiers. The cause of this movement is economic.

XINJIANG'S ECONOMIC DEVELOPMENT IN THE 1980S

It might be expected that, given Xinjiang's economic backwardness, its development would open rifts with Beijing. And indeed it was true that for much of the 1980s Xinjiang suffered from the consequences of the opening of the economy to outside forces, and the preferential treatment accorded by the central government to the coastal provinces. In the Seventh Five-year Plan during the second half of the decade, the western provinces of China were explicitly relegated to the role of providers of minerals and raw materials, with large-scale modernisation projects only to be expected in the twenty-first century. It was true that during the 1980s output grew on average by just over 10 per cent annually, i.e. slightly more than the national average. Nevertheless, the share of industry in the total of industrial and agricultural output combined was, at 60 per cent, lower than in other minority regions such as Inner Mongolia and Ningxia. Within the province there was a sense that Xinjiang was being allowed or forced to fall further behind in the race to develop a modern, industrialised economy. Given all its potential for developing agriculture, animal husbandry, cotton, construction materials, non-ferrous metals, not to mention oil, there was a sense that not enough was being done to develop it. There were also obvious deficiencies in terms of inadequate transport infrastructure.[13] All of this contributed to the view that Beijing was exploiting Xinjiang by 'taking' its raw materials and failing to give adequate recompense.

Paradoxically, the government of the autonomous region was also dependent upon the central government for subsidies to keep operating. Anything up to 50 per cent of its operating budget had to be subsidised. This situation was replicated at lower levels. Eight per cent of all the counties and townships could only operate with subsidies from higher levels of government.[14] Thus the centre seemed at the same time to be both subsidising and exploiting Xinjiang.

The consequence of all this was that economists in Xinjiang began to search for alternative trading opportunities. Their minds were concentrated by the sharp cuts in investment funds which occurred in 1988 as part of the government's attempts to prevent the economy from overheating, and which hit the western provinces hardest.

In particular they began to talk of turning towards a 'Great Islamic

Circle', by which they meant turning to neighbouring states in the northwest, but also to the Middle East.[15] Following in the steps of Ningxia, which began its first joint ventures with partners from the Gulf states in 1986, Xinjiang also began to try to take advantage of its Muslim identity and trade with partners in the Middle East.

Another possibility was to try to enter markets in South Asia. Connections with Pakistan originally served as the basis, and these are now being supplemented by opportunities to enter the Indian market, especially now that government-to-government relations are making progress.

Most activity, however, has centred upon the opening of markets to the north in the FSU. The rapid collapse of the Soviet and then the Russian economy led to new opportunities for cross-border trade. The failure of light industry in the former Soviet republics in Central Asia to supply the needs of the local population created new opportunities for entrepreneurs in the south of the autonomous region to export there. Markets in Almaty and Tashkent became well-stocked with Chinese consumer products. To a limited extent the Central Asian republics, especially Kazakhstan, could reciprocate by exporting oil exploration equipment, tractors and fertilisers.

At the same time the then Soviet government was seeking to expand contacts and trade with China as a way of strengthening the relationships and building upon the *de facto* arms reductions which were taking place.

In the past few years this cross-border trade has mushroomed. Where in 1988 it was estimated to be worth $88 million, in 1991 it rose to $1 billion, and then in 1992 alone it doubled to $2 billion. In 1992 the Chinese government attempted to stimulate it still further by granting five cities in Xinjiang equivalent rights to the ten open cities on the east coast for attracting foreign investment, whilst in 1993 it opened ten highways to land ports on the frontiers of republics of the FSU. One Xinjiang official, the Vice-Chairman of the region, predicted that this border trade in 1993 would constitute half of the province's total foreign business.[16]

In the period 1991–93 this two-way trade spread into investments. There is now quite a flourishing trade in investments too, with Chinese investing in the newly privatised enterprises in Russia, especially Siberia, and also, although to a lesser extent, in Central Asia.[17] In 1992 Xinjiang firms signed a deal to build the largest hotel in Almaty. Clearly this is a trend pointing in the direction of more integrated economies in Central Asia.

And people-to-people contacts have multiplied too. In 1991 visas were abolished for citizens of China and Kazakhstan visiting each other's country. In 1992 roughly 130,000 business people and tourists visited Xinjiang, whilst it was expected that figure would rise by 100,000 in 1993. It has also led to a more permanent migration of people from Xinjiang to Kazakhstan and this worries the authorities in Almaty. According to a recent newspaper article, no one there knows how many ethnic Chinese are living there, either legally or illegally, but it reported estimates of 300–350,000. The 1989 Soviet census did not even list Chinese as one of the ethnic groups living in Kazakhstan. On average one in ten Chinese crossing the frontier remain in Kazakhstan. According to the same article, 'Chinese business[men] are perhaps the most self-assured, energetic and aggressive in Kazakhstan today'. More worrying for the Kazakhstan authorities is the involvement of Chinese mafias in the supply and transport of drugs estimated at $2 million per year.[18]

Yet the idea of counterposing the opportunities for an opening to the west for Xinjiang, as against those for developing links with markets in China to the east may itself be simplistic. One of the realisations of recent years has been that market success in one place can then lead to greater success in markets elsewhere. For example in Xinjiang a vacuum flask manufacturing plant which had been making losses for years began a joint venture with a partner in Kazakhstan. After a few years it established four joint ventures in Kazakhstan which have proved enormous successes. This is now a firm which is making a profit and paying significant taxes. And it is also now more successful in selling to consumers elsewhere in China.[19]

On a broader scale it has been argued that Xinjiang's opening to the north could not have been conceived without a similar expansion of its integration into the national economy as a whole.[20] Xinjiang needed the latter so as to supply goods to Central Asia. Equally important is the fact that by 1989–90 economists in Beijing seemed to have accepted that the discrimination against the western provinces of China in terms of cutbacks on investment funds was counterproductive.

A second factor which strengthened the hand of Xinjiang in its dealings with Beijing was the realisation in Beijing that China's existing oil reserves are reaching a point where they can at best only meet her domestic demand. In 1993 China became a net oil importer. And the more rapid economic growth of 1992/3 which at around 12/13 per cent per annum is roughly double what the government decided was 'optimal' in 1991, even though it has impressed foreign investors and has created the impression of an economy striding faster ahead, also has the effect of making the energy balance even worse. There is a pressing need for China to develop new sources of oil. And given the failure to discover significant new reserves off-shore, this has meant that Xinjiang is likely to benefit most.

Yet the central government is being increasingly squeezed for resources, as provinces drag their feet over forwarding the tax revenues which they had committed. And the China State Oil Corporation has itself been squeezed by a reluctance on the part of the government to allow oil prices to rise to a level approximating to world market levels, for fear of it provoking an upsurge of inflation. Thus the two main domestic sources of potential investments to develop the reserves in Xinjiang are both under strain. It was for these reasons that the government in Beijing allowed in 1993 for the first time foreign oil companies to participate in on-shore oil exploration. Above all this has led to joint exploration in Xinjiang.

It has meant that the authorities in Xinjiang, in collaboration with the central government, were forced or enabled to look further afield for major investment. Now a whole series of oil multinationals are cautiously evaluating the opportunities and risks.

If any of them do decide to go ahead with serious exploitation of oil fields there, they will be confronted by the enormous task of shipping the oil to markets. This in turn will require enormous investments in the shape of added railway lines, or an oil pipeline. For this none of Xinjiang's neighbours will have sufficient resources. So in summer 1993 the Mitsubishi Corporation was commissioned by the Japanese government to begin evaluating the possibilities for a gas pipeline linking Xinjiang with the east coast. Rough estimates have suggested that trillions of yen, as well as nearly a decade, would be needed to build it. All of this is a reminder that Xinjiang cannot build her own future without significant outside help.

CONCLUSION

Compared to other provinces on the periphery of China, there is a greater possibility for the links developing between Xinjiang and the states across the border to gel into a new economic region which could pull the autonomous region further from Beijing's control. There are both the re-emerging cross-border ethnic ties, which could underpin economic relations, and also the opportunities for complementary cross-border trade.

Yet at the same time trade is not the only thing which Xinjiang needs. It also needs investment, so as to be able to open up its rich mineral resources. Here Central Asia itself will be of little assistance. The former republics of the Soviet Union themselves are poor, and need large amounts of foreign investment if they are to develop their own resources. They will not have anything left to aid the significant needs of Xinjiang. Moreover, the former Soviet republics are themselves competitors rather than partners of Xinjiang in terms of mineral endowment. They will want to ensure maximum exploitation of their own resources rather than someone else's.

For investment Xinjiang will have to look further afield. It can look to Beijing, and the fact of the PRC's growing oil shortages will no doubt spur the central authorities into sympathetic consideration of enhanced rail links, as well as an oil pipeline. On the other hand the growing relative impoverishment of the central government compared to the provinces will act as a brake upon what any province, however, significant, can expect.

In that case the authorities in Xinjiang will wish to look abroad for potential investors. For example, they have been courted by Turkey and Iran – and there have been important visits by the presidents of both states to Central Asia and to Xinjiang. Yet neither country possesses abundant financial resources. The most important sources of foreign investment would be either oil-rich Muslim states in the Middle East, or Western oil multinationals, or Japan. In any of these cases the source would be relatively distant. Whatever may be the attraction of a regional economic grouping in Central Asia, such as has been mooted by the President of Uzbekistan, it would have to be a region relatively open to the outside world.

In addition Xinjiang's ability to win significant amounts of foreign investment is still, for the moment at least, extremely limited. In 1992 Xinjiang attracted the second lowest amount of FDI of any provincial-level administration (Tibet was not included in the list). Xinjiang signed contracts for just $10.5 million, which was more than Qinghai, but only a quarter of what Ningxia attracted. It was only 0.01 per cent of all foreign investment contracted to China in that year, and only 0.17 per cent of the total contracted to provincial-level authorities. This does not compare at all with the 33 per cent which went to Guangdong.[21]

One of the obvious difficulties which would confront a Xinjiang trying to go it alone would be the fact of being land-locked. As far as transport is concerned, land-locked countries have little leverage over the neighbours across whose territory trade has to pass. Xinjiang, like the republics of the FSU in Central Asia, would quickly discover the necessity for preserving reasonably amicable ties with its large neighbours, both Russia and China, through whose territory any products would necessarily have to go before they could reach international markets. If China needs Xinjiang's oil, Xinjiang needs China's transport facilities, and probably China's markets, if its oil and other resources are to be sold at competitive prices.

The real threat to harmonious relations with China therefore stems not from economics, but from politics, i.e. the dangers of an ethnic upsurge which would spring from resentment over past humiliations, and over the past colonisation and misuse of the region's land. This could be reinforced, or sparked, by grievances over past religious repression. It is impossible to rule out the possibility that minority resentments in some part of Central Asia might cross frontiers and reach Xinjiang, even if they did not originate there. This could result either from economic success or from economic and political failure. On the one hand growing economic success in Xinjiang might encourage some to press for 'full' independence, on the grounds that now they could be economically self-sufficient. There is no guarantee that economic success in Xinjiang would lead to a more stable, and more quiescent relationship with Beijing. On the other hand the government in Beijing might also feel provoked into intervening in political turbulence on the other side of existing frontiers so as to pre-empt destabilisation from spreading.[22] In turn that could lead to military commitments which could evolve in all sorts of directions.

Another possible development could be the re-emergence of rivalries and frictions between the various peoples of Central Asia themselves. We have already seen fighting in places like the Fergana valley in Uzbekistan, not to mention the civil war in Afghanistan which has spread into Tajikistan. In those cases Beijing, like Moscow, could well have the role of mediator, or even peacemaker, thrust upon it. The peoples of Xinjiang have always found it difficult to maintain a long-term alliance against the Chinese. Many rebellions have crumbled as a result of internal dissension. In so far as that was sometimes the pretext for colonisation, there is a danger of history repeating itself. Neither can China insulate itself from events in Central Asia, nor can Xinjiang afford to cut itself off from China without enormous costs. But neither are China or Xinjiang in complete control of their own destinies.

NOTES

1 Owen Lattimore, *Inner Asian Frontiers of China* (Boston: Beacon Press, 1940), p. 171.
2 Morris Rossabi, *China and Inner Asia: From 1368 to the Present Day* (London: Thames and Hudson, 1975), pp. 166–218.
3 Allen S. Whiting and General Sheng Shih-ts'ai, *Sinkiang: Pawn or Pivot?* (East Lansing: Michigan State UP, 1958), pp. 14, 19
4 *Far Eastern Economic Review*, 25 August 1988, pp. 28–9.
5 Quoted in Thomas Heberer, *Nationalitätenpolitik und Entwicklungspolitik in den Gebieten nationaler Minderheiten in China* (Universität Bremen, Bremer Beiträge zur Geographie und Raumplanung, Heft 9, 1984), p. 152.
6 i.e. old ways of thinking, old culture, old customs and old habits.
7 *Far Eastern Economic Review*, 25 August 1988, p. 29.
8 Yuan Ming, 'Missed Historic Opportunity Recalled', *Minzhu Zhongguo*, no. 8, February 1992, pp. 17–18 (translated in JPRC-CAR-92–039).
9 June Dreyer, 'The PLA and Regionalism in Xinjiang', *The Pacific Review*, vol. 7, no. 1, Spring 1994.
10 *Ibid.*
11 *Renmin Ribao*, 17 November 1992.
12 'Xinjiang Secretary Addresses Prefectural Meeting', *FBIS-CHI*–93–162, 24 August 1993, p. 63.
13 Li Fang, 'Xinjiang jingji he shehui fazhandi jige wenti', *Minzu Yanjiu*, 1993(2), pp. 17–18.
14 Li Fang, *ibid.*, p. 17.
15 Gayle Christofferson, 'Xinjiang and the Great Islamic Circle: the Impact of Transnational Forces on Chinese Regional Economic Planning', *China Quarterly*, 133 (March 1993), p. 133.
16 *Beijing Review*, 1–7 February 1993, p. 27.
17 E. Grebenshchikov, 'Voucher kak predmet eksporta', *Aziia i Afrika Segodnia* 1993(5), pp. 49–50.
18 'China-Towny v Kazakhstanskikh gorodakh', *Nezavisimaia gazeta*, 7 October 1993.
19 Fang Li, *op. cit.*, p. 21.
20 Gayle Christofferson, *op. cit.*
21 *JETRO China Newsletter*, No. 105, July–August 1993, p. 22.
22 For a discussion of the issues related to Mongolia, see *Far Eastern Economic Review*, 9 April 1992, pp. 16–20.

11 Regional economic integration in Yunnan

Ingrid d'Hooghe

China's economic integration with different parts of the Asia–Pacific region is no longer limited to the coastal areas. Recently, there have been clear indications of increasing economic cooperation between China's border provinces and their neighbouring countries, with one of them being southwestern Yunnan Province.

Yunnan has long been regarded as an inaccessible, backward and remote frontier, with hardly any potential for economic development, let alone foreign trade. Although in ancient times it flourished as a part of the Southern Silk Road, for most of the time the landlocked and inaccessible province remained a forbidding place. After a promising start in the closing years of the nineteenth and the first decades of the twentieth centuries, when the French and British developed trading relations with Yunnan from their respective colonies in Vietnam and Burma, the province fell into oblivion again. It was only after 1978, when Deng Xiaoping began the nation's modernisation drive and decreed that China should open its doors, that Yunnan gradually developed its economy and renewed the ties with its neighbours.

Now, fifteen years later, foreign economic relations are no longer a negligible part of Yunnan's economy and the province aims, eventually, to obtain a leading position in China's trade with South-east Asia. With varying success, it is developing border trade with the neighbouring countries of Burma (Myanmar), Laos and Vietnam and forging links with nearby countries such as Thailand. For example, Yunnan is one of the promoters of the Golden or Mekong growth quadrangle which also includes parts of Burma, Laos and Thailand.

Yunnan's lack of capital, which is needed in its drive towards development, has prompted its leaders to look abroad in the attempt to attract foreign investors, especially from rich countries such as Hong Kong, Singapore, Thailand and Taiwan. Given the promising potential of many South-east Asian countries and the increasing popularity of the concept of 'growth triangles' in Asia, it is quite conceivable that Yunnan's economy will become inextricably bound with the South-east Asian region.

This chapter will discuss Yunnan's possible integration with the region and its neighbours in particular, by looking at some aspects of Yunnan's modernisation drive, including macro-economic trends over the last fifteen years, the role of foreign capital in Yunnan's strategic economic planning and government plans for the development of the economy. In particular, the focus will be on Yunnan's foreign trade and economic relations with its neighbouring countries, since this is where the trend towards regional economic integration can best be observed.

As Yunnan's economic potential is the decisive factor in the development of foreign economic relations, this chapter will start with an outline of the province's assets and liablities with respect to its economic development.

GEOGRAPHY

With an area of 394,000 square kilometres, Yunnan is China's seventh biggest province. Because 94 per cent of its surface comprises mountains and plateaus, transport is very difficult and the construction of roads and railways is both laborious and expensive. The landlocked province shares its borders with Burma, Vietnam and Laos. The nearest sea ports are Beihai and Fangcheng in Guangxi and Haiphong in Vietnam. Only 7 per cent of the land is cultivated, which is below the national average of 10 per cent. Yunnan's climate comprises characteristics of both equatorial monsoon and tropical types, thus allowing for the cultivation of two to three crops per year. The province has a population of 39 million and is inhabited by 24 ethnic minority groups which constitute roughly one-third of the entire population. The biggest minority group is the Yi, who make up 10 per cent of the entire population. Other important minorities include the Bai (3.6 per cent), Hani (3.3 per cent), the Zhuang, Dai, Miao and Hui.[1] Most of these minorities live in eight autonomous prefectures. In total, regional autonomy is exercised by minority nationalities in 79 (61 per cent) of Yunnan's 127 districts.[2]

The large presence of minorities in Yunnan is a significant feature of the province's demography. At present there are no signs of political unrest or a striving for independence among Yunnan's minorities. However, the central authorities are apprehensive about ethnic turmoil and Yunnan's history, up till the 1970s, has indeed been punctuated by ethnic rebellion.[3] Thus it is very important for the authorities to foster good relations with and among the minorities and to improve their economic and social position. As things stand, the economic position of minorities within the province, especially those living in the remote mountain areas, is very weak. More than 75 per cent of Yunnan's poorest counties are located in minority areas.[4] Every year, more than 2 billion yuan in subsidies is provided for both direct/incidental aid and for structural projects. These projects are aimed, for instance, at improving local production forces or helping people tap new sources of income by exploiting Yunnan's large deposits of mineral and other resources or by developing businesses in the tourist sector.[5]

Yunnan is rich in various kinds of resources. Firstly, it has more than fifty kinds of mineral resources that are foremost on the national list of reserves. The reserves of six of them, including lead, zinc and phosphorous ore, are the largest in the country. Secondly, thanks to its many rivers and lakes, the mountainous Yunnan Province has an abundant supply of industrial water and hydroelectric power. The province's water power potential is estimated at 71 million kilo-watt, which constitutes 18.7 per cent of the country's total and is second only to Sichuan.[6] Other resources include forests and animal species. However, the exploitation and utilisation of resources is still at a low level. In general, the level of utilisation in proportion to their practical potential is less than five per cent.[7]

Yunnan's considerable wealth lies in the abundance of raw materials and potential energy resources (hydropower). However, its rough and mountainous terrain poses great difficulties in the full development of this promising potential. The fact that the province is landlocked and borders three countries again implies both obstacles and opportunities. On the one hand, Yunnan has to do without any sea ports but on the other hand, having so many neighbours provides Yunnan with ample opportunities to engage in foreign trade.

YUNNAN'S ECONOMY

Yunnan's economy is relatively underdeveloped. The level of pro-duction is low, the per capita income is far below China's average, and over 40 per cent of the population is still illiterate.[8] Widespread poverty is very much in evidence in the province. Approximately 2 million people have not yet achieved the minimum level of subsistence.

Table 11.1 Main economic indicators of Yunnan Province[9]

		1978	1985	1991	1992
Gross provincial products	(billion yuan)	6.9	16.5	43.0	49.0
Provincial income	(billion yuan)	6.2	14.3	38.0	43.0
Per capita provincial income	(yuan)	203	424	1011	—
Agricultural output	(billion yuan)	4.0	8.9	22.3	24.0
Industrial output		5.5	13.6	39.4	46.0
– light industry	(billion yuan)	2.4	6.6	20.4	—
– heavy industry	(billion yuan)	3.2	7.0	19.0	—
Electric energy	(billion kWh)	5.25	7.55	14.09	—
Investment in fixed assets	(billion yuan)	1.5	4.6	9.8	—
Retail sales	(billion yuan)	3.1	9.3	18.8	23.5

In 1992 the Gross National Product (GNP) was 48.7 billion yuan, a mere 2 per cent of the country's total. However, economic growth is fast. Yunnan's growth rate in 1991 was almost 11 per cent. Although somewhat lower than the national growth rate in the same period (12.8 per cent), this can still be considered a good achievement.[10] Agriculture and industry have an almost equal share in the province's GNP (with the latter having a slightly bigger share), while the tertiary sector, which currently accounts for roughly one-fifth of the GNP, is quickly expanding.[11]

In 1992, Yunnan's industrial output totalled more than 46 billion yuan, a rise of 16.5 per cent over 1991, which is quite an impressive performance.[12] Although the majority of industrial enterprises are privately or collectively owned village and township enterprises, still more than 76 per cent of industrial output comes from state-owned enterprises.

Yunnan has to rely mainly on itself to raise the capital needed for further development. The central government only provides financial support for some key projects, mainly in transport and infrastructure, and foreign investment is still limited. The province's financial situation is, therefore, tight. To raise the necessary capital, the province, in its economic plans, including the Eighth Five-year Plan and Ten-year Plan for Development, has developed its own version of Deng Xiaoping's 'some should get rich first' by identifying a number of key industries that are certain of bringing in good profits in a short time. In the initial stage, most of the investment is poured into these key industries and the profits they make are subsequently used to set up infrastructural support in key sectors such as transport, energy and telecommunications.

YUNNAN'S MONEY-EARNERS

In accordance with the principle of comparative advantage, the following industries have been identified as key industries that should provide the province with investment capital. In the category of foodstuffs and drinks: tobacco, sugar and tea; in the category of tropical crops processing: rubber and spices; in the category of mineral resources processing: phosphorus chemical and nonferrous and ferrous metals industry; and finally the tourist industry.[13]

Construction, expansion and the upgrading of industries in the first two categories had already begun during the Sixth Five-year Plan (1981–86). Over the last decade, Yunnan imported new processing technologies and packaging equipment which led to a considerable

Table 11.2 Development of key industries[14]

	1978	1985	1991
Agricultural products:			
sugar cane (million tons)	1.6	4.8	8.2
tobacco (million tons)	0.12	0.41	0.58
Industrial products:			
sugar (million tons)	0.14	0.33	0.60
cigarettes (million boxes)	0.63	2.06	4.37
non-ferrous metals (10 kinds)			
(million tons)	0.15	0.25	—

improvement in the quality of the products concerned. Most successful was the development of the tobacco industry. During the sixth and
seventh five-year plans, $250 million was invested in the techno-
logical renovation of tobacco factories.[15] In the period 1978–91 the
average annual growth of the production of cigarettes increased by
16.1 per cent.[16] At present, the tobacco industry is Yunnan's biggest
money-maker, generating more than 60 per cent of provincial financial revenue.[17] Furthermore, Yunnan is the biggest tobacco producer
in China, accounting for almost one-fifth of the country's total. In the
near future, Yunnan plans to invest another $200 million worth of
funds in order to effect the technological transformation of the
tobacco industry, and locate new international markets for its
tobacco products.[18]

The development of a processing industry that should enable
Yunnan to reap more benefits from its mineral resources started
somewhat later, during the Seventh Five-year Plan (1986–90). Currently Yunnan sells its resources mainly as raw materials, without any
value added. Furthermore, a great part of the output of raw materials
is still distributed by the central government. This leads to a considerable loss of potential profit. With the gradual abolition of the
central distribution system and the development of new core industries such as phosphorus chemical, nonferrous and ferrous metal, and
rubber processing industries, the province plans to reverse this
process.[19] Within the nonferrous metals sector, the focus is on the
development and expansion of zinc and lead processing, which in
their turn should boost the development of copper and tin industries.

The third of the money-making sectors is the tourist industry. With
its tropical climate, primeval forests and variety of minority groups,
Yunnan has a considerable potential for the development of tourism,
which is already an important source of income. Table 11.3 shows the

Table 11.3 Development of tourism[20]

	1980	1985	1990	1992
Tourists (1000 persons)	20.5	72.2	148.2	233.0
foreigners (1000 persons)	7.9	46.6	49.8	—
HK/Macao/Taiwan (1000 persons)	18.6	97.5	—	—
FEC earnings from tourism (million FEC)	1.7	26.8	77.6	160.0

increase in both revenue and the number of tourists, in particular from the Asian region. In 1992, more than 313,000 foreign tourists visited Yunnan and the province's revenue from tourism was $67.5 million.[21] Although still modest in scope, the province hopes that tourism will become the second pillar of its economy, after the tobacco industry. It has taken measures to improve the efficiency of the tourism sector and is opening up new resorts and increasing facilities, as well as developing the souvenir industry and transport. It is expected that the development of tourism will lead to a boost to the service sector in general.

Money-swallowers

Transport and telecommunication

Transport is Yunnan's Achilles' heel and its biggest obstacle to smooth development. This concerns the infrastructure within the province itself as well as its links with other provinces and other countries. Currently, the transport system can handle only 10 million tons of materials a year. However, the actual demand is 25 million tons.[22] To overcome this obstacle, Yunnan Province has drawn up an infrastructure construction scheme for the next ten years and plans to invest more than 10 billion *yuan* (about $1.72 billion) in the construction of modern transport and telecommunication networks.

The construction or reconstruction of four railways currently under way includes provincial lines and a railway linking Kunming with Nanning in Guangxi. The latter will be finished before 1996 and is expected to bring about a modest breakthrough in the province's foreign trade as it will provide Yunnan with access to two seaports: Beihai and Fangcheng. In the following decade, the total length of railways in Yunnan will be increased from its present 1,684 kilometres to 2,390 kilometres.[23]

Major highways will be expanded and upgraded: the total length will be expanded from 50,000 kilometres at present to 70,000 kilometres by the year 2000. Six high-grade highways are targeted for completion by 1995, many of which will provide a link with the countries in the region. For example, the 800-kilometre long Yunnan–Burma Road, will run through Burma and connect Yunnan with India and Bangladesh; the 800-kilometre Kunming–Daluo Road will provide a link with both Burma and Thailand. Other examples are the road from Mengla to Laos' capital Vientiane, and the road to the Vietnamese border, Kunming–Hekou.[24]

Much attention is being paid to the improvement of water transport. This is primarily concerned with developing transport on the Lancanjiang (Mekong). Within the region, Yunnan is taking the leading role in developing shipping services on the Mekong between Jinghong in Xishuangbanna and Chiangrai in northern Thailand. As Chiangrai is a popular tourist destination, Yunnan expects that the realisation of the Mekong transport corridor will not only boost exports but also greatly expand tourism.[25] In order to coordinate activities and avoid conflicts, China, Laos, Burma and Thailand jointly established a Mekong Observation Group, that made proposals on the exploitation and utilisation of the Mekong in the areas of navigation, tourism, hydroelectricity and trade.

Special emphasis is to be placed on the construction and renovation of airports. The renovation of six airports will be completed by 1995 and two new airports, Lijiang and Dali, will be constructed. Furthermore, national and international air routes, especially to South-East and South Asia, will be increased. At present, international air routes include Bangkok, Singapore, Hong Kong, Rangoon and Vientiane; the first two yield a considerable reduction in the travelling time for people coming from South and South-West Asia and Europe.

Telecommunications is another weak point, especially outside Kunming. Progress in this field over the last few years was largely limited to Kunming where urban telephone exchanges have been expanded from 7,400 connections in 1985 to 48,000 connections at present, and the city has introduced advanced technologies such as programme-controlled telephone exchanges and optical-fibre transmission.[26] With a few exceptions, telecommunications with the border areas is troublesome or even totally impossible, thus constituting a deterrent to foreign investors.

Energy supply

Another obstacle to the swift development of industries is the energy supply. Although abundant energy can be produced in Yunnan, its distribution is not yet adequately developed. Nevertheless, Yunnan strives to become a major power supplier for the region. The production of electricity rose from 5.25 billion kWh in 1978 to 14.09 billion kWh in 1991. The development of the energy sector focuses on hydropower. In 1984, Yunnan initiated a national–provincial joint venture to develop power generation on the Lancanjiang and 1985 saw the beginning of the construction of the river's first big hydropower station: the Manwan Dam, located in Yunxian county. In June 1993, the first unit of the Manwan Power Station became operational and, in July, Yunnan began the supply of electricity to Guangdong.[27] When fully operational, Manwan will become the main supplier of energy to eastern China, where the rapid industrialisation has created an urgent demand.[28] It is estimated that Yunnan and Guizhou will transmit 1.1 million kW of electricity to Guangdong in 1995 and that in the year 2010, the two provinces together with Guangxi will transmit more than 20 million kW to the east annually.[29] Furthermore, Yunnan has begun work on the Jinghong power plant. This station, which will be run by foreign investors, aims to become the centre for navigation and electric power transmission to the Southeast Asian market, primarily Thailand which has already signed an agreement with Yunnan. As Thailand, according to some reports, already has to rely on its neighbours for up to 60 per cent of its energy supply, the market is practically guaranteed.[30] In all, Yunnan has planned 14 power stations for the Lancanjiang.[31] The next major project is the construction of the Xiaowan plant on the upper reaches of the Manwan, which will have a capacity of 4.2 million kW. The preliminary design is expected to be finished by 1995 and financing will be provided by Yunnan, Guangdong and the central government.[32]

The development of the energy sector is not limited solely to hydropower. Thermal power and coal production are growing in importance as well, and the province has designated the Zhaotong Nos 1, 2 and 3 power plants, currently scheduled for construction, to become another power-export base.[33]

It can be concluded that Yunnan has considerable economic potential, especially in agriculture-related industries (with the tobacco industry being the most important), and in the development of its natural and energy resources. These sectors could be developed not only into a prominent national, but also a South-east Asian regional base. However, to do so the province will have to surmount many obstacles, poor transport and lack of investment capital being the most pressing. To overcome these developmental bottlenecks, the Yunnan authorities have turned to foreign investors for the provision of both export opportunities and badly needed capital. Moreover, Yunnan has joined forces with other southwestern Chinese provinces in the Southwestern Cooperation Zone.

Southwestern Cooperation Zone

In 1984, the Southwestern Cooperation Zone was established. Initially, this zone consisted of the provincial-level administrations of Yunnan, Sichuan, Guangxi, Guizhou and Chengdu; later it was expanded to include Tibet and Chongqing. The idea behind this zone was to pool efforts and bring the attention of the central government, which at the time was focusing on the coastal area, to the common problems shared by its members. The other aims were to facilitate and coordinate cooperation in the areas of resources, technology, capital, technical and management expertise, business, transport and energy resources. In the beginning of the 1990s, some even argued for the conversion of the zone into a coordinated region for foreign trade and economy which could then compete with economic blocs such as ASEAN, South China (Guangdong/Hong Kong) and even NAFTA and the EU.[34] Although this seems far-fetched and the significance of the cooperation zone must not be overestimated, in actual practice it *does* facilitate the realisation of joint infrastructural projects and strengthen Yunnan's role in regional trade.

Beijing assigned to the zone the task of taking the lead in opening up the South-east Asian market. In mid-1992, the State Council decided that, from 1993 onwards, a large-scale export commodities fair targeted at the South-east Asian market would be organised every August. Chengdu and Kunming were the major contenders in the bid to host permanently the yearly event. The latter won the bid. With that, Kunming's position as the centre of the (new) Southern Silk Route was confirmed and the city can look forward to a boost in local investment and trade. It built an enormous trade centre in the outskirts near the airport and from 8–18 August 1993, the first Kunming Export Commodities Fair (KECF) was held. According to the first reports, business transactions during the fair resulted in $87 million worth in contracts actually signed and $96 million worth in tentative contracts.[35]

At this point, it is useful to scrutinise more closely the main indicator of Yunnan's integration with the neighbouring countries: foreign economic relations. This section begins with an outline of Yunnan's foreign trade and economic relations in general, and subsequently the focus shifts to the Asian region and border trade in particular.

YUNNAN'S FOREIGN ECONOMIC RELATIONS

Yunnan has a long tradition of foreign contacts and trade in the region. Its routes to Burma and Vietnam were important arteries of the Southern Silk Road which flourished in the early centuries AD. The same routes regained their prominence in the second half of the last century when Britain and France colonised Burma and Vietnam and saw great opportunities to turn Yunnan into a profitable hinterland. In the beginning of this century a French traveller wrote:

> Yunnan must be regarded as the necessary economic extension of our Indo-China: its fortress as well as its hospitals, its storehouse full of corn, barley, cattle, sheep, horses, and in general all the products of a moderate climate, and not forgetting the vast mining reserves open to our activities.

On their part, the Chinese authorities in Yunnan were also interested in trade and made purchases such as military equipment and wire telegraph technology from the French and the British. By the end of the 1880s, the French and British forced Yunnan into unequal treaties. This is not to say, however, that the province did not profit from the foreign presence. The French, for instance, made huge investments by setting up the Yunnan–Vietnamese Railway Company and building the Kunming–Hanoi railway. After its opening in 1910, trade developed quickly and foreign banks and consulates were opened in Kunming. Other investments, in particular in coal mining, followed, and soon the USA joined in as well. New communications and mining technologies were introduced, transport and industries developed and trade flourished.[36]

Yunnan's importance as a gateway to China continued throughout the first half of this century. During the war against the Japanese, when the coastal areas and shipping on the Yangzi were controlled by the enemy, Yunnan's Burma Road, officially opened in 1938, formed a crucial connection with the outside world. The road was used not only for transportation of merchandise but also for weapons supplied to the Kuomintang by the United States and Britain.

Table 11.4 Yunnan Province foreign trade[37]

	1980(a)	*1985(a)*	*1991(b)*	*1992(c)*
Total imports & exports				
(million US $)	110	210	757	965
Exports (million US $)	69	129	525	649
Border trade (million US $)		45	206	295
Exports (million US $)		21	124	182

Furthermore, thanks to its good prevailing weather conditions, Kunming airport played an important role in the supply of goods. In fact, Kunming served as the unofficial military capital of unoccupied China and also became a sort of intellectual centre, as more than 60,000 refugees, including many scholars and students, streamed into the city.[38]

After 1945, Yunnan's significance in foreign contacts disappeared quickly. Between 1949 and 1978, there was hardly any foreign trade in Yunnan. Simple barter trade among inhabitants in the border regions was negligible and the only foreign goods that reached Yunnan – technology and equipment from Russia and Eastern Europe – were distributed by the central government. It was not until 1978 that Yunnan started direct foreign trade again. Table 11.4 gives an overview of the development of foreign trade in the period 1980–92. In spite of rapid growth, it should be realised that in 1991, Yunnan's total of imports and exports was less than 0.5 per cent of the country's total.

At present, Yunnan exports to 67 countries and imports from 24 countries. Its main trading partners in 1992 were Burma (34 per cent), Hong Kong (22 per cent), Taiwan, Japan, the US, Singapore, and Thailand. Major export products include tobacco, nonferrous metals, chemicals, machinery, textiles and food products. Imports consist mainly of machinery for tobacco, packaging and textile industries, telecommunications equipment and medical appliances.

During the decade 1982–92, the composition of export commodities underwent a significant change. In the early 1980s, Yunnan's exports consisted mainly of agricultural products, whereas imports consisted mainly of electrical appliances and equipment. By 1992, the picture was completely reversed, something local leaders are very proud of. Now, thanks to the development of its industries, it is Yunnan which exports the more profitable industrial products and imports agricultural products.

Although Yunnan at present dumps a lot of cheap and low-quality

Table 11.5 Composition of Yunnan's exports[39]

	1986	1992
Agriculture and sideline products	36%	12%
Light industrial products	30%	46%
Heavy industrial products	34%	42%

products across the border (a situation arising from the combination of the rising living standards within the province and the underdevelopment of the surrounding external region), it eventually wants to focus on the more developed export markets. However, many of its high-quality export products are not (yet) suitable for the world market because packaging and design are still underdeveloped. Therefore, in Yunnan's search for new outlets, much attention will have to be given to the import of packaging and design equipment and know-how.

Foreign investment has been growing rapidly over the last two years. In 1992, a total of 202 new foreign-invested enterprises were given the approval to be set up in Yunnan; 142 of these concern industry and 27 concern real estate and service.[40] Foreign investment in industry is concentrated in the chemistry branch, bamboo processing, garment factories, tourism and hydropower. As table 11.7 below illustrates, the biggest investors in 1992 were Hong Kong, Taiwan, the USA, Burma and Thailand. By the end of 1992, there were 275 enterprises with foreign investment in the province. However, these growth rates should not hide the fact that, compared to the rest of the country and even to many of the other interior provinces, Yunnan's performance is poor with respect to attracting foreign contacts and capital. For example, in 1991 Yunnan's enterprises involving foreign capital made up only 0.18 per cent of China's total, ranking the province 25th; in the same year the amount of direct foreign investment in Yunnan accounted for 0.11 per cent of the country's total.[41] To attract more foreign capital, the local authorities, in line with current practice throughout China, are developing so-called 'cooperation zones' and wholesale centres, where foreign investors are granted the benefits of preferential policies.

Yunnan received three foreign economic aid projects: from the United Nations World Food Program (UNWFP) ($14 million), United Nations Development Project (UNDP) ($1.5 million) and the United Nations High Commissioner for Refugees (UNHCR) ($550,000) in 1992.[42]

Table 11.6 Foreign investment in Yunnan[43]

	1985(a)	1991(b)	1992(c)
Foreign contracts (number)	15	22	202
Contracted foreign capital (million US $)	18	26	234
Implemented foreign capital (million US $)	2	3	29
Contracted foreign loan (million US $)	—	34	98
Implemented foreign loan (million US $)	—	46	98

Table 11.7 Major direct foreign investors in Yunnan in 1992[44]

Country	No. of projects	Value (US $ million)
Hong Kong	101	100
Taiwan	49	37
USA	12	9
Burma	18	7
Thailand	5	5
Japan	5	2

In order to encourage foreign investment, the provincial government issued the 'Provisions of Yunnan Province for the Encouragement of Foreign Investment' in September 1992, which made provisions in the areas of taxation, supply of water, electricity and the utilisation of local raw materials.[45] Another recent encouragement was the announcement by the authorities in Beijing concerning the intention to open up part of its gold mines to foreign investors. The mines in Yunnan are thought to be a likely choice.[46]

Yunnan's capital Kunming is the economic and science and technology centre of the province. In 1992, it accounted for 40 per cent of the province's industrial output. The city's importance and potential as the centre of the so-called 'revived' Southern Silk Route has been recognised by Beijing. In 1992, the central government ratified the establishment of the Kunming Hi-tech Industrial Zone. The 12 square kilometre zone – the home of 150 industrial enterprises – will focus on biological engineering, new materials, electrical information and photoelectric-machinery industries; by the end of 1992, there were ten foreign-funded or joint venture projects in the zone with a committed foreign investment total of $29.6 million.[47] In addition, an economic and technological development zone on the provincial level, which will focus on export and advanced processing industries, was established in Kunming in May 1992. To date, 43 domestic and overseas firms with a total investment of $210 million, 16 of which are joint ventures with a combined investment of $57 million have moved to the zone. The hosting of the annual Export Commodities Fair of the Southwestern Region mentioned earlier, is another illustration of Kunming's pivotal position.

Border trade

The role of border and regional trade in the province's total foreign trade is steadily gaining importance. Furthermore, border and regional trade has been made a priority in Yunnan's current attempt to accelerate the development of an export-oriented economy. A much-used slogan in Yunnan is 'open up the southern gate and head for the Asia Pacific'. In early 1993, Yunnan's Governor He Zhiqiang put it this way:

> We should fully exploit the geographical advantage of Yunnan to open up markets in the Asia-Pacific region, develop large-scale trade and border trade simultaneously, and, through border trade, establish tens of thousands of enterprises which do both import and export business with foreign countries in the areas along the borderline, where a number of large, medium, and small power stations will be set up in five to six years, and electricity will be considered a major export commodity.[48]

The development of border trade is a result of both China's open door policy and the improvement of diplomatic relations with the neighbouring countries from the late 1980s onwards. Border trade took off in 1984, when 27 border districts were allowed to establish trading ties with their neighbours. Soon after, in December of the same year, the State Council approved the 'Provisional Regulations for the Management of "Small Volume" border trade', which gave practically full autonomy to local governments to conduct small-volume border trade.[49] They were followed on the provincial level by the promulgation in 1985 of the 'Yunnan Province Temporary Provisions on Border Trade'.[50] These and many local-level measures gave an enormous boost to the development of border trade, which in turn gave rise to the development of processing industry, trade in technology and information, joint ventures and direct foreign investment. However, the poverty and underdevelopment of Yunnan's direct neighbours, pose serious limits to the growth of border trade.

To date, there are 94 open cities and counties in Yunnan, constituting 74 per cent of the province's total area.[51] Since September

1992, 7 state-level (responsible to the central government) and 10 provincial-level (responsible to Yunnan provincial government) ports and 92 outlets have been established in Yunnan.[52] The most important ports are the state-level trading ports of Ruili and Wanding on the China–Burma border, Mengla on the China–Laos border and Hekou on the China–Vietnam border. The development of these ports will be examined later. In 1991, Yunnan's border trade ranked fourth in the country, after Heilongjiang, Guangxi and Inner Mongolia.

Trade between the border residents is facilitated by the fact that the people on both sides of the border often belong to the same minority group. They share the same language and customs, and marriages across the border are common. Local officials in many areas stress that, in spite of past problems in foreign relations on the national level, relations between the local residents on both sides of the border have always been close.

In Yunnan, the regulations on border trade are drawn up and implemented by the Provincial Government Border Trade Administration Office. However, precise details are left to local offices and the rules may differ from place to place. The same variation can be found in local preferential policies that have been created to attract investment. Kunming, Ruili and Wanding enjoy the same preferential policies as the cities in the open coastal areas. According to the official regulations, people must carry an entry and exit pass when crossing the border. These passes have been issued to all border residents and are available to non-border residents upon application. Apart from Hekou, which is a so-called international port, people from a third country cannot cross the border through state-level ports in Yunnan, which of course is a negative factor in the development of regional trade and tourism. According to local officials, this restriction is imposed by the other parties, that is Burma and Laos.[53] Another obstacle is the fact that, at present, investors from a third country cannot directly engage in border trade. Their participation is limited to the setting up of joint ventures or cooperation projects.

A few remarks on the statistics of border trade are necessary here. These statistics are not likely to give a full picture of all transactions across the border. In the first place, the small-scale free trade between border residents is not included in the statistics; secondly, Yunnan's border extends over 4,061 kilometres and is impossible to control completely. It is known that a growing volume of goods passes the border without being registered. The problem of smuggling is recognised by the local governments and primarily involves drugs, cars and home appliances.[54] In most border ports in Yunnan, the import of cars is prohibited or otherwise subject to high taxation. Despite efforts by the local authorities to fight smuggling, the number of cases is on the increase. Cars are brought in illegally from Thailand, Burma and Laos. It is, for example, reported that Chinese buyers cross the border and head for the northern market town of Muong Hay where they can select from hundreds of vehicles.[55] The issue of drug smuggling will be treated separately.

YUNNAN'S RELATIONS WITH THE EXTERNAL REGION

Mekong subregion

Although Yunnan's activities in expanding its foreign trade have up to now been focused on cross-border trade with Burma, Vietnam and Laos and on establishing links with Thailand, the province and Beijing have more ambitious plans. It is their intention to link up various parts of Yunnan with the whole of South-east Asia. For example, eastern Dehong Prefecture has been assigned to establish, via Burma, trading links with Bangladesh, India and Pakistan; southern Xishuangbanna Prefecture, via Burma and Laos, links with Thailand, Malaysia and Singapore.

Presently, much of Yunnan's attention is aimed at the promotion of the Mekong subregion, which comprises all six Mekong nations (China, Burma, Laos, Thailand, Cambodia and Vietnam), and the Mekong growth quadrangle which includes parts of Yunnan, Burma, Laos and Thailand. The latter is often referred to as the Golden Quadrangle but Chinese officials do not seem to like this name as it suggests associations with the drug-producing Golden Triangle.[56] For all six countries, the Mekong offers the potential of hydropower, transport and irrigation. However, the issue of conflicting interests will have to be dealt with. Hydropower projects in one country may well affect irrigation systems or the environment in a neighbouring country. For example, Thailand has plans for large-scale irrigation projects using water from the Mekong, whereas the Vietnamese Mekong delta, which is vital to the country's rice production, already experiences water shortage in the dry season.[57] Thus, a thorough coordination of projects is necessary and potential dangers make countries like Laos and Vietnam wary of hasty action.

In August 1993, the six countries met at the Second Conference on Subregional Economic Cooperation held at the Asian Development

Bank (ADB) Headquarters in Manila. The conference was also attended by representatives of organisations such as the United Nations Development Programme (UNDP), the Economic and Social Commission for Asia and the Pacific (ESCAP), and the Mekong Secretariat. The discussions focused on subregional cooperation in the areas of transport, energy, environment, human resource development, trade and investment, and tourism, and resulted in a prioritised list of transport development projects, to be coordinated by the ADB. Three of the five projects on the list involve Yunnan: the Chiangrai–Kunming Highway via Burma, the Kunming–Chiangrai Highway via Laos, and the Kunming–Lashio (Burma) Highway via Dali. The ADB aimed to round off feasibility studies on these road projects in the first half of 1994.[58]

The fact that it has already provided much investment and loans for the reconstruction of major roads across its borders in Burma and Laos, which in turn will link Yunnan with Thailand, illustrates China as one of the most enthusiastic promoters of Mekong subregional cooperation. Furthermore, China proves a strong advocate of making the Mekong navigable for commercial traffic that could transport Yunnan's export products as far downstream as Thailand. This would require dynamiting rapids, dredging, and setting up loading and unloading facilities. However, the smaller Mekong nations and Laos in particular, being apprehensive of China's ambitions, placed the project on a second list for further study and discussion.[59]

In the last few years China has made efforts to restore and improve foreign relations within the area and settle border disputes with its neighbours. Nevertheless, China is viewed by many as a threat to the region's security. They fear that China is seeking political as well as economic domination and has strategic goals in mind.[60] These claims are encouraged by Chinese actions, such as assisting Burma in building naval facilities.[61] Furthermore, many of the Mekong nations have already incurred trade deficits with China.

Yunnan's relations with Thailand

Links with Thailand – the most developed nation in the vicinity – hold a great attraction for Yunnan. Thailand is the only member of the Mekong growth quadrangle which can provide Yunnan with the much-needed investment capital and technology. In this respect, Thailand can play a role for Yunnan similar to that of Hong Kong for Guangdong. Thailand and China established regular political,

economic and military ties after 1978 and relations have been rather
stable ever since.

The interest in economic cooperation in the Mekong subregion is
mutual.[62] Both sides see opportunities in expanding their tourist
industry and exports via the Mekong transport corridor. In this
respect, Thailand has not only Yunnan but also the populous province of Sichuan in its sights. Although at present investment in
Yunnan makes up only a small percentage of its total investment in
China, Thailand considers the province important enough to have
opened a consulate in Kunming in 1993. In addition, Thailand is
the first foreign country to establish a commercial bank in Kunming.[63] Furthermore, it hopes to benefit from the lower wages in
Yunnan by relocating its factories and creating a new market for its
technology, and services industry. Finally, Thailand is interested in
Yunnan's energy resources and will be the first foreign destination of
the province's export of hydroelectricity.

Basically, there are two routes between China and Thailand: one
through Laos and one through Burma. Both routes pose their specific
problems. The road through Laos is made difficult by the terrain and
the notorious Laotian bureaucracy; the road through Burma which
runs through the Burmese area bordering southwest Yunnan is still
under control of rebellious minority groups. For example, the area
west of Daluo in Xishuangbanna, is under the control of the Wa tribe
that charges transit fees. Nevertheless, the northern Thai tourist
town of Chiangrai, expressed interest in cooperation with the
Xishuangbanna and Simao prefectures and has already approached
Burma with respect to a road link from the Thai–Burmese border
town of Mae Sai to the Chinese–Burmese border town of Daluo.[64] In
spite of the problems posed by Burmese rebel groups, it is expected
that by 1995–96, there will be a highway between the Thai–Burmese
border and Daluo, a regular boat service on the Mekong between
Jinghong and Chiang Saen–Chiang Khong, extending to Vientiane
and an improved road from Yunnan through Luang Nam Tha to the
Mekong.[65] In the summer of 1993, Thailand and China signed an
agreement to start dredging the Mekong River.[66]

On the other hand, doubts are being voiced in Thailand: some
worry that improved connections will lead to a flood of cheap
Chinese goods into northern Thailand, including low-priced consumer goods as well as onions, garlic and fruit.[67] Others worry
about a further increase of activities such as illegal labour, the
smuggling of migrants via Thailand into the US and the smuggling
and selling of Chinese women into prostitution in Thailand. Some

estimate that there are already more than 10,000 illegal Chinese workers in Thailand and that, since 1989, about 5,000 Chinese women, mostly from small villages in southwestern China, have been sold as prostitutes into Thai brothels.[68]

Yunnan's relations with Burma

China became one of the first countries to establish close ties with the Burmese State Law and Order Restoration Council (SLORC) after the latter assumed power in September 1988. Subsequently, Beijing reversed its policy towards the Burmese rebel groups it had supported for decades. It dropped financial and military aid to groups such as the Communist Party of Burma (CPB) and compelled them to enter into an agreement with Rangoon. This resulted in a pacified area along the Burma road and direct trade links with Rangoon instead of with the rebel groups.

The close alliance is favourable for both sides. China provides the isolated Burmese regime with political support, economic aid, infrastructure, military assistance and weapons. Burma provides China with strategic links with South-east Asia and the Indian Ocean, a market for its weapons and cheap consumer goods, and resources such as jade and timber. However, despite increased cooperation, the growing Chinese influence in Burma is met with resentment from the Burmese population. In some parts of Burma the Chinese economic presence is very strong and, for example, a number of residents of Mandalay already refer to their city as 'China Town'. This resentment may impede the future development of Yunnan's relations with Burma. Furthermore, many countries in the Asia–Pacific region, especially India, which considers the Bay of Bengal its strategic backyard, and Japan, are apprehensive of China's growing influence on the regime in Rangoon which could turn Burma into a Chinese satellite.[69]

The good bilateral relations are reflected in close contacts on the provincial level. Visits from the Burmese side to Yunnan include provincial and commercial delegations as well as state-level visits. For example, in February 1993, Burma sent a deputy minister to attend a meeting held in Kunming on the opening up of the south-western region of the PRC to the outside world.[70]

Yunnan plays an important role in China's trade with Burma. In 1992, the province's trade with Burma constituted more than 80 per cent of the trade of the country as a whole.[71] Mutual investment is on the increase and both sides cooperate in ventures involving the extraction of manganese ore, coal and teak and the construction of roads and even a new international airport near Mandalay.[72] Another area of cooperation is health services. For example in April 1993, the Burmese Vice-Minister of Public Health paid a visit to Yunnan to discuss cooperation in the field of reducing the incidence of contagious diseases.[73] At the moment, however, further development is hampered by Burma's lack of capital, lack of infrastructure, poor investment climate, high taxes and political and economic isolation.

Sino-Burmese border trade

With a share of more than 90 per cent of the province's total border trade volume, Burma is by far Yunnan's most important border trade partner. For Burma the proportion of this border trade is even more outstanding: China's border trade with Burma represents a third to half of Burma's total foreign trade.[74] An important reason for the smooth development of bilateral trade is the fact that the prices of Chinese commodities are considerably lower than those on the world market. Furthermore, Burma has no means of processing its raw materials such as timber, jade, and other precious stones. A very lucrative business for Burma is the motor vehicle transit trade. In the first half of 1993, Burma is reported to have earned $ 0.5 a million from allowing cars to transit from Thailand to China.[75] Although border trade between the two countries commenced in 1984, Burma only legalised it by the end of 1988. In 1989, the Governor of Yunnan visited Burma and signed an agreement for the opening of department stores and the marketing of Chinese goods in Burma. In the last few years, simple barter trade with Burma has advanced to cash trade and the exchange of technology and services. Exports make up 70 per cent of trade and include textiles, small household items, electrical appliances, building materials and machinery. Yunnan's imports from Burma consist mainly of cotton, foodstuffs, wood, jade and aquatic products.

More than 80 per cent of Yunnan's trade with Burma goes through Dehong Prefecture, which also used to be the main corridor of the Southern Silk Route. In addition, the Burma (Stillwell) Road crosses the prefecture. Of all Chinese prefectures on the Sino-Burmese border, Dehong has the best transportation connections with Burma and borders, importantly, with an area under control by Burma's official authorities, the State Law and Order Restoration Council (SLORC). Other areas, for example Xishuangbanna on the border,

Table 11.8 Border trade with Burma via Wanding and Ruili (in million yuan)[76]

Year	Wanding	Ruili
1984	10	22
1985	38	45
1987	100	200
1989	233	340
1991	271	600
1992	279	770
Jan–June 1993	115 (−29%)	480 (+ 20%)

are still in the hands of rebellious minority groups, a fact which seriously hampers transport and trade.

Trade in Dehong is mostly handled by two state-level ports, Wanding and Ruili. Foreign investment in these ports comes from Burma, Singapore, the Philippines, Thailand, Hong Kong and Taiwan, bearing testimony to the extent of Asian interests in this area. Both Ruili and Wanding obtained approval from the State Council in 1992 to set up a national-level 'cooperation zone', but Beijing's concrete support is limited to a loan of 10 million *yuan* to each city, whereas many hundreds of millions of *yuan* are needed to develop the basic infrastructure alone. In addition, Ruili is developing the Jiegao Border Trade and Economic Experimental Zone, which is expected to become a major channel between Yunnan and Burma. The zone, which has a surface of 3.4 square kilometres, is surrounded by Burma on three sides. Jiegao is an experimental zone and will focus on bonded warehousing and the service sector, whereas in the cooperation zones, industries will be developed.

Of growing significance is Dehong Prefecture's flourishing tourist industry, which is concentrated in Ruili. Every day, more than 1,000 Chinese tourists from all over the country make a day trip to the Burmese border town of Nankan. These trips are organised by several travel agencies in Ruili that cooperate closely with the Burmese side. The Chinese tourists, ironically, buy Chinese electrical appliances which happen to be cheaper on the Burmese side of the border.

In addition to the official merchandise, a number of other commodities, such as weapons and drugs, cross the Yunnan–Burmese border. The weapons are exported by the Chinese government and form part of the Sino-Burmese military cooperation, while drugs are smuggled in from Burma. These factors pose a thorny issue on China's relations within the Asian region.

Drugs and weapons

There are numerous reports on military cooperation between the
SLORC and the Chinese military. This cooperation includes weapon
manufacturing (for example in Mergui), weapon trade and joint
military exercises. In October 1989, China and Burma allegedly
signed an arms deal of $1.2–1.4 billion.[77] In exchange for Chinese
military assistance, Burma imports Chinese household goods, allows
Chinese businesses to be set up in Burma, allows the Chinese to
extract natural resources from Kachin State, and, according to some
reports, refuelling facilities or even the entire use of a naval installation.[78] Furthermore, Burma and China signed an agreement in
January 1993 to construct three major highways from Yunnan to
Kachin State. These highways will not only stimulate trade but are
primarily of military importance. Many observers suspect that Burma
pays for Chinese weapons with drug money.[79]

For the past few years, southern China has become a much-used
smuggling route to Hong Kong for drugs originating from the Golden
Triangle. Yunnan's hilly areas, with over sixty major border-crossing
routes used by the local population, are beyond both governments'
control and drug barons have slowly intensified infiltration into
China. Their initial aim was to set up a drug route from Yunnan to
Hong Kong by which Western markets could be reached. Soon,
however, the South-East Asian drug business as a whole, including
production and sale, was extended northward into China and Yunnan
was opened up as a new market. This development coincided with a
shift of Burma's major drug producing area from the southern border
with Thailand to the northeastern Kokang area, bordering Yunnan,
where a new chain of refineries was established. Many of the drug
barons in this area are of Chinese descent or belonged to the
Communist Party of Burma (CPB), which used to cooperate with
Chinese security authorities in the border area. Some of them still
have good relations with Chinese border officials, enabling them to
cross the border in spite of the official prohibition.[80]

Drugs are not an entirely new phenomenon in the province. Before
1949, poppy growing was widespread in Yunnan and in Dehong
Prefecture in particular, but both drug production and drug abuse
were claimed to have been eradicated in the early 1950s. At present,
drugs are becoming a major social problem again. According to
official sources, the Yunnan authorities seized 4,075 kilogrammes
of drugs in 1992, a rise of 152 per cent over 1991, uncovered
3,643 trafficking cases and arrested over 5,000 traffickers. The actual

number of drug addicts in Yunnan Province, where intravenous use of heroin dominates, is unknown. Chinese sources reported that 23,515 addicts gave up drug abuse in 1992 after taking part in short-term rehabilitation courses. As the same report stated that in 1992, the number of drug addicts was reduced by 38 per cent, this would mean that the province had more than 58,000 registered drug addicts by the end of 1991.[81] According to another report of the Yunnan authorities, the number of officially registered addicts in the province, has decreased from 45,000 in 1991 to 36,000 in 1992.[82] However, as these data omit unregistered addicts, for example those living in remote villages, they do not reveal the real magnitude of the problem. A 1990 survey with 319 samples in an unindentified city in the province, found that 20 per cent of the drug users came from cadre families, 47 per cent from working families and 10 per cent were farmers.[83]

The province claims that the success in reducing drug addiction, can be attributed to the 'war against drugs' it launched in 1990 and the development of rehabilitation programmes. In fact, Yunnan already set up an anti-drug apparatus in 1982 and was the first Chinese province to do so.[84] Heavy punishment awaits drug criminals and, in serious cases, the death penalty. For example, in 1991 at least 277 drug traffickers were executed and in 1992 and 1993 there have been numerous, often public, mass executions of people who were involved in drug-related crimes.[85]

The social consequences of the drug trade and drug abuse include a rise in corruption, crime and cases of AIDS. In Dali Prefecture, more than 80 per cent of the crimes committed in 1990 were reported to be committed by drug addicts.[86] The widespread intravenous use of heroin in Yunnan has led to a high concentration of AIDS cases in Yunnan and in the Sino-Burmese border town of Ruili in particular. By the end of 1993, there were 885 registered cases of HIV-infection in Yunnan.[87] China recognised the necessity of international cooperation on AIDS and AIDS-related issues and signed agreements with Thailand, Burma and the United Nations. In 1992, Burma and China established close cooperative arrangements in anti-narcotics activities, including the exchange of information on drug trafficking and related activities along the common borders, training of drug enforcement personnel and transfer of technology.[88] A subregional cooperation accord was signed by China, Burma, Thailand and the UN International Drug Control Programme (UNDCP), stipulating the sharing of intelligence information, the encouragement of alternative crop cultivation, joint training of personnel and coordinated

enforcement activity on drug abuse and AIDS education for minority groups living in mountain areas, and a supply of vehicles and communication equipment for law enforcement through the UNDCP.[89] In September 1992, Kunming hosted a United Nations-sponsored conference on AIDS.[90]

As events in Pingyuan in August 1992 demonstrate, the increasing drug trade in Yunnan is not only a social problem but has a political dimension as well. The local government of the remote southern town of Pingyuan, already well known in Yunnan for its intractability, was deeply involved in the drug trade and other forms of criminality, and in order to protect its interests had organised a local army. Their criminal networks expanded across Yunnan's international borders, and Pingyuan, behaving like an independent state, challenged provincial and national authorities. After several failed attempts to regain control over the area, the Chinese government decided to launch a large-scale attack. In the summer of 1992, China's paramilitary police needed three months of battling with Pingyuan's guerrillas before it was able to break up the drug gangs and restore order.[91]

There are more reports that suggest involvement of local cadres in the drug trade.[92] Not all government officials will be able to resist the temptation of sharing the new wealth of legitimate and illegitimate traders.[93] As noted before, it is often rumoured that Burma's SLORC, descendants of KMT refugees in Burma and Yunnan officials cooperate closely with the opium traders.[94] Some argue that, given the enormous scope of drug trafficking inside China, official complicity cannot be limited to just local border security officers.[95]

Yunnan's relations with Laos

Bilateral contacts between China and Laos have been hostile for decades. The two countries restored diplomatic relations in 1987 and have only recently settled their border disputes.[96] Thus business relations between China and Laos developed relatively late, but a promising start has been made. China is not only interested in Laos as a trade partner but also, or maybe even primarily, as a corridor to Thailand. Furthermore, it is in China's interest to counterbalance Vietnam's influence in Laos.

Most border trade with Laos takes place via Mengla (Mohan), located in Xishuangbanna Autonomous Prefecture, which was only opened as a provincial-level port in 1992. Border trade via Mengla totalled 35 million *yuan* in 1991, and increased to 104 million *yuan* in

1992.[97] China's activities in Laos vary greatly and are not limited to trade. By the end of 1992, PRC businesses had won bids for construction projects worth $45 million and were involved in 13 investment projects in Laos worth $19 million. Furthermore, over 30 PRC companies have sent some 200 personnel on study tours in Laos.[98] For example, China is involved in a joint survey to build a hydroelectric dam and in the construction of a small hydroelectric power station. It is engaged in livestock raising and irrigation projects. In addition, China has set up factories, built garages, houses and hotels in Laos.[99] Yunnan is actively involved in many of these projects. Both sides opened air routes and started utilising the Mekong as a means of developing waterway transport services, although as noted above, Laos is wary of any rash action by China.

In April 1994, a new bridge over the Mekong, connecting Laos and Thailand, opened to traffic. The bridge is considered a key link in an emerging network of roads connecting Yunnan and South-east Asia. In 1996, an asphalt road will extend from Yunnan to the bridge leaving only the notorious Laotian border formalities as the obstacle in the passage through Laos.[100]

Contacts between the two countries, especially on the local level, are on the increase, often validated by official agreements. For example, in early June 1993, a memorandum on economic cooperation in various fields and the protection of the Laotian–Chinese border was signed in Xishuangbanna.[101] A few weeks later, the Laotian Ministry of Trade sent a ministerial delegation to Yunnan, to hold consultations on the implementation of bilateral cooperation. In August, two delegations from the Laotian border districts paid a 15-day visit to Xishuangbanna and Kunming in order to consolidate and expand the relations at the local level between the two countries.[102] However, the significant position of Yunnan in bilateral relations is perhaps best illustrated by the 5-day visit of Laos' Foreign Minister, Somsavat Lengsavat, to the province in spring 1993.[103] Furthermore, Laos was the first foreign country that opened a consulate in Kunming.

Nevertheless, there are major obstacles to a smooth development of trade between the two countries. One of the most obvious obstacles, the underdevelopment of Laos' communications and transport sectors, was also emphasised by Vice-Premier and Foreign Minister Qian Qichen during his visit to Laos in early 1993.[104] Further obstacles are poverty and trade and transit restrictions on the Laotian side, the latter mainly affecting trade with Thailand. For example, officials in Mengla complain of unpaid accounts. Finally, Laos is apprehensive of the increasing foreign presence. It worries that by opening up too fast, it may lose control of its economy and rich timber and mineral resources and, on the other hand, that it will become merely a transit route.[105]

Yunnan's relations with Vietnam

Although relations between Vietnam and China were officially normalised in 1989, they are still strained by a number of factors. It was only 15 years ago that the two countries fought a short but bloody border war. A second source of tension is derived from the territorial sea conflicts: both sides disagree on official demarcations of the border in the Tonkin Gulf region, and both sides claim the Paracels and the Spratly archipelago. A third issue, discrimination against ethnic Chinese in Vietnam, which used to be a constant source of irritation for Beijing, has diminished in importance but could flare up again. On top of this, the Vietnamese harbour historically motivated suspicions of Chinese intentions in their dealings with Vietnam.

From the beginning of this century until 1942, especially after the French had built the Sino-Vietnamese railway, foreign trade was booming in what today is the Honghe Prefecture, which borders Vietnam. In 1930, the Chinese border town of Hekou had 90 trade houses including 5 foreign companies and a French consulate. China imported cotton yarn, kerosene and exported *cilang*, brown sugar and medicinal materials. On 24 October 1942, however, the Japanese bombed Hekou and trade virtually stopped. After the establishment of the PRC, trade resumed for a while. For example, in 1954 more than 82,000 border crossings were registered and the amount of trade was valued at 937,000 yuan. In 1955, however, Vietnam started to reform its trade and introduced a state monopoly on purchase and marketing, after which trade decreased swiftly. In 1957, bilateral trade was dealt a further blow when Vietnam prohibited small retailers from engaging in border trade and China followed suit. Only small-scale daily barter trade between border residents continued until 1978, when relations between Vietnam and China were virtually frozen. In 1985, border crossing resumed, and only in 1989, after the normalisation of Sino-Vietnamese relations, China started to prepare for the full-scale restoration of border trade. China sent various investigative missions to Vietnam and trade between the two neighbours gradually resumed.

Almost all trade between Yunnan and Vietnam is conducted through Hekou, which became a national-level port in 1992 and which is the province's only so-called international border port, which means that people from a third country are allowed to cross the border. In the same year, the railway from Kunming to Hekou was restored, providing the border area with a vital connection to the rest of the province. According to local officials, China would like to see the railway connected with Hanoi and Haiphong again, and although Vietnam recently restored a vital part of its section of Haiphong–Kunming railway line, it remains very hesitant to allow the Chinese use of it.

Situated relatively close to the Vietnamese sea harbour of Haiphong and with a railway connection to Kunming at hand, the development of Hekou as a border port has potential; more so given the growing Western interest in Vietnam, which will only increase now that the US embargo has been lifted. However, after September 1992, Yunnan's trade with Vietnam started to diminish, a trend which continued into the first half of 1993. According to Chinese officials at the border, this negative trend is partly due to the Vietnamese side. The large quantities of Chinese merchandise that began to flood the North Vietnamese market were perceived to damage Vietnamese enterprises and infant industries. On 16 October 1992, Vietnam imposed restrictions on the import of 17 categories of Chinese merchandise, including bicycles, textiles and beer.[106] The Vietnamese also limited their exports of rice and copper to China and stopped entrepot trade through Vietnam, the latter mainly affecting Yunnan's trade with third countries.[107] On the other hand, as total foreign trade between China and Vietnam, as well as Guangxi's border trade with Vietnam have only been on the increase, Yunnan must be responsible for the fall in trade as well. A major reason could be that since Hekou became a national port and established a customs office, trade was hampered by all kinds of regulations. The port has, for instance, imposed more than 77 different fees. Added to the fact that Hekou is located in a hilly area which limits the development of basic facilities such as storage space, this might have prompted potential

Table 11.9 Border trade of Hekou[108]

	Value (in million yuan)
1989	0.03
1990	0.06
1991	132
1992	141
1993 (Jan–June)	60

314   *Ingrid d'Hooghe*

investors to shift their attention to Guangxi. However, the visit Vietnamese President Le Duc Anh paid to Kunming in November 1993, could be interpreted as a sign that Vietnam is still interested in close economic cooperation with Yunnan.[109] In comparison, Guangxi's trade with Vietnam in 1992 totalled 2.6 billion yuan.[110]

CONCLUSIONS

Yunnan, as China's southwestern overland gateway, has undoubtedly opportunities to develop trade with South and South-east Asia. Transport to nearby countries in the region, whether by rail, road, water or air is being improved at a fast pace. Kunming is closer to foreign harbours such as Rangoon in Burma and Haiphong in Vietnam than it is to major domestic harbours such as Shanghai or Guangzhou. Even more importantly, in some cases it is cheaper to export via its own borders than via Guangdong.[111] Furthermore, apart from being a trade corridor to and from China, Yunnan has the potential to develop into a significant base for energy production – a factor which has already attracted regional attention – and for processing natural resources, both its own and those of its neighbours, particularly Burma. In general, Yunnan's outward-looking policy has led to modest successes, judging from the increasing number of regional leaders visiting Yunnan and the number of treaties and contracts that have been signed.

An examination of border trade illustrates that Yunnan's relations with its neighbours are in some ways almost the reverse of, for example, those of Guangdong with Hong Kong, Fujian with Taiwan or Shandong with South Korea. Laos, Burma and Vietnam are all much poorer and less developed than Yunnan. Thus, it is primarily Yunnan which invests across the border, Yunnan which is engaged in the construction of infrastructure and Yunnan which exports services and technology. That Yunnan is willing to do so points to its confidence in its economic position within the region. In return, it has obtained road and water connections with the more developed parts of South-east Asia, raw materials, and a market for its products.

This being the case, it is also clear that the external region's underdevelopment is one of Yunnan's biggest comparative disadvantages in the further development of foreign trade. The province is already experiencing difficulties in financing its own infrastructural projects, let alone raising enough capital to develop Burma and Laos as well. In spite of all the ongoing construction, transport and telecommunications will remain inadequate in the years to come.

Furthermore, where Yunnan is already suffering from a serious lack of trained personnel, managers as well as technicians and officials, it also does not have much to gain from its neighbours with respect to the transfer of knowledge and the exchange of experts. Finally, the respective foreign policies of Yunnan's neighbours are characterised by a lack of openness to the outside world. This constitutes a negative impact on integration and on the development of foreign trade in the region as a whole.

As far as China's foreign policy is concerned, China has given more attention to the Asian region from the early 1990s, as reflected in the restoration of ties with Vietnam in 1989, and with Indonesia and Singapore in 1990. Furthermore, there has been an increasing number of reciprocal visits by various heads of governments in the region, including countries that are important to Yunnan, such as Thailand, Burma and Laos and Vietnam. Although this shift is more a result of China's intention to gain dominance in the region than of Yunnan's aim to link up with its neighbours, it does serve both purposes. Yunnan's economic significance is (still) too small to exert influence on China's foreign affairs. On the contrary, it seems more likely that Yunnan's opening up to South-east Asia is merely one of China's vehicles to achieve its desired key position in the region. This explains why, during recent visits to and from countries like Vietnam, Laos, Burma and Thailand, the issue of regional cooperation with Yunnan Province was always brought up.[112]

The Chinese government will have a hard job intensifying relations with its southeastern neighbours. Although the latter do have an interest in a certain level of economic cooperation, they are at the same time wary of political and economic dominance by their big neighbour. This is particularly true for Vietnam which harbours political suspicions of Chinese activities in the region and strongly opposes the practice of dumping by the Chinese. The same kind of suspicions have been voiced by other countries in the Asia–Pacific region, and these sentiments may lead to anti-Chinese sentiments, which would not be conducive to regional integration.

All things considered, in spite of references to rapid increases in trade and cooperation with other countries in the region and the 'growth quadrangle', and cooperative projects such as in the fight against drugs, it would be premature to speak of Yunnan's 'regional integration' with South-east Asia. In the first place, the volume of trade between Yunnan and South-east Asia and the amount of foreign investment from the region still make up only a small part of Yunnan's total foreign trade and investment. Secondly, given the current poverty and closedness of its neighbours as described above, the growth of regional trade will, for the years to come, certainly have its limits. Finally, the development of Yunnan's regional trade depends to a great extent on the development of foreign relations with the region on the central level. At present, bilateral political relations with Yunnan's neighbours are still too immature, too precarious and too restricted to enable a sustained growth and ensure a smooth integration.

This is not to say, however, that Yunnan will not integrate with the South-east Asian region, but to what extent and how fast this will happen, depends as much on Beijing and all countries concerned as on Yunnan's own efforts.

NOTES

The author is grateful to the Koninklijke Nederlandse Academie voor Wetenschappen (Royal Netherlands Academy of Arts and Sciences) and the Chinese Academy of Social Sciences, especially the Yunnan branch, for financial support and assistance for the research trip in Yunnan.

1 Figures for 1991. Source: Yunnansheng tongjiju, *Yunnan tongji nianjian 1992* (Yunnan Statistical Yearbook 1992) Zhongguo tongji chubanshe 1992, p. 97.
2 Yunnansheng tongjiju, *Yunnan sishi nian* (Yunnan's Forty Years) Zhongguo tongji chubanshe 1989, p. 19.
3 For example, in the previous century, the big Muslim Uprising in Yunnan in 1855, which spread to Miao tribes and religious sects, only to be quelled in 1873; for minority resistance or rebellion after 1949 see Dorothy J. Solinger, *Regional Government and Political Integration in Southwest China, 1949–1954* (Berkeley: University of California Press 1977), for the mid-1950s see *China News Analysis* (hereafter called *CNA*), No. 159, and for ethnic unrest after the Fall of the Gang of Four, see Wang Hsiao-hsien, 'The turmoil in Yunnan: 1976–1977', *Issues and Studies* (hereafter *I & S*), Vol. 13, No. 12 (1977), pp. 41–52.
4 Li Zhong, 'Yunnon sheng pinkun diqu renkou suzhi wenti tanqiu' (Investigation into the problem of quality [of life] of the population in Yunnan's poor areas), *Yunnan jiaoyu xueyuan xuebao*, Vol. 9, No. 3 (June 1993), p. 52. These are situated in the northwest, bordering Burma and Tibet Province, and in the south, bordering Vietnam.
5 He Zhiqiang, 'Renzhen zongjie lishi jingyan, shixian wending xietiao fazhan – Yunnan jingji gongzuo de huigu yu zhanwang' (Earnestly summing up our historical experience and accomplishing a stable and coordinated development – review and prospect of Yunnan's economic work), *Yunnan shehui kexue*, 1992, No. 1, pp. 1–9.
6 *Yunnan sishi nian*, p. 4.
7 Sources: *Yunnan sishi nian* and *Yunnan tongji nianjian, 1992*.
8 He Zhiqiang, *op. cit.*, p. 1.

9 Sources: figures of 1978, 1985 and 1991: *Yunnan tongji nianjian*, 1992; figures of 1992: 24 April 1993, p. 1.
10 *Yunnan ribao* (hereafter *YNRB*), 24 April 1993, p. 1
11 *Yunnan tongji nianjian 1992*, p. 33.
12 *YNRB*, 24 April 1993, p. 1
13 *Yunnan sishi nian*, p. 15.
14 Source: *Yunnan tongji nianjian 1992*.
15 He Zhiqiang, *op. cit.*, p. 3.
16 *Yunnan tongji nianjian 1992*, p. 23. However, the annual growth rate decreased after 1988; see *Yunnan sishi nian*, p. 27.
17 He Zhiqiang, *op. cit.*, p. 3
18 *BBC Summary of World Broadcasts* (hereafter *SWB*), FE/W 0277, 14 April 1993.
19 *US Foreign Broadcast Information Service* (hereafter *FBIS*), CHI–93–045, 10 March 1993, p. 66.
20 Sources: figures for 1980, 1985 and 1990: *Yunnan tongji nianjian 1992*; concerning 1992: *YNRB*, 20 March 1993, p. 1.
21 *Yunnan Supplement by China Daily*, 30 July 1993 (hereafter *Supplement*); and information provided by the Yunnan International Trade Research Institute.
22 *YNRB*, 24 April 1993, p. 3.
23 *FBIS*, CHI–93–145, 30 July 1993, p. 45
24 He Zhiqiang, *op. cit.*
25 E.C. Chapman and Peter Hinton, 'The Emerging Mekong Corridor: A Note on Recent Developments (to May 1993)', *Thai–Yunnan Project Newsletter* (hereafter *TYPN*), No. 21 (June 1993), pp. 12–16.
26 *SWB*, FE/W0273, A/5, 17 March 1993.
27 *SWB*, FEW/0301, W6/4, 29 September 1993.
28 *JPRS*, CEN–93–010, 5 November 1993, p. 28. The Manwan Power Station was the first large power station built jointly by the central government – the former Ministry of Hydroelectricity – and a province instead of solely by the central government. *Supplement* and *SWB*, FE/W0276, A/3, 7 April 1993.
29 *SWB*, FEW/0301 WG/4, 29 September 1993.
30 E.C. Chapman and Peter Hinton, *op. cit.*
31 *Ibid.*
32 *SWB*, FE/W0290, A/3, 14 July 1993.
33 *JPRS*, CEN–93–010, 5 November 1993, p. 28.
34 Han Shilong, 'Shilun jianli da xinan duiwai jingji maoyi xiezuoqu' (Essay on the establishment of the big southwestern cooperation zone of foreign economic relations and trade). *Yunnan shehui kexue 1990*, No. 4, pp. 26–31.
35 *SWB*, FEW/0299, 15 March 1993, W6/7
36 Chen Xi, 'Shilun jinxiandai yunnande waizi liyong he jishu yinjin' (Essay on contemporary Yunnan's use of foreign capital and import of technology), *Yunnan shehui kexue 1989*, No. 5, pp. 47–54.
37 Sources: (a) *Yunnan tongji nianjian 1992*; (b) Zhongguo duiwai jingji maoyi nianjian bianji weiyuanhui, *Zhongguo duiwai jingji maoyi nianjian* (Almanac of China's Foreign Economic Relations and Trade 1992), Beijing: Zhongguo chubanshe 1992 (hereafter *Almanac 1992*); (c)

318   *Ingrid d'Hooghe*

The Editorial Board of the Almanac of China's Foreign Economic Relations and Trade, *Almanac of China's Foreign Economic Relations and Trade 1993/4*, Beijing: Zhongguo chubanshe 1993 (hereafter *Almanac 1993/94*).

38 See Joseph E. Passantino, 'Kunming, Southwestern Gateway to China', in *The National Geographic Magazine*, Vol. XC, No. 2, p. 138.

39 Zhongguo duiwai jingji maoyi nianjian bianji weiyuanhui, *Zhongguo duiwai jingji maoyi nianjian 1987* (Almanac of China's Foreign Economic Relations and Trade 1987], Beijing: Zhongguo zhanwang chubanshe 1987; *Almanac 1993/94*.

40 *Almanac 1993/94*, pp. 380–83.

41 Wang Shilu, 'Yunnan yu dongnanya jingji guanxi yanjiu' (A study of the economic relations between Yunnan and South-East Asia), *Yunnan shehui kexue 1992*, No. 4, p. 23.

42 *Almanac 1993/94*.

43 (a)*Yunnan tongji nianjian 1992*; (b) *Almanac 1992*; (c) *Almanac 1993/94*.

44 Author's calculation from data in the *Almanac 1993/94*.

45 For a translation of this document see, The Research Department of the Hong Kong Trade and Development Council, *Trade Developments, Market Report on Yunnan Province*, Hong Kong, 1992, Appendix 7.

46 *International Herald Tribune* (hereafter *IHT*), 1 October 1993.

47 *Supplement*.

48 Governor of Yunnan Province, He Zhiqiang, at the Yunnan Provincial Economic Relations and Trade Work Meeting in March 1993; *FBIS*, CHI–93–051, 18 March 1993.

49 These regulations were issued by the Ministry of Foreign Economic Relations and approved by the State Council on 15 December 1984. See Li Maoxing, Shi Benhi and Zhang Jitao (eds), *Bianjing maoyi lilun yu shiwu*, (Theory and practice of border trade), Dehong minzu chubanshe 1992, p. 12. 'Small volume border trade' (*xiao'e bianmao*) is one of three types of border trade and refers to trade between local companies and merchants on both sides of the border. The other two types are 'regional trade' (*difang maoyi*), which refers to border trade carried out by governmental organizations, and 'border residents exchange market' (*bianmin hushi*), which refers to small-scale tax-free trade between individual border residents, most often agricultural products, daily use items and handicrafts.

50 Li Chengding and He Ming (eds), *Yunnan bianjing kouan maoyi zhinan* (A guide to trade in Yunnan's border ports), Guangxi renmin chubanshe 1992, p. 12.

51 *FBIS*, 5 March 1993.

52 State-level ports are Kunming, Ruili, Wanding, Mengla, Hekou, Tianbao and Jinshuihe; the provincial-level ports are Pianma, Tengchang, Yinjiang, Zhangfeng, Nansan, Mengding, Menglian, Simao, Jinghong and Daluo. *FBIS*, CHI–92–211, 30 October 1992, p. 40, and *SWB*, FE/W0308, WB/2, 17 November 1993, and *YNRB*, 28 November 1993, p. 2.

53 Interviews with government officials in Mengla, Wanding and Ruili in July 1993.

54 *Ibid*. and *FBIS*, CHI–93–173, 9 September 1993, p. 62.

55 Talks with Chinese officials in Mengla in July 1993. Paul Handley,

'River of Promise' and 'Seeds of Friendship' in *Far Eastern Economic Review* (hereafter *FEER*), 16 September 1993, pp. 68–69 and 71–72.
56 Interviews with various local officials in Yunnan, July 1993.
57 Jan Willem Paijens, 'Hevige Twist Aziatische Oeverstaten over Mekong' (Hot Dispute in Asian Riverain States about the Mekong', *NRC Handelsblad*, 2 December 1993.
58 'The Draft Summary of Proceedings of the Second National Conference on Subregional Economic Cooperation' (Hereafter 'Proceedings'), Manila, 30–31 August 1993.
59 Paul Handley, 'River of Promise', *FEER*, 16 September 1993. pp. 68–69; E.C. Chapman and Peter Hinton, *op. cit.*; 'Proceedings'.
60 Paul Handley, 'Shadow Play', *FEER*, 16 September 1993, p. 70.
61 'Old Enemies Build Economic Bridges in South-East Asia', *Guardian*, 28 October 1993.
62 *FBIS*, CHI–93–141, 26 July 1993, p. 17.
63 *YNRB*, 30 April 1993. p. 1.
64 E.C. Chapman and Peter Hinton, *op. cit.*, p. 13.
65 *Ibid.*
66 *Supplement.*
67 Handley, 'Seeds', p. 72.
68 Handley, 'Seeds', p. 72; Bertil Lindner, 'Rocks and a Hard Place', *FEER*, 9 September 1993. pp. 26–27. Kim Gooi, 'Cry of the Innocents', *FEER*, 9 September 1993, pp. 36–37.
69 Edward Neilan, 'China's Influence in Burma Causes Fear in Southeast Asia', *San Francisco Chronicle*, 27 February 1993, in *China News Digest*, 28 February 1993.
70 *FBIS*, 8 February 1993: Myanmar delegation led by Brigadier General Win Tin, Deputy Minister for Planning and Finance.
71 Calculation based on statistics from the *Almanac 1993/94*, pp. 380–83 and 482.
72 News Brief, AP-DJ 21 September 1993 in *China News Digest* (*News Global*, 22 September 1993.
73 *YNRB*, 24 April 1993, p. 1.
74 Mya Than in Gehan Wijeyewardene, 'Southeast Asian Borders: Report of a Seminar held at the Australian National University, 28–30 October 1993' in *TYPN*, No 23, p. 4.
75 *SWB*, FEW/0303, WB/1, 13 October 1993.
76 Sources: Wanding Bureau for Management of Domestic and Foreign Trade and Ruili Government. This table shows that border trade in Wanding is stagnating. Ruili, however, is more successful and aims to generate 2 billion yuan in border trade in 1997.
77 Bertil Lintner, 'Rangoon's Rubicon: Infrastructure Aid Tightens Peking's Control', *FEER*, 11 February 1993, p. 28.
78 *Ibid.*, and see *Burma Alert*, Vol. 4, No. 3, 1993, and Edward Neilan, *op. cit.*
79 See for example, Bertil Lintner, 'Fields of Dreams, Heroin Trade Flourishes along China-Burma Border', *FEER*, 20 February 1992, pp. 23–24.
80 Bertil Lintner, 'Triangular Ties: Burma's New Drug Warlords linked with China's Yunnan Province', *FEER*, 28 March 1991, pp. 22–24.

81 *FBIS*, CHI–93–085, 5 May 1993.

82 *YNRB*, 2 December 1993, p. 1.

83 Zhi Shi, 'Xidu diaocha yu zonghe zhili chuyi' (A survey of drug use and my opinions on dealing with it comprehensively), *Chuxiong sheke luntan*, No. 1 (1991), pp. 65–69, in Dali L. Yang, 'Illegal Drugs, Policy Change, and State Power: The Case of Contemporary China', draft for the article published in *Journal of Contemporary China*, December 1993.

84 Dali L. Yang, *op. cit.*

85 Sources: Reuter report, 15 July 1992; street poster seen in Kunming, July 1993; *YNRB*, 27 October 1993; see also Dali L. Yang, *op. cit.*

86 Geoffrey Crothall, 'Documents Suggest Drug Problem "More Serious"', *South China Sunday Morning Post*, May 17, 1992, pp. 1, 7; in Dali L. Yang, *op. cit.*

87 *YNRB*, 2 December 1993, p. 6.

88 *FBIS*, 23 January 1991, p. 20.

89 *SWB*, FE/1603, 3 February 1993, A2/2; *SWB*, 15 June 92, in Allen F. Anderson, 'Mainland China at the AIDS Crossroads: Competing Directions and Hard Choices', in *Issues and Studies*, July 1993, pp. 43–54.

90 'Puritan China Faces Homosexuality', *Chicago Tribune*, 27 September 1992, C6, in Allen F. Anderson, *op. cit.*

91 UPI report, 23 December 1992.

92 Dali L. Yang, *op. cit.*

92 'Report of the Preliminary Joint Survey Team on Opium Production and Consumption in the Union of Burma', in *TYPN*, No. 22, September, 1993.

94 See, for example, the 'Dialogue Program on Oslo Democratic Voice of Burma', in *FBIS*, 24 February 1993.

95 Bertil Lintner, 'Triangular Ties'.

96 *FBIS*, 10 May 1993, *FBIS*, EAS–93–095, 19 May 1993, and *FBIS*, EAS–93–235, 9 December 1993, p. 54. In May 1993, the Minister of Foreign Affairs of Laos, Somsavat Lengsavat, visited China at the invitation of Chinese Vice-Premier and Foreign Minister Qian qichen. Both parties exchanged a ratification document of the protocol of the Laotian–Chinese border demarcation line. During a five-day official visit to Laos by a CPC delegation headed by Ding Guangen in December 1993, the two sides signed a border demarction treaty to legalise their common border.

97 This does not include profits from illegally imported cars with which the local government is said to enlarge its revenue. Figures provided by Mengla government.

98 *SWB*, FE/W0264, A/7, 13 January 1993.

99 *FBIS*, EAS–93–088, 10 May 1993, p. 46.

100 'Old Enemies Build Economic Bridges in South-East Asia', *Guardian*, 28 October 1993; Michael Richardson, 'New Bridge to Link Mekong Lands', *IHT*, 11 November 1993.

101 *FBIS*, EAS–93–112, 14 June 1993.

102 *FBIS*, EAS–93–167, 31 August 1993.

103 See note 63.

104 *SWB*, FE/1603, A2/3; and *FBIS*, 2 February 1993.

105 Michael Richardson, *op. cit.*
106 'Li Peng's Vietnam Visit set to Gloss over Border Disputes', *Japan Economic Newswire*, 28 November 1992, in *China News Digest*, 29 November 1992.
107 *FBIS*, CAR–93–047, 9 July 1993.
108 Source: Hekou Customs, July 1993.
109 *SWB*, FE/1846, G/1, 15 November 1993.
110 'Boom im Grenzhandel mit Vietnam' in *China Aktuell*, August 1993, pp. 760–61.
111 Information provided by Dehong Prefecture Economic Research Institute.
112 For example, for a report on a visit by Qian Qichen to Burma in early February, see *SWB*, FE/1603, A2/p2.; for his visit to Laos, see *SWB*, FE/1603, A2/p.3 and *FBIS*, 2 February 1993.

12 Deconstructing foreign relations

Gerald Segal

Chinese foreign policy has been described as that of a nineteenth-century mercantile power in a twenty-first-century, 'post-modern' region where state sovereignty is a 'Victorian value'. Yet this description is defective both because most states in East Asia still have important features of state sovereignty, and because China is more complex. It is true that East Asia increasingly contains Natural Economic Territories (NETs) that straddle old sovereign frontiers, including those of China.[1] But East Asia is also burdened with unresolved conflicts over sovereign frontiers and longer-term worries about major shifts in the balance of power.

China and its neighbours share, to varying degrees, an ambivalence about Victorian and post-modern values of international affairs. China's position is all the more complex because its size and the extensive decentralisation of economic decision-making involve it in more NETs than any other state. The result is pulling at the fabric of the country and these 'pull' factors are increasing because the process of interdependence with the outside world is gaining strength. Under ordinary conditions this would be difficult enough to control, but it is complicated by the fact that, in terms of military security, China remains a nineteenth-century power with unsettled territorial claims, willing to use force to settle disputes and re-order the balance of power. Thus China is not only in conflict with the outside world, but at times its own interests conflict. Are the incentives of interdependence stronger than the pressures to pursue irredentist claims or re-order the balance of power? This chapter identifies how much the pull factors of interdependence affect China's foreign and security policy. To what extent is China's pattern of trade being redefined by the emergence of more powerful provincial actors in China, and which countries exert the most important pull on the provinces and the country as a whole?

THE PROVINCES AND THE OUTSIDE WORLD

It makes sense to begin with some basic data on Chinese foreign trade.[2] In the first decade of reform, from 1978, China's foreign trade more than tripled (GNP increased by 2.5 times). In 1993, China's total trade stood at $167 billion, up from some $70 billion in 1985. In the same year it was ranked tenth among world exporters, and set to become Asia's second largest exporter after Japan. It was also the United States' second largest and the EC's third largest source of imports. Trade as a ratio of GDP roughly doubled to some 10.2 per cent in 1986–90 compared to the 1976–80 period. However, China's dependence on a single trade partner declined from over 50 per cent in the 1951–55 period (the Soviet Union) to some 27 per cent in the 1961–65 period, and then rose to 37 per cent in the 1986–90 period (Hong Kong).[3]

As impressive as this growth undoubtedly is, presenting it in this way misleadingly suggests that such prosperity can be understood as a national phenomenon. As in domestic economic growth, expansion in foreign trade has been very uneven. Brantly Womack has usefully divided Chinese provinces into three broad groups: coastal; border (some can be coastal and border); and inland. The model coastal province is Guangdong, whose exports increased seven-fold between 1978 and 1990, and by that year accounted for 21.9 per cent of total Chinese exports, up from 17.2 per cent in 1987.[4] In 1992 Guangdong's total exports reached $18 billion, nearly the same as that of India.[5] Guangdong's dependence on any single trade partner (in this case Hong Kong) was by far the highest in the country (82 per cent). Another coastal (and border) province, Liaoning, accounted for 11 per cent of national exports and also had a relatively high dependency of 47 per cent (with Japan).

A key indicator of the importance of international factor is a province's exports as a percentage of its GDP. There is an almost perfect fit between major exporting provinces and those with a high percentage of exports. Guangdong leads the table with 18 per cent, followed by Shanghai with 13 per cent, Fujian and Liaoning with 12 per cent and Tianjin with 10 per cent. Hainan's figure of 15 per cent is distorted by its small GDP. The general conclusion is that trade is vital to coastal China, but is this trade skewed in any particular way?

Although these coastal provinces ranked top of China's export league (see Table 12.1), they could be divided into two groups, according to the extent of their dependence on a single trade partner. Coastal provinces that are not border provinces tend to have lower rates of dependence on a single trade partner, even though trade remains a very important part of GDP. Shanghai, a coastal province which also accounted for 11 per cent of national exports, had a dependency rate well below the national average (29 per cent). Jiangsu, Zhejiang, Shandong, Beijing, Shanghai and Tianjin ranked below the national average of dependence, while Guangdong, Hainan, Guangxi, Fujian and Hebei topped the dependency league.

The second group of provinces is on China's land borders. Excluding those with coastal frontiers, inland border provinces apparently have only incidental advantages, or else have not made much of the advantages they do have. Patterns are harder to identify in this category. Trade is often less well reported because of smuggling, and often depends on the province's level of development and that of its trade partner. Heilonjiang, which ranks twelfth on the league table of exporters (2.2 per cent of national exports in 1990), is similarly ranked on the table of trade dependence (41 per cent on Russia). Neighbouring Jilin accounts for 1.5 per cent of national exports with a trade dependency of 43 per cent. Yunnan, Xinjiang, Inner Mongolia and Tibet are all relatively insignificant as provincial exporters and none has a strikingly high trade dependence.

In short, being an inland border province usually means having obvious trade links across frontiers, but none of these bridges (perhaps apart from Heilongjiang) makes the provinces especially dependent on land neighbours. While these provinces could increase their trade relations across the frontier to improve their relative economic position, they have so far not done so. There are some signs, especially in Xinjiang, Inner Mongolia, Yunnan and Tibet, that trade is growing especially fast across the frontier. This may emerge as a more clear-cut pattern in the coming years. The current result must be mixed feelings in Beijing, for although these provinces remain a greater burden on the state budget, they are less trouble in international affairs because they have not struck up major international trade links like some coastal provinces. Beijing's ambivalence is a major and inherent problem in the debate over decentralisation.

The third group of provinces fills most of the bottom half of the table of provincial exporters. Some, such as Hubei, Henan and Hunan, each have close on 2 per cent of national exports. Anhui, Jiangxi, Shaanxi and Shanxi each have close on 1 per cent, while Gansu, Guizhou, Ningxia and Qinghai bring up the rear. Most of these provinces have trade dependencies above the national average. The most striking cases are Qinghai (54 per cent on Japan), Hunan (47 per cent on Hong Kong), Hubei (47 per cent on Hong Kong) and

Shanxi (45 per cent on Hong Kong), appearing in the top ten provinces ranked according to trade dependence.

Since none of these provinces is close to its main export markets, it is hard to see a relationship of real dependence. Only in Hunan, where relatively high levels of dependence and provincial exports coincide, can it be argued that trade is important, but the dependence seems to be a secondary effect of Guangdong's dependence on Hong Kong. This argues in favour of looking more at regional patterns of dependence on the outside world than just on provincial boundaries.

Further evidence of this complexity comes from David Zweig, who argues that the role of township enterprises is rising so sharply – 20 per cent of total national exports in 1991 – that certain townships, especially in border provinces, have developed particularly heavy dependence on foreign trade.[6] To complicate matters further, these townships and village enterprises also power the growth of such provinces as Jiangsu and Zhejiang where dependence on foreign trade is not nearly as high as it is in southern China.[7] There are some 19 border towns in Heilongjiang facing Russia that have mean growth rates well above the national average because of trade across the frontiers.[8] Therefore the argument can be widened to show the danger of looking too closely at the provincial level of trade when the process often focuses on areas smaller or larger than the province.[9]

One basic pattern which does emerge is a limited, but nevertheless still important form of dependence linking some regions of China with the outside world. The two obvious regions are southern China linking Guangdong, Fujian, Hainan and neighbouring hinterland provinces with Hong Kong and Taiwan; and a northern coastal region focused on Liaoning which links with Japan. Less clear evidence suggests that Shandong can be linked to this second region, or else has a special connection with South Korea. Another possibility is Heilongjiang and perhaps Jilin becoming more tied to Russia, or Guangxi and Yunnan connecting with Vietnam and Myanmar. But like other inland border regions, there is scope for far more regional connections across frontiers before the NETs can begin to emerge as really important features.

From Beijing's point of view, the pattern of NETs is still manageable. Only two NETs are powerful and because China as a whole benefits from close relations with Hong Kong, Taiwan and Japan, the effect can be diffused, especially as overseas finance seeks cheaper labour further inland. Yet it is also clear that the opening up of the provinces to foreign trade, based as it is on 'market localism', has great potential to develop according to market forces and outside central control. Market specialisation has replaced the Maoist ideal of self-sufficiency, and material incentives have spurred local initiative.[10] As provinces and regions diversify and grow they will be more difficult to handle. One can already begin to conceive of several provinces as independent trading powers. The logical outcome should be greater diversification of production and more complex trade relations between provinces. The provinces will also be less inclined to need Beijing's services and more likely to resent its interference. If interprovincial relations become more akin to North–South relations in the international system, Beijing may be called upon to be more involved in settling trade disputes.

Beijing also derives strength from the fact that China is seeking wider membership in, and contacts with, international economic institutions. Although these institutions, such as the IMF and World Bank, do have teams working in different parts of China, central government has retained basic control of the relationship. Chinese membership in the General Agreement on Tariffs and Trade (GATT) is especially desired by Beijing because if membership requires the regions to provide more reporting of data, then the centre will gain power over otherwise freer enterprise in coastal regions. The same transparency that GATT requires of China as a whole will be required by Beijing of its provinces. Indeed, Beijing and international institutions often share common interests. The most egregious cases of Chinese enterprises receiving GATT-violating subsidies or flouting intellectual property rules are to be found at the provincial or township and village enterprise level.[11] Beijing may want to abide by international agreements on these matters, but it simply does not control that part of the economy.

While the functioning of the NETs is made possible by the growing autonomy of certain provinces, it is also dependent on specific policies of China's neighbours. But these neighbours are not only concerned with the economic basis of the relationship with parts of China, they are also concerned with security issues. One of many complications in the operations of these NETs is that, while economic relations are increasingly localised in specific parts of China, security issues still concern Beijing and not the provinces.

HONG KONG

By far the tightest NET is that which links Hong Kong to Guangdong Province and includes virtually all of southern China. Within this

NET are unusual security issues concerning the fate of Hong Kong.[12] On 1 July 1997 Hong Kong will become part of China, and what were once considered external relations will become a special sort of internal affairs. It is not surprising that the decade or so since the 1984 Anglo-Chinese accord on Hong Kong has been taken up with managing the convergence of the colony and China.

Conventional wisdom suggested that China would take increasing charge of convergence as 1997 approached. But the Hong Kong problem has been far more complex. In fact southern China (and especially Guangdong) is changing faster than Hong Kong on its way to convergence with the British colony. This process both pulls southern China further away from Beijing and strengthens the hand of foreigners who operate in and through Hong Kong. The extent to which Beijing has lost control of this process is evident in the way in which the Chinese trade surplus with the United States has grown into a major problem in Sino-American relations, even though it is largely due to the transfer of a large part of Hong Kong's (and Taiwan's) trade surplus to production within China. As the United States threatened China with restrictions on exports and thereby forced concessions on trade and human-rights policy, most of this American power was made available by decisions taken in Hong Kong and Taiwan.

The power of Hong Kong also derives from the fact that it is essential to the growth of southern China, and growth in southern China is essential for the growth of the country at large. Without this growth, the legitimacy of the Communist Party in Beijing is at risk.

The close connection between Hong Kong and southern China is evident in a number of ways. Most important is the undoubted dependence of Guangdong on Hong Kong for investment and trade. Some 75 per cent of total Guangdong exports pass through Hong Kong, and the British colony employs some 3 million people in the Chinese province. In 1990, some 55 per cent of Hong Kong's massive imports from China came from Guangdong and Fujian. Hong Kong was by far the most important trade partner for all of China, and most Chinese provinces had Hong Kong as their main export market. In 1992, 44 per cent of Chinese exports and 25 per cent of its imports passed through Hong Kong, up from 26 per cent and 12 per cent respectively in 1984. Hong Kong and Macao accounted for 70 per cent of all direct investment in China in 1992, up from 52 per cent in 1984. In 1990 the colony accounted for 37 per cent of all provincial exports, up from 30 per cent in 1987. But the volume of trade and investment flows remain heavily weighted towards southern China.[13]

The cross-border connections also include ties between local gang-sters and a flourishing narcotics trade.[14] By 1993 the problems had grown so serious that the PLA navy was called in to deal with anti-smuggling operations. But the navy itself had been so corrupted by the vast amounts of money to be made in southern China that it proved ineffective in stopping the smuggling.[15] The problem at sea is in fact part of a wider one that China is experiencing since provinces were given responsibility for managing territorial waters in 1992.[16] Piracy has become a more prominent problem in the 1990s, in part because it is related to the booming drug and gun running in Guangxi Province. Criminal gangs in Fujian are key players in the smuggling of Chinese into the United States, thus helping to create wider international problems.[17] Thus, as even the reliability of the PLA was being called into question, there could be no doubt that Hong Kong was having a major impact on Chinese foreign policy and, from Beijing's perspective, often a deleterious impact.

Cross-border links are also well grounded in close ethnic and family ties and are fuelled daily by the tens of thousands of people who cross the frontier for work and social reasons. Some 30 per cent of Hong Kong dollar notes circulate in southern China.[18] Some 21 per cent of Guangdong's industrial output is generated by joint ventures and foreign-owned enterprises (the national total is 4 per cent), and Guangdong's foreign enterprises account for some 37 per cent of the industrial output of all such enterprises in China. Over 75 per cent of realised foreign direct investment in Guangdong comes from Hong Kong, and 57 per cent of total foreign investment in China in 1979–92 came from Hong Kong.[19]

As the NET connecting Hong Kong and southern China grows tighter because of explicit Hong Kong and Chinese policy, the implications extend well beyond the economic prosperity of the region. The wider political and security implications derive primarily from the fact that the fate of Hong Kong is part of the wider issue of how China manages national reunification. The intensified row between London and Beijing over Hong Kong has demonstrated the extent to which Britain's (and Hong Kong's) hand is strengthened by the convergence of Hong Kong and southern China. When Beijing tried to shake confidence in the colony in 1992–93 to undermine support for Governor Chris Patten, it was investment from southern China into the Hong Kong stock market in early 1993 that buoyed up confidence in the colony and undermined Beijing. The mixture of flight capital from China and sound investment decisions by Chinese firms have made Hong Kong a net importer of capital from China since 1992. As Hong Kong grows more important to the prosperity of southern China, Chinese officials have grown increasingly worried that Britain and Hong Kong are deliberately using their new economic power to improve their bargaining on the colony's political fate. China's recent concern that Britain sees Hong Kong not just as an economic centre, but also as a political entity, with demands of its own, is a vivid case in point.[20]

The best explanation for recent events is that as Hong Kong and China have converged, contrary to Beijing's initial expectation, central government has lost some control over how the Hong Kong issue is resolved. As a result, Beijing is also less in control of how the wider issue of national reunification is managed. When it failed to force Britain to withdraw its proposals for greater democratisation, Beijing set in motion plans to set up an alternative structure of government for Hong Kong. Beijing hoped that it, rather than the southern Chinese, would run Hong Kong after 1997, although the outcome of that power struggle will only be known after the British withdraw. By acting as the service hub for the southern Chinese economy, Hong Kong is trying to ensure that it has a closer relationship with Guangdong and that after 1997 their combined forces will be better able to resist Beijing. So long as growth in the coastal regions remains essential to the strategy that keeps the Communist Party in power in Beijing, Hong Kong will continue to exert important leverage over policies in Beijing. The NET that includes Hong Kong is obviously the tightest and most important on China's periphery, and its strength demonstrates the extent to which China's foreign policy is altered by domestic decentralisation and international interdependence.

TAIWAN

One reason why the relationship with Hong Kong is so sensitive, and the loss of power by Beijing so significant, is that more is at stake than just the fate of Hong Kong. The fate of the 21 million people of Taiwan is also bound up with this issue. In fact, it is far more accurate to talk of a southern Chinese NET, where Hong Kong and Taiwan are joined with Guangdong, Fujian and Hainan into an increasingly tight economic unit. Taiwan once had a particular interest in strengthening ties with Fujian across the straits, but what has evolved is a wider NET in southern China.[21]

Data on trade are scarce and unreliable, if only because until recently most of Taiwan's trade with China passed through Hong

Kong. Recent estimates suggest that Taiwanese investment in China in 1992 was $5.5 billion, over and above the cumulative investment of $3.4 billion in the previous decade.[22] By April 1993 there were reportedly some 12,000 Taiwanese-funded enterprises in China. Two-way trade in 1992 stood at some $7 billion, and was up 25 per cent in 1993.[23] About 1.5 million Taiwanese visited the mainland in 1992, triple the figure in 1989, and nearly 30 million phone calls were made to China in 1992, an increase from less than 10 million in 1990.[24] Data on the extent of concentration of these links in southern China are not reliable, but anecdotal evidence points to the conclusion that, as in the case of Hong Kong, investment is present in impressive totals around the country, but the heaviest concentration is in the southern Chinese NET. As Taiwanese investment in Shanghai grows rapidly, Taiwanese firms speak of developing separate regional strategies for investment.[25]

The fact that Taiwan and China held their first high-level talks in Singapore in April 1993 indicates the extent to which economic convergence has caused changes in the political relationship. The selection of the predominantly ethnic Chinese city-state of Singapore worried those who feared the power of Greater China. But it is clear that China does not have commanding authority over a wider, ethnically based community. Unlike Hong Kong, Taiwan is not necessarily destined to accept unity on China's terms. As Taiwan has grown richer, its emerging middle class has changed the political system, with a resulting increase in support for political parties favouring greater independence. The more Taiwan is able to operate as a normal international actor, the less it will feel the need to surrender its *de facto* independence. Taiwan's trade with China has several advantages for Taipei. Not only does it bring economic benefits, but it makes it harder for third parties to refuse decent relations with Taiwan if China is prepared to be pragmatic. Because the trade is so heavily focused on southern China, like that of Hong Kong, the result is a more powerful southern Chinese NET able to resist the will of Beijing.

Taiwan's encouragement of regional autonomy, at least in trade, gives it a role different from that of Hong Kong. The greater the autonomy given to China's provinces, the more *de facto* independence for Taiwan is made plausible. Economic interdependence buys greater political independence. Taiwan's wealth and its ability to resist pressure from Beijing are connected, and offer a model of sorts to China's own more independently minded provinces. Greater China means closer economic relations with the mainland, but greater political fragmentation of China in its widest sense.

In part because of the growing worries about the basis of social order in China, Hong Kong and Taiwan, investors have been ensuring that their investment is not too heavily concentrated in southern China. Jiangsu Province has been especially assiduous in courting Taiwanese investment, and by mid-1993 had 423 enterprises with a total investment value of $768 million.[26] By giving a wider area of China a stake in seeking investment from Hong Kong and Taiwan, other regions can be strengthened in competition with southern China. By bargaining with different provinces, investors risk Beijing's ire, but in general Beijing will welcome such a trend if it makes managing the most powerful NET in southern China easier. Yet such an ability to fine-tune investment for strategic reasons is unlikely. Money is invested for a mixture of good business reasons and cultural factors and is therefore most likely to remain concentrated in southern China. But if such concentration and convergence is sustained in the southern Chinese NET, there are major implications for Beijing's ability to maintain China's unity. Short of a looser, informally federal structure, market and political forces are likely to pull southern China further from Beijing's grasp. As this process gathers pace, Beijing may well find that its richer coastal regions are reluctant to risk their prosperity for the sake of a forced reunification with Taiwan.

SOUTH-EAST ASIA

The role of the overseas Chinese demonstrates that the 'pulling' on the fabric of China that comes from Hong Kong and Taiwan is also part of a process involving the wider Chinese world. Most of the overseas Chinese who do not live in Hong Kong and Taiwan live in South-east Asia, and their presence is only one of a number of reasons for the region's distinctive approach to China and its unity.

China is becoming an increasingly important trade partner for many states in South-east Asia, but its relationships are many and varied. There is the case of Mandarin-speaking Singapore which, despite cultural connections to southern China, is trying very hard to operate throughout China. Total Singapore trade with China is the largest among South-east Asian states. In 1991 its $3 billion of total trade was 37 per cent of South-east Asia's total trade with China. China's exports to Singapore were nearly 3 per cent of China's total. In 1979–91 total Singapore investment in China was $897 million, but in 1992 alone it was $997 million. Provincial exports from China in 1990 were only 1.8 per cent, up from 1.2 per cent in 1987, but still low enough to suggest that Singapore was notable for focusing on trade with national rather than provincial enterprises. A recent Singapore investment scheme concerns plans to invest some \$20 billion in a township in Suzhou near Shanghai. The initiative came from Beijing, which wanted to encourage the creation of another model of development involving overseas Chinese not tied to Hong Kong or Taiwan.[27] But Lee Kuan Yew also took a delegation to Shandong and, by his own admission, implicitly suggested that Singapore was bargaining over terms of investment by playing off Shandong, Suzhou and other provinces anxious for investment.[28]

Singapore is, ethnically, mainly a Chinese state and its impressive trade links with China can be explained by the strong trading advantages that overseas Chinese have in the China market. Given the distance between Singapore and the Chinese coast, it is clear that Singapore's economic relations are not tied up with questions of national reunification. But Lee Kuan Yew has seen himself as an elder statesman of the overseas Chinese and a voice in the debate about China's role in the world. He has argued against those in the West who would press China on human rights and trade issues, and has urged quiet diplomacy in order to make China a more cooperative player in East Asian affairs. Such a line of argument endears him to Beijing, but garners little support outside the ethnic Chinese world. In fact, Lee's approach raises suspicions about the powers and intentions of China and overseas Chinese. While the overseas Chinese as a business community help pull coastal China further out into the world of international interdependence, Lee Kuan Yew is seen to be strengthening Chinese nationalism and in effect souring relations in South-east Asia, especially among those who worry about China's irredentist agenda.

South-east Asians are unsure whether China is a threat, and if so, what kind of threat precisely. One way that China copes with its concern over the impact of its reforms is to take a tough line on nationalist issues – hence Beijing's active and vigorous pursuit of claims in the South China Sea. Leaving aside the question of whether China's claim is stronger than others, the regular use of force in seizing islands demonstrates that nationalism comes before a cautious calculation of the impact on regional trade relations. Surely it makes no economic sense for China to continue to scare South-east Asians and the wider international community with its determination to regain lost territory? It only makes sense if China feels that its neighbours and the rest of the world need to learn that China will be ruthless in taking what it claims to be rightfully its own. China's strategy is nationalist and constrained only by the limits on its military power and potential political costs.[29] Energy supplies and other resources are set to become even more vital to a growing Chinese economy, and China would rather control these by itself than be required to trade with others. Military officials in China are thus quick to make the geo-economic case for the use of force.

The use of force in the South China Sea has apparently been determined by the leadership in Beijing and, unlike the case of Hong Kong, there are not yet any clear signs of regional opposition to a hard, nationalist policy.[30] Yet it is not impossible to imagine situations in which regional leaders object to actions ordered by the centre that could damage them economically.

There is also evidence that China's agenda is not just nationalist in the sense of regaining lost territory, but also in the sense of demonstrating dominance in the region. China's systematic humiliation of Vietnam, even in the years following Hanoi's withdrawal from Cambodia and normalisation of relations with China, is a case in point.[31] The problem is that China defines 'normal' relations with Vietnam as ones where Vietnam is subservient to China. Even the growing cross-border trade relations between Chinese and Vietnamese provinces follow a pattern of Chinese domination.[32]

The unique problems of Yunnan and Guangxi indicate where the Chinese can lose some control of policy towards South-east Asia. Drug and gun running are rapidly increasing, and the problem is beyond the control of central and provincial government. Some villages even straddle the frontier. The commerce is part of a 'black NET' linking these provinces with Vietnam, Myanmar and Thailand. Narcotics use is also on the increase throughout China, and the inability to block supply routes is part of the reason. Hong Kong is also involved in the drug and gun trade. These problems contribute to social decay and make the maintenance of order, especially in major cities, more difficult.[33].

Although Thailand and Myanmar are most concerned with managing the drug trade, the rest of South-east Asia is also anxious to control the problem. Whether the trade is in drugs and guns or other less unpleasant products, China has a large trade surplus with its southern neighbours. Vietnam tried to deal with the problem by raising import tariffs in October 1993, but as most of the trade was illegal anyway, the measures were expected to have little impact.[34]

The wider question for many South-east Asians is whether China is better placated or deterred. Vietnam, Malaysia, Indonesia, the Philippines and perhaps even Thailand have good reason to seek early answers. A China that is aware of its vulnerabilities when contemplating the agenda for economic interdependence, and yet free to use force in the region as it sees fit, will want to use such power as it has to tip the balance of advantage its way. Japanese economic investments in South-east Asia seem already to have passed their peak, and in any case could never be an effective counter to either fully developed Chinese economic or military power. Without a balance of power, South-east Asians are vulnerable.

Arguments that increasing economic interdependence will keep China from using force are simply not borne out by recent events. China's neighbours in South-east Asia may be too politically divided to prevent China pursuing its nationalist agenda. To the extent that China has had a security dialogue with the Association of South-East Asian Nations (ASEAN) states, it has dealt with generalities. In the meantime China has continued to assert control over its claimed territory in the South China Sea and refuses to discuss shared sovereignty.[35] South-east Asians have improved economic relations with China, but increasingly worry about having to 'pay tribute' to a China that grows strong. Their interests would no doubt be better served by finding new ways to use their trading relations with China's coastal regions to nudge China into more neighbourly political relations.

JAPAN

Japan is already emerging as China's largest trade partner. In 1991 it accounted for some 16 per cent of Chinese trade, and the same percentage of China's total provincial trade. But just as there are special links between Taiwan, Hong Kong and southern China, so there is an evolving northern coastal NET. In 1990 Japan ranked first as the destination for exports from four Chinese provinces (Liaoning, Shandong, Qinghai and Xinjiang), and second for a further twenty provinces. Liaoning and Qinghai had high trade dependency ratios, while Shandong and Xinjiang were near the national average. Some 28 per cent of total provincial exports to Japan were accounted for by exports from Liaoning – the obvious nexus of the northern coastal NET. Japanese relations were also particularly close in the Shanghai/ Jiangsu region.

Comparing the trade figures for 1987 and 1990 suggests little change in the pattern of Japanese trade. In September 1992, twenty Japanese firms joined together to develop a special industrial park and half the foreign direct investment in Liaoning came from Japan. Some two-thirds of all foreign investment in Dalian came from Japan, in part because of the persistence of Japanese expertise on the region, as well as a large number of Chinese in Dalian who still spoke Japanese. The historical record of Japanese involvement can be a problem, since many memories remain of harsh Japanese rule, but at a time of competition between China's cities and provinces for investment, past memories are often suppressed to ensure contemporary advantage.[36]

Despite the emergence of a northern coastal NET, there has been far less discussion of its importance compared to that of southern China. There are many reasons for this, one of them being the role of South Korea in the region (see below), but another is to be found in Japan's twentieth-century history. Having already occupied vast parts of China in the 1930s and 1940s and spent years trying to divide and manipulate it, modern Japanese are rightly careful about being accused of harbouring similar intentions now.

This delicacy about the past which hinders discussion about the present and future is, in fact, part of a broader and more serious problem in Sino-Japanese relations.[37] It is clear that each country sees the other as a problem in the post-Cold War world, and yet officials are reluctant to speak in public about the risks they perceive. Optimistic Japanese speak of their ability to control China by weaving it into webs of interdependence. Some Japanese even speak of their ability to manipulate China because Tokyo controls access to high technology and finance. But as Japan itself changes, so it expresses concern about a China unchecked by other powers. Recent projections about the size of the Chinese economy only fuel Japanese worries. They are concerned about the military dimensions of Sino-Japanese relations as China acquires in-flight refuelling or possibly even aircraft carriers. They wonder why China wants to enter into long-term defence-production arrangements with Russia when there are no major threats to Chinese security. They puzzle over why China's defence budget is growing while nearly all other great powers are reducing theirs. Why does China criticise Japan's modest plans to take part in United Nations (UN) peacekeeping forces, while Beijing is reluctant to see Japan join the roster of permanent members of the UN Security Council? Could it be that China is trying to keep Japan from becoming a more normal power and trying to reassert the traditional role of Chinese pre-eminence? In 1993 Japan and China agreed to resume a high-level security dialogue, broken off in 1989, which may help ease some of the tensions in the relationship.[38] Other potential disputes include the damage done to the Japanese environment by pollution from China – a problem that is bound to grow as the Chinese economy expands.[39] Concrete confidence-building measures and a wider dialogue on multilateral issues are clearly necessary.

If Japan views China as seeking a more hegemonic role, then Tokyo may well rethink its economic and technological assistance to it. Might Japan seek closer Group of Seven (G–7) cooperation over policy towards China? Will Japan continue to put its trust in American protection and in its own ability to manage China through economic interdependence? To some extent the question is also whether Japan is prepared to work with other East Asians in dealing with a rising China. As Japanese economic interdependence is focused on the northern coastal NET, Japan has the potential either to work with other major players in other NETs, or to go it alone. By working together, but in separate NETs, China's neighbours, including Japan, will have the opportunity to make different parts of China compete for the favours of the outside world. Japan has leverage, but there are reasons why it will find it difficult to articulate an explicit strategy that seeks to make use of the regional differences in China. Nevertheless, there are ways in which Japan can maintain a formal dialogue with Beijing, while developing new forms of influence in the regions in the hope of moderating Chinese behaviour.

KOREA

Korea, sometimes described as 'the Palestine of East Asia' because of claims by rival empires, sits uneasily between Japan and China. As a divided country it was also a battleground in the Cold War. It was only in the 1980s that China began to explore potential economic relations with South Korea, and relegated North Korea to a containment zone because of its economic backwardness and its odd and uncooperative policies. As Sino-North Korean trade dropped sharply, Sino-South Korean trade increased rapidly. Yet China's trade with South Korea has only recently become direct, and diplomatic relations between them were only established in 1992. There had been insufficient time for an economic NET to be established, although given the relatively small size of the South Korean economy this may not really be formed until after the two Koreas are reunified.

For the time being, Sino-South Korean relations are best seen as part of the larger northern coastal NET led by Japan. China describes this as the Bohai Rim and claims it has the potential to rival the growth zones in the south or around Shanghai. China's trade with

South Korea stood at some $5 billion in 1992. There is a strong regional focus to that trade, most notably with the provinces of Shandong, Liaoning and Jilin. The Korean Autonomous Prefecture of Yanbian has a large concentration of Korean nationals (850,000) and in 1991 claimed to have sent one-third of its total export volume (or $4 million) to South Korea. China's first ethnic-minority economic-development zone was created in the Yiyuan country of Shandong in order to attract Korean investment.[40] The much larger and more prosperous Liaoning Province has been the largest provincial trade partner with South Korea. Trade has mostly been with smaller Korean companies who are most desperate for China's cheaper labour costs, although Beijing continues to hope that the larger Korean Chaebol will eventually become involved and make it easier for Beijing to manage the trade from afar.[41]

There are few prospects for South Korea, or even a unified Korea, evolving an especially powerful NET on its own. Neither is Korea likely to work well with Japan in a northern coastal NET because of the already wary state of their relations. As a result, China and its provinces have far more leverage and opportunity to play off one partner against the other than in any other NET. The Japanese and Koreans are likely to be competitors for Chinese favours, and therefore all levels of the Chinese government may well find that they are able to drive tougher bargains on trade and technology transfer terms by encouraging the Japanese and Koreans to outbid each other. China also exerts important influence on North Korea, and as both South Korea and Japan grow more concerned about succession in Pyongyang and the risks of nuclear conflict, China's diplomatic leverage becomes more important. While there may eventually be prospects of a NET that includes what was once North Korea, China will retain important leverage over Japan and South Korea. As a result, South Koreans are finding that not all of China's neighbours can make use of regionalism in China. Similar conclusions are evident on China's most northern frontier with Russia.

RUSSIA/MONGOLIA

There is perhaps no other bilateral relationship for China that is both so important and so ambivalent as that with Russia. As the Soviet Union, and in earlier days as Russia, China's northern neighbour has been both close comrade-in-arms and most evil of enemies. In the 1950s it was far and away China's major trade partner, but by the 1970s the Soviet Union might as well not have existed when considering patterns of Chinese trade. All those extremes were unnatural, but because they have existed so recently, there is little firm guidance on the normal state of Sino-Russian relations.

Current trade relations are distorted by the legacies of the past and the chaos in modern Russia. The total trade volume in 1991 was some $4 billion, rising to $7.7 billion in 1993. Total provincial export volume was $1.5 billion in 1990. As might be expected for a country whose trade with East Asia was heavily focused on the north-east, Russia's trade with China could be narrowed down to very few provinces.[42] Although Russia ranked third for six Chinese provinces, it only ranked second for one (Xinjiang) and first for two others (Inner Mongolia and Heilongjiang). Trade as a percentage of GNP was low for Inner Mongolia (3.2 per cent) and a bit higher for Heilongjiang (4.2 per cent). Both had trade dependencies above the national average, but not exceptionally high.

From Russia's point of view, trade had grown more localised since the 1980s. This is primarily because of changes in the pattern of trade by Chinese provinces, as only the northern bordering provinces had an enduring need for trade with Russia because trade became based more on market forces than on state command. But even in 1990 Heilongjiang was the major provincial trade partner, followed by Shangdong, Jilin, Jiangsu and only then Inner Mongolia. Whether this less than tightly knit trade along China's northern frontier constituted a NET is in part a matter of degree. Certainly there were distinctive trade orientations for northern provinces towards Russia, but they were not very strong when compared to the northern coastal and southern NETs. As Womack has suggested, many of these inland frontier connections are thin.

Perhaps these connections are just underdeveloped, at least in the case of Heilongjiang's connection with Russia. With 50,000 Chinese working and trading on the Russian side of the frontier and a good basis for economic complementarity, there are decent prospects for growth in trade. In 1992 a number of new towns and counties were given special status in order to enhance trade prospects. As in other parts of China, the decentralisation process often meant that economic decision-making was devolved well below the provincial level.[43] What problems there were seemed to stem primarily from the uncertainty and economic difficulties on the Russian side of the frontier. Nevertheless, border trade increased to $6 billion in 1993, five times the 1991 figure, and new rail and air links were established. There was much talk (and a great deal of hype) about the prospects of multilateral cooperation in the Tumen River region that would bring

Japanese capital to help exploit Chinese labour and Russian and North Korean resources. But given the serious concerns about the economic viability of the projects already discussed, let alone fundamental uncertainty about Korean politics and even the shape of Russia, it is not surprising that the discussions on the Tumen project never developed very far.[44]

But Russia has good reason to be wary of China as a unified great power. The relatively small Russian population in the Far East sitting on top of valuable natural resources feels highly vulnerable. It would feel even more so if Russia should fragment further and not have the protection of what is left of the Russian armed forces. If China grows fast it will require precisely those minerals and energy resources that are so close to it in the Russian Far East, and Russia knows it took much of this territory from a weak China in earlier centuries.

Perhaps for those reasons there is tension in Russia's view of China. On the one hand, in 1992 Russia sold 27 Su-27 aircraft and 144 aviation missiles and has since discussed a number of other possible ways for the defence industries of the two countries to collaborate. (Russian engineers are apparently working in various parts of the Chinese military industry.)[45] On the other hand, longer-term fears about Chinese intentions are fed by the infiltration of Chinese smugglers across the open frontier, and the piratical actions of Chinese officials and bandits in Pacific waters.[46] Decentralisation of policy on the Russian side, in the form of the break-up the Soviet Union, is also responsible for the failure to reach a border agreement.[47] But there are also longer-term worries in Russia about the wisdom of becoming too close militarily with China.

It has been argued in Russia that in the medium and longer term, China rather than Japan is Russia's main enemy in the region and that Russia and Japan thus need to work more closely together. Russia may be so weak in its Far Eastern territory that it may grow ever more wary of China. Major economic development in the Far East may require large-scale Chinese involvement, but to do so would make Russia highly dependent on China. At a minimum, while there are prospects for closer economic cooperation and the formation of a tighter NET in the region, Russia will find itself the weaker partner. Neither can Mongolia be of much help, for it is even more dependent on, and vulnerable to, China.[48] The prospects are more for Chinese pressure on Russia than the other way around.

CENTRAL ASIA

A geopolitician with anthropological training might see great potential for a NET in Central Asia that straddles Xinjiang and the newly dependent states of the former Soviet Union, even as far as the frontiers of the Middle East.[49] With major ethnic populations on both sides of the frontiers, the basis for cooperation seems obvious. Yet such speculation is much too premature, given the basic uncertainty in the Central Asian states about their statehood and priorities. By contrast, the Chinese side of the frontier appears to be an area of relative tranquillity and prosperity.

There are millions of minority peoples and Muslims with affiliations across the frontier in the new Central Asian states. In all the important cases, the larger portion of the minority was on the former Soviet side of the frontier, except for the Uygurs (only 185,000 on the Kazakh side). Illegal immigration of up to 100 Chinese each day in 1993 to Kazakhstan has already been reported.[50] The Kazakhs across the border worry about being swamped and losing control of their economy, although they recognise that the level of Chinese technology may be better suited than that from the West. The Chinese model of economic and political reform also has its attractions for those in Central Asia who like the notion of 'enlightened authoritarianism'.[51] In 1992 total Chinese–Kazakh trade was $430 million or 21 per cent of Kazakhstan's total trade. By 1993 China had become Kazakhstan's major trade partner (after Russia), accounting for roughly 27 per cent of imports and 20 per cent of Kazakh exports. Discussions have been held about setting up a special economic zone, including the participation of Hong Kong companies.[52]

There is every expectation that China will remain a major trade partner for the Central Asian states. Beijing sees a possible NET as one led by itself and would hope to extend it further across the region to Pakistan, a long-standing ally of China. Both Urumqi and Beijing recognise that they are just starting out on this road of widening contacts in the region, but the tone of the initiative is distinctly confident. China's talk of a 'golden opportunity' may be optimistic, but it does reflect the feeling that it has the economic initiative in the region.[53]

As noted above, there are reasons for China to be wary about the openness implied in a Central Asian NET. Under certain circumstances, China could find its problems with its minorities growing, especially if economic growth in Xinjiang cannot be sustained. The fact that China changed its policy on Kashmir in 1993 to one that no longer supported the notion of self-determination for a mainly Muslim population, suggests serious Chinese concern with what its own Muslim population across the border might learn.[54] But under current conditions the prospects of a NET in either the north or west look far more likely to play into Beijing's hands than to serve the interests of those hostile to Chinese unity. Only conditions of privation in China's regions, or drastic decay and disarray in the centre, would work against China's interests.

The new Central Asian states bordering China all have deep, and probably growing, worries about Chinese intentions. President Nazarbayev of Kazakhstan is openly concerned about China's intentions in allowing large numbers of migrants to cross the frontier from Xinjiang. He also worries about China's nuclear capability and has noted that it has territorial claims against his country. In fact China has long-standing territorial claims to Tajikistan and Kyrgyzstan as well, and officials can often be heard musing about China's long-term intentions.[55] Kyrgyz officials routinely blame China for natural disasters – for example, the earthquake in April 1992 was popularly believed to have been deliberately caused by a nuclear test in Lop Nor. In 1993 President Nazarbayev obtained China's agreement for a mechanism to monitor nuclear radiation from Lop Nor.[56] In short, the new Central Asian states seem more worried than the Chinese about the risks of closer relations in a Central Asian NET.

The brief surveys of these prospective northern and western NETs make clear that the implications of interdependence around China's rim can differ widely. In the north and west, the relative poverty and disarray of China's neighbours make the Chinese regions less subject to pull factors. China's southwestern frontier with Myanmar and Vietnam is a difficult case, because central government control is lacking on all sides. The most ominous challenge for Beijing is along coastal China, and primarily in the southern NET. The challenge is in fact that of neighbours who are rich and serve up poles of attraction. When coupled with rising aspirations in parts of China connected by these NETs, the challenge is powerful and growing. In short, China is both pushed and pulled in very different directions, but there is no doubt that the definition of the future shape of China is in flux.

FORCES FOR CHANGE

The signs that China is changing shape are increasingly clear. A closer look at its national identity reveals fissures and pressures that have long been masked by an official determination to uphold the myth of national unity. Yet rapid and radical economic reforms are transforming the structure of the Chinese economy and have even begun to affect its political system. These reforms are taking place at a time of the greatest uncertainty about the leadership of China since the communists came to power in 1949. As the central leadership loses some of its influence through the decentralisation of economic and some political power, it is harder for it to keep China's minorities in place. Chinese unity is also challenged by forces outside the country. Perhaps the most surprising pull on the national fabric comes from the overseas Chinese, who are keen for parts of China to compete in the global market economy. The overseas Chinese are part of the broader process of international interdependence. By pulling parts of coastal China into different relationships, these forces are helping to form NETs.

Evidence shows that the central government in Beijing first surrendered power willingly, but in recent years has discovered how difficult it is to recover that power when it wishes to do so. Some key decisions on how to run the economy can no longer be enforced by Beijing, and, to the extent that managing economic success is an important part of the regime's legitimacy and hence a key part of its political power, the decentralisation of economic power is also a decentralisation of political power. Indeed, it would be strange for a Communist Party leadership to argue that economics and politics could be anything but closely linked.

Yet evidence has also made clear that power has not simply been transferred to another player, for example a provincial leadership. Power has been devolved to a range of actors, including township and village enterprises, individuals and even overseas Chinese and other outsiders. Thus there is no simple struggle for control between centre and province.

Provincial leaders are aware of the relative increase in their powers, although their jousting with the centre and other levels of government is not generally manifest in formal statements. But interprovincial protectionism, trade wars and the refusal to accept central decisions on the economy, all suggest that real disputes exist and that real power has increased at the provincial level. Provincial trade with the outside world has also grown rapidly, while interprovincial trade has decreased in real terms. This is because the outside world is often a more reliable (not to mention more profitable) partner. As the World Bank suggests, China's provinces are becoming more independent actors.

One important reason why power has not flowed back to Beijing is the uncertainty surrounding the succession to Deng, and the state of factional politics. A central feature of the analysis here has been the extent to which the mixture of sweeping reforms and impending succession struggles has made officials at all levels wary of how they express their loyalities. This has resulted in signs of social decay, as well as a reluctance to restore powers to a central government that may not last very long. It makes little sense for the leaders of a reforming province along China's coast to make major sacrifices for the centre when it is not yet known who will be wielding power or controlling money in Beijing over the years to come.

RESHAPING FOREIGN RELATIONS

In an age of increasingly close links between domestic and foreign policy, major changes in China's domestic affairs have a significant impact on foreign relations. Thus China's relations with the outside world have changed, but in different ways for different parts of the country. This process has four levels.

First, Beijing has quite deliberately decentralised decisions on some issues. The vast increase in legitimate cross-border trade has led to the creation of different types of NETs. Whether in Central Asia, along the northern frontier or along the coast, cross-border trade has boomed. Even though much of this trade is outside central control, Beijing does not mind. Similarly, Beijing is generally pleased with its creation of special economic zones and has used their very diversity to ensure that no one region grows too strong. In short, not all decentralisaton has had unwanted consequences for Beijing.

Second, and at the core of this study, are the unwanted consequences of decentralisation. Because such a range of China's economic interactions with the outside world has developed outside Beijing's control, the centre has found that it has worryingly little control over some key elements of its foreign economic policy. In some aspects of its foreign relations power has simply been decentralised, and no one, except assorted individuals acting independently, has taken up that power. These include the sharp increase in problems with piracy, unsanctioned migration (even to the USA), the drug trade and gun running. Many of these problems result from Beijing's decision not to micro-manage border controls in order to encourage greater foreign trade. Any market economy often has such unsavoury features, but in the current Chinese case the results create a whole series of problems for central and regional government.

Uncontrolled migration affects relations with neighbours, as well as countries as far away as Australia or the United States. Piracy has worried neighbours and upset the international community anxious to maintain open sea lanes. The gun and drug trades also affect social order right across China, as well as provoking complaints from neighbours from Central Asia to Hong Kong.

Unwanted consequences of decentralisation are also evident in evolving trade and investment relations, especially along the coast. China now finds that the United States has enormous leverage on it because investors from Hong Kong and Taiwan have ensured that the Chinese trade surplus with the United States remains huge. What is more, the trade practices of these enterprises along the coast are often beyond the control of central government. Beijing may sign international agreements on textile exports, protecting intellectual property or halting trade subsidies, but the central authorities are unable to control the violations of such accords. China may wish to join GATT and be ready to accept its rules on trade transparency, but provincial and township authorities are unwilling to be equally transparent in their dealings with Beijing, let alone the outside world. In short, China's ability to enforce accords on its own territory is affected by the decentralisation of economic power, as is its international reputation.

There are also strong signs that greater power for the regions and greater involvement of key NETs, including Hong Kong or Taiwan, have begun to affect Chinese policy towards parts of the outside world. China's ability to browbeat Hong Kong into accepting its political or constitutional terms is circumscribed in part by the new power Hong Kong exerts over the economy of southern China. More disconcerting for Beijing is that, as the regions grow stronger, Taiwan becomes less likely to unite with a non-unified mainland. On the contrary, Taiwan is more likely to exert a 'pull' of its own on coastal China. As Taiwan emerges as a more independent actor, it encourages greater independence of mind in those areas of China with which it deals.

Third, conditions are being created that may cause the centre to lose further control if the process of decentralisation continues. For example, as Japanese trade becomes increasingly focused on neighbouring parts of coastal China, and as Japan grows increasingly concerned about Chinese military power, ther may be an increase in the as yet small number of people tempted to use Japan's economic influence to encourage parts of coastal China to moderate Beijing's political ambitions. Similar sentiments are beginning to be heard in

South-east Asia about the virtues of interdependence in tying China down.

In Central Asia or Tibet, the risks of decentralisation are of a very different kind. Here, local elite groups, while beholden to Beijing, are aware of the serious potential for unrest on the part of local people. Greater economic decentralisation provides greater prosperity, but also rising expectations and rising resentment of foreign rule. As coastal China develops more political and economic power, the national bonds are loosened still further. This is not to say that regional separatists in Central Asia will lead the movement for change, but it does suggest that Chinese leaders have good reason to be worried about what they acknowledge to be increasingly powerful 'separatist tendencies'.

Fourth, it should be acknowledged that, for many aspects of Chinese foreign policy, the centre continues to hold great power. If the outside world wants to negotiate arms control or obtain a Chinese vote on the UN Security Council, they will have to talk to Beijing. So far there is no sign that regionalism has affected these aspects of foreign policy.

The centre is also apparently in control of such issues as human-rights policy and defence spending. Yet even on these issues there may soon be a greater independent role for the provinces. If foreign governments increasingly slap embargoes on exports from prisons, for example, the vested interests concerned are both local and national. The structure of defence spending may be affected the more the economy is decentralised and large defence manufacturers seek to convert to civil production for export. It has already been suggested that the foreign sales of the defence industry are often the result of local initiative or the actions of well-connected individuals.

WHAT SHOULD BE DONE?

How can the outside world handle this Muddle Kingdom? The new reality of China requires the outside world to adopt a more complex policy if it wishes to be effective. The forces at work are primarily within China, but outsiders can be effective at the margins of this process of change. Any analysis of what the outside world should do must satisfy those who would ask 'to what end?' As has been posited, the strategic goals of outsiders will vary depending on their national interest and the part of China with which they are dealing. Trade relations are especially differentiated. But most outsiders will agree on the desirability of encouraging a China that is peacefully interdependent with the world beyond its borders. A goal of more complex interdependence will be harder to manage then if China had remained more centrally run. If China manages to hold together, even if only as a looser system, the outside world will find it easier to fashion more differentiated policies to suit specific interests. As China itself changes, the world has to face a new reality, and by adapting policy, this new reality can be made to suit basic Western goals towards China. To do nothing in the face of these major changes in China would be to retain an outdated China policy, to miss new opportunities and to fail to deal with new problems that emerge as decentralisation changes China's domestic and foreign policy.

Although the nature of decentralisation means that different countries will have more specialised trade relations with China, this does not mean that there will be more disputes among outsiders on how to handle China. Disputes about whether to pursue human rights or arms control as the priority will continue to divide outside governments, not to mention causing division within and between individual ministries. Similarly, debates about public or private diplomacy will continue. Regionalism in China adds yet another layer to these debates. For example, while some in the United States might seek to exert strong public pressure on coastal provinces to encourage Beijing to adopt a more accommodating attitude towards Hong Kong or territorial disputes, Japan and the ASEAN states might prefer to be more private and subtle in their diplomacy. The point is that all outsiders will increasingly adapt the way they deal with China to take into account the impact and opportunities of decentralisation.

It will be very difficult to develop and articulate a policy for dealing with a less centralised China that will not be interpreted in Beijing as an attempt to divide the country. There is no easy way around this problem, although China's own rhetoric about the virtues of decentralisation can be used to make the strategy of dealing in a less centralised fashion with a decentralising China more palatable. At least three clusters of policies can be identified, with many possible variations on, and connections between, them.

First, remarkably little is known about the localities, provinces and regions of China and far more needs to be known. How do the new institutions and interest groups operate? Who are the new individuals who benefit from decentralisation and who benefits most from imports or exports? At what point does the centre pass power down to the localities and when does it become harder to take that power back? What role do foreigners play in these struggles? This involves more study of local culture (including language), as well as local economic and political conditions. Far more needs to be known about local political and military elite groups and how they relate both to other regions and to the centre. Few of these questions are asked systematically and only a small number of Sinologists are working on the foreign-policy dimensions of decentralisation. Sinologists have curiously mirrored their country of study by also tending to accept relatively uncritically the myth of a unified national identity. It is no longer enough to go to Beijing and talk to officials in central government to understand events in a wider entity called China. Far more may by learned about real economic policy in all its facets by visiting Guangzhou or Shanghai. Nor is it any longer possible to visit any one part of China and come away with much more than a local snapshot.

Second, governments are already finding it necessary to develop far more local expertise. This involves the more expensive process of establishing and maintaining consulates or trade offices around China and in the parts of Asia connected to it by NETs. Governments are often reluctant to do this because of high staff costs at a time when funds and staff must be found for the new states that are emerging in Europe and Central Asia. China might even be reluctant to agree to the opening of more consulates or trade offices. An obvious answer, especially for like-minded states, would be to pool resources, especially outside the major coastal cities where the business opportunities are greatest. Similar arrangements are already made for new representation in Eastern Europe and Central Asia, and Australia and Canada agreed in September 1993 to establish shared facilities in many Asian and Latin American countries.

The purpose of such new consulates or trade offices would be both vastly to improve the range of information on local conditions and officials, and to support investment and trade in the region. It has long been inappropriate to assess China's economy in a centralised way and it similarly makes little sense to confine political and military analysis of China to staff in Beijing. For some purposes, a visit to Beijing is no more essential than it is for a Japanese investor in the United States to visit Washington when seeking to choose between a green-field site in Tennessee or California. There is a great deal that localities can do to encourage foreign investment without angering Beijing, especially if it is kept below the current ceiling of $50 million before Beijing's permission is required. Foreign lending institutions already often think in these regional terms.

These reforms in the way the outside world handles China will also require changes in foreign ministries where there will be a need for more staff and more complex decision-making procedures. Such a policy will not necessarily be opposed by Beijing for, as has already been seen, greater transparency on GATT issues or observation of intellectual property rules are supported by Beijing, even though they may be violated at the lower levels. By encouraging international business to think in terms of a more decentralised China, it will be easier to achieve the kinds of changes desired by the international community. So long as it is a goal of Western policy, a China that is more open to liberal political ideals or to international trade can be achieved both by dealing with Beijing, and by dealing with new centres of power in the regions. Thinking in such decentralised terms would only be a recognition of reality, and as a result provide better prospects for international trade and a more open China. Of course, governments should be wary about tampering with market forces, especially when overseas Chinese investment is far more sophisticated than most outside governments could possibly be. The need to think regionally is more a problem for Western investors who lack the local connections of the overseas Chinese.

Third, foreign governments can begin to treat China's provinces or regions as more independent levels of government, and to do so would merely be to recognise the new reality. This is not just a matter of information gathering, although that is essential. It is also a matter of evolving new policies that encourage China's provinces to feel more confident about their own position and ability to deal with the outside world. Broadcasting to China might be targeted more specifically at regional and local elite groups in order to provide less biased information about the course of decentralisation at home and the interests of foreigners abroad. From the point of view of the outside world, such policies would allow the point to be put across more directly, and provide more information about how decisions are taken at the increasingly important local level. Just as such information is needed about newly decolonised states or newly liberated ones in Eastern Europe or the former Soviet Union, so the outside world needs to know more about the thinking and operation of new actors in the international system, even if they happen still to be within China's frontiers.

Regional leaders in neigbouring countries, for example in Japan or South Korea, might establish regular channels of communication with provincial leaders in China. This should go beyond the usual banalities of twinning cities, and include funding of exchange programmes on technical and cultural matters. Regular channels might even be established to discuss such security issues as piracy or environmental matters such as pollution. By establishing more regular connections, greater openness would be developed. Aid given to regional broadcasters could be especially helpful in this regard. The basic desire should be to understand the new diversity and perhaps help shape it in ways that meet foreigners' needs. The West already expresses this desire in its policies towards Beijing, for example, on human rights or trade policy, so it is only sensible to extend this policy to the new centres of power at the local level. If outsiders wish to end exports by Chinese enterprises which violate intellectual property regulations, use prison labour or violate GATT regulations by benefiting from massive injections of capital from local government, their policies need to be tailored to reach China's local levels.

An expanded range of openness to local leaders might also include extending invitations to them to be guests of other governments, perhaps supported by 'know-how' fund projects for training, as Europeans currently do for Eastern Europeans. Assistance to China in the form of development aid or even educational grants and exchange programmes might be established at the provincial or even lower levels, rather than exclusively at the national level, thereby building more specific networks of influence. As China becomes more open, there are new opportunities for more varied contacts. In good times this enhancement of openness at local levels will be good for trading interests. In bad times, for example if centre–local relations should deteriorate sharply, the outside world will know more about the process and be better able to judge what policies might be more appropriate. These provincial officials should be specifically invited to join national delegations visiting other countries and take part in events sponsored by international institutions. Identification of the people involved should be done by foreign governments and not left to the nomenklatura system of the Beijing regime.

The most controversial aspect of a greater international status for Chinese provinces is the way in which provincial governments may need to be consulted on security issues. While it is true that most issues on the international security agenda will still be dealt with on the national level – for example, arms control or UN peacekeeping – it is possible that efforts undertaken at the provincial level to reinforce messages delivered in Beijing may well be worth considering. States that worry about China's possible use of force, whether against Taiwan or in the South China Sea, could encourage local leaders in southern China to realise that they may suffer a loss of investment and prosperity if they do not urge Beijing to limit its ambitions. Japan might send a similar message to coastal China if it should wish to use its influence to encourage China to avoid a military build-up. Provinces with large defence industries might be given special aid to convert to civilian industry. Provinces with factories producing exports using prison labour might be targeted for international pressure, just as complaints are lodged at the national level. In short, provinces can be singled out for special treatment both in the area of incentives and penalties.

INTO THE BEYOND

Given the complexity of the internal and external forces involved, it is impossible to be certain about the future shape of China. A return to rigidly centralised rule is highly unlikely, but should not be entirely ruled out. Nor should a break-up of China be entirely ruled out. There are certainly powerful forces that could explain such a development, especially at a time of major uncertainty about the succession to Deng Xiaoping. When examining what held states together (the USA in the 1860s) or allowed them to split (the USSR in the 1990s), the final outcome was rarely obvious from the start. But what does appear clear is that, even though external forces have helped pull at the fabric of China, they will not be a determining factor in any specific crisis that might emerge. The fate of China will be in the hands of the Chinese and will depend critically on how they manage their reforms. If things go badly for the centre, the outside world may fear the calamitous consequences of mass migration or worry about damage to the international economy, but some would also applaud the end of 'the China threat'.

The most likely outcome is a prolonged crisis of national identity, where changes short of complete collapse have an important impact on the lives of the Chinese and their neighbours. The preceding analysis has argued that China's crisis is in part the result of the failure of the old ideology and the consequent failure to evolve a new and coherent system for governing the country. It may be that the country is simply heading into a more chaotic era, or what optimists might prefer to call pragmatic government. But the evidence also suggest that this is not just a crisis of the regime; it has important elements of a crisis of national identity.

The notion that China faces a crisis of national identity has led some dissidents to discuss the role that federalism might play in a new China. Current discussions of federalism stress the advantages that might be obtained from a looser form of government that allows for the incorporation of the more liberal ideas of government found in Taiwan and Hong Kong. They are in part an antidote to the discussions of 'new authoritarianism' that were supported by some of Zhao Ziyang's associates before his purge in 1989. The discussions represent the restoration to Chinese political thought of the debate on how to reconcile the Great and Little Traditions.

Yet it is unlikely that China will adopt a formally federal structure. A crucial component to effective federalism is a firm legal tradition and Confucian political culture lacks anything of the sort. Indeed, one of the key features that distinguishes East Asian from transatlantic political cultures is the relative absence in East Asia of legal forms for settling disputes and managing social relations. The implications of this are evident in everything from trade disputes to debates over human rights. Interestingly, there are virtually no countries in East Asia (apart from Malaysia) with a federal form of government.

There can, however, be informal variants of federalism. China might best be seen as evolving a distinctive type of informal federalism where power is managed in different ways at different levels, and even varies in form at the same level. It seems unlikely that a mechanism for government could be introduced, whether formal or informal, which could micro-manage or micro-administer such diversity. Whether one adopts the Euro-speak of 'subsidiarity' and 'variable geometry', or the political science concept of 'polycentrism', the reality in China is tending increasingly towards devolved power. Effective authority can now be found at very different levels, both within and outside China, depending on the specific issues at stake. This is already evident in much of China's foreign economic relations. The role of external power and authority is especially novel in Chinese history, for China has never been as interdependent with the outside world as it is today.

The motive for developing a more differentiated policy towards China is at least twofold. First, it is clear that China is already decentralising key aspects of its policies, and it is simply prudent to be better prepared for this process and better able to manage change that is already taking place under the twin pressures of domestic and international forces. Even if the outside world undertook none of the steps outlined above, China would continue to decentralise power and change would be forced upon the outside world.

A second motive is simply that if China is left to manage its own regionalism it might only be able to contain fissiparous tendencies by strengthening its nationalist and irredentist policies. If China is left to grow economically strong and more ruthlessly nationalist at the same time, it is likely to be far more difficult for the outside world to deal with. The advantages of undertaking a more engaged attitude towards Chinese regionalism will be perceived in different ways by Beijing. On the one hand, the Chinese would be right in supposing that many foreign governments would welcome a more decentralised China because it would weaken Beijing's ability to pursue a nationalist agenda, for example as regards territorial disputes.

On the other hand, Beijing can also see ways in which the outside world can play a positive role in dealing with regionalism. If foreigners positively engage with the process of decentralisation, they might make a formal break-up less likely. A strategy of engagement with China's regions is intended to gain more information about the process and minimise the risks of chaos. On many issues, the outside world has an interest in a more decentralised China. But it also has an interest, at least on some issues (e.g. GATT or arms sales), in an effective government in Beijing. If the outside world seriously believes that it can best accommodate China's rising power by weaving it into webs of interdependence, then the strongest webs will be built on regional and local lines. The outside world has no interest in the formal break-up of China. But there is much that stops short of a formal break-up which offers the outside world the opportunity of creating a more realistic and constructive dialogue with China. It may be that the only way to ensure that China does not become more dangerous as it grows richer and stronger is to ensure that in practice, if not in law, there is more than one China to deal with.

NOTES

1 The NET is a useful concept because it stresses the extent to which contacts can develop despite existing internal and external frontiers. The strength of NETs can be 'measured' by the intensity of trade and financial flows, as well as by the movement of people or even ideas.
2 There are huge problems with the data. Data on Chinese trade is skewed because of the problems of counting indirect trade with South Korea and Taiwan which used to pass mainly through Hong Kong. Smuggling has also increased in recent years along various frontiers. In short, the data should be taken as indicating trends rather than providing precise calculations. See Nicholas Lardy, *Foreign Trade and Economic Reform in China* (Cambridge: Cambridge University Press, 1992).
3 Calculations in Brantly Womack and Guangzhi Zhao, 'The Many Worlds of China's Provinces: Foreign Trade and Diversification', chapter 5 in this volume.

4 These calculations are based on various years of the *Almanac of Chinese Foreign Economy and Trade*, cited in Stefan Landsberger, *China's Provincial Foreign Trade* (London: RIIA, 1989), and Womack and Zhao, 'The Many Worlds'.
5 *China Daily*, 22 May 1993, p. 1.
6 David Zweig, 'Internationalizing China's Countryside', *China Quarterly*, no. 128, 1991, p. 718.
7 Junhua Wu, 'Economic Growth and Regional Development Strategy in China', *Japan Research Quarterly*, no. 3, 1993.
8 Womack and Zhao, 'The Many Worlds'.
9 Zweig, 'Internationalizing China's Countryside', p. 718.
10 Womack and Zhao, 'The Many Worlds'.
11 David Zweig, 'Reaping Rural Rewards', *China Business Review*, November–December 1992, pp. 12–17.
12 Unless otherwise noted, this section relies heavily on Gerald Segal, *The Fate of Hong Kong* (London: Simon and Schuster, 1993).
13 *Financial Times*, 19 December 1993.
14 *Ming Pao* (Hong Kong), 30 June 1992, in FBIS-CHI-92-126, 30 June 1992, p. 17; *Zhongguo Tongxun* (Hong Kong), 13 May 1993, in FBIS-CHI-93-097, 21 May 1993, pp. 14–15; and *IHT*, 9 April 1993.
15 *Wen Wei Po* (Hong Kong), 12 September 1993, in *FE/1802/G/9–10*.
16 See, for example, the case of Liaoning, *Xinhua*, 19 October 1992, in FBIS-CHI-92-204, 21 October 1992, p. 49. See also *Zhongguo Tongxun She*, 13 May 1993, in *FE/1702/B2/3*.
17 *Zhongguo Xinwen She*, 21 July 1993, in FE/1748/B2/4, and *The Economist*, 24 July 1993.
18 David Goodman, *Southern China in Transition* (Canberra: AGPO, 1992).
19 Goodman, 'The PLA and Regionalism', and *Financial Times*, 7 June 1993.
20 *Xinhua*, 10 July 1993, in *FE/1739/A2/1–2*, and *Far Eastern Economic Review*, 14 October 1993, p. 74.
21 Ting Wai, 'The Regional and International Implications of the South China Economic Zone', *Issues and Studies*, December 1992.
22 *IHT*, 27 April 1993, and *South China Morning Post Weekly*, 1 August 1993, p. 5.
23 *Financial Times*, 27 April 1993. *Far Eastern Economic Review*, 20 May 1993, p. 66, puts the figure for total trade in 1992 at $14 billion. For early 1993 data, see China News Agency, Taiwan, 24 May 1993, in FBIS-CHI-93-099, 25 May 1993, p. 55.
24 *Far Eastern Economic Review*, 1 July 1993, pp. 21–22.
25 *Asian Wall Street Journal*, 6 December 1993.
26 *Xinhua*, 24 May 1993, in FBIS-CHI-93-099, 25 May 1993, p. 52.
27 *Financial Times*, 14 May 1993.
28 *Xinhua*, 11 July 1993, in *FE/1739/A2/3–4*. Of course Lee pledged to consult with Beijing before making the decision. See reports of his Suzhou trip in *Xinhua*, 12 May 1993, in FBIS-CHI-93-099, 25 May 1993, p. 9.
29 John Garver, 'China's Push Through the South China Sea', *China Quarterly*, December 1992.
30 Details on the Hong Kong debate are subject to the usual caveats about

reading Chinese tea-leaves. On the resort to nationalism among hard-liners see, for example, *Chiushih Nientai* (Hong Kong), no. 5, 1 May 1993, in *FE/1681/B2/4–5*. See also Hong Kong's *Cheng Ming*, 1 January 1993, in *FE/1577/A2/3–7*, in the midst of the recent Sino-British row over Hong Kong.

31 Michael Williams, *Vietnam* (London: Pinter for the RIIA, 1992). For more recent evidence of humiliation, see the violation of Vietnamese territorial waters by Chinese-sponsored oil drillers just before Chi Haotian visted Hanoi, *Far Eastern Economic Review*, 27 May 1993, p. 14.

32 *Wen Wei Po* (Hong Kong), 7 December 1991, in FBIS-CHI-91-243, 18 December 1991, pp. 10–11, *South China Morning Post*, 31 December 1992, p. 8, *Financial Times*, 9 July 1993.

33 *Zhongguo Xinwen She*, 11 June 1993, in *FE/1738/B2/4*, and the same agency on 6 July in *FE/1746/B2/3*. See also *Far Eastern Economic Review*, 3 June 1993, pp. 26–27, and *Asia Inc*, November 1993, pp. 37–47.

34 *Zhongguo Tongxun She*, 25 October 1993, in *FE/1834/G/1*.

35 *IHT*, 10 June 1993, and *The Economist*, 10 July 1993.

36 *The Economist*, 24 April 1993.

37 Gerald Segal, 'The Coming Confrontation Between China and Japan', *World Policy Journal*, Summer 1993.

38 *Financial Times*, 1 June 1993.

39 *The Economist*, 21 August 1993.

40 *Xinhua*, 2 September 1992, in FBIS-CHI-92-171, 2 September 1992, p. 11, and *Xinhua*, 24 August 1993, in *FE/0300/WG/3*.

41 Yao Jianguo, 'A Dynamic Bohai Rim Looms on the Horizon', *Beijing Review*, 13–19 December 1993, and *Asian Wall Street Journal*, 7 December 1993.

42 On the regional pattern, see Gerald Segal, *The Soviet Union and the Pacific* (Boston, MA: Unwin/Hyman for the RIIA, 1990), especially chapter 6. For recent data, see Mayak Radio, 15 August 1993, in SU/WO296/A/8–9.

43 *Xinhua*, 29 August 1993, in *FE/0298/WG/6*.

44 *Liaowang* (Hong Kong), no. 40, 5 October 1992, in FBIS-CHI-92-211, 30 October, pp. 21–23, *Christian Science Monitor*, 14 August 1992; *Financial Times*, 23 February, 1992; *Far Eastern Economic Review*, 8 July 1993, pp. 40–43, 21 October, 1993, pp. 20–21, and *Zhongguo Xinwen She*, 11 December 1993, in *FE/1871/G/5*.

45 Despite wilder stories, these are the only confirmed deals as reported by Russia to the United Nations Arms Register. See *Moscow News*, no. 29, 16 July 1993, p. 5.

46 ITAR-TASS, 3 June 1993, in SU/1707/A1/5, ITAR-TASS, 19 June, in *FE/1734/A1/5*, *Postfactum*, 6 July 1993, in SU/1740/A1/1–2, ITAR-TASS, 9 July 1993, in SU/1737/i, and Ostankino Channel 1 TV, 4 July 1993, in SU/1733/A1/5. Mayak Radio, 10 September 1993, in *FE/1794/G/2*.

47 *Kommersant*, Moscow, 17 April 1993, in SU/1676/A1/3–4, and *Krasnaya Zvezda*, 7 May 1993, reporting that some disputes had become 'an acute issue', SU/1689/A1/1. See also Pi Ying-hsien, 'China's Boundary Issues with the former Soviet Union', *Issues and Studies*, July 1992.

48 *South China Morning Post*, 28 June 1993, and *Far Eastern Economic Review*, 17 June 1993, p. 2.
49 Lillian Craig Harris, 'Xinjiang, Central Asia and the Implication for China's Policy in the Islamic World', and Gaye Christoffersen, 'Xinjiang and the Great Islamic Circle', *China Quarterly*, no. 133, March 1993.
50 *KazTag*, 9 July 1993, in SU/1739/A1/4–5.
51 Roland Dannreuther, *Creating New States in Central Asia*, Adelphi Paper 288 (London: Brassey's for the IISS, 1994), and Radio Moscow, 6 September 1993, in SU/1791/G/1.
52 *Xinhua*, 30 April 1993, in SU/W0280/A7, and *Xinhua*, 29 May 1993, in *FE*/W0286/A7. See also an interview with Nazarbayev on Ostankino Channel 1 TV, Moscow, in SU/1845/G/1–2.
53 *Xinhua*, 24 July 1992, in FBIS-CHI-92-147, 30 July 1992, pp. 60–61, *Xinhua*, 2 August 1992, in FBIS-CHI-92-151, 5 August 1992, pp. 62–63, and *Xinhua*, 21 March, 1993, in FBIS-CHI-93-054, 23 March 1993, p. 9. See also J. Richard Walsh, 'China and the New Geopolitics of Central Asia', *Asian Survey*, no. 3, March 1993.
54 *Daily Telegraph*, 4 January 1994, reporting details of Prime Minister Bhutto's trip to China in December.
55 Kazakh TV, 5 October 1993, in SU/1817/G1–5, and various reports on his visit to China in October 1993 in SU/1824/G/1–2. *The Washington Post*, 6 May 1992. See also Nazarbayev's interview, 10 November, Ostankino Channel 1 TV, in SU/1845/G/1–2.
56 Dannreuther, *Central Asia*.

Index